MODERN PER[

ELEMENTARY LEVEL

MODERN PERSIAN, ELEMENTARY LEVEL

Like a Nightingale

Iago Gocheleishvili

ANTHEM PRESS

Anthem Press
An imprint of Wimbledon Publishing Company
www.anthempress.com

This edition first published in UK and USA 2020
by ANTHEM PRESS
75–76 Blackfriars Road, London SE1 8HA, UK
or PO Box 9779, London SW19 7ZG, UK
and
244 Madison Ave #116, New York, NY 10016, USA

British Library Cataloguing-in-Publication Data
A catalogue record for this book is available from the British Library.

Library of Congress Cataloging-in-Publication Data
Library of Congress Control Number: 2019949289

ISBN-13: 978-1-78527-513-5 (Hbk)
ISBN-10: 1-78527-513-5 (Hbk)
ISBN-13: 978-1-78527-106-9 (Pbk)
ISBN-10: 1-78527-106-7 (Pbk)

This title is also available as an e-book.

CONTENTS

1   Hello!   1

Function	Greeting and introducing yourself and others, saying where you are from and where you live, describing how you are feeling, saying where and what you study, counting (0–10), saying your phone number, talking about the days of the week, using nouns with numbers. Key verbs: *to be, to have, to study, to work, to live, to read*
	Alphabet. Differences between spelling and pronunciation in Persian. Writing your name in Persian
Vocabulary	Pronouns, greetings and introduction
	What do you do? I am a student. Verbs *to be, to study*
	Where are you from? How many siblings do you have? Counting (0–5). Verbs: *to have, to live*
	What is your major? Verb *to work*
	What is your phone number? Counting (0–10)
	Days of the week
Letters	ذ د ژ ز ر و آ,
	ب پ ت ث ن ک گ
	س ش ص ض ل ف ق
	ط ظ م ه ی
	Initial vowels ã, ee, oo

ACKNOWLEDGEMENTS

Throughout the work on this book so many colleagues and students at Cornell University and elsewhere have offered their suggestions, specific and general comments and ideas for this textbook that I am bound to fail to mention each and everyone to whom I am so grateful for their encouragement and support. In particular, I would like to express my gratitude to professors Seema Golestaneh of Cornell University, William Reyes-Cubides at the American Association of University Supervisors , Coordinators and Directors of Language Programs and Academic Specialist of Curriculum Development at Michigan State University, Brisa Teutli of Cornell University and Damien Tissot of Cornell University for carefully reading the manuscript and offering invaluable feedback and practical suggestions that have made this book infinitely better.

I would also like to express my special gratitude to Rambod Mirbaha for contributing so much of his time and talent to the audio, video and photo material that accompany this volume and for providing so generously his help and feedback.

I am also very thankful to Sama Azadi, Parastou Ghazi, Sahar Tavakoli, Mansourh Ghertassi, Isaa Tavakoli, and Pauniz Salehi for their contributions to the audio presentations of this book and for their feedback.

My grateful thanks to the anonymous reviewers who read the manuscript and provided most helpful and most useful feedback that has made the book so much better.

I am also thankful to Soroush Karimi, a photographer and true artist who generously contributed his works to this volume.

My special thanks are due to my students, in particular Abdul Rahman Al-Mana, Afsaneh Faki, Chris Hesselbein, Daniel Sabzghabaei, Darren Chang, Ian Wallace, Kayla Scheimreif, Leo Luis, Nadia Palte, Raas Goyal, Thomas Nolan, Talia Chorover and Talia Turnham for being so enthusiastic and encouraging about this book and for providing their feedback and thoughts regarding the various exercises, classroom activities and drills that have inspired the material of this textbook.

I would also like to thank my wife for being so patient and so incredibly supportive of this project. I would like to dedicate this book to my son, Maxi, who brings so much happiness and meaning to every minute of every day of my life.

INTRODUCTION TO THE PERSIAN LANGUAGE SPOKEN IN IRAN

Persian belongs to the Indo-European language family, and is related to Germanic and Slavic languages, which means that Persian has major similarities with the European languages in grammar, syntax and word formation. There are only two consonantal sounds in Persian that differ from consonantal sounds that English speakers can easily pronounce: sound **kh** as in German *Bach*, and a soft glottal sound **q** similar to the first sound in French "rouge" but with a harder glottal quality. Persian language has no cases, no noun inflection, no gender categories, no irregular conjugation of verbs, and no capital letters. Persian is, perhaps, the easiest language of the Middle East for the speakers of Western languages to learn. Modern Persian of Iran is a language of Indo-European origin with a multitude of English, French, Turkish and Arabic cognates combined with the core Persian vocabulary and built upon a basic and uncomplicated grammar. Persian is spoken by over one hundred million people around the world including one million people in the United States. Farsi of Iran, Tajiki of Tajikistan and Dari of Afghanistan are all variants that share roots in the same Persian language. Until 1964, the variant of Persian spoken in Afghanistan was called Farsi, and its native speakers in Afghanistan still widely refer to it as Farsi, even though officially it is now called Dari. The Tajiki variant of Persian is also spoken in various parts of Uzbekistan, most notably Bukhara, Samarkand and Surxondaryo areas. In the English language, *Persian* is a reference to the modern live language, while *Farsi* is indeed the name used by native speakers in Iran to refer to this language in their native tongue. Old Persian, Middle Persian and modern Persian refer to different stages in the development of the same language, present-day Persian.

THE ALPHABET

The Persian alphabet contains thirty-two letters and a few special signs that can be used when needed as pronunciation and grammatical markers in order to avoid occasional ambiguity. The Persian sound system contains twenty-one consonant sounds, six vowels and two diphthongs.

Peculiarities of the Persian script:

(1) Persian is written from right to left. Due to this fact, Persian books start on the right side of the cover, that is, diametrically opposite to the format of books printed in the Western scripts.
(2) There are no capital letters in the Persian script.

(3) Like the letters of the Latin alphabet, Persian letters are written using lines combined with dots. However, in Persian, some linear shapes can be combined with one, two or three dots to give them different phonetic values, for example, ر (r), ز (z), ژ (zh).

(4) Unlike English that has printed and cursive styles of penmanship, Persian has only one style—cursive, which is a combination of joins and pen lifts. This means that all letters must be connected one to another. For example, if written separately, the following letters do not make up a word, even though they are written in correct order:

ل ب ل ب

If connected, they spell the word بلبل (bolbol) *nightingale*.

(5) Because of the above characteristic, the connecting line between letters may replace a part of the letter's shape. Thus, the appearance of the same letter might change from the way it looks between two other letters to the way it looks at the end of a word where it is only joined by another letter on one side. That is why the letters of the alphabet are presented to students in their initial, medial and final positions. Initial position means that the letter is connected to another letter only on the left, or, for some letters, is not connected at all. Medial position means that the letter is joined by other letters on both sides when possible. Final position means that the letter is joined by another letter only on the right. Although having three positions might sound complicated, you will be surprised at how fast you will learn to write and distinguish the letters of the Persian alphabet.

(6) Persian has six vowels. Three of those vowels are represented by the corresponding letter symbols that are always written. The other three are represented by special signs called diacritics or vowel signs. These vowel signs are only written by native speakers when it is necessary to avoid ambiguity. In written material intended for native speakers these three vowel markers are normally omitted, and the reader recognizes the word without them. You too will easily learn how to do that. When you learn a new word, you learn its spelling and pronunciation and will know how to recognize and pronounce the word, even without those vowel signs. The context of the sentence will also help you recognize the word and its pronunciation.

For comparison, look at the following phrase written twice—once with the vowel signs and the second time without them:

مَن پِسَرعَمو و دُختَرعَمو دارَم.
من پسرعمو و دخترعمو دارم.
/man pesar amoo va dokhtar amoo dãram./

In the English transliteration above, the red letters are the ones represented by the vowel signs in Persian spelling.

If you are writing the word and also would like to add the vowel signs, first write the shapes of the letters with respective dots, and then add the vowel signs. For your convenience, all new words that appear in the glossaries and also readings and texts in Persian in the initial chapters of this textbook are spelled with the vowel signs. As we progress through the course, though, the vowel signs will disappear in readings and texts, but not in the glossaries. You will recognize the words without the vowel signs when you see them in texts, just like native speakers do.

(7) Letters of the alphabet are introduced and learned in groups of several letters. The groups are created based on the following: the basic shape shared by several letters; the way in which the letters connect or do not connect to other letters; the shape of the final arabesque.

(8) There are several letters in the Persian script that represent the same sounds. The presence of these superfluous letters is due to the fact that modern Persian alphabet is based on a foreign, Arabic alphabet that was adopted in the early Middle Ages to replace the original Persian alphabet. Persian, an Indo-European language, and Arabic, an Afro-Asiatic language, are not related, and some of the Arabic sounds, particularly the glottal sounds, do not exist in Persian language. Because of this, the letters that represented those Arabic sounds ended up being superfluous in everyday Persian. Those letters still remain in use in modern Persian in order to avoid confusion over the spelling, especially in the case of borrowed words which were adopted in their original spelling, but are now pronounced according to the Persian sound system. On the flip side, Persian writers had to introduce several new letters as the original alphabet lacked symbols to represent all the Persian sounds. You will see several letters that represent the same sound *z*. You will also see the added letter پ *p* that does not exist in the Arabic alphabet. The absence of the sound *p* in the original version of the adopted Arabic alphabet is the reason why today we refer to the language of Iran as *Farsi*, and not *Parsi* which is how it was originally pronounced. The other added letters are used to represent the Persian sounds *ch*, *zh* and *g*.

ABOUT STRESS AND INTONATION

(1) **In the Word.** In the vast majority of Persian words, the stress falls on the last syllable of the word. There are very few exceptions from this rule (e.g., **ba**leh (yes), **khey**lee (very, very much), **mer**see (thank you)). Stress shifts to the first syllable in personal names and titles when these names and titles are used to call on someone (**khaa**nomeh Kermani!). The prefixes *mee, be, ne* in the conjugated base verbs (i.e., one-word verbs) are also stressed (e.g., **mee**ram, **be**nevees, **ne**meeram).

(2) **In the Sentence**. A Persian sentence is pronounced with a rise in pitch at the end of the sentence before the verb. Although there is an enunciated stress on the first word (i.e., its last syllable), primary stress (rise in pitch) in the sentence falls on the last stressed syllable before the verb. However, if the verb is negated, the primary rise of pitch will fall on the negated verb of the sentence.

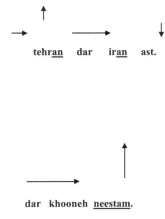

tehr<u>an</u>   dar   ir<u>an</u>   ast.

dar   khooneh   <u>neestam</u>.

If the sentence comprises multiple clauses, there is usually one rise in pitch per clause.

The rise in pitch, however, may shift to a different word in the sentence if the speaker wishes to emphasize it in the context of his statement. Compare:

man dar ketãb-khooneh **dars** mee-khoonam (In the library I **study**).
man dar **ketãb-khooneh** dars mee-khoonam
(I study in the **library**, i.e., not in my room, classroom, or somewhere else).

Persian lacks auxiliary verbs, and thus a question sentence differs from a statement by the use of question words, or by the intonation if question words are not present. In a question sentence, the pitch is generally distributed as in a statement, but if no question words are present, the last syllable is stretched out.

faarsee bala**deen?**

A NOTE ON SYLLABLES

Persian words are composed of syllables that always have one vowel combined with one, two or three consonants. The consonants of the syllable can appear with the vowel in between them (*rãd*), or as a consonantal cluster after the vowel (*eest, rãst*). The Persian syllable may end in two (or sometimes three) consonants, but it may not begin with more than one single consonant. Thus, the word *rãstee* breaks into two syllables *rãs* and *tee* (not 'rã' and 'stee').

If a word borrowed from a foreign language starts with two consonants clustered together, Persian speaker will add a vowel to break that consonantal cluster. Thus, the English name

xvii

Steve will be pronounced as ***es-teev,*** and the word *plastic* as ***pe-lãs-teek*** in order to separate the two consonants in the beginning of the word. The usual rule is that the vowel *e* will appears in the initial position to break up the consonantal cluster if the first sound in that cluster is *s* (e.g., *es-pã-ge-tee, est-rã-te-zhee*). If the word starts with any other consonant, the vowel *e* appears after that first consonant in order to break up the initial consonant cluster (e.g., *kelãs*).

ABOUT THE TEXTBOOK

This is a textbook of the modern Persian language (Farsi) spoken in Iran. It is intended for university-level learners and features material for two consecutive courses or semesters of the Elementary level. The textbook is designed to facilitate the implementation of the two most recent trends in second language instruction: communicative approach and flipped learning. This textbook is an integrated and self-contained way of acquiring functional proficiency in spoken and written Persian. The textbook's theoretical framework and underlying linguistic philosophy, its practical approach to language instruction and learning objectives are based on the latest trends in foreign language instruction as defined by the Modern Language Association (MLA) and American Council on the Teaching of Foreign Languages (ACTFL). The material of the textbook also reflects the 5 Cs of National Standards in Foreign Language Education. The textbook is inspired by the author's 17 years of experience of designing and teaching university-level courses in less commonly taught languages and is informed by the experiences, research and data gathered across various modern languages. The textbook features all the attributes necessary for the implementation of modern practices in foreign language instruction such as content-based activities for real-world objectives in a student-centered classroom, an integrated approach toward teaching all language skills (speaking, listening, reading and writing) from the outset, differentiating between proficiency (being able to use a skill) and competence (knowing a skill), teaching of language through culture and teaching culture through language, thematic presentation of the material, and use of authentic material produced by native speakers for native speakers. The textbook's learning objectives and curriculum are designed with the ACTFL proficiency guidelines in mind, and students who complete the textbook should be able to score on Elementary High to Intermediate Low levels, depending on individual progress in class and a language skill.

KEY FEATURES OF THE TEXTBOOK

The textbook is designed to facilitate the implementation of the communicative approach and flipped learning in a student-centered classroom with the integration of all skills (speaking, listening, reading, writing and cultural competence) from the outset. Besides speaking exercises and listening sections, each chapter contains separate sections for Reading and Writing practice.

Each chapter is designed with a clearly discernable progression and gradually increasing complexity of tasks. Chapters start with the new Vocabulary learning exercises, followed by the Grammar (new structures), Listening, Reading, Writing and even Translation sections. All sections were designed to complement and reinforce each other and are tied together by the common Topic and Vocabulary of the given chapter. The practical approach toward the implementation of this textbook's curriculum is rooted in the notions that **Speaking a Language is a Skill**, and that we learn the skill by doing, and that a **Language Classroom is a Language Student's Lab**, that is, that learning happens outside of the classroom, while the classroom is where the student acquires practical experience in putting the skill to use for real-world purposes. Students must have a venue and opportunities to use the language daily and, very importantly, use it in a real-world context to communicate with other students. With this textbook, students speak in the target language with multiple peers in class from the very beginning. They engage in speaking activities in Persian every single day for the entire duration of the two semesters covered by the textbook. Some of the key features of the textbook are as follows:

- Companion website.
- Answer key.
- Appendix Instructor's Resources that contains handouts, activity cards, color images, maps, tables and templates for a variety of engaging, task-based classroom activities in pairs and groups.
- A Searchable English-Persian and Persian-English Dictionary with pronunciation audio for every word entry (on the companion website).
- Video instructions that demonstrate how to write and connect the letters of the Persian alphabet and feature a voice-over that provides verbal explanations to writing.
- Audio presentations in Persian that accompany every word entry in all glossaries in all chapters in order to facilitate the correct pronunciation from the beginning.
- Over 200 audio presentations throughout the book as to help develop listening comprehension and facilitate flipped learning. Speaking homework assignments are presented with audio and transliteration as to help students learn and prepare Persian utterances with correct pronunciation and intonation at home.
- Diacritics that appear in every word entry in all glossaries in all chapters. Diacritics also appear in all new words in all exercises throughout the given chapter so as to reinforce correct pronunciation. In order to replicate the real-world use of the language, diacritics are not present in the words learned and reinforced in preceding chapters.
- A guide to differences between Spelling and Pronunciation in Persian along with illustrative examples..
- Transliteration in English that is straightforward and easy to follow for an English speaker appears in all glossaries (in Chapters 1–4).
- Jargon-free and straightforward language is used to explain grammar in practical context and is accompanied by plenty of illustrative examples.
- The spoken Persian form is always given alongside the written form of phrases and sentences in all speaking assignments so as to teach the real-world spoken language.
- Unscripted audio material by native speakers for students' greater exposure to the authentic use of the language is part of the chapters' listening exercises. These presentations (e.g.,

audio "My Apartment" in Chapter 6, audio "My Daily Routine" in Chapter 5, etc.) expose students to completely authentic speech of native speakers and to their natural selection of vocabulary and structures. Real native speakers tell real stories in unscripted, real-world spoken Persian. The textbook's glossaries, grammar sections and exercises are then designed to enable students comprehend and work with the material that is as authentic as it gets.

- A guide to the formation and comparison of high frequency verb categories in Persian (with examples).
- A guide to understanding Persian base and composite verbs that is accompanied by the list of high frequency verbs in their present, past and subjunctive forms.
- Dedicated Homework, In Class, Grammar, Listening, Reading, Writing and Translation sections in the chapters for easy reference by instructors and students. These sections feature carefully designed, research-based and practice-proven exercise that serve to reinforce and complement each other and to make for the most comprehensive learning experience and a greater material retention rate.
- The textbook emphasizes teaching High Frequency Topics, High Frequency Vocabulary and High Frequency Structures for real-world purposes.
- The textbook facilitates the implementation of the communicative approach. Class meetings are designated for speaking. *In Class* section of the textbook features multiple speaking exercises and activities for pairs and groups assigned for every day of classes throughout the entire two semesters covered by the textbook.
- Material is presented thematically to facilitate communicative proficiency rather than focusing on grammatical competence. Grammar is presented as a complement to the topic of the chapter in the form of the most common and important structures necessary for the implementation of the communicative tasks related to the topic of the given chapter.
- Words in the glossaries are presented in categories.
- The letters of the alphabet are taught in batches of letters that share similar ways of connecting to other letters or have similar shapes.
- Culture is introduced in the form of vocabulary and structures-focused Homework and In Class exercises that appear in the main body of the chapters as opposed to being after-chapter addenda. For example, we practice the use of the subjunctive mood by using an anecdote about Molla Nasreddin, where students are required to use the verbs in subjunctive mood in order to complete the task. Other exercises require students to do online research about Iran and complete the exercise using their findings. Authentic cultural material (e.g., Persian tongue twisters, Persian proverbs, Persian poem, anecdotes about Molla Nasreddin, etc.) and information about the target country and people are integrated in a natural and utilitarian way into the exercises throughout the chapters of the book. Culturally authentic material is carefully selected to reflect the vocabulary and structures covered in the given chapter.
- All exercises and activities are designed for a specific purpose such as Preparation (e.g., pre-listening), Comprehension, Follow-up and Practice, Review and Reinforcement. Emphasis is made to differentiate between comprehension on the one hand, and reinforcement and retention on the other hand.

- Vocabulary of the chapter is continuously repeated in the Homework, In Class, Grammar, Listening, Reading and Writing sections for better retention. Glossaries are followed by Input exercises for Visual and then for Auditory learners. These are followed by vocabulary exercises that encourage students' Output in spoken and in written forms. Then follow the exercises that prepare students for class discussions in the target language.
- Grammar sections are followed by Input exercises, which are further followed by exercises that encourage students' Output.
- Listening section is preceded by a series of brief audio presentations and speaking exercises throughout the chapter and is then introduced at the end of the chapter after students have learned and used the new words and structures repeatedly. After such preparation, students are able to perform tasks of greater complexity aimed at discussing and analyzing the content, message and context of the Listening section rather than trying to understand individual words and phrases uttered by the native speakers in the audio.
- Each Listening section is accompanied by a pre-listening activity and is followed by a series of follow-up exercises and activities to be completed as homework and in class.
- Each Reading section is accompanied by a pre-reading activity and is followed by a series of follow-up exercises.
- The appendix Grammarian's Corner features further elaborations and illustrative examples, especially for the structures that have alternative or additional forms in formal and written language.

LEARNING OBJECTIVES

The textbook teaches the standard Persian language of contemporary Iran. In order to reflect the authentic use of modern Persian by native speakers, the book teaches colloquial pronunciation to practice speaking and listening comprehension, and teaches proper spelling for reading and writing purposes. Grammar and spelling rules which the textbook relies on are the official grammar and spelling conventions published by the Academy of Persian Language (فرهنگستان زبان و ادب فارسی) the official regulatory body of the Persian language headquartered in Tehran, Iran. Two major sources we rely on are the official Grammar of Persian (دستور زبان فارسی) and Orthography of Persian (دستور خط فارسی).

The textbook's ultimate objective is to train students to acquire a functional proficiency in colloquial Persian, along with becoming literate in the target language, that is, being able to read and write in proper Persian.

Themes and topics that students will have learned by the end of the book include the following: greetings and introductions, talking about themselves, describing where they come from and where they live now, describing their academic schedules, what they study and what work they do, their daily routines, talking about their families and friends, likes and dislikes, home and living, cityscape, landscape and geography, clothing and shopping, travel and transport, describing location and asking for directions, describing people's appearance and personal traits, describing feelings and emotions, understanding weather forecast and talking about the seasons of the year, the months and days of the week, numbers (saying age, dates, time, quantities) and colors. Students will have learned how to describe events in Present, Past and Future tenses, how to use Subjunctive and Imperative moods to make requests and suggestions, communicate intentions and wishes, how to structure a sentence and arrange properly direct and indirect objects, how to build sentences with multiple clauses and use most common conjunctions and prepositional phrases, how to say what they think and support their opinion, how to relay information and describe chronology, how to explain cause and effect, how to describe possession, how to compare things, how to use a specific direct object in Persian, and how to understand the basics of Persian social etiquette, the *taarof*. Importantly, students will learn how to accomplish these tasks in a culturally appropriate and authentic way, and learn about the target country, culture, and people. Students will learn how to read and also write one- to two-page essays (on familiar topics) like an educated Persian speaker.

SOME PRACTICAL POINTS

The textbook features 12 chapters that are designed around high frequency communicative tasks, and not around grammar. Grammar is selected based on the most common and useful categories and structures needed to perform the communicative tasks assigned in the given chapter. The instructor has an option of distributing six chapters per semester for the academic calendar that is semester-based, or to teach four chapters per period if the academic calendar comprises trimesters.

The book designates between 10 and 15 contact hours per chapter. The detailed breakdown of hours per chapter is give below. This will allow students to digest and reinforce the material of a given chapter on a functional level without feeling like they are rushing through topics, vocabulary lists and structures without really retaining any of them well. For every 50 minutes in the classroom, the instructor may plan for two activities of 20 minutes or three activities of 15 minutes each. The time needed to complete a single activity will depend on the nature of the activity and on the number of students in class. The other 5–10 minutes of class are left for answering students' questions, explaining the activities to be done in class, summarizing the day's material or other organizational matters.

There are 12 chapters in the book, which can be distributed according to semesters or quarters.

Semester system	
Semester I	**Semester II**
Chapter 1	Chapter 7
Chapter 2	Chapter 8
Chapter 3	Chapter 9
Chapter 4	Chapter 10

Semester system	
Chapter 5	Chapter 11
Chapter 6	Chapter 12

Trimester system		
Quarter I	**Quarter II**	**Quarter III**
Chapter 1	Chapter 5	Chapter 9
Chapter 2	Chapter 6	Chapter 10
Chapter 3	Chapter 7	Chapter 11
Chapter 4	Chapter 8	Chapter 12

Suggested contact hours distribution per chapter:

Chapters	**1**	**2**	**3**	**4**	**5**	**6**	**7**	**8**	**9**	**10**	**11**	**12**
Academic Hours	15	7	10	9	11–12	11–12	7	13	7	10	14	15

STRUCTURE OF THE CHAPTERS

Chapters start with a Vocabulary list on the topic of the given chapter followed by a series of input and output exercises focused on Comprehension and Application and aimed at both visual and auditory learners. After students have become comfortable with the vocabulary, new grammar and structures are introduced and are followed by a brief series of exercises focused on grammar competence in order to provide the instructor with an opportunity of holding a Grammar day (Lecture) or giving the students extra grammar exercises if the performance of the given class requires it. These are then followed by daily task-based speaking activities and drills through which students practice the vocabulary and structures of the chapter in a variety of contexts for real-world purposes and focus on speaking and listening skills. The Listening and Reading sections accompanied by the Follow-up drills are introduced toward the end of the chapter. As students are already familiar with the vocabulary and structures featured in the Listening and Reading sections, they can engage in more complex activities and discussions in the target language, rather than focusing on basic comprehension objectives. The chapters end with the Translation and Writing sections that serve to reinforce the vocabulary and topic of the given chapter.

A NOTE ON TRANSLITERATION

Because students will start speaking in the target language before they will have finished learning the entire alphabet, they will have to say words that they will not be able to read or write in Persian. Using transliteration should be a solution to that difficulty. Throughout the Chapters 1–4, the glossary lists include transliteration in order to serve as a supplement to the diacritics and audio. In the initial chapters, Persian texts and readings also include the vowel signs in order to aid learning the correct pronunciation from the very beginning. Later in the book, diacritics are omitted in readings and texts so as to reflect the real-world use of the written language. Wherever transliteration is used, it is written in a straightforward, easily comprehensible manner without the special signs and symbols used by librarians and linguistics specialists.

Symbols

       In order to complete this exercise students will listen to an audio.

       In order to complete this exercise students will work in pairs.

       In order to complete this exercise students will work in groups of 3–4 people.

   In order to complete this task student will speak to everyone in class.

The subtitle of this book, *Like a Nightingale*, is an allusion to the long-standing Persian tradition of comparing somebody's eloquence and fluency to the singing of nightingale. In Persian, to say that a person speaks Persian like a nightingale is to say that the person speaks Persian beautifully and fluently.

TO THE STUDENT

Hello! Salaam! Welcome to the amazing world of the Persian language—the world of mesmerizing and internationally acclaimed Iranian art cinema, of eternally beautiful Persian poetry and infinitely enigmatic Persian mysticism. "To learn a language is to have one more window from which to look at the world", says an old saying. Indeed, you are about to take a journey that will open for you a window to extraordinarily rich culture and civilization that have given us many of the world's firsts in the diverse fields of animation, architecture, medicine, religion, philosophy, forms of social and political organization, cuisine and the art of good living. I am excited to accompany you on this journey through my textbook! I hope that you enjoy the learning process and come to love Persian as much as I do!

My textbook was inspired and guided, in many of its aspects, by my students. My intention was to make the learning process interesting and enjoyable, while still creating practically useful and structured material appropriate for a formal language classroom. I have designed this textbook keeping in mind the invariable diversity of learning styles, interests, needs and backgrounds that I always encountered in my Persian classes. Some of my students liked to focus primarily on communicative proficiency and have learned grammar implicitly, on the go, while the others preferred having explicit and thorough grammar explanations in the chapters, so that they could truly internalize the mechanics of the language in order to make progress in the learning process. Almost all my students liked to have readily available grammar sections for a quick reference, whenever they needed to prepare for exams or simply review the material from earlier chapters. Some of my students were visual learners, and others were auditory learners. Some of them needed to focus mostly on learning how to write and read, while others started from zero and aimed at learning all four skills. This textbook includes a variety of activities and exercises with the purpose of addressing the different learning objectives and needs and different learning styles. I have also selected diverse and authentic practice material for this textbook that includes humorous anecdotes, tongue twisters, Persian poetry, passages about modern Iran and about Iranian Americans, information about the dress code and about universities in Iran, and proverbs. I hope that no matter what your learning style and needs, most of you will find in this textbook something that appeals to your specific interests. However, I realize that it is impossible to write a language textbook that is perfect or personalized for everyone. If you have any thoughts and suggestions for the textbook, please get in touch with me. I will be glad and grateful to hear your feedback!

Here, I would like to share with you few ideas that my students and I found helpful for achieving success in the language class, especially when using this textbook. This textbook differs from traditional Persian language textbooks in the way it: selects the high frequency vocabulary; views and teaches grammar topics; the extent to which it focuses on communicative proficiency; and the way it is geared toward completely student-centered approach to classroom instruction. The overall philosophy and approach on which the textbook is based, rely on modern practices in language instruction informed by experiences, research and data across languages. Therefore, the books will be more helpful if you keep in mind the following points.

First and foremost, remember: **speaking a language is a skill.** In order to get better at it, you have to put it to active use and regular practice. The more you do it, the better you get at it. Regular practice and repetition are crucial to your success in acquiring language proficiency. It is not enough to read *about* the language and memorize the rules *about how* to use it. You must make a conscious effort to use the language daily and, importantly, to use it to communicate with others. I encourage you to take full advantage of the time available to you in class and speak in Persian as much as you can during the class meetings. Even if you complete a speaking task with your conversation partner early, continue speaking in Persian with your partner while you are waiting for the others to finish. When you get to class, speak in Persian to your classmates and instructor—simply greeting them and inquiring about their health every day is a good starting point for implementing this rule. Speak in Persian even if you think you are making mistakes. Only by speaking regularly will you perfect your use of vocabulary and structures and improve your overall speaking proficiency. Before entering the classroom, prepare mentally to switch to Persian and try to speak only in Persian till the end of class.

Come to class Prepared. Think of your language class as of your Lab. It is not the place where you start learning things, but the place where you put to use the things you have already read about and learned. It is the place where you gain practical experience using the skill—speaking the language. Do your homework regularly as it: (1) provides you with the preparation and theory which you then put in practice and context during the class activities, and (2) provides you with the instructor's regular feedback on your comprehension of the material and aids you in identifying the areas you still need to improve. Whenever you feel a need for additional vocabulary to express yourself or prepare for class, look up those new words, don't wait for others or the instructor to bring them up.

Take Initiative! Don't wait to *be taught* the language! Instead, take charge and *learn* the language. Your instructor is there to help and guide you. But, ultimately, it is your responsibility and job to follow through with the learning process. Make a habit to regularly analyze your performance, and identify aspects of the language that are still problematic for you. Then refer to your instructor for guidance. Take charge of the process and be an independent and responsible learner!

Be Enthusiastic. Be Active. Speak Up. Do not expect your instructor to speak throughout the entire class time with you listening silently. This textbook is designed with a student-centered classroom in mind. We expect YOU, the student, to dominate the class and speak for the most part of the class time every day. In class, aim to speak in Persian more than the minimum requirements of a given class drill call for.

Pronunciation. Every chapter starts with a vocabulary list needed for the entire time designated for the given chapter. Make sure to listen to the pronunciation of the new words from the audio presentation that accompanies every vocabulary list, and read the spelling of the words as you listen. Repeat each word a few times aloud so that you can hear your voice! This will make sure that muscles of your tongue and throat get used to the movements that might not be usual for your mother tongue, but are necessary to produce individual sounds and sound combinations in the target language. Pronounce each word at least five times. Start slowly and pay attention to the pronunciation of consonants and vowels as well as to stress in the word. Gradually increase the speed with which you say the word until you can easily pronounce it at a natural speed. To aid you with the pronunciation, I have included the vowel markers in the Persian spelling of the words, and also added English transliteration for every word in the list. By the time you get to class, you should be able to easily pronounce individual words that appear on the vocabulary list.

Vocabulary. This textbook focuses on high frequency topics and high frequency functional words introduced to you in various contexts for real-world purposes. I have tried to rid you of the tedious exercise of memorizing lists of words that you might not even encounter in real-life situations. Acquiring vocabulary is an essential and crucial aspect of language learning. This is a task that no one can do for you or instead of you. It will be your responsibility to make a conscious effort to learn and regularly review vocabulary. The textbook is designed in a way that chapters reuse material from previous chapters for review and reinforcement purposes, but that does not mean that you can relinquish all responsibility for learning the words on your own and expect the learning to just happen for you. One of the first things you might want to do in the very beginning of the semester is to figure out how you learn vocabulary best, that is, do you learn words better by hearing them or by seeing them in writing? Identify one or more techniques that are most effective specifically for you. You will use those techniques regularly to learn vocabulary throughout the semester. As you learn a new word, it might be helpful to give it some meaningful context, association or even imagery in order to memorize the word's meaning. If you have time, write or say a brief but meaningful sentence that would allow you to put the word you are learning in a context, preferably, something related to you and your personal experiences. As you walk in the street, say to yourself in Persian the numbers you see on the buildings, on the bus, on your car or on the elevator buttons, and, if you are using stairs, count the steps in Persian. Name in Persian the items you see around you, for example, the words for different rooms if you are in your dorm, words for stationery if you are in a bookstore or words for clothing items if you are in a department store. Make Persian vocabulary an integral part of your daily life.

Have fun writing. Thanks to its very nature, Persian script with its curves, dots and strokes is a form of art of its own that offers a lot of flexibility and freedom for artistic expression. Think of yourself as of an artist, when writing in Persian, and have fun doing it! As you learn new words, write each word numerous times—at least one full line per word—until writing the unfamiliar letter shapes of the foreign script starts to turn into a natural and easy process for your hand.

Seek opportunities to learn and practice outside of the classroom. That can mean having a conversation group with your classmates, engaging with a student organization or looking for opportunities in the local community outside of the university. Also, listen to songs, daily news, watch commercials, short films and movies in Persian, search online for cartoons or familiar films dubbed in Persian. Listen to Persian while you walk to and from your classes, ride the bus, workout in gym, and so on. Even if you don't understand what you hear, you still benefit from getting used to continuous native speech with its intonation, stress, pitch and natural speed. You will learn to identify where one word or sentence ends and the other one begins. As the course progresses, you will start to hear and recognize the words that you had learned in class, and vice versa, you will begin to recognize in your class assignments the words you heard while listening to a random song in Persian. This will help you bridge the classroom activities with the real world, which will provide a greater context and meaning to what you do in your class.

And, lastly, remember to always ask, if you cannot find an answer on your own. Ask your instructor or other students in class. Don't be shy. In Persian we say *nadãnestan eyb neest, naporseedan eyb ast* ("There's no fault in not knowing, the fault is not asking").

TO THE INSTRUCTOR

Dear Ostãd! Thank you for considering this textbook for your class. I hope you find it practical, effective and easy to use for you as well as for your students. Being a language educator and classroom instructor myself, I have always kept your role and needs in mind while writing this textbook. The structure and contents of the textbook were created in a way that strives to facilitate your day-to-day work and save you from extra logistical work that instructors often end up doing on their own in the absence of a modern language textbook. Here are some specific aspects of the textbook that serve the above purpose.

I have included in this textbook an appendix that is specially created for your use (Appendix **Instructor's Resources**). It contains activity cards, color images, maps, templates, and so on, for a variety of engaging task-based activities and group exercises in class. This should rid you of unduly and disproportionately laborious practice of designing and creating all these classroom materials for your students on your own.

Each vocabulary list throughout the textbook is accompanied by an audio presentation which serves as a pronunciation guide for your students. Persian spelling of the words in those lists includes the diacritics, the *harakat*. Each word is also accompanied by a simple-to-follow English transliteration to further aid students with the pronunciation. You don't need to read all new words in class and have students repeat each one of them after you. This should save you time during the class meetings and let you focus more on communicative activities. Every new vocabulary list is followed by Homework exercise where students use the new words in context by completing listening, reading or pronunciation assignments. This way, by the time students come to class, they have already heard, pronounced and used the words in a meaningful context, and hopefully, they feel comfortable with the words that they now have to use during class exercises.

From my own experience, I have learned all too well that most textbooks on the market do not have a sufficient number of speaking and, in many cases, even other types of activities to support enough hours of classroom meetings to allow students to really learn a topic and related vocabulary on a functional level. Keeping this in mind, I have designed a textbook that offers you and your students multiple carefully designed, research-based, and practice-proven communicative activities and homework exercises to cover every single day of classes for as many days as the textbook has designated for the given chapter. The number of designated contact hours differs from chapter to chapter depending on the nature of the topic and complexity of the given chapter's objectives. Homework assignments and classroom exercises are clearly distributed in corresponding sections and are carefully matched to complement each other. All you have to do it to follow the presented sequence of assignments.

The textbook is accompanied by a comprehensive Answer Key that is available on the textbook's companion website. You do not need to correct daily homework assignments.

I have never had a class where all students had the same learning style. Similarly, their preference for Grammar presentation varied. Some liked implicit introduction of grammar points, mainly through illustrative examples, while others preferred explicit and thorough grammar explanations. I have included thorough grammar sections in the chapters, along with numerous illustrative examples and answer key for exercises where the given structures are put to use. This way, even if you have in class those who prefer explicit grammar presentation, you will not need to hold Grammar sessions and, possibly, switch to English in order to explain mechanics of the language in class. Students will be able to read about the grammar points, see them in context, put them to use on their own and even see feedback about their application of new grammar rules, all before coming to class. In order to make for a transition between theory and hands-on activities, I have included in the In Class section additional exercises focused on grammatical competence, which will provide you with the flexibility to focus on grammar as little or as much as the class requires while still keeping the main focus on communicative proficiency.

Homework is to be assigned every day. Homework serves to prepare students for practice in the classroom and to provide students with feedback on the work they are doing. Homework also helps to make Persian a part of students' daily routine outside of the classroom. However, homework should not interfere with the speaking time in the classroom. In the beginning of class, instructor can ask if students have questions about homework due that day and, if needed, take 5-10 minutes to address those questions. Students can also take advantage of the instructor's office hours for additional guidance relating to grammar. With the comprehensive Answer Key, Grammar sections in the chapters and appendix Grammarian's Corner that all together provide detailed grammar explanations along with a multitude of illustrative examples, a need for extensive grammar lectures should not arise.

I would like to close this section by thanking you for giving your students an incredible gift of one of the world's most beautiful languages. "To learn another language is to have one more window from which to look at the world", states a Chinese saying. Indeed, after graduating from your class, your students will see the world in a different way, and will be able to interact with the world in a more effective and personal manner. By teaching a language, you train individuals who will be able to bridge cultures and peoples, and bring the world together. To some of your students still you give that "one more window from which to look" and understand their own selves, their identity and roots, which, perhaps, will allow them reconnect with their families and relatives on a deeper, more personal and emotional level. یک زبان جدید یک زندگی جدید است, we say in Persian. Thank you for giving your students an incredible gift of another life, Ostãd. *khasteh nabãsheen!*

IMAGE CREDITS

Opening images for chapters: 2 by Kamyar Adl; 3 by Soroush Karimi; 4 by Rambod Mirbaha; 5 by Soroush Karimi; 6 by Mjforoughi, 7 by Hansueli Krapf, 8 by Ali Safdarian, 9 by Hesam. montazeri; 11 by ehsanahmadnejad; 12 : by Parastou Ghazi.

Icon for speaking exercises Colorful People Communicating is Created by Freepik and modified.

Images in Chapter 1: Kavir National Park sign by HaDi, Kish island sign by خسرو حيرت, تابلو نگاری , Lady leaning on her hands by Ramtin AK, Tablo Zachekan by Hajiloo 1365, فروشگاه دنیای دیگیتال زرفسنجا by Mojpaydar, روستا سفیداله by S.morteza.

Images in Chapter 2: Family tree genealogy tree diagram chart free vector Created by Iconicbestiary—Freepik.com modified, Iranian family walking in the street by Soroush Karimi

Images in Chapter 3: Photographer in red headscarf by Mohammad Ali Jafarian on unsplash. com, Man walking in the street by Soroush Karimi, Young lady in headscarf by Soroush Karimi, Guitarist by Ashkan Forouzani

Images in Chapter 5: Headphones by Tomasz Gawlowski on unsplash.com Pen by Mike Tinnion on unsplash.com, Pencil by Kelly Sikkema on unsplash.com, Laptop by jannoon028 on Freepik, Notebook by Ashley Edwards on unsplash.com, Smart phone by Jannoon028 on Freepik.

Images in Chapter 6: USA map design with vibrant colors free vector created by Freepik modified. Image Blue Wall with a brown furniture designed by Javi_Indy / Freepik, Modern studio apartment designed by katemangostar / Freepik, Modern House Three Storey designed by vectorpocket / Freepik.

Images in Chapter 7: Sarvelat by Mojtaba Hoseini on Unsplash, Resalat tunnel in Tehran by Ivan Milnaric, Jamshidie Park, Niavaran by Amin Gholamali.

Images in Chapter 8: Jeans, casual men short pants , top long casual beautiful , pair of socks, blue hat Created by Mrsiraphol—Freepik.com, Young lady in red scarf by Soroush Karimi, sweater by Freepik,

Images in Chapter 10: Blue weather icons free vector created by Lyolya_profitrolya—Freepik.com, weather app template free vector created by Freepik, Mellat park in winter by Milad Mosapoor, Manjeel windmills by Ali Madjfar, Map of Iran by Ali Zifan.

Images in Chapter 11: Handsome guy enjoying education at university, created by Katemangostar—Freepik.com, elegant businesswoman by Pressfoto on Freepik, Student man presenting something by Luis Molinero on Freepik, Young blond woman by Abbas Maleki Hosseini on unsplash.com, Man with moustache and glasses, Young man by Ashkan Forouzan on unsplash.com, Man with grey hair by Soroush Karimi, woman in red scarf by Bardia Hashemirad, woman in yellow scarf by Farshad Rezvanian, smiling man by Alireza Attari, woman leaning on her hand by Sobhan Joodi.

Chapter 12: Road sign icon collection free vector created by Zandern – Freepik.com, yellow road signs free vector created by Freepik, Customs line in Tehran airport by Parastou Ghazi

فَصلِ اَوَل
Chapter 1

سَلام
Hello!

Hello, Persian class!

Function Greeting and introducing yourself and others, saying where you are from and where you live, describing how you are feeling, saying where and what you study, counting (0–10), saying your phone number, talking about the days of the week. Key verbs: *to be, to have, to study, to work, to live, to read*.

The alphabet. Differences between spelling and pronunciation. Writing your name in Persian.

Listening Parsa introduces himself and his family.

Structures Building simple phrases, using nouns with numbers.

UNIT 1

Vocabulary: Hello, how are you? What is your name? Pronouns.

Letters: ذ د ژ ز ر و آ

The following are the most common forms of greeting in Persian. There are several different registers of greetings in Persian on formal and casual levels. They may include references to third persons and employ various aspects of the Persian social etiquette, the *taãrof*. Greetings are often accompanied by smile and gestures, such as placing one's hand on the chest as a sign of gratitude. It is important to use the appropriate form (formal or casual) of greeting so as to not appear impolite and disrespectful.

A formal greeting is a must when addressing individuals who are older or have a higher—actual or perceived—social, professional or other status, unless your familiarity with and relation to the person allows you to deviate from this rule. A formal greeting is also usual when addressing strangers, but the casual form is sometimes used by strangers who belong to the same age group.

In Iran, upon greeting, women usually shake hands and kiss once on each cheek. Iranian men greeting each other would act the same way. However, if a man and a woman greet each other they don't kiss and might only shake hands, unless they are relatives or close acquaintances. In the Islamic Republic of Iran, Islamic customs prevent strangers of opposite sex (men and women) from shaking hands upon greeting. In such situations, a verbal greeting, polite smile and gentle bow are common.

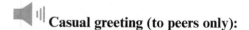
Casual greeting (to peers only):

salãm, cheto-ree?	Hi, how **are** you?
khoobam, mersee!	I am well, thank you.

Formal greeting:

salãm, hãleh shomã cheto-reh?	Hello, how **is** your health/condition?
khoobam, mersee!	I am well, thank you.

There are situations when the environment or time does not allow for elaborate and extended greetings. For example, if familiar individuals quickly pass each other in a hallway at work, the short phrase /salãm, hãleh shomã!/ is used, to which one may reply with /mam-noon, *hāleh shomā!/* or simply */hāleh shomā!/*. These are, sometimes combined with a gentle nod or respectful smile.

In Unit 1 we will learn how to say *hello*, how to say your name, how to ask somebody's name, how to say *nice to meet you* and say *good-bye*. You will need those words to meet students of your Persian class and introduce yourself.

LISTEN AND REPEAT. At this point, you do not need to try and learn the Persian spelling of the words as you are not familiar with all the letters of the alphabet. Learn the pronunciation and meaning of the words. Listen to the audio and repeat each word several times aloud until you can easily pronounce it. Try to imitate the native speaker's pronunciation and intonation. Speaking a language is a skill, so repetition and practice are crucial to your success in the process of language acquisition.

Pronouns		
I	man	مَن
You (formal, i.e., royal *you* in reference to one person), also: plural you (i.e,. you all)	shomā	شُما
you (casual *you* in reference to one person)	toh	تو
s/he	oon	او
they	oon-hā	آنها

Introductions and Greetings		
Name, First name	esm	اِسم
Last name	nāmeh khāne-vāde-gee	نامِ خانوادِگی،
	esmeh fāmeelee fāmeelee	اِسمِ فامیلی، فامیلی،
	fāmeel	فامیل
What	chee	چه

3

Introductions and Greetings		
Hello, Hi	sa-lãm	سَلام
Good-bye	khodã hã-fez	خُدا حافِظ
Condition, health, state of being	hãl	حال
Good, well	khoob	خوب
Bad, badly	bad	بَد
Very well, very good	khe-ee-lee khoob	خِیلی خوب
How	che-tor	چِطور
Thank you	mer-see	مِرسی
You are welcome	khã-hesh mee-ko-nam	خواهِش میکُنَم
And	va	و

Verbs and Phrases		
Is	ast/hast/eh	آست
What is?	chee eh?	چه است؟
How is?	che-toreh?	چِطور آست؟
Your first name?	es-meh shomã	اِسمِ شُما
What is your first name?	es-meh shomã chee eh?	اِسمِ شُما چه آست؟
What is your last name?	fãmeelee-yeh shomã chee eh?	فامیلیِ شُما چه آست؟
My first name is Amir	es-meh man Amireh	اِسمِ مَن امیر آست
My last name is Amin	fãmeelee-yeh man Amin-eh	فامیلیِ مَن امین آست

Verbs and Phrases		
His first name is Amir	es-meh oon Amireh	اِسمِ او امیر آست
How are **you** (casual greeting)	che-toree	چِطوری
How is your health (formal greeting)	hã-leh shomã che-toreh	حالِ شُما چِطور آست؟
I am good, well	khoob-am	خوبَم
I am not feeling well	hãlam khoob neest	حالم خوب نیست
Nice to meet you	khosh vaqt-am	خوش وَقتَم
It was nice meeting you	khosh vaqt sho-dam	خوش وَقت شُدَم

LETTERS

ذ د ژ ز ر و آ

The letters are presented in groups. The first group comprises the letters that only connect to one side-the right side, that is, they do not connect to the left. This group is abbreviated using the word وارد that combines all basic shapes of the letters that make up this group and means *entrant*, symbolically representing the starting point for learning the alphabet.

آ   *alef maddeh* (vowel *ã* as in English words *far, father*)
و   *vav* (consonant *v*; vowel *oo*; diphthong *ow*)
ر   *re* (soft *r*)
ز   *ze* (sound *z*)
ژ   *zhe* (soft sound *zh*)
د   *dal* (sound *d*)
ذ   *zal* (sound *z*, same as above)

The letter آ alef maddeh

This letter represents a deep vowel sound **ã** similar to the vowel in the English words *far, father*. In our transliteration this sound is represented by the symbol *ã*. Note that *ã* carries the tilde, the so-called hat in order to imitate its Persian counterpart letter *alef maddeh* آ that too carries the "hat." Don't confuse this sound with the vowel sound that occurs in the

5

beginning of the English word **afternoon** and also in the Persian word صف *saf* and is represented in our transliteration by the symbol *a*. Think of the difference in pronunciation of the sound *a* in two English words **far** (roughly corresponds to *ã*, the *alef maddeh*) and **apple** (roughly corresponds to *a*). Similar difference exists between the Persian sounds *ã* (the *alef maddeh*) and *a*, and the two sounds are not interchangeable in Persian. Replacing *ã* with *a* may lead to the change of the meaning of the word, for example, Persian word *bãd* means **wind**, whereas Persian word *bad* means **bad, badly**. Note that the "hat" (*maddeh*) on top of the letter *alef maddeh* is present only when *alef maddeh* is in beginning of the word. The *maddeh* disappears when *alef* is in the middle or end of the word.

1.1 Watch the video and learn how to write the letter Ī (alef *maddeh*) in the initial, medial and final positions within a word. Write the letter *alef* several times in each of the three positions.

1.2 Listen to the words and check the appropriate number for the words in which you hear the sound *ã* (as opposed to the sound *a*).

1.	2.	3.	4.	5.	6.

1.3 Listen to the words and circle the number for the words in which you hear the sound *a* (as opposed to the sound *ã*).

1.	2.	3.	4.	5.	6.

1.4 Look at the image and identify the letter Ī.

The letter و vav

This is a chameleon letter. It may represent the consonant *v* (as in English words *voice, venture*), the vowel *oo* (as in English word *scoop*), the diphthong *ow* (as in English word *throw*). Sometimes it can also carry the vowel *o* (as in English word *joy*). The rule of thumb, albeit not without exceptions, is that when و precedes a vowel, it acts as the consonant *v*, and when و follows a consonant, it acts as the vowel *oo* or the diphthong *ow*.

1.5 Watch the video and learn how to write the letter و in the initial, medial and final positions within a word. Write the letter *vav* several times in each position.

1.6 (a) Listen to the words and check the number of the words in which you hear the sound *oo* (as opposed to the sound *o* as in English *bolt*).

1.	2.	3.	4.	5.	6.	7.

(b) Listen to the words and check the number of the words in which you hear the sound *o* (as opposed to the sounds *oo* as in English *tool* and *ow* as in English *throw*).

1.	2.	3.	4.	5.	6.

1.7 Look at the image and identify the letter و. Count how many و you see in the image and underline all of them.

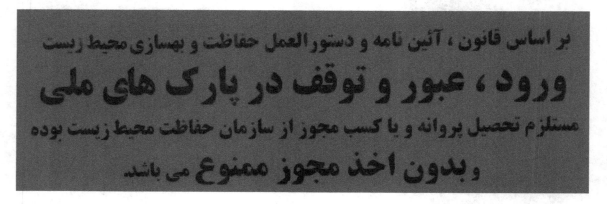

بر اساس قانون ، آئین نامه و دستورالعمل حفاظت و بهسازی محیط زیست

ورود ، عبور و توقف در پارک های ملی

مستلزم تحصیل پروانه و یا کسب مجوز از سازمان حفاظت محیط زیست بوده

و بدون اخذ مجوز ممنوع می باشد.

The letters ژ ز ر

These letters have the same basic shape and therefore connect to other letters in the same manner. These letters differ from each other by the presence and number of dots placed above that basic shape. Like the previous two letters we have already discussed, the letters ژ ز ر only connect to the right, that is, they do not connect to the left.

The letter ر *re* represents a soft *r* sound.

The letter ز *ze* represents the *z* sound as in English *zeal*.

The letter ژ *zhe* represents the soft *zh* sound similar to the sound that appears in the beginning of the French words *joli, Juliette*, or at the end of the English word *beige*.

1.8 Watch the video and learn how to write the letters ژ ز ر in the initial, medial and final positions within a word. Write these letters several times in each position.

1.9 Listen to the words and check the number for the words in which you hear the sound *zh* (as opposed to the *j* sound as in English Jim).

1.	2.	3.	4.	5.	6.	7.	8.

1.10 Look at the image and count how many letters ز and how many letters ژ you see.

The letters د ذ

These letters have the same basic shape and therefore connect to other letters in the same manner. These letters differ from each other by one dot placed above the basic shape. Similar to the letters we have already discussed, the letters ذ د only connect to the right, that is, they do not connect to the left.

The letter د *dal* represents the sound *d* as in the English word *dorm*.

The letter ذ *zal* represents the *z* sound identical to the sound of the letter ز.

1.11 Watch the video and learn how to write the letters د ذ in the initial, medial and final positions. Write these letters several times in each position.

1.12 Listen to the words and circle the appropriate number for the words in which you hear the sound *d*.

1.	2.	3.	4.	5.

1.13 Look at the following passage and underline the letter ‏د‎ in it. In the Persian paragraph below, increase spacing between all lines otherwise letters from different lines overlap and students will not be able to complete the exercise.

کوه دماوند بلندترین کوه ایران و بلندترین کوه خاور میانه و همچنین بلندترین قله آتشفشانی آسیا است. کوه دماوند در استان مازندران در کشور ایران قرار دارد. کوه دماوند از شهر تهران و همچنین کرانه های دریای مازندران دیده میشود

HOMEWORK   تَکلیف

1.14 Read the new vocabulary list for this lesson. Now, listen to the audio presentation of this exercise and arrange the words in the order that you hear them.

khoob, eh, shomã, esm, hãl

1.15 (a) Listen and read along. Now, complete the English translation based on what you hear and see.

/esmeh man tomeh. fãmeelee-yeh man jonsoneh./
My _____ is _____. My _____ is _____.

(b) You will hear the person in the photo below introduce herself. Listen and prepare to answer the following questions in class.

1. es-meh oon chee-eh?
2. fãmeel-eh oon chee-eh?

1.16 Below are the transcripts of two short conversations: one is performed in a casual register between two individuals who are familiar to each other, and the other is performed in a formal register between two strangers who are meeting each other for the first time. (1) Read the transcript and complete the translation. (2) Prepare to read aloud the transcripts. In class, your instructor will ask you and one other student in class to take on the roles of different characters in the dialogue and read their lines.

Dialogue 1

Transcript	Translation
S: salām, Keyvan! chetoree? K: salām, Sahar! man khoobam, mersee! to chetoree? S: khoobam, mersee! K: khodā hāfez. S: khodā hāfez.	S: Hi, Keyvan! _____? K: _____, Sahar! _____, thank you! _____? S: I am _____! K: good-bye. S: _____.

Transcript	Translation
A: salām, hāleh shomā chetoreh? esmeh man Amireh. S: salām, esmeh man Sahareh. A: khoshvaqtam! S: khoshvaqtam!	A: Hi, _____? My _____ is Amir. S: _____! _____ name is Sahar. A: Nice to meet you! S: _____.

1.17 Watch the video and write each word several times.

_____

_____

_____

_____

_____

11

1.18 The following combinations of letters make up actual words. Transcribe them in Persian. Write each word several times. Remember that Persian is written from right to left. The letter you see on the right is the first letter of the word.

_____ vav + dal 1.

_____ dal + re + alef + vav 2.

_____ dal + vav + re 3.

_____ dal + vav + re + vav 4.

_____ dal + alef + re 5.

_____ dal + ze + dal 6.

_____ re + ze 7.

_____ dal + ze 8.

_____ ze + alef + re + dal 9.

IN CLASS

دَر کِلاس

1.19 Your instructor will go around and ask you questions about your first name and last name using the vocabulary list given in the beginning of the chapter. Answer the questions in Persian. Your instructor will then go around again and ask you about the first name and last name of the person next to you. If you do not remember that person's name, ask them in Persian what their name is and then answer the instructor's question.

1.20 Your instructor will pair you up with a random student in class. The two of you will read aloud lines from the two dialogues from Homework 1.16 that you have prepared to read aloud in Persian.

1.21 Arrange the chairs so that you face a classmate. Strike up a conversation with your classmate in Persian using the greeting phrases you have learned. Greet your classmate, inquire about their health and ask their first name and last name. Be prepared to answer the same questions about yourself. Don't forget to say in Persian *nice to meet you*, and close your conversation with *good-bye*. Now, move one seat over to the left or right and start a similar conversation with a different classmate. Repeat. These basic phrases for greeting and introductions should come automatically to you. You should not have to stop and think about the words when you need to use these phrases, so practice as much as needed in order to achieve that fluency.

1.22    You will be working in groups. Prepare and perform for the class a very brief dialogue using the greeting and farewell phrases you know. Speak in Persian only. Your instructor will assign to each group either a formal or informal register in which to perform the dialogue, and say if the characters in the dialogue are familiar or unfamiliar with each other. Familiar characters in the dialogue will greet each other. Unfamiliar characters will greet and introduce themselves to each other.

1.23   Read the following words aloud.

داد، راد، رو، واد، دار، دارا،روز، دور، راز، آزاد، زور، آزار.

1.24   Close your textbook for this drill. Your instructor will pronounce a word from the list below. Write that word on the board in Persian

وادار، آژور، رود، آزادوار، زاو، دارو، دود، زود، زاد، دارا، واد، رو

UNIT 2

Vocabulary: What do you do? The verb *to be*. I'm happy, sad, tired, sleepy, and so on.

Letters: گ ک ن ث ت پ ب

Listen to the audio and repeat the words. Say each word several times until you can easily pronounce it. Try to imitate the native speaker's pronunciation. Speaking a language is a skill. Repetition and practice are crucial to your success in the process of language acquisition.

Translation	Pronunciation	Spelling
Student	dã-nesh-joo	دانِشجو
PhD student	dã-nesh-joo-yeh dok-to-rã	دانِشجوی دُکتُرا
Professor, teacher	ostãd	اُستاد
Occupation, job	shoql	شُغل
Class	ke-lãs	کِلاس
Persian class	ke-lã-seh fãrsee	کِلاسِ فارسی
University	dã-nesh-gãh	دانِشگاه
University of ...	dã-nesh-gãh-eh ...	دانِشگاهِ ...

13

Adjectives		
I'm happy	khosh hāl-am	خوشحالَم
I'm sad, feeling down	del-gee-r-am	دِلگیرَم
I'm in a good mood	sar-eh hāl-am	سَرِ حالَم
I'm excited	haya-jān zad-am	هَیَجان زَده آم
I'm sleepy	khā-bam mee-yād	خوابَم میاید
I'm tired	khasteh-am/ khast-am	خَسته آم
I'm feeling under the weather	ke-sel-am	کِسِلَم
I'm upset	nā-rā-hat-am	ناراحَتَم
I'm comfortable	rā-hat-am	راحَتَم
I'm anxious, worried	moz-ta-reb-am	مُضطَرِبَم
I'm hungry	gosh-na-meh	گُشنه ام است
I'm thirsty	tesh-na-meh	تِشنه ام است
I'm nervous	dast-pācham	دستپاچه ام

Verbs and Phrases		
I am	has-tam	هَستَم
You (pl., formal) are	hasteed/hasteen	هَستید
you (sing., casual) are	hastee	هَستی
Is (used in colloquial register instead of است /eh/ often after the words that end with vowels); in formal language, this word means *there is/there are*	hast	هست
We are	hasteem	هَستیم
They are	hastand/hastan	هَستَند
I am not	nees-tam	نیستَم
You (pl., formal) aren't	nees-teed/nees-teen	نیستید
you (sing., casual) aren't	nees-tee	نیستی
It, s/he isn't	neest	نیست
Are you well? (use to say *how are you?* in casual register)	khoobee?	خوبی؟
I'm pleased (lit.: happy) to meet you	az āshnā-ee-toon khoshhālam!	از آشنایی اتان خوشحالَم!

14

Verbs and Phrases		
Likewise, So am I (lit.: I also the same way)	manam hameen-tor/man ham hameen-tor	مَن هَم هَمینطور
Who is that?	oon kee-eh?	آن کی است؟
What is your occupation?	shoq-leh shomã chee-eh?	شُغلِ شُما چه است؟
What is his/her occupation?	shoq-leh oon chee-eh?	شُغلِ او چه است؟
I am a student too	man-am dã-nesh-joo hast-am	مَن هَم دانِشجو هَستَم
In what class?	dar cheh ke-lã-see?	در چه کلاسی؟
In what university?	dar cheh dãnesh-gã-hee?	در چه دانشگاهی؟

When using the question word *che* چه, add the unstressed ending *ee* to the end of the word to which that question word چه refers.

Useful Words		
That	oon	آن
This	een	این
Who?	kee	کی؟
Which	koo-doom/ko-doom	کُدام؟
Yes	ba-leh	بَله
No	nah	نَه
In	dar (too)	دَر (تو)
Also, too	ham/am	هَم

The word *also* (ham) in Persian is placed immediately after the word to which it refers, for example: She too is a professor /oon ham ostãdeh/ او هم اِستاد است

TO KEEP IN MIND

The verb میخوانم /mee-khoo-nam/

The verb *to study* is a compound verb in Persian, where میخوانم /mee-khoo-nam/ is combined either with the word درس /dars/ *lesson* or with the name of a specific class or subject matter. When combined with the word /dars/ درس, the whole compound verb refers to the general notion of studying, writing or reading class assignments, preparing for classes, and so on. When combined with the name of a subject matter, major or a field of study, the whole composite verb refers to the process of studying that particular subject, major, and so on.

E.g., در کتابخانه درس میخوانم /dar ketābkhooneh dars meekhoonam/
I study in the library;
زیست شناسی میخوانم /zeest shenāsee meekhoonam/ I study Biology.

The verb *to read* is a compound verb in Persian, where میخوانم /meekhoonam/ is combined either with the word کِتاب /ketāb/ *book* or with the name of a specific item that you are reading, for example, email (ایمِیل).

خیلی کتاب میخوانم. /khe-ee-lee ketāb meekhoonam/ I read a lot.

ایمیل میخوانم. /ee-me-eel meekhoonam/ I read email.

LETTERS

ب پ ت ث ن ک گ

These letters connect to both sides. Several of them share one basic shape and are only distinguished from each other by the use of dots and oblique dashes.

ب	*be*	(sound *b*)
پ	*pe*	(sound *p*)
ت	*te*	(sound *t*)
ث	*se*	(soft sound *s*, as in English word **seek**)
ن	*noon*	(sound *n*)
ک	*kaf*	(sound *k*)
گ	*gaf*	(sound *g*, as in English word **geese**)

The letters ب پ ت ث

These letters have the same basic shape and differ from each other by the position and number of dots. Their basic shapes are written and connected in the same manner.

2.1 Watch the video and learn how to write the letters ب پ ت ث in the initial, medial and final positions. Write each word several times!

2.2 Listen to the words and check the number of the words in which you hear the sound *p*.

1.	2.	3.	4.	5.

2.3 Look at the following passage and count how many times the letter ب appears in it.

شِهر بابل که معروف به شِهر بهار نارنج است در شِهرستان بابل در شِمال ایران قرار دارد. در گذشته به دلیل تجارت و عبور و مرور تاجران و بازرگانان در این شِهر، آن را بارفروش میگفتند.

The letter ن

This letter might look similar to the letters ب پ ت ث in shape, but it differs from those letters by the fact that its body extends below the line, while the letters ب پ ت ث always stay on the line. In the medial position, however, ن looks almost identical to the above four letters, but ن is distinguished from the other four letters by a single dot on top. Don't confuse ن with the letter ب that is written with a dot under the line.

2.4 Watch the video and learn how to write the letter ن in the initial, medial and final positions. Write each word several times!

2.5 Look at the following passage and count how many times the letter ن appears in it.

شِهر بابل که معروف به شِهر بهار نارنج است در شِهرستان بابل در شِمال ایران قرار دارد. در گذشته به دلیل تجارت و عبور و مرور تاجران و بازرگانان در این شِهر، آن را بارفروش میگفتند.

The letters گ ک

The letter ک (k) is pronounced similarly to the sound *k* in the English word **keep**. It is usually pronounced much softer when it appears at the end of the word. The letter گ is pronounced similarly to the sound *g* in the English word **geese**. It is usually pronounced much softer when it appears at the end of the word. These two letters share the same basic shape and therefore connect to other letters in the same manner. They differ from each other by the number of oblique lines on top.

2.6 Watch the video and learn how to write the letters گ ک in the initial, medial and final positions. Write each word several times!

2.7 Listen to the words and check the number for the words in which you hear the sound *g*.

1.	2.	3.	4.	5.	6.

2.8 Look at the image and identify the letter ک on it.

HOMEWORK   تکلیف

2.9 (a) Read the new vocabulary in this lesson. Now, listen to the audio presentation of this exercise and complete the translation of the sentences you hear.

(1) I am a _____ at the _____ of California. (2) I also _____ Persian. (3) The _____ of my _____ in the Persian class is Ali. (4) I'm _____ (5) I am not a _____.

2.9 (b)  Let's learn more about the person from the photo. From her introduction in Unit 1, you already know her name. Now, she will be talking about what she does. Listen and prepare to answer these questions in class in Persian. Useful word: /yã/ *or*.

(a) esmeh oon chee-eh?
(b) fãmeelee-eh oon chee-eh?
(c) oon ostãdeh?
(d) oon dãneshjoo yã dãneshjooyeh doktorã hast?
(e) oon dãneshjoo dar cheh dãneshgãhee-eh?

2.10 Below are transcripts of two short dialogues. Dialogue 1 takes place between two strangers who meet and introduce themselves to each other for the first time and therefore speak in a formal register. Dialogue 2 takes place between three individuals, where one of the individuals introduces the other two people to each other. In Dialogue 2, the speakers choose casual or formal register based on whether they are friends or they are meeting for the first time. (1) Read the transcripts and complete the translations. (2) Prepare to read aloud the transcripts. In class, your instructor will ask you and one other student in class to take on the roles of different characters in the dialogue and read their lines.

Dialogue 1 between two individuals Sogand and Ramtin who meet for the first time.

Transcript	Translation
S: salãm, khoob hasteen? man Sogand hastam. R: salãm, man Ramtin-am. az ãshnãeetoon khoshhãlam! S: man ham hameen-tor!	S: Hi, _____? I _____ Sogand. R: _____, I'm Ramtin. _ _____! S: So am I!

Dialogue 2 between Keyvan and Sahar who are friends, and Marjan who is Sahar's friend.

Transcript	Translation
S: salãm, Keyvan! K: salãm, Sahar! S: chetoree? K: man khoobam, mersee! to khoobee? S: khoobam, mersee. Keyvan, een Marjaneh. Marjan, een Keyvaneh. K: salãm, hãleh shomã chetoreh? az ãshnãeetoon khoshhãlam! M: mersee! man ham hameen-tor!	S: Hi, Keyvan! K: _____, Sahar! S: _____? K: I'm well, _____! Are you _____? S: _____, thank you. Keyvan, _____ is Marjan. Marjan, this _____ Keyvan. K: Hi, _____? I'm pleased to meet you! M: _____! So am I.

2.11 Listen to the words and, for each word that you hear, write an antonym.

(a)	(d)
(b)	(e)
(c)	(f)

2.12 Answer in Persian the following questions about yourself. Prepare to ask and answer these questions aloud in class.

(a) esmeh shomã chee-eh?
(b) shoq-leh shomã che-eh?
(c) dãneshjoo dar cheh dãneshgãhee hasteen?
(d) dãneshgãh-eh shomã khoobeh?
(e) dãneshjoo dar cheh kelãsee hasteen?
(f) esmeh ostãdeh shomã dar kelãseh fãrsee chee-eh?
(g) kelãseh fãrsee khoobeh?

2.13 Watch the video and connect the letters to form words. Write each word several times.

ا.‏ ۱. و د ر گ ا

ب.‏ ۲. ر آ و گ ر ز ب

ن.‏ ۳. ن و ت پ ن

ر.‏ ۴. ر آ گ ن

2.14 The following are the names of the letters of the Persian alphabet. Write them out in Persian and connect them when possible. Remember that Persian is written from right to left. In the series of letters below, the letter on the right is the first letter of the word. Write each word several times.

_____ gaf, re, gaf, te 1.

_____ kaf, nun, alef, be 2.

_____ zhe, alef, re, alef, gaf 3.

_____ dal, vav, kaf 4.

2.15 🔊 Listen and write the words you hear in Persian. Use ز when you hear *z*.

1.	2.	3.	4.	5.	6.
7.	8.	9.	10.	11.	12.

IN CLASS   دَر کِلاس

2.16 👥 A large number of Iranian last names are structured by adding the stressed ending *ee* to a place of origin, such as a town, city, province, and so on. Some of the examples of such last names are Tehrani /tehrãnee/, Kashani /kãshãnee/. Another common suffix is /eeyãn/ often attached to a personal name. Some examples are Jamshidian /jam-shee-dee-yãn/, Rashidian /ra-shee-dee- yãn/, and so on. Another common Persian last name ending is Zad or Zadeh, for example, Pirzad /peer-zãd/, Jamalzadeh /ja-mal-zãdeh/. The stress in these last names falls on the last syllable. In Persian pronunciation, the first name and last name are connected with the unwritten and unstressed glide /eh/ that is pronounced between one's first name and last name, for example, Kamran-eh Kashani. The names are preceded by the prefix Mr. /ã-qã-yeh . . ./ or Mrs./Ms. /khã-noo-meh . . ./.

Now, make up a Persian name for yourself using the suffixes mentioned above. Working in a group, introduce yourself using the Persian name you have chosen for yourself, and then ask others in the group to say their Persian names. Don't forget to say *hello*, inquire about the respondents' health, say *nice to meet you*, and say *thank you*.

2.17 👥 (a) Arrange the chairs so that you face a classmate. Start a conversation with your classmate by greeting him/her and inquiring about his/her health. Ask questions about your classmate's name, occupation and place of occupation. Ask what class s/he

21

is taking and if it's any good. Close by thanking your conversation partner and taking leave. Refer to the questions you have prepared as Homework. Be prepared to answer the same questions from your classmate. Now, move one seat over to the right and start a similar conversation with a different person. You will see that you can maintain a longer conversation today than you did yesterday.

(b) Once you have finished talking to the last person, the instructor will ask you to introduce to the class your last conversation partner by sharing with the class his/her first name, last name, occupation, place of occupation, and so on. Your objective is to say as much as you know about the other person.

(c)  Role Play. You will be working in groups. Prepare and perform in Persian a skit in order to demonstrate to the class how to introduce a friend to a third person. Your instructor will assign to your group a setting (university hallway, an office, classroom, etc.) where the introductions should take place. Do the introductions considering the appropriate cultural norms discussed in the beginning of the chapter.

2.18 Read these following words aloud.

تاب، پا، گاراژ، بازار، پارو، ناز، باکو، کود، داراب، نان

2.19 Close your book. Your instructor will read a random word from the list below. Write on the board the word you hear. Keep in mind that only the deep *ã* sound is written (using the letter آ), whereas the other *a* sound is not written.

آبدار، کارد، تودار، بانک، کباب، برگ، توانا، توپ، بد، باد، کدو، تب، پاک، بند، پارک.

UNIT 3

Vocabulary: Where are you from? How many brothers and sisters do you have? Numbers (0–5). Verbs: *to have, to live.*

Letters: ق ف ل ض ص ش س

Listen and repeat the words. Repeat each word several times aloud until you can easily pronounce it. Try to imitate the native speaker's pronunciation and intonation. By the time you get to class, you should be able to pronounce the words fluently.

Translation	Pronunciation	Spelling
Family (immediate family)	khã-nevã-deh/ khoo-nevã-deh	خانِواده
Relative	fãmeel	فامیل
Dad	bãbã	بابا
Mom	mãmãn	مامان
Parents	pedaroh mãdar, mãmãnoh bãbã, mãmãn-bãbã	پِدَرومادَر، مامان و بابا، مامان بابا
Sister	khã-har	خواهَر
Brother	ba-rã-dar	بَرادَر
Doctor, physician	dok-tor	دُکتُر
Life	zen-de-gee	زِندِگی
Being from	a-h-l	اَهل
Where?	ko-jã	کُجا؟
From	az	اَز
From where? (stress falls on final *ee*)	ko-jã-*ee*	کُجایی؟
Now	al-ãn	آلان
My mom	mãmã-neh man	مامانِ مَن
Your dad	bãbã-yeh toh	بابای تو
Other, another	dee-geh	دیگر
American	ãm-ree-kã-ee	آمریکایی
Iranian	ee-rã-nee	ایرانی

The word *other* /deegeh/ in Persian is a modifier and follows the word it describes.

My other sister /khã-har-eh dee-geh-yeh man/ خواهَرِ دیگرِ مَن
My other sister's name /es-meh khã-har-eh dee-geh-yeh man/ اِسمِ خواهَرِ دیگرِ مَن

Numbers		
How many?	chan tã	چَند تا؟
0	sef-r	صِفر (۰)
1	yeh	یِک (۱)

23

Numbers		
2	doh	دو (۲)
3	se	سه (۳)
4	chãr	چَهار (۴)
5	panj	پَنج (۵)

Verbs and Phrases		
I have	dã-ram	دارَم
you (singular, casual) have	dã-ree	داری
You have (formal), Also: You all have (plural)	dã-reen	دارید
S/he has	dã-reh	دارد
They have	dã-ran	دارَند
We have	dã-reem	داریم
I don't have	na-dã-ram	نَدارَم
I live	zen-de-gee mee-ko-nam	زِندِگی میکُنَم
You live (singular)	zen-de-gee mee-ko-nee	زِندِگی میکُنی
You live (formal), Also: You all live (plural)	zen-de-gee mee-ko-neen	زِندِگی میکُنید
S/he lives	zen-de-gee mee-ko-neh	زِندِگی میکُند
They live	zen-de-gee mee-ko-nan	زِندِگی میکُنَند
Where are you from?	ko-jã-ee has-teen?	کُجایی هَستید؟
I am American.	ãm-ree-kã-ee has-tam	آمریکایی هَستَم
I am from America.	az ãm-ree-kã has-tam	اَز آمریکا هَستَم
Where are you from (when inquiring about city, town)	ah-leh ko-jã has-teen?	آهلِ کُجا هَستید؟
I am from New York	ah-leh New York has-tam	آهلِ نیویورک هَستَم
How many brothers do you have?	chan tã ba-rã-dar dã-reen?	چَند تا بَرادَر دارید؟
I have two brothers	doh tã ba-rã-dar dã-ram	دو تا بَرادَر دارَم

LETTERS

ق ف ل ض ص ش س

These letters connect to both sides. Two of them have the same basic shape and are distinguished from each other by the use of a dot.

- س   **sin** (soft sound *s*, as in English word *seek*)
- ش   **shin** (sound *sh*)
- ص   **sad** (same sound *s* as described for the letter س above)
- ض   **zad** (sound *z*, same as ذ ز)
- ل   **lam** (soft sound *l*)
- ق   **qaf** (*q/gh* a soft glottal consonant sound)
- ف   **fe** (sound *f*)

The letters س ش

These letters connect to both sides. They share the same basic shape and are distinguished from each other by the use of dots. Don't confuse the letter *shin* ش in the medial position with the letter ث (se) in the medial position. The letter ش has three spikes, whereas the letter ث only has one spike in the medial position.

3.1 Watch the video and learn how to write the letters ش س in the initial, medial and final positions. Write each word several times!

3.2 Look at the image and identify the letters س and ش.

3.3 Distribute the following words in the columns according to the letter that appears in the word.

آش ، شانس ، استثنا ، ثابت ، شور ، ثور ، وارث ، پشت

ث	ش

The letters ص ض

These letters connect to both sides. Be careful not to confuse ض in its medial position with the letter ف in its medial position. The letter ض has an elongated top, whereas ف has a round top.

3.4 Watch the video and learn how to write the letters ص and ض in the initial, medial and final positions in a word. Write each word several times!

The letter ل

This letter connects to both sides. Don't confuse it with the letter آ (alef) which only connects to the right.

3.5 Watch the video and learn how to write the letter ل in the initial, medial and final positions. Write each word several times!

3.6 Look at the image and identify the letter ل.

3.7 Distribute the following words in the columns according to the letter that appears in the word.

آرد ، لر ، وارد ، ولگرد ، گل ، دانا ، گلگشت ،کانون

آ	ل

The letter ق

This letter connects to both sides. This is a soft glottal consonant sound that is, in a way, similar to the first sound in the French word "rouge" but with a harder glottal quality. Your throat will contract inward when you pronounce it. As you write words from the following video, try to repeat the words after the speaker as he pronounces them.

3.8 Watch the video and learn how to write the letter ق in the initial, medial and final positions. Write each word several times!

3.9 Look at the following passage and identify the letter ق on it.

قهوه خانه، کافه و کافی شاپ به مکان هایی گفته میشود که در آنها قهوه،
چای و نوشیدنی های دیگری سرو میشوند. در گذشته، قهوه خانه جای تبادل
افکار، قصه گویی و نقالی هم بوده است.

3.10 Listen to the audio and check the appropriate number for which you hear a word with ق in it.

1.	2.	3.	4.	5.
6.	7.	8.	9.	10.

3.11 Listen and write the words you hear. For the sound *s* in these words use the letter س

The letter ف

This letter connects to both sides. Do not confuse the letter ف in the medial position with the letter ق in the medial position. The letter ف is written with only one dot, whereas the letter ق is written with two dots.

3.12 Watch the video and learn how to write the letter ف in the initial, medial and final positions. Write each word several times!

3.13 Listen to the audio and check the appropriate number for which you hear a word with ف in it.

1.	2.	3.	4.	5.	6.

3.14 Listen and write the words you hear.

3.15 Distribute the following words in the columns according to the letter that appears in the word.

فر، قرض، بنفش، نقش، ساق، نصف

ق	ف

HOMEWORK  تَکلیف

3.16 (a) Listen and read along. Complete the translation based on what you hear and see.

/salãm, esmeh man Nikeh. man dar New York zendegee meekonam. man yeh khãhar va yeh barãdar dãram. esmeh khãhareh man Taraeh. Tara dãneshjooyeh dãneshgãheh New Yorkeh. esmeh barãdareh man Keyvaneh. Keyvan dãneshjooyeh doktorã dar dãnesh-gãheh Columbiaeh. bãbãyeh man doktoreh va mãmãneh man ostãdeh dãneshgãheh./

Hi, my _____ is _____ . I _____ in New York. I have _____ sister and one _____ . My _____'s name is Tara. Tara is a _____ at the New York _____ . My _____'s name is _____ . Keyvan is a _____ at _____ . My _____ is a doctor, and my _____ is a _____ .

(b)   Listen to Parisa as she tells you more about herself. She will be speaking about her hometown and her family. Prepare to answer in class the following questions.

- esmeh oon chee-eh?
- oon kojãee-eh?
- alãn kojã zendegee meekoneh?
- chan tã barãdar vah khãhar dãreh?
- esmeh khãhareh oon chee-eh?
- esmeh barãdareh oon chee-eh?
- shoq-leh bãbãyeh oon chee-eh?
- shoq-leh mãmãneh oon chee-eh?

3.17 Answer the following questions about yourself. Prepare to say the questions and your answers aloud in class.
- esmeh shomã chee-eh?
- shomã kojãee hasteen?
- khoone-vãde-yeh shomã kojã zendegee meekonan?

- esmeh bābā-yeh shomā chee-eh?
- esmeh māmāneh shomā chee-eh?
- shomā chan tā barādar va khāhar dāreen?
- esmeh barādar-eh shomā chee-eh?
- barādar-eh shomā dāneshjoo-eh? barādar-eh shomā dāneshjoo dar cheh dāneshgāhee-eh? oon dāneshgāh kojās?
- esmeh khāhar-eh shomā chee-eh?
- khāhar-eh shomā dāneshjoo-eh? khāhar-eh shomā dāneshjoo dar cheh dāneshgāhee-eh? oon dāneshgāh kojās?
- shomā alān kojā zendegee meekoneen?

3.18 Watch the video and connect the following letter combinations into words. Write each word several times.

_____	۱. ض ر ب
_____	۲. ل آ ف
_____	۳. ص آ د ر ت
_____	۴. ف آ ر س
_____	۵. ق ر ض
_____	۶. ب ش ق آ ب
_____	۷. ق ف س آ ت
_____	۸. گ ل آ ب
_____	۹. ق ب و ل
_____	۱۰. ل ذ ت
_____	۱۱. ق آ ش ق

3.19 Prepare to read the following words aloud in class. Pay special attention to pronunciation. In class, your instructor will help you with the pronunciation when needed.

شال، قاب ، لاف ، نان ، صاف ، پاساژ ، لال، دانا ، نور، سال ، آن، داس ، قاز، لاک ، ساک، کانادا

3.20 Listen to the audio presentation and write down the number of the words in which you hear the letter ق (as opposed to گ).

3.21  Listen to the audio presentation and circle the numbers that you hear.

(a) 1 2 4　　(b) 4 5 0　　(c) 3 5 2　　(d) 0 3 5　　(e) 1 2 5

IN CLASS
دَر کِلاس

3.22 You instructor will ask you the questions for which you have prepared at home. Answer you instructor's questions. Now, arrange the chairs so that you face one or two of your classmates. Prepare to ask your classmates the questions (about family) that you have prepared at home. Be ready to answer similar questions from your classmates.

3.23 Now the instructor will ask you questions about your conversation partner's family.

3.24 Read aloud the words that you have prepared at home. Your instructor will help you with pronunciation if needed.

3.25 Close your book. Your instructor will call on you and read for you a random word from the following list. Write on the board the word you hear. You instructor will tell you which Persian letter *s* to use in your word.

صاف ، ساق ، گول ، لاس ، ساک ، نادان ، بال ، ضاد ، شاد ، شوفاژ ، فال ، صور ، سارا ، صابون ، قاپو

UNIT 4

Vocabulary: What do you study? The verbs *to study*, *to work*. Differences between the spelling and pronunciation of the verb ending *eh*.

Letters: ط ظ م ه ی

 Listen to the audio presentation and repeat. Say each word several times until you can easily pronounce it. Try to imitate the native speaker's pronunciation.

Field of study, major	resh-teh	رِشته
University	dā-nesh-gāh	دانِشگاه
High school	da-bee-res-toon	دَبیرِستان
Office	daf-tar	دَفتَر
Homework	mash-q	مَشق

	tak-leef	تَكلیف
Exercise	tam-reen	تَمرین
Lesson	dars	دَرس
Book	ke-tāb	کِتاب
Library	ke-tāb-khoo-neh	کِتابخانه
Engineering	mo-han-de-see	مُهَندِسی
English Language	za-boo-neh een-glee-see	زبانِ انگلیسی
Usually	ma-moo-lan	مَعمولا
Semester	ter-m	تِرم
Like me	mes-leh man	مِثلِ مَن
Like my mom	mes-leh mā-mā-neh man	مِثلِ مامانِ مَن

Ask your instructor to tell you the name of your field in Persian!

Verbs and Phrases		
I study	dars mee-khoo-nam	دَرس میخوانَم
I study Persian	fār-see mee-khoo-nam	فارسی میخوانَم
I read a book, I read books	ke-tāb mee-khoo-nam	کِتاب میخوانَم
What do you study, What is your major?	cheh resh-teh-ee mee-khoon-een	چه رِشته ای میخوانید؟
I study engineering	man mo-han-de-see mee-khoo-nam	من مُهَندِسی میخوانَم
I work	kār mee-ko-nam	کار میکُنَم

— I study and also work.   مَن هَم دَرس میخوانَم هَم کار میکُنَم.

— I study /dars meekhoonam/   دَرس میخوانم

— You study /dars meekhooneen/   دَرس میخوانید

— S/he studies /dars meekhooneh/.   دَرس میخواند

— I work /kaar meekonam/   کار میکنم

— You work /kaar meekoneen/   کار میکنید

— S/he works /kaar meekoneh/   کار میکند

On the differences between spelling and pronunciation:

The written verb ending د (for *s/he, it* in present tense) is pronounced *eh* in colloquial speech. You may also pronounce this ending as *ad*, but that would sound very bookish and formal. After the word's final ã however, this ending is pronounced /d/ even in colloquial speech, for example, /meeãd/ *s/he is coming*.

Written	Pronounced
میکند	**mee**-kon-*eh*
میخواند	**mee**-khoon-*eh*
دارد	dãr-*eh*

Letters

ط	*ta*	(sound *t*, same as ت)
ظ	*za*	(sound *z*, same as ز ذ ض)
م	*mim*	(sound *m*)
ه	*helhe-ye docheshm*	(sound *h*, as in English word *hey*)
ی	*ye*	(sound *ee*)

The letters ظ ط

These letters connect to both sides. They have the same basic shape and are distinguished from each other by the use of one dot.

4.1 Watch the video and learn how to write the letters ظ ط in the initial, medial and final positions. Write each word several times!

4.2 Look at the following passage and note how many times the letter ظ appears in it. Identify the letter ظ throughout the passage.

ظهر نجومی به لحظه ای گفته میشود که در آن خورشید در بالاترین ارتفاع خود در آسمان قرار میگیرد. مترادف ظهر نیمروز است. متضاد ظهر، نیمه شب است.

The letter م

This letter connects to both sides. Be careful not to confuse م in its medial position with the letter ف in its medial position. The latter has a dot on top of it.

4.3 Watch the video and learn how to write the letter م in the initial, medial and final positions. Write each word several times!

4.4 Look at the following passage and identify the letter م in it.

استان مازندران در شمال کشور ایران و جنوب دریای مازندران قرار دارد. شهرستان های مازندران عبارتند از رامسر، میان دورود، آمل، محمودآباد، قایم شهر، فریدونکنار و غیره. مرکز استان مازندران شهر ساری است.

The letter ه

This letter connects to both sides. It represents the consonant *h* as in English word *hey*. At the end of the word, this letter also serves as a carrier for the vowel *e*, that otherwise does not have a separately assigned letter symbol. The rule of thumb is that if the letter ه at the end of word follows a vowel, then that letter ه represents the consonant *h* (as in ماه،دانشگاه), and if the ه at the end of word follows a consonant, then the letter ه carries the vowel *e* (as in دانه، سه). However, in few cases, the ه at the end of the word follows a consonant but stays true to its consonantal nature as *h* (as in /meh/ and /dah/ مِه، دَه) as, in fact, in such words it follows unwritten vowel sounds. In the word *no* نه /na/ the letter ه at the end of the word represents the vowel *a*.

4.5 Watch the video and learn how to write the letter ه in the initial, medial and final positions. Write each word several times

4.6 Listen to the audio presentation and mark the numbers for the words in which you hear the *h* sound.

1.	2.	3.	4.	5.	6.	7.	8.

4.7 Look at the following passage and count how many times the letter ه appears in it.

من در شمالِ ایران زندگی میکنم و اهل لاهیجان هستم. لاهیجان از مکانهای مهم شمال ایران است. من هجده ساله هستم و در خانه مامان بابایم زِندِگی میکنم. یک خواهر دارم. خانه ما سه طبقه است.در طبقه همکف چهار تا اتاق خواب، هال، یک دستشویی و یک حمام هست. پدر و مادرم در این طبقه زندگی میکنند.

The letter ی

The letter ی represents the vowel *ee* as in *bee, feel*. This letter connects to both sides.

4.8 Watch the video and learn how to write the letter ی in the initial, medial and final positions. Write each word several times!

4.9 Look at the image and identify the letter ک on it.

4.10  Listen to the audio presentation. Check the numbers for words in which you hear the vowel *ee* as in English word *bee* (as opposed to the sound *e* as in English word *get*).

1.	2.	3.	4.	5.	6.	7.	8.

4.11 Listen to the audio presentation and circle the numbers for words where you hear the vowel *e* (as opposed to *ee*).

1.	2.	3.	4.	5.	6.	7.	8.

Initial vowels ã, ee, oo.

When you need to write the vowels *ee* or *oo* in the beginning of the word, first write the symbol ا and then write the letter that corresponds to the vowel you need, for example, eerãn (ایران), oot (اوت). When a vowel is the first sound of the word, it is, in fact, preceded by a slight glottal stop. Think of the words *uh-oh, early*. The glottal stop occurs in many languages, but in most languages that glottal stop is not written. In Persian, however, this glottal stop is represented by the symbol ا, which is then followed by the symbol that represents the vowel sound. Thus, the vowel *ã* in the beginning of the word is represented by one ا symbol with a short horizontal line on top of it (instead of writing two ا symbols side by side).

اوت (oot) August, ایران (eerãn) Iran, آب (ãb) water.

Prepare to read the following words aloud.

آن، آمار، آثار، او، اوف، این، ایتالیا، ایندیانا، ایستاد.

35

HOMEWORK  تَکلیف

4.12 (a) Listen and read along. Complete the English translation based on what you hear and see.

/salãm, esmeh man Nikeh. man dãneshjooyeh mohandesee dar dãneshgãheh California has-tam. een term dar chãr tã kelãs hastam. een term dar kelãseh fãrsee ham hastam. een term ham dars meekhoonam ham kãr meekonam/.

Hi, my _____ is Nik. I am an engineering _____ at the _____ of California. This _____ I am taking four _____. This _____ I am also taking Persian. This semester I _____ and also _____.

(b) Let's learn more about Parisa as she tells you about her classes at the university. Listen and prepare to answer these questions in class.

1. esmeh oon chee-eh?
2. oon dars meekhooneh yã kãr meekoneh?
3. oon chee meekhooneh?
4. oon dãneshjoo dar cheh dãneshgãhee-eh?
5. een term dar chan tã kelãs-eh?
6. oon engleesee ham meekhooneh?
7. dar kelãseh eengleesee-yeh oon chan tã dãneshjoo-eh?

4.13 Answer the following questions about yourself. Prepare to answer and ask these questions aloud in class.

- (1) es-meh shomã chee-eh? (2) fãmeelee-yeh shomã chee-eh? (3) shomã ah-leh kojã hasteen? (4) esmeh bãbã-yeh shomã chee-eh? (5) esmeh mãmã-neh shomã chee-eh? (6) shomã chan tã barãdar va khãhar dãreen? (7) esmeh barãdar-eh shomã chee-eh? (8) esmeh barãdareh deegeyeh shomã chee-eh? (9) esmeh khãhareh shomã chee-eh? (10) shoq-leh shomã chee-eh? (11) shomã dãneshjoo dar cheh dãneshgãhee hasteen? (12) shomã cheh reshteh-ee mee-khoo-neen? (13) een term chan tã kelãs dãreen? (14) Fãrsee ham meekhooneen?

4.14 Do you study and also work? Prepare to talk to everyone in your class and find out who is a student and who is a student who also works. Here are the questions and answers you will need:

/een term kãr mee-kon-ee?/
/baleh, een term ham dars meekhoonam ham kãr meekonam/
/nah, een term dars meekhoonam, kãr nemeekonam/.

Once you have talked to everyone, share with the class who has a lifestyle and workload similar to yours, for example:

Like me /mes-leh man/
Like me, Kamran takes classes and does not work
/kãmrãn mesleh man, dars meekhooneh, kãr nemeekoneh/.
Like me, Kamran takes classes and also works.
/kãmrãn mesleh man, ham dars meekhooneh ham kãr meekoneh/.

4.15 Watch the video and connect the following letters to form words. Write each word several times.

گ و ی   _____

ن ی   _____

م ی م   _____

ی ک   _____

ظ ه ر   _____

م ط ه ر   _____

ف ق ط   _____

ت ص م ی م   _____

ه ر   _____

ب ل ه   _____

4.16 Listen and write the words you hear. Write the letter ه when you hear *h*, use ط when you hear *t*. Remember that the vowels *a*, *e*, and *o* are not written, while *ã*, *oo* and *ee* are written.

4.17 Prepare to read the following words aloud.

سه، لیوان ، هالو ، مو، ما ، فالوده ، زیاد ،سیما ، فامیلی ، طول ، گیلاس ، ژاله.

4.18 Spelling and Pronunciation. Prepare to read the following words and phrases aloud in class. Pay attention to the differences between spelling and pronunciation of the verb ending. You don't need to know the meaning of the words to pronounce them correctly.

دارد، میکند، میخواند، میگیرد، میبیند، میداند، میسوزد، میجوشد، میبازد، میاویزد، میتابد، میباشد.

۱ . استاد ماژیک دارد. ۲ . برادر من کلاس دارد. ۳ . او خواهر ندارد. ۴ . خواهر فارسی میخواند. ۵ . او فوتبال یاد میگیرد. ۶ . او من را میبیند. ۷ . مادر او را نمیبیند. ۸ . خدا میداند. ۹ . اسم من را نمیداند. ۱۰ . آب میجوشد. ۱۱ . ماه میتابد. ۱۲ . او نمیبازد. ۱۳ . او فارسی میاموزد. ۱۴ . بابا در دانشگاه کار میکند.

IN CLASS   دَر کِلاس

4.19 Arrange the chairs so that you face a classmate. Ask him/her the questions you have prepared at home. Your objective is to inquire about your conversation partner's family and occupation. Try to maintain a conversation as long as you can. Start with greetings and close by saying "Was nice meeting you, good-bye." Answer your conversation partner's questions. Once you are done, move one seat over and strike up a conversation with a different classmate. Repeat. Your objective is to get to the point when answering and asking basic questions about someone's identity becomes automatic. You should not have to stop and think about words to ask these simple questions.

4.20 Think about yourself. Do you take classes or do you also work? How many classes are you taking this semester? What is your field? Now, talk to everyone in class and find all those who pursue the same activities as you do at the university, that is, they study or they both study and work, they take same number of classes this semester or they study the same field. From those you have spoken to, pick one student who shares the most with you and introduce that student to class. Say that person's name, major, the number of classes taken this semester, whether he or she takes classes or also works this semester. Use the phrase /mesleh man/ when you want to point out a similarity between you and that student, for example, /kãmrãn mesleh man ham dars meekhooneh ham kãr meekoneh/.

4.21 Read aloud the words you have prepared at home.

4.22 Close your book. Your instructor will call on you and read for you a random word from the list below. Write the word in Persian on the board.

ایست ، ایرلند ، اینترنت ، اینها ، ایمن ، ایشان ، ایراد ، اوکراین ، آبادان ، او ، ایران ،
ایرج ، ایستگاه ، ایمیل ، اومانیسم ، آبی.

UNIT 5

Letters: ج چ ح خ ع غ

Pronunciation practice: Consonants گ ، خ ، غ/ق

Letters

ج	*jim*	(sound *j* as in **Jay**)
چ	*che*	(sound *ch* as in **cheese**)
ح	*helheye jimi*	(sound *h*, same as the sound of the letter ه as in English word *hey*)
خ	*khe*	(sound *kh* as in German **Bach**)
ع	*eyn*	(slight glottal stop, often omitted all together in modern Persian)
غ	*gheyn*	(soft glottal sound *q/gh*, same as the sound described for the letter ق)

The letters ج چ ح خ

These letters connect to the right and to the left. They have the same basic shape and are distinguished from one another by the number and position of dots.

5.1 Watch the video and learn how to write the letters ج چ ح خ in the initial, medial and final positions. Write each word several times!

39

5.2 🔊 Listen to the audio presentation. Circle the numbers for the words in which you hear the sound *kh* (خ) (as opposed to the sounds *h* and *k*).

1.	2.	3.	4.	5.	6.
7.	8.	9.	10.	11.	12.

5.3 🔊 Listen to the audio presentation and circle the numbers for the words in which you hear the sound *kh* (خ) as opposed to the sound *q* (ق).

1.	2.	3.	4.	5.	6.	7.	8.	9.	10.

5.4 🔊 Listen to the audio presentation and in each pair of words mark the word that you hear.

1. خالی – قالی	2. خم – غم	3. خار – غار
4. قیام – خیار	5. خانه – قانع	

The letters ع غ

These letters connect to the right and to the left. They have the same basic shape and are distinguished from each other only by the use of a dot. The letter ع is a slight glottal stop or a brief pause that is often omitted all together in colloquial speech, especially in the beginning and at the end of the word. In such cases, ع simply becomes an extension of the vowel that precedes or follows it (بَعد bad/baad; راجِع rãje). When ع appears in the beginning of the word, it plays the role similar to that of ا that is used to introduce vowels in the beginning of the word (see Initial Vowels above).

The letter غ is a glottal consonant that, in Persian, sounds the same as the letter ق. Be careful not to confuse غ in the medial position with the letter ف in the medial position. The letter غ in the medial position looks like an inverted triangle with clearly defined corners (for example, بغداد), whereas the letter ف appears as a circle (for example, سـفت).

Don't confuse the letters ع غ in the final position with the letters from the ج group in the final position. The top of the letters غ ع looks like an inverted triangle, for example, تیغ – غ while the final خ does not form a triangle, for example, میخ – خ.

5.5 Watch the video and learn how to write the letters غ ع in the initial, medial and final positions. Write each word several times!

5.6 Look at the image and identify the letter ع.

بر اساس قانون ، آئین نامه و دستورالعمل حفاظت و بهسازی محیط زیست

ورود ، عبور و توقف در پارک های ملی

مستلزم تحصیل پروانه و یا کسب مجوز از سازمان حفاظت محیط زیست بوده

و بدون اخذ مجوز ممنوع می باشد

5.7 Distribute the following words into the columns according to the letter that appears in the word.

فال، غار، مفرد، مغرب، نفت، نغمه، بغض، برفی، بفرمایید، بغداد.

ف	غ

HOMEWORK   تَکلیف

5.8 Watch the video and connect the following letters where possible to form words. Write each word several times.

١. چ ه آ ر   _____

٢. ب چ ه   _____

٣. و ح ش ی   _____

۴. گ چ _____

۵. ق ر چ _____

۶. ع ش ق _____

۷. د ع آ _____

۸. ت ع د آ د _____

۹. ب غ ل _____

۱۰. و ض ع _____

۱۱. و س ی ع _____

۱۲. د آ غ _____

5.9 🔊 Listen to the audio and repeat the words. Pay special attention to the difference between the sounds ق/غ and خ. Prepare to read these words aloud in class.

داغان، باغ، غاش،خیابان، خالی، خاموش، غاغاله، عادی، عاق، عامیانه، عید، خیال، قوری، غاز، قاب، خانه، قیام.

IN CLASS	دَر کِلاس

5.10 Close your book. Your instructor will read out a random word from the list below and call on you to write that word in Persian on the board.

All words in the following series start with the letter ع:

علم، عابر، عشق، عجیب، علی، عدد.

In all words in the following series, the letter ع is the second written letter of the word:

بعد، بعید، تعمیر، ، فعل.

42

5.11 Your instructor will read one of the following words for you. Repeat and try to imitate his/her pronunciation.

قشنگ، غرق، غمگین، قالی، غایب، حقوق، فقط، قاشق، رقص، قهوه،

قرباقه، حق، غیبت، قشقرق، خالی، خام، خیال، خام، خدا، خانه، خامه.

5.12 Your instructor will read words in pairs. Repeat after your instructor and pay special attention to the pronunciation of the consonants.

قم – گم/ غاز – گاز/ مگر – مقر/ قاب – گپ/ گرم – غرب/

قالی – خالی/ آخر – اگر/ غنچه – گُنده/ غم/ خم/ خار – غار/

غیره – خیره/ قانع – خانه/ قیام – خیار/ قند – خنده

5.13   Talk to your classmate and ask them the following questions in Persian. Pay special attention to the conjugation of the verb *to be* in singular and plural. Your objective is to find those who have something in common with you. Now, introduce to class the individuals you have found by saying /oon mesleh man az New Yorkeh/, / māmāneh oon mesleh māmāneh man ostādeh/, and so on.

Ask your classmate if:

- S/he is a student, PhD student, Iranian, from New York, happy, in good mood, his or her name is Iranian, his or her field is engineering.
- Her or his sister is a high school student, studies linguistics, works, lives in New York.
- His or her father is Iranian, from New York, works, is a professor.
- His or her mother is Iranian, lives in New York, is a professor, has sisters and brothers.

UNIT 6

Vocabulary: Numbers 0–10. What is your phone number?
Letters: vowel signs (diacritics) and diphthong; additional signs. Writing your name in Persian.

Listen and Repeat.

0	1	2	3	4	5	6	7	8	9	10
۰	۱	۲	۳	۴	۵	۶	۷	۸	۹	۱۰
صفر	یک	دو	سه	چهار	پنج	شش	هفت	هشت	نه	ده
sefr	yek/ yeh	do	seh	chãr	panj	sheesh	haft	hasht	no-h	da-h

Number	sho-mã-reh	شُماره
Phone number	sho-mã-reh-yeh te-le-fon	شُماره ِ تِلِفُن
Cell phone	mo-bã-eel	موبایل
Apartment	ã-pãr-te-mãn	آپارتِمان
House	khoo-neh	خانه
Dorm	khãb-gãh	خوابگاه
Building	sãkh-te-moon	ساختِمان
Number of the building (lit.: plaque)	pe-lãk	پِلاک
Street	khee-ã-boon	خیابان
On Steward street	dar khee-ã-boo-neh Stewart	دَر خیابان ِ Stewart
Address	ãd-res, ne-shoo-nee	آدرِس، نِشانی
What's Your (formal) phone number?	sho-mã-reh-yeh te-le-fo-neh-toon chan-deh?	شُماره ِ تِلِفُنِتان چَند است؟
My phone number is …	sho-mã-reh-yeh te-le-fo-nam hast …	شُماره ِ تِلِفُنَم است....
On what street?	dar cheh khee-ã-boo-nee (stress falls on *boo*)	در چه خیابانی؟
In what city?	dar cheh shah-ree (stress falls on *shah*)	دَر چه شَهری؟
In what neighborhood?	dar cheh ma-ha-leh-ee (stress falls on *leh*)	دَر چه مَحَله ای

Vowel Signs (Diacritics). As we have mentioned before, the vowels 'a', 'e', 'o' have no letter symbols to represent them. There are, however, special signs to mark these vowels in the text. These signs are, as a rule, omitted in all published and written material, and are only used when it is necessary to clarify the meaning of the word or to clarify the pronunciation of foreign names and words.

The vowel *a* is represented by a diagonal dash placed on top of the letter which it follows and with which it forms a syllable. This diacritic is called *zebar*.

$$\text{تَن} \qquad \text{/ta-n/}$$

The vowel *e* is represented by a diagonal dash placed under the letter it follows. This diacritic is called *zeer*.

$$\text{دِل} \qquad \text{/de-l/}$$

The vowel *o* is marked by a diagonal shape that looks like small number 9 or small letter و *vav*. This diacritic is placed on top of the letter which it follows. This sign is called *peesh*.

$$\text{دُر} \qquad \text{/do-r/}$$

Keep in mind that we do not end words with vowel signs. If a word ends with the sounds 'e' or 'o', a carrier letter (as opposed to a vowel sign) is required to represent those sounds at the end of the word. As we have mentioned before, we use the letter ه to carry the vowel *e* at the end of the word (usually after a consonant), for example, خانه، بله، سه. Remember that the letter ه in such cases is a silent carrier and only the vowel 'e' is pronounced at the end of such word.

To carry the vowel *o* at the end of the word, we use the letter و as in دو /do/.

If the sounds *a, e* and *o* appear in the beginning of the word, they are represented by the corresponding diacritic placed on top of (for *a* and *o*) or under (for *e*) the symbol ا that we have disussed in the section *Initial Vowels* above. This symbol ا represents initial glottal stop that precedes the first vowel of the word in pronunciation (think of the English words *uh-oh, early*). For example:

ast –   آسـت

emrooz –   اِمروز

ostâd –   اُستاد

Read the following words and pay attention to the diacritics.

اُلگو، اُستاد، اُملِت، آسـب، آدَب، آسـاتید، اِسکی، اِمشَب، اِمسـال

45

Diphthongs. There are six vowels and two diphthongs in modern standard Persian of Iran. Diphthongs are sounds formed by the combination of two vowels, where the sound starts with one vowel and moves toward another. There are two diphthongs in Persian: the diphthong *ow* as in the English word *throw,* and the diphthong *ey* as in the English word *grey*. The diphthong *ow* is written using the letter و combined with the diacritic for the vowel *o* written on top. The diphthong *ey* is written using the letter ی combined with the diacritic for the vowel *e* written under it.

مُوج /mowj/

مِیل /mey-eel/

Read the following words aloud.

مِیل، غِیر، سِیر، حِیوان، اِیوان، زُوج، اُوقات، فُوری.

Additional signs

Hamzeh is the sign ء that is used to represent a glottal stop. In modern Persian, it is also used to represent the sound *e* in foreign words (تئاتر teâtr, سئول Seoul). It is also used to represent a slight glottal stop in the middle of the word and in between two vowels (سُؤال so'âl, مسئله mas'ale; and هاوائی ، آمریکائی). However, the most recent trend is to replace it with ی whenever it is not used to carry the sound /e/ in foreign words, that is, آمریکایی.

Tashdid (emphasis) is a sign that looks like a small letter double *u* which is placed above a consonant. It means that the marked consonant has to be pronounced twice. It occurs almost exclusively in words borrowed from Arabic, but few Persian words require the *tashdid* (e.g., بچّه *bach-che* child).

Tanvin is a sign that looks like two parallel diagonal dashes placed above the final ا with the entire combination pronounced as *an* (not as *â*). It is used to create adverbs and is an equivalent of the English adverbial suffix *ly* (e.g., قبلاً" /qablan/ previously).

A Quick Guide to Transliteration of the Letters of the Alphabet

Name of the letter	Pronunciation of the letter as in English word	Representative letter in English transliteration	Persian letter
Alef	far	ã	آ
Be	bay	b	ب
Pe	pay	p	پ
Te	tone	t	ت

Name of the letter	Pronunciation of the letter as in English word	Representative letter in English transliteration	Persian letter
Se	seek	s	ث
Jim	jay	J	ج
Che	cheese	ch	چ
he (heye jimi)	hey	h	ح
Khe	in German word *Bach*	kh	خ
Dâl	dorm	d	د
Zâl	zeal	z	ذ
Re	soft sound *r*	r	ر
Ze	zeal	z	ز
Zhe	in French words *joli, Juliette*, or English *beige*	zh	ژ
Sin	seek	s	س
Shin	sheep	sh	ش
Sâd	seek	s	ص
Zâd	zeal	z	ض
Tâ	tone	t	ط
Zâ	zeal	z	ظ
Eyn	pronounced as a short pause or a slight glottal stop, and often omitted all together		ع
Qeyn	soft glottal consonant	q	غ
Fe	face	f	ف
Qâf	soft glottal consonant	q	ق
Kâf	keep, key	k	ک
Gâf	geese	g	گ
Lâm	lap	l	ل
Mim	may	m	م
Nun	night	n	ن
Vâv	voice/scoop/joy	v/oo/o	و

Name of the letter	Pronunciation of the letter as in English word	Representative letter in English transliteration	Persian letter
he (heye docheshm)	hey/get	h/e	ه
Ye	bee	ee	ى
Vowel Signs			
Zebar	afternoon	a	◌َ
Zeer	get	e (**eh**, when it appears at the end of the word)	◌ِ
Peesh	joy	o	◌ُ
Diphthongs			
	grey	ey	◌َى
	throw	ow	◌ُو

READING THE VOWEL SIGNS AND LETTERS

خانه‌ِ مَن /khooneh-yeh man/. The vowel sign you see after the word خانه is there to represent the connector sound *yeh* between the two words (not the sound *eh* that is part of *khooneh*).

If the letter *vav* و is not accompanied by vowel signs, then the letter *vav* is itself a vowel: مو /moo/. If the letter *vav* is preceded or followed by vowel signs *a* or *e*, or a vowel letter, then the letter *vav* is a consonant: مَوارد /ma-vã-red/, سیوُم /sev-vom/, جاوید /jãveed/. In the letter cluster خوا the *vav* و is silent: خواب /khãb/, خواهش /khãhesh/, میخواهم /meekhãm/.

If the letter *he* ه is preceded by a vowel letter or vowel sign, then that letter *he* is a consonant: دِه /de-h/, دانشگاه /dãnesh-gã-h/. If the final letter *he* ه is not preceded by a vowel letter or vowel sign, then that letter *he* is itself a vowel carrier: خانه /khooneh/, سه /seh/.

Sound Mates

Different Letters that Represent the Same Sounds

Letters	س ، ص ، ث	ز ، ذ ، ض ، ظ	ت ، ط	ه ، ح	غ ، ق
Sound	s	z	t	h	q
Examples	سیب ، صَف مِثال ،	زیر،گُذَر،ضَرب، ظُهر	تیم ، طَرح	هیچ ، حال	قالی ، غَرب
	mesãl, saf, seeb	zohr, zarb, gozar, zeer	tarh, teem	hãl, heech	qarb, qãlee

Chameleon Letters

Single Letter that May Represent Several Different Sounds

ه (heyeh docheshm)	
After a consonant at the end of the word	**sound _eh_ as in:** /baleh/ بله
Before and after a vowel	**sound _h_ as in:** /havā/ هوا /dāneshgāh/ دانشگاه

و (vav)	
Before and between vowels	**consonant sound _v_** /vāred/ وارد /āvāz/ آواز
After and between consonants	**vowel sound _oo_** /bood/ بود
When the vowel _o_ has to be represented at the end of the word	**vowel sound _o_** /do/ دو
cluster خوا	**silent letter** خواهَر /khāhar/ خواهِش /khāhesh/

The following are the letters that are commonly mispronounced and mistaken for other letters. In order to illustrate the difference in pronunciation between these letters, the narrator will pronounce pairs of words where the sounds occur. Listen and read along.

1. 🔊 _ã_ and _a_:

Sound	Letter	Examples
_ã_ as in _far_	آ	آب، آقا، ما، تا، چاه، بابا، بالا، دانا، با ما، ناهار
_a_ as in _afternoon_	◌َ (vowel sign _zebar_)	مَن، بَس، سَر، تَن، بَدَن، نَمَک، سَبَب ، وَ
Listen and Compare _ã_ to _a_:		
بار ـ بَر، زار ـ زَر، دار ـ دَر، صاف ـ صَف ، باد ـ بَد، دام ـ دَم، نام ـ نَم		

49

2. 🔊 *j* and *zh*:

Sound	Letter	Examples
j as in *Jay*	ج	جا، جور، جیم، آجیل، تاج، باج، کج
zh as in French words *joli, Juliette*	ژ	ژاله، ژَرف، ژوبیه، ژیلا، رِژیم، گاراژ
Listen and Compare ج to ژ		
جَم – ژَرف، جیب – ژیلا، جور – ژورنال، تاج – گاراژ ، آبجو – آباژور		

3. 🔊 *k* and *kh*:

Sound	Letter	Examples
k as in *keep*	ک	کار، کیش، کوچ، اِکران، اَفکار، نوک، ساک
kh as in German word *Bach*	خ	خار، ، خیره، آخَر، میخ، سِخاوَت
Listen and Compare ک to خ		
کار – خار، کیش – خویش، یک – یخ، کِی – خِیلی		

4. 🔊 *q* and *kh*:

Sound	Letter	Examples
Soft glottal sound	ق/غ	قاب، قالی، آقا، مَقاله، ساق، عَرَق، قورباقه
kh as in German word *Bach*	خ	خام، ، خالی، آخَر، میخ، بُخار
Listen and Compare ق/غ to خ		
غَم – خَم، قیام – خیال، ساقی – سَخی، قاب – خواب ، قارچ – خارِج		

HOMEWORK  تَکلیف

6.1 Watch the video and write the numbers. Write each number several times.

6.2 Listen to the audio presentation and for each series mark the number that you hear.

1	۵	۴	۱
2	۹	۲	۶
3	۴	۳	۷
4	۸	۵	۲

6.3 Listen and write the numbers that you hear.

1.   2.   3.   4.   5.   6.   7.   8.   9.   10.

6.4 Complete the sequence with the missing numbers.

۱۰			۷	۶			۳	۲		۰

6.5 (a) Listen and complete the English translation based on what you hear and see.

۱. او دَر تِهران زِندِگی میکُند. ۲. او دَر خیابانِ وَلی عَصر زِندِگی میکُند. شُمارهِ آپارتِمانِ او ۹ اَست. ۳. شُمارهِ تِلِفُنِ او ۶۰۷۲۵۵۶۴۶۷ اَست.

1. S/he _____ in _____. 2. She lives on Vali Asr _____. 3. Her/his apartment _____ is _____.
4. Her/his phone _____ is _____.

(b) Listen to Parisa as she tells you more about herself. Prepare to answer the following questions in class.

51

1. oon kojã zendegee meekoneh?
2. shomãreyeh ãpãrtemãneh oon chandeh?
3. oon dar cheh khee-ã-boonee zendegee meekoneh?

6.6 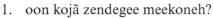 Answer the following questions about yourself. Prepare to answer and ask these questions in class.
(a) shomã ahleh kojã hasteen?
(b) shomãreyeh telefonetoon chandeh?
(c) neshoonee-yeh shomã chee-eh?

6.7 Complete the equations. Use Persian digits.

۴ – ۱ = __	۵ – ۴ = __	۴ – ۴ = __	۲ – ۱ = __	۱ + ۱ = __
۵ – ۱ = __	۰ + ۲ = __	۲ + ۲ = __	۳ + ۱ = __	۲ + ۱ = __

6.8 Complete the equations by filling in the blanks.

۴ + ۵ = __	۳ – __ = ۱	۲ + __ = ۵
۶ + __ = ۰۱	۰ + __ = ۱	۱۰ – ۵ = __

6.9 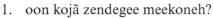 Listen to the narrator and repeat the following words. Mark the ones you have difficulty in pronouncing, so that you practice them with your instructor in class. Add diacritics based on what you hear, so that you are able to read the words in class.

قبول، قالب، قالی، قانون، خالی، خار، خیال، قاشـق، گاز، گرگ، گوجه، کارتون،
کتری، کانون، ژرف، ژاله، ژانویه، ژاپن، پژوهش، ژاکت، ژولیده، جیم، جگر، ترجمه،
جمشید، جامعه، جایزه.

6.10 Watch as the writer writes the words and pronounces them. The writer will only write the linear shapes and will omit the dots. Copy the linear shapes based on what you see, and then add dots based on what you hear.

6.11 🔊 The following is a short poem (quatrain) by the Persian poet Baba Koohee, who lived and loved in the 11ᵗʰ century CE. Listen to the recitation of his poem, and complete the transliteration with the missing letters *ã* and *a* accordingly. Write *ã* when you hear آ as in باد /bãd/. Write *a* for the vowel represented by the vowel sign *zebar* as in بَد /bad/.

bee …tesheh eshq k…r kh…m …st, ey del!

h…r del keh n…sookht, n…t…m…m …st, ey del!

meesooz sh…boh rooz choo p…rv…neh-oh sh…m,

zolfoh rokheh y…r sobh-o sh…m …st, ey del!

Without Love's fire, any work is incomplete, hey heart!

Any heart that hasn't burnt for Love, is imperfect, hey heart!

Burn night and day like the candle and moth,

The beloved's curls and face is what makes the morning and night, hey heart!

6.12 🔊 Listen to the pronunciation of the following words and add the diacritics as needed.

امشـب، امسـال، امروز، استقلال، اقامت ،اسـم، استاد، اردو، امید، الگو، اسـب،
اسـت، ابر، گپ، جمعه ، سـلام، من، شـما، کلام، پنج، دانشـگاه، کلاس، قشـقرق،
خیلی، میل، دور، طور.

6.13 Tongue twisters. Now that you are familiar with all the sounds and letters, let's practice pronouncing them. The following are Persian tongue twisters (زبان پیچ ها). Prepare to read them fluently and fast in class. Repeat each tongue twister three times. Practice before coming to class.

1. /lee**reh** roo loo**leh**, loo**leh** roo lee**reh**/

لیره رو لوله، لوله رو لیره

(A lyre on a pipe, a pipe on the lyre)

2. /**shee**sh seekh jee**gar**, **see**khee **shee**sh he**zār** ree**āl**/

شیش سیخ جیگر، سیخی شیش هِزار ریال

(Six skewers of liver, each for six thousand Rials)

3. /kalā**qeh** bā malā**qeh**, baa ka**mā**leh alā**qeh**, **zad** too **sa**reh olā**qeh**/

کَلاغه با مَلاقه با کَمالِ عَلاقه زَد تو سَرِ اُلاغه

(A crow with a ladle enthusiastically hit a donkey on the head.)

IN CLASS   دَر کِلاس

6.14 Ask your classmates the following questions. You task will be to find someone who lives on the same street, in the same building, or in the same area of campus or town as you do.

* Insert the name of the town where your university is located

۱. دَر ...* یا دَر دانِشگاه زِندِگی میکُنی؟

۲. دَر چه خیابانی زِندِگی میکُنی؟ (دَر چه خیابونی زِندِگی میکُنی؟)

۳. شُماره‌ِ ساختِمان‌ِ تو چَند است؟ (شُماره‌ِ ساختِمون‌ِ تو چَنده؟)

۴. شُماره‌ِ آپارتِمان‌ِ تو چَند است؟ (شُماره‌ِ آپارتِمان‌ِ تو چَنده؟)

6.15 Talk to all your classmates and find out the following information:

اِسمِ پِدَرِ تو چه است؟ (اِسمِ پِدَرِ تو چیه؟)   اِسمِ مادَرِ تو چه است؟ (اِسمِ مادَرِ تو چیه؟)

او کُجایی است؟ (اون کُجاییه؟)   او کُجایی است؟ (اون کُجاییه؟)

او کار میکُند؟ (اون کار میکُنه؟)   او کار میکُند؟ (اون کار میکُنه؟)

اِسمِ خواهَرِ تو چه است؟ (اِسمِ خواهَرِ تو چیه؟)

او آلان کُجا زِندِگی میکُند؟ (اون آلان کُجا زِندِگی میکُنه؟)

او دَرس میخواند یا کار میکُند؟ (اون دَرس میخونه یا کار میکُنه؟)

اِسمِ بَرادَرِ تو چه است؟ (اِسمِ بَرادَرِ تو چیه؟)

او آلان کُجا زِندِگی میکُند؟ (اون آلان کُجا زِندِگی میکُنه؟)

او دَرس میخواند یا کار میکُند؟ (اون دَرس میخونه یا کار میکُنه؟)

6.16 Your instructor will ask a couple of students in class some of the following equations in order to provide an example. Now, pick a classmate and ask your classmate one of the following equations in Persian. Be ready to answer similar questions from your classmates.

دو با دو چَند است؟ (دو با دو چَنده؟) - دو با دو چهار است (دو با دو چاره)

۷ + ۳ =	۴ + ۱ =	۱ + ۱ =	۱ + ۴ =
۸ + ۱ =	۳ + ۴ =	۲ + ۱ =	۲ + ۶ =
	۵ + ۴ =	۲ + ۲ =	۳ + ۳ =

6.17 Start counting in Persian. Your classmate will say the next number, and the next person will say the number after that. Once you reach number ten, start counting back in descending order. Start and finish with zero.

6.18 Now, start counting again, but only say the even numbers. When you reach number ten, start counting back in descending order.

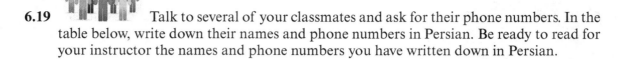

6.19   Talk to several of your classmates and ask for their phone numbers. In the table below, write down their names and phone numbers in Persian. Be ready to read for your instructor the names and phone numbers you have written down in Persian.

شُماره ِ تِلِفُن ِ شُما چَند است؟ (شُماره ِ تِلِفُن ِ شُما چَنده؟)

شُماره ِ تِلِفُن ِ مَن ... است (شُماره ِ تِلِفُن ِ مَن هَست ...).

اِسم	شُماره ِ تِلِفُن

6.20 Read the following words. Pay special attention to the difference between the sounds **â** and **a** in the words.

(a)   The following words only have *â* sound represented by the letter آ

بابا، بالا، با ما، بادام، سارا، دانا، ناهار، ما، باران، ماه

(b) The following words only have the sound ***a*** that is written using the vowel sign.

مَن، بَس، دَم، سَر، دَر، بَد، بَدَن، تَن، بَر

c)   The following words have both *â* and *a* sounds. The sound *â* is represented by the letter آ, while the sound *a* is represented by the vowel sign (diacritic).

سَلام، آمَد، فَردا، بَهار، مادَر، آهَن، بَهار، نَدارد، با مَن، باوَر، فَرار، با هَم، بَرادَر.

d)   باد - بَد / صاف - صَف / زار - زَر/ دَر - دار/

داستان - دَستان / بَر آن - باران / بَر - بار

6.21 Close your books. Your instructor will read aloud two words, one of which has the sound *ee* and the other one has the sound *e* in it. Write on the board the words you hear. Use the letter ی to write the vowel *ee* and use the diacritic for sound *e*.

سه - سی ، یِم - بیم ، مِس - میز ، کِشمِش - کیش ، شِیش - شیک

6.22 Close your book. Your instructor will read a random word from the list below and call on you to write that word on the board. The word will have both sounds *ee* and *e* in it. Use the letter ى to write the vowel *ee* and use the diacritic for sound *e*.

تِنیش، شِلیک، گِلیم، بِلیت، دِنیم، رِژیم

6.23 Close your book. Your instructor will read out a random word from the list below and call on you to write that word on the board. Write the word on the board and add the vowel signs (diacritics) where applicable.

مُشکِلات، پَریشان، اِستِقلال، اِنتِخاب، مالی، بادِنجان، کوچه، کوچِک، اُمید، اِمروز، خاکِستَری، اِقامَت، اُستاد، دامَنه، آسان، اُلگو، اِمشَب، خاموشی، قانون، مَعمولی، عُمودی، چَهاردَه، اُتاق، اِنحِصار، اِمتِحان، اِنسان، اُمیدوار، آرامِش، آسایِشگاه.

6.24 Write your name and last name on the board and add the diacritics. Transcribe non-Persian names phonetically using Persian letters. When writing non-Persian names, use س to represent *s*, write ز to represent *z*, write ه to represent *h*, write و to represent the sounds *v*, *oo*, and *o*. Use the diacritics as needed.

UNIT 7

Vocabulary: Days of the week. The verb *to be* in past tense (was). Some of the common differences between pronunciation and spelling in modern Persian.

DAYS OF THE WEEK  روزهای هَفته

 Listen and repeat.

Week	haf-teh	هَفته
Day	rooz	روز
Today	em-rooz	اِمروز

57

Tomorrow	far-dã	فَردا
Yesterday	dee-rooz	دیروز
Was	bood	بود
Day-off	(roozeh) ta-teel	تَعطیل (روز)
What day of the week?	chan-sham-beh?	چَندشَنبه

In Iran, the week starts on Saturday. Friday is the end of the week and a day-off.

sham-beh	شَنبه	Saturday
yeh-sham-beh	یِک شَنبه	Sunday
do-sham-beh	دو شَنبه	Monday
se-sham-beh	سه شَنبه	Tuesday
chãr-sham-beh	چَهار شَنبه	Wednesday
panj-sham-beh	پَنج شَنبه	Thursday
jo-meh	جُمعه	Friday

em-rooz chan-sham-bas?	اِمروز چَند شَنبه اَست؟
	What day of the week is today?
em-rooz do-sham-bas.	اِمروز دوشَنبه اَست.
	Today is Monday.
deerooz chan-shambeh bood?	دیروز چَند شَنبه بود؟
	What day of the week was yesterday?
deerooz yeh-shambeh bood.	دیروز یِک شَنبه بود.
	Yesterday was Sunday.
fardã chan-shambas?	فردا چند شنبه است؟
	What day of the week is tomorrow?
fardã seh-shambas?	فردا سه شنبه است.
	Tomorrow is Tuesday.

7.1 Prepare to answer the following questions in Persian.

۱. یِک هَفته چَند روز اَست؟ (یه هَفته چَن روزه؟)

۲.دَر آمریکا یِک هَفته چَند تا روز تَعطیل دارد؟ (تو آمریکا یِه هَفته چَن تا روزِ تَعطیل داره ؟)

۳. دَر ایران یِک هَفته چَند تا روز تَعطیل دارد؟ (تو ایران یِه هَفته چَن تا روزِ تَعطیل داره ؟)

۴. اِمروز چَندشَنبه اَست؟ (اِمروز چَنشَمبَس؟)

۵.فَردا چَند شَنبه اَست؟ (فَردا چَنشَمبَس؟)

۶. فَردا تَعطیل است؟ (فَردا تَعطیله؟)

۷. دیروز چَند شَنبه بود؟ (دیروز چَنشَمبه بود؟)

۹. دیروز تَعطیل بود؟

7.2 Your instructor will name a date from the calendar in October below. Say what day of the week that date is. For example,

پَنجِ اُکتُبر چَند شَنبه اَست؟ (پَنجِ اُکتُبر چَنشَمبَس؟)

پَنجِ اُکتُبر شَنبه اَست (پَنجِ اُکتُبر شَمبَس).

چَهارِ اُکتُبر چَند شَنبه بود؟ (چارِ اُکتُبر چَنشَمبه بود؟)

چَهارِ اُکتُبر جُمعه بود (چارِ اُکتُبر جُمه بود).

7.3 Ask your classmates how many classes they have every day of the week and complete the chart below using Persian digits. Answer your classmates' questions and help them to complete their own charts. Your instructor will then ask you questions about the schedule of the individuals whose information you have written down. Be prepared to say this information in Persian. For this drill you will use the verb *to have* in first, second and third person singular.

🔊 Examples:

اِمروز چَندشَنبه آست؟ (اِمروز چَنشَمبَس؟)

اِمروز چَند تا کِلاس داری؟ (اِمروز چَن تا کِلاس داری؟)

دوشَنبه چَند تا کِلاس داری؟ (دوشَنبه چَن تا کِلاس داری؟)

	تعدادِ کِلاسها	روز
		شَنبه
		یِک شَنبه
		دو شَنبه
		سه شَنبه
		چَهار شنبه
		پَنج شنبه
		جُمعه

7.4   Talk to everyone in your class and find out who has the same number of classes this semester or on the same day of the week as you do. Prepare to share with the class what you have found out.

🔊 Examples:

این تِرم دَر چَند تا کِلاس هَستی؟ (این تِرم تو چَن تا کِلاس هَستی؟)

اِمروز چَند تا کِلاس داری؟ (اِمروز چَن تا کِلاس داری؟)

On the Differences between Spelling and Pronunciation

The present tense verb *is* that is spelled است is pronounced *eh* after the words that end in consonants and vowel *ee*. If the word ends in the sound /e/ and is followed by the verb است, that verb است is pronounced /as/ or /ast/ instead of the word's final /e/ sound. Alternatively, the verb است is replaced by هست /hast/ after the word's final /e/ sound. Same phenomenon takes place after the word's final /ā/ sound that is followed by the verb است. For a complete guide to the differences between spelling and pronunciation in Persian, please refer to Appendix E.

Translation	Pronounced	Written
(It) is good	khoob**eh**	خوب است
... is in University	dar dāneshgāh-**eh**	در دانِشگاه است
... it's Persian class	kelāseh fārsee-**eh**	کِلاسِ فارسی است
Is Monday	doshambeh **hast** / doshamb**as**	دوشَنبه است
NY is in America	dar āmreekā **hast** / dar āmreek**ās**	NY دَر آمریکا است

7.5 Read the following sentences in accordance with the pronunciation rule described above.

۱. حالِ شُما چِطور است؟ مِرسی، خوب است. ۲. بَرادَرِ شُما چِطور است؟ مِرسی، خوب است. ۶. او آدَمِ خوبی است. ۷. اِسمِ مامانِ تو چه است؟ ۸ . اِسمِ او اِنی است. ۹. اِسمِ بَرادَرِ تو چه است؟ ۱۰ . اِسمِ او ریکی است. ۱۱ . او کُجایی است؟. ۱۲ . او از سین سیناتی است.

Question Word چه *what*

Pronounced	Written
Chee	چه

7.6 Pronounce the following sentences in accordance with the pronunciation rule described above.

۱. اِسمِ تو چه است؟ ۲. او کی است؟ ۳. او کُجایی است؟ ۴ . او ایرانی است. ۵. دوستَم آمریکایی است. ۶. او آدَمِ خوبی است. ۷ . اِسمِ مامانِ تو چه است؟ ۸ . اِسمِ او اِنی است. ۹. اِسمِ بَرادَرِ تو چه است؟ ۰۱ . اِسمِ او ریکی است. ۱۱ . او کُجایی است؟ . ۲۱ . او از سین سیناتی است.

> The combination of the letters spelled ان and ام are pronounced /**oon**/ and /**oom**/ respectively.

61

Written	Pronounced
آن	oon
میخوانم	mee-khoon-am
کُدام	kod-oom
عَصبانی	a-sa-boon-ee

7.7 🔊 Read the following words in accordance with the pronunciation rule described above.

آن، نان، دانه، میداند، خانه، آنجا، بادام، کُدام، چانه، لانه ، شانه ، تَمام، جان.

7.8 🔊 Listen to Parsa. Pay attention not only to pronunciation but also to the intonation and stress in the sentences. Now, prepare to read the sentences aloud just as the narrator did. Imitate the native speaker's pronunciation and intonation.

فَرانسه   France /fa-rãn-seh/

مِعماری   Architecture /me-mã-ree/

فَلسَفه   Philosophy /fal-sa-feh/

اِسمِ مَن پارسا است. فامیلیِ مَن نیکزاد است. مَن آهلِ نیو یورک هَستَم. پِدَرِ مَن ایرانی است. مادَرِ مَن آلمانی است. مَن یِک بَرادَر و یِک خواهَر دارَم. اِسمِ بَرادَرِ مَن عَلی است. عَلی آلان دَر کالیفرنیا است. او دانِشجوی دُکتُرا دَر دانِشگاهِ کالیفُرنیا است. اِسمِ خواهَرِ مَن لیفکه است. لیفکه آلان دَر فَرانسه است. او دَر پاریس مِعماری میخواند. مَن هَم دانِشجو هَستَم. مَن دانِشجوی دانِشگاهِ نیویورک هَستَم. رِشتهِ مَن فَلسَفه است.

فَصلِ دُوُم
Chapter 2

خانِواده
My Family

Affordable price, fuel efficiency and maneuverability make motorcycle a common means of family transportation for low-income families in Tehran. Guess what all three passengers are missing here! Helmets!

Function Describing your immediate and extended family, asking and telling age, saying dates, counting (10–100), asking common questions. Key verbs: *to be related, to be … years of age.*

Listening Ashkan's family.

Structures Word order, high frequency question words.

🔊 Listen, read along and try to imitate the native speaker's pronunciation. Repeat each word aloud several times until you can easily pronounce it.

Family and Friends		
Family	khoone-vã-deh	خانِواده
Relative	fã-meel	فامیل
Parents	pedaroh mãdar, mãmãn-bãbã	پِدَرومادَر، مامان بابا
Father	pe-dar	پِدَر
Dad, my dad	bã-bã, bãbã-yeh man	بابا، بابای مَن
Mother	mã-dar	مادَر
Mom, my mom	mã-mãn, mãmãn-eh man	مامان، مامانِ مَن
Daughter, girl	dokh-tar	دُختَر
Son, boy	pe-sar	پِسَر
Brother	bar-ã-dar	بَرادَر
Sister	khã-har	خواهَر
Grandfather	pe-dar bo-zorg	پِدَر بُزُرگ
Grandmother	mã-dar bo-zorg	مادَر بُزُرگ
Grandchild	na-veh	نَوه
Paternal aunt	am-meh	عَمه
Paternal uncle	amoo	عَمو
Paternal male cousin	pe-sar amoo, pe-sar am-meh	پِسَرعَمو، پِسَرعَمه
Paternal female cousin	dokh-tar am-meh, dokh-tar amoo	دُختَرعَمه، دُختَرعَمو
Maternal uncle	dã-ee	دایی
Maternal aunt	khã-leh	خاله
Maternal male cousin	pe-sar khã-leh, pe-sar dã-ee	پِسَر خاله، پِسَردایی
Maternal female cousin	dokh-tar dã-ee, dokh-tar khã-leh	دُختَر دایی، دُختَرخاله
My older sister	khã-har-eh bo-zor-geh man	خواهَرِ بُزُرگِ من

Family and Friends		
My younger brother	bar-ã-dar-eh koo-chee-keh man	بَرادَرِ کوچکِ من
Man	mard	مَرد
Woman; also: wife	zan	زَن
Husband	show-har	شُوهَر
Wife, woman	zan	زَن
Child	bach-cheh	بَچه
Children	bach-cheh hã	بَچه ها
Friend, my friend	doost, doosteh man / doostam	دوسـت، دوسـتِ مَن / دوسـتَم
Boyfriend	doost pe-sar	دوست پِسَر
Girlfriend	doost dokh-tar	دوست دُختَر
My best friend	beh-ta-reen doos-teh man	بِهتَرین دوسـتِ مَن
Married	mo-ta-ahel, mo-te-a-hel	مُتأهِل
Single	mo-ja-rad	مُجَرَد
Marriage	ez-de-vãj	ازدواج
S/he is married	ez-de-vãj kar-deh	ازدواج کَرده
Pet	pet, hey-voo-neh khoo-ne-gee	پِت also حِیوانِ خانِگی
Dog	sag	سَگ
Cat	gor-beh	گُربه
How is s/he related to you?	oon bã sho-mã che nes-ba-tee dãr-eh?	او با شُما چه نِسبَتی دارد؟
She is my aunt	oon am-me-yeh ma-neh	او عَمهِ مَن است
We are friends	bã ham doost-eem	با هَم دوستیم
My grandmother and I are very close	manoh mãmãn bo-zor-geh man khe-ee-lee bã ham samee-mee hasteem	من و مامان بُزُرگِ من خِیلی با هَم صَمیمی هَستیم
To see the relatives	bar-ã-yeh dee-da-neh fã-meel	بَرای دیدَنِ فامیل

65

Miscellaneous		
Why?	cherã	چِرا ؟
Because	bar-ã-yeh een-keh	بَرای اینکه
Because of …	be-da-leeleh …	به دَلیلِ ...
Person (used when counting)	na-far	نَفَر
How many people?	chan na-far	چَند نَفَر؟
How many?	chan tã?	چَند تا؟
Several (used with nouns in singular)	chan-deen	چَندین
Whether, if	ãyã	آیا
Approximate equivalent of آیا that is used in a negated question	ma-gar/ma-geh	مَگَر
With	bã	با
But, however	valee, am-mã	وَلی، آما
During the day	rooz-hã/roozã	روزها
What type?	che-no/che no-oo	چه نُوع؟
What type of restaurant?	cheh no-oo restoorãn	چه نُوع رِستوران؟
City	shah-r	شَهر

Numbers and Age		
Ten	dah	دَه (۱۰)
Twenty	beest	بیست (۲۰)
Thirty	see	سی (۳۰)
Forty	che-hel/chel	چِهل (۴۰)
Fifty	pan-jah	پَنجاه (۵۰)
Sixty	sha-st	شَصت (۶۰)
Seventy	haf-tãd	هَفتاد (۷۰)
Eighty	hash-tãd	هَشتاد (۸۰)
Ninety	na-vad	نَوَد (۹۰)

Numbers and Age		
Hundred	sa-d	صَد (۱۰۰)
Ninety-five	na-va-doh panj	نَوَد و پَنج (۹۵)
Year	sãl	سال
Age (of a person)	senn	سین
How old are you?	chan sã-leh hast-ee?	چَند ساله هَستی؟
I am twenty	beest sã-leh hast-am	بیست ساله هَستَم
How old are you? (colloquial style)	chan sã-le-teh?	چَند سالِته؟
I'm twenty (colloquial style)	beest sã-la-meh	بیست سالَمه
How old are you? (formal style)	chan sãl dãr-ee?	چَند سال داری؟
I'm twenty years old	beest sãl dãr-am	بیست سال دارَم

Quantifier تا is used to reply to questions about the number of items without naming that item, for example,

اِمروز چَند تا کِلاس داری؟ – دو تا!

Note that in Persian, when we count things and persons the counted items are used in singular, that is, *two brother, three cousin,* دو بَرادَر، سه دُختَر خاله

On Numbers

To form numbers such as *twenty-one, twenty-two* in Persian, say *twenty and one, twenty and two,* for example, بیست و یِک ، بیست و دو

For the ease and fluency of pronunciation, the و here is pronounced *o* as if it were the ending of the first word in the compound, that is, /beestoh yek/, /beestoh doh/.

If you are writing Persian digits, arrange them as you do in English, that is, from left to right.

95	۹۵
162	۱۶۲
2018	۲۰۱۸

67

HOMEWORK تَکلیف

1. Look at Mitra's family tree. Read in Persian the sentences that describe these individuals' relationships to each other, and then complete the English translation based on what you read in the sentences and see in the image.

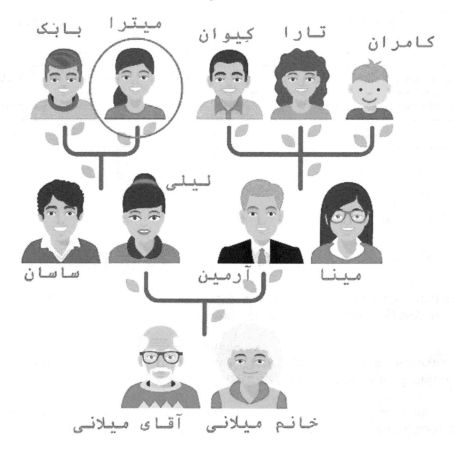

۱ بابک پِسَرِ ساسان اَست. ۲. میترا خواهَرِ بابک اَست. ۳. کیوان بَرادَرِ تارا اَست. ۴. خانُمِ میلانی مادَربُزُرگِ میترا اَست. ۵. میترا دُختَرعَمه تارا اَست. ۶. کیوان پِسَردایی بابک اَست.۷. آقای میلانی شُوهَرِ خانُمِ میلانی اَست. ۸. لیلی و ساسان مادَر و پِدَرِ میترا هَستَند. ۹. لیلی عَمه کیوان اَست. ۱۰. آرمین دایی میترا اَست.

(1) Babak is Sasan's _____. (2) Mitra is Babak's _____. (3) Keyvan is Tara's _____. (4) Mrs. Milani is Mitra's _____. (5) Mitra is Tara's paternal female _____. (6) Keyvan is Babak's

maternal male _____. (7) Mr. Milani is Mrs. Milani's _____. (8) Lily and Sasan are Mitra's _____. (9) Lily is Keyvan's paternal _____. (10) Armin is Mitra's maternal _____.

2. 🔊 Listen and read along. Roya is talking about her family. Complete the English translation based on what you hear and read. Answer the questions about Roya's family in Persian.

سَلام، اِسمِ مَن رویا است. من تِهرانی هَستم. خانوادهِ من هَفت نَفَر است. دو تا بَرادَر و دو تا خواهَر دارم. پِدَرِ من یک بَرادَر دارد. اِسمِ بَرادَرِ پِدَرِ من کامران است. کامران عَموی من است. من یک پِسَرعَمو دارم. پِسَرعَموی من آلان در شَهرِ نیویورک زِندِگی میکُند. پِسَرعَموی من دانِشجو ی زیست شِناسی در دانِشگاهِ نیویورک است. او با خانوادهِ خاله ِ من در نیویورک زندگی میکند.

پِدَرِ من خواهَر نَدارد. مادَرِ من یک خواهَر دارد. اِسمِ آن خواهَر زیبا است. زیبا خالهِ من است. مادَرِ من یک بَرادَر دارد. اِسمِ آن بَرادَر امیر است. امیر دایی ِ من است. من یک پِسَرخاله و یک دُخترخاله دارم. آنها آلان در نیویورک زِندِگی میکُند. من یک پِسَردایی و یک دُختَردایی دارم. آنها در شَهرِ کِرمان زِندِگی میکُند. پِسَردایی و دُختَردایی من هَر دو تایِشان دانِشجو هَستَند.

Translation

Hi, my name is Roya. I am from Tehran. There are _____ people in my _____. I have two _____ and two _____. My _____ has one _____. My father's _____ name is Kamran. Kamran is my _____. I have one paternal _____. My paternal male cousin now _____ in the city of New York. My _____ is a biology student at NYU. He lives with the family of my _____ in New York. My _____ does not have _____.

My _____ has one _____. That _____ name is Zeeba. Zeeba is my _____. My _____ has one _____. That _____ name is Amir. Amir is my _____. I have one maternal _____ and one maternal _____. They _____ in New York now. I have one maternal _____ and one maternal _____. They _____ in the city of Kerman. My _____ and _____ are both students.

Questions

۱.دَر خانوادهِ رویا چَند تا بَچه آست؟

۲.رویا عَمو دارد؟

۳. رویا عَمه دارد؟

۴. رویا دایی دارد؟

۵. خالهِ رویا چَند تا بَچه دارد؟

3. Complete the following sentences with the words that describe your relation to your family members.

۱ . پِدَر و مادَرِ بابای مَن ....ِ مَن هَستَند.

۲ . مادَرِ پِسَرخاله ِ مَن .... مَن است.

۳ . مَن .... ِ پِدَر بُزُرگ و مادَر بُزُرگِ مَن هَستَم.

۴ . مَن ....ِ پِدَر و مادَرِ مَن هَستَم.

۵ . پِدَرِ دُختَرعَموی مَن ....ی مَن است.

4. On the family tree below, next to each person, write in Persian the word that reflect their relation to Kamran (in Table 1) and to Mitra (in Table 2). For example, the gentleman in the bottom third row is grandfather (پدربزرگ).

میترا

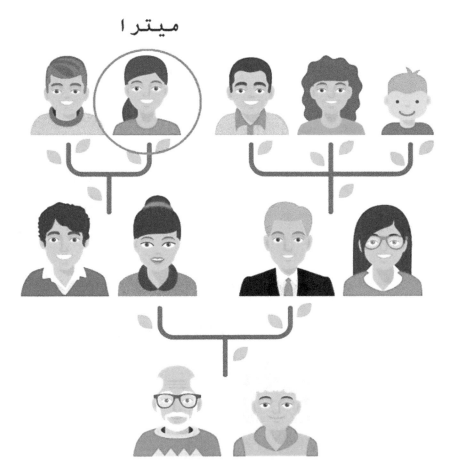

5. Prepare to ask and to also answer these questions in Persian. Before coming to class, say the sentences a few times aloud until you can easily pronounce them. In class, you will work with a classmate and ask him/her these questions in Persian.

۱. دَر کِلاسِ فارسیِ تو چَند تا دانِشجو هَست؟ (تو کِلاسِ فارسیِ تو چَن تا دانِشجو هَست؟)

۲. دَر کِلاسِ فارسیِ تو چَند تا زَن و چَند تا مَرد هَستَند؟ (تو کِلاسِ فارسیِ تو چَن تا زَن و چَن تا مَرد هَستَن؟)

۳. خانِواده‌ِ تو چَند نَفَر هَستَند؟ (خونِواده‌ِ تو چَن نَفَر هَستَن؟)

۴. چَند تا بَرادَر و خواهَر داری؟ (چَن تا بَرادَر و خواهَر داری؟)

۵. عَمو یا دایی داری؟

۶. عَمه یا خاله داری؟

۷. بَرادَرِ تو مُتاهِل یا مُجَرَد است؟ خواهَرِ تو مُتاهِل یا مُجَرَد است؟ (بَرادَر/خواهَرِ تو مُتاهِل یا مُجَرَده؟)

۸. بَرادَرِ تو دَرس میخواند یا کار میکُند؟ خواهَرِ تو دَرس میخواند یا کار میکُند؟ (بَرادَر/خواهَرِ تو دَرس میخونه یا کار میکُنه؟)

6. 🔊 Prepare to answer and ask the following questions in class.

۱. تو چَند ساله هَستی؟ (تو چَن ساله هَستی؟)

۲. پِدَرِ تو چَند ساله است؟ (پِدَرِ تو چَن ساله هَست؟)

۳. مادَرِ تو چَند ساله است؟ (مادَرِ تو چَن ساله هَست؟)

۴. بَرادَر داری؟ او چَند ساله است؟ (اون چَن ساله هَست؟)

۵. خواهَر داری؟ او چَند ساله است؟ (اون چَن ساله هَست؟)

۶. پِدَربُزُرگ داری؟ او چَند ساله است؟ (اون چَن ساله هَست؟)

۷. مادَربُزُرگ داری؟ او چَند ساله است؟ (اون چَن ساله هَست؟)

۸. پِسَردایی و دُختَردایی داری؟ آنها چَند ساله هَستَند؟ (اونا چَن ساله هَستَن؟)

۹. پِسَرخاله و دُختَر خاله داری؟ آنها چَند ساله هَستَند؟ (اونا چَن ساله هَستَن؟)

۱۰. بِهتَرین دوستِ تو چَند ساله است؟ (بِهتَرین دوستِ تو چَن ساله هَست؟)

۱۱. دوست پِسَر/دوست دُختَر داری؟ او چَند ساله است؟ (اون چَن ساله هَست؟)

7. 🔊 Do research online and complete the sentences with data pertaining to your university and the city in which your university is located. Prepare to read the completed sentences aloud. Useful word: هِزار /he-zăr/ thousand.

دانِشگاهِ ما دَر شَهرِ ـــــــ است. (دانِشگاهِ ما دَر شَهرِ ـــــــه)

دَر شَهرِ ما ـــــــ تا دانِشگاه هَست. (تو شَهرِ ما ـــــــ تا دانِشگاه هَست)

دَر دانِشگاهِ ما ـــــــ دانِشجو هَست (تو دانِشگاهِ ما ـــــــ دانِشجو هَست).

دَر دانِشگاهِ ما ــــــــــ دانِشجوی لیسانس هَست

(تو دانِشگاهِ ما ــــــــــ دانِشجوی لیسانس هَست).

دَر دانِشگاهِ ما ــــــــــ دانِشجوی دُکتُرا هَست (تو دانِشگاهِ ما ــــــــــ

دانِشجوی دُکتُرا هَست).

دَر دانِشگاهِ ما ــــــــــ اُستاد هَست (تو دانِشگاهِ ما ــــــــــ اُستاد هَست).

دَر دانِشگاهِ ما ــــــــــ تا دانِشکَده هَست (تو دانِشگاهِ ما ــــــــــ تا دانِشکَده

هَست).

8. Now, do research online and write sentences which are identical to the ones in the exercise above, but about the University of Tehran (دانِشگاهِ تِهران). Write your sentences in Persian and prepare to read your sentences aloud.

9. 🔊 Prepare to ask and answer the following questions in Persian.

۱. دَر کِلاسِ فارسیِ ما چَند تا دانِشجو هَست؟ (تو کِلاسِ فارسیِ ما چَن تا دانِشجو هَست؟)

۲. اِمروز دَر کِلاسِ ما چَند نَفَر هَستَند؟ (اِمروز تو کِلاسِ ما چَن نَفَر هَستَن؟)

۳. دَر کِلاسِ فارسیِ ما چَند تا اُستاد هَست؟ (تو کِلاسِ فارسیِ ما چَن تا اُستاد هَست؟)

۴. دَر کِلاسِ فارسیِ ما چَند تا تی اِی هَست ؟ (تو کِلاسِ فارسیِ ما چَن تا تی اِی هَست؟)

۵. دَر کِلاسِ فارسیِ ما چَند تا دُختَر هَست؟ (تو کِلاسِ فارسیِ ما چَن تا دُختَر هَست؟)

۶. دَر کِلاسِ فارسیِ ما چَند تا پِسَر هَست؟ (تو کِلاسِ فارسیِ ما چَن تا پِسَر هَست؟)

۷. دَر آمریکا، یِک هَفته چَند روز اَست؟ (تو آمریکا، یِه هَفته چَن روزه؟)

۸. دَر ایران، یِک هَفته چَند روز اَست؟ (تو ایران، یِه هَفته چَن روزه؟)

۹. دَر آمریکا، یِک هَفته چَند روز تَعطیل دارَد؟ (تو آمریکا، یِه هَفته چَن روزِ تَطیل داره؟)

۱۰. دَر ایران، یِک هَفته چَند روزِ تَعطیل دارد؟ (تو ایران، یِه هَفته چَن روزِ تَطیل داره؟)

۱۱.دَر دانِشگاهِ تو، یِک تِرم چَند هَفته است؟ (تو دانِشگاهِ تو، یِه تِرم چَن هَفتَس؟)

۱۲. اِمروز چَندشَنبه است؟ (اِمروز چَن شَمبَست؟)

۱۳.فَردا چَند شَنبه است؟ (فَردا چَن شَمبَست؟)

۱۴. فَردا روزِ تَعطیل یا روزِ کاری است؟ (فَردا روزِ تَطیل یا روزِ کاریه؟)

10. Listen and write down the equations you hear. Use Persian digits. Prepare to read the equations aloud.

For example, 10 + 15 = 25   ۱۰ + ۱۵ = ۲۵

Useful words: با /bã/ plus (colloquial) / میشود /meesheh/ equals

for example, بیست با پَنج میشود بیست وپَنج /beest bã panj meesheh beestoh panj/.
۲۰+۵=۲۵

۶.	۱.
۷.	۲.
۸.	۳.
۹.	۴.
۱۰.	۵.

11. Complete the equations. Spell out the numbers using words not digits.

۱. چَهاردَه با _____ بیست و هَشت میشود. ۲. بیست و پَنج با پَنج _____ میشود.

۳. بیست و پَنج با پانزدَه _____ میشود. ۴. چِهِل با _____ پَنجاه میشود.

۵. سی با سی _____ میشود. ۶ . _____ با پانزدَه شَصت و پَنج میشود.

۷. بیست و پَنج با _____ شَصت میشود. ۸. هَفتاد و پَنج با پانزدَه _____ میشود.

۹. سی با بیست و پَنج _____ میشود. ۱۰. دَه با _____ چِهِل و پَنج میشود.

IN CLASS

دَر کِلاس

12. Look at the image and answer the following questions.

۱. این خانِواده چَند نَفَر هَستَند؟ (این خونِواده چَن نَفَر هَستَن؟)

۲. دَر این خانِواده چَند تا مَرد و چند تا زَن هستَند؟
(تو این خونِواده چَن تا مَرد و چَن تا زَن هستَن؟)

۳. دَر این خانِواده چَند تا بَچه هَست؟ (تو این خونِواده چَن تا بَچَست؟)

۴. این پِسَربَچه چَند تا خواهَر دارد؟ (این پِسَربَچه چَن تا خاهَر داره؟)

۵. این دُختَربَچه چَند تا برادَر دارد؟ (این دُختَربَچه چَن تا برادَر داره؟)

۶. در این خانِواده چَند تا مادَربُزُرگ و چند تا پِدَربُزُرگ هَستَند؟ (تو این خونِواده چَن تا مادَربُزُرگ و چَن تا پِدَربُزُرگ هَستَن؟)

13.   You will work with a classmate. Look at the image below and describe the family.

14.   Using the family tree below and the individuals' names, ask your classmates how they are related to Mitra. For example,

ساسان با میترا چه نِسبَتی دارد؟ (ساسان با میترا چه نِسبَتی داره؟)

ساسان پِدَرِ میترا است (ساسان پِدَرِ میترا ه/هَست)

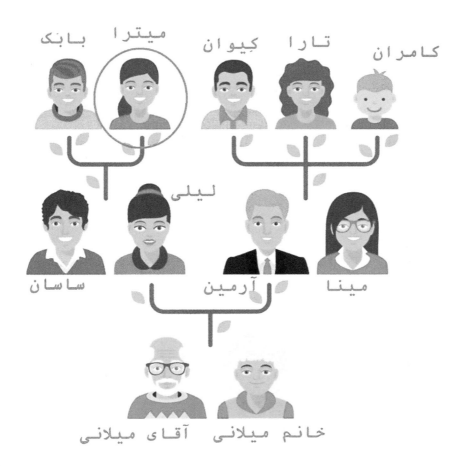

15. Talk to a classmate. Inquire about his/her family members and draw their family tree. The family tree should include your classmate's immediate family, grandparents, uncles/aunts and cousins. Prepare to answer the instructor's questions about the family tree you drew.

16. **My Family.** Your instructor will give you a card with the description of your fictional family. Other students will get cards that describe their "families." Some of your classmates belong to your "family," but you don't know who they are. The card will tell you whether you are a son or daughter in your family, and how many brothers and sisters you have. Look for classmates with matching information. Talk to everyone in class and find your "family members." There are several families in class. Don't show your card to others. You have to communicate the information verbally.

Instructor, please see the appendix Instructor's Resources.

17. Your instructor will give you and each one of your classmates a card with word(s) in Persian. All those words together make up two sentences. Your objective is to talk to all your classmates and get all words from them in order to reconstruct and write down in Persian the original two sentences. Your classmates will only provide you with the definitions of their words in Persian and you will have to guess their words based on the definitions. Be ready to do the same for your classmates. You must speak only in Persian.

Instructor, please see the appendix Instructor's Resources.

18. Talk to everyone in class and find out how many of your classmates are of your age. Share with class the results of your inquiry, for example,

او مِثلِ مَن ۲۰ ساله است (اون مِثلِ مَن ۲۰ ساله هست)/ oon mesleh man beest sãleh hast/ Like me, s/he is 20 years old.

19. You will receive a card with equations in Persian. Read the equations to your classmate, so that s/he can write them down in Persian. Your classmate will read his/her equations to you. Listen to him/her and write those equations down. Compare notes.

Instructor, please see the appendix Instructor's Resources.

20. Talk to your classmate(s) and find out the age of the following family members. Write down the numbers that reflect their ages. Your instructor will ask you to say the age of selected family members from the list.

	دانِشجوی ۱	دانِشجوی ۲
پِدَرِ او		
مادَرِ او		
عَموی او		
عَمهِ او		

		داییِ او
		خاله ِ او
		مادَربُزُرگِ او
		پِدَربُزُرگِ او

21.   Talk to your classmates and find out who in your class:

- is of the same age as you are
- has the same number of siblings
- has siblings of the same ages as your siblings
- has parents of the same age as yours
- has the same number of uncles and/or aunts

Be ready to answer your instructor's questions about your inquiry in Persian, for example,

بَرادَرِ او مِثلِ بَرادَرِ مَن بیست ساله آست (بَرادَرِ اون مِثلِ بَرادَرِ مَن بیست ساله هَست).

22.   Look at the Homework assignments 7 and 8 (data about your university and the University of Tehran). Pick a sentence. Pick a classmate and ask him/her a question about the data reflected in the sentence you have chosen, for example,

دَر دانِشگاهِ تِهران چَند تا دانِشکَده هَست؟

(تو دانِشگاهِ تِهران چَن تا دانِشکَده هَست؟)

23.   **Sentence charades.** You will work with a classmate. Speak in Persian only and say the definitions of the words in your sentence, so that your classmate can guess the words and write down your exact sentence in Persian. Your classmate will do the same for you. You will receive the cards with the sentences from your instructor.

Instructor, please see the appendix Instructor's Resources.

GRAMMAR

دَستورِ زَبان

Word Order in Persian

Simple sentence:

3. Verb	2. Object	1. Subject
دارم	یک خواهر	من
have	one sister	I

Typical Persian sentence starts with the subject. The subject is followed by the object with its modifiers. The sentence concludes with the Verb. If the sentence has multiple objects, then the direct object (not accompanied by a preposition) precedes the indirect object (accompanied by a preposition). If the sentence communicates even more information, then the extra words are normally placed between the subject and object(s). For explanations of what the subject, indirect and direct objects mean, refer to the appendix Grammarian's Corner.

Sentence with Multiple Objects:

Verb	Indirect object (and modifiers)	Direct object (and modifiers)	Place	Time	Subject
دادم	به استاد	مشقم را	در کلاس	دیروز	من
Gave	to the Professor	my homework	in class	yesterday	I

I am a student.	مَن دانِشجو هَستَم.
We saw him in class.	ما او را دَر کِلاس دیدیم.
Mom gave the car to my brother.	مامان ماشین را بِه بَرادَرَم داد.
This year I am going for a trip with my friend.	اِمسال با دوستَم بِه مُسافِرَت میرَوم.

The word order can be modified for the purpose of applying emphasis. The part of the sentence that needs to be emphasized may be moved to the beginning of the sentence:

Who lives in this house?   کی دَر این خانه زِندِگی میکُند؟

Who lives in *this house*?   دَر این خانه کی زِندِگی میکُند؟

If the sentence comprises several clauses, each clause constitutes a mini-sentence with its own word order as described above.

The subject of the sentence is the person or thing who/what is doing or being something. In Persian, the subject (e.g., I, you, she, we, etc.) is reflected in the verb's ending (conjugational suffix). Therefore, if the subject of a Persian verb in the sentence is a pronoun (e.g., I, you, she, we, etc.), that subject becomes superfluous and is usually omitted.

من به خانه میرَوَم ← به خانه میرَوَم.

Question words. Place the question word where the answer word would usually go in the sentence. For example, the word کی (who?) would go in the beginning of the sentence if it refers to the subject, but would be placed in the middle of the sentence after a preposition if it refers to indirect object. For example,

کی در این خانه زِندِگی میکند؟   Who lives in this house?

شُما با کی زندِگی میکُنید؟   With whom do you live?

The question word چه (what?) is usually placed right in front of the verb unless it refers to a modifier, for example,

What do you want from me?   از من چه میخواهی (از من چی میخای)؟

What kind of book is this?   این چه نوع کِتابی است (این چه نوع کِتابیه)؟

The question word چِرا (why?) usually comes in the beginning of the sentence.

اِسمِ شُما چه است؟ - اِسمِ مَن پارسا است.

شُما چه میخورید؟ - مَن نوشابه میخورم.

شُما کُجا زِندِگی میکُنید؟ - مَن دَر نیویورک زِندِگی میکنم.

کی اَهلِ نیویورک است؟ - مَن اَهلِ نیویورک هَستَم.

اِسمِ کی پارسا است؟ - اِسمِ مَن پارسا است.

شُما با کی زِندِگی میکُنید؟ - مَن با دوستِ پِسَرَم زِندِگی میکُنم.

شُما چَند تا بَرادَر دارید؟ - مَن دو تا بَرادَر دارَم.

حالِ شُما چِطور است؟ - حالِ مَن خوب است.

81

Building Multiple Questions for a Statement

Statement:

دوستِ مَن جُمعه ها دَر رِستوران غَذای ایرانی میخورد.

Questions:

About the subject: ؟ کی جُمعه ها دَر رِستوران غَذای ایرانی میخورد

About the time: دوستِ مَن کِی دَر رِستوران غَذای ایرانی میخورد؟

About the place: دوستِ مَن جُمعه ها کُجا غَذای ایرانی میخورد؟

About the object: دوستِ مَن جُمعه ها دَر رِستوران چه میخورد؟

The words آیا and مَگَر are placed in the beginning of the sentence.

The word آیا serves to start a question sentence if no other question word is present. In this case, it serves as the equivalent in English of "Are/Is …", "Do/Does …" in the beginning of a question sentence.

Are you Iranian? آیا ایرانی هَستید؟؛

Do you know that …? آیا میدانید کِه...؟

In a statement, آیا serves to connect different clauses of the sentence and translates as *whether*, *if*, for example,

نِمیدانَم آیا دَر این شَهر رِستورانِ ایرانی هَست یا نَه.

I don't know **if** there is an Iranian restaurant in this city.

In proper Persian we would not say: نمیدانم اگر در این شَهر رستوران ایرانی هست.

The word مَگَر is a close equivalent of آیا but it is used in negative questions.

Am I not your friend? مَگَر مَن دوستِ تو نیستَم؟

Am I a stranger? (i.e., I am not a stranger!) مَگَر مَن غَریبه هَستَم؟

High Frequency Question Words

 Listen, read along and try to imitate the native speaker's pronunciation. Repeat each word aloud several times until you can easily pronounce it. You already know some of these words.

Who	kee (che ka-see)	کی، چه کَسی
What	che/chee	چه/چی
Where	ko-jã	کُجا
When	ke-ee	کِی
Why	che-rã	چِرا
How	che-tor	چِطور
Which	koo-doom	کُدام
Which one	koo-doom ye-kee	کدام یکی
What type	che no-oo, che-no	چِه نُوع
Of what origin	ko-jã-ee	کُجایی
How much	che-qad	چِقَدر
How many	chan-tã	چَند تا
How many people	chan na-far	چَند نَفَر
How many times	chan bãr	چَند بار
How often	chan vaq-t yeh bãr	چَند وَقت یِک بار
How much time	che-qad vaq-t	چِقَدر وَقت
How long	che mod-dat-ee	چِه مُدتی

HOMEWORK   تکلیف

24.   Create sentences using the given words.

۱. مَن، زِندِگی میکُنم، خوابگاه، دَر، الان

۲. اِسم، شُما، است ،چه ، بَرادَر ؟

۳. تو، هَستی، دانِشجو، کِلاسی، چِه، دَر ؟

۴. چِه، بَرادَر، است، او، اِسم؟

83

۵. شُما، دوست، کُجا، اَهل، است ؟

۶. کُجا، است، شُما، دانِشگاه ؟

۷. مَن، میخوانَم، تاریخ، دانِشگاه، دَر

۸. با، کی، زِندِگی، شُما، میکُنید، ؟

۹. مَعمولا، دَر، مَن، دَرس میخوانَم، با، دوستِ مَن، کِتابخانه

۱۰. او، کار، میکُنَند، و، خانُمِ او، دانِشگاه، دَر

۱۱. مَن، زِندِگی میکُنَم، نیویورک، دَر، وَلی، زِندِگی میکُنَند، خانِواده ِ ، مَن، واشینگتُن، دَر

۱۲. بِهتَرین دوستِ مَن، میخوانَد، و، میخوانَم، مَن، تاریخ، مُهَندِسی

25. Complete the sentences with the given question words. Translate the sentences into English.

کی ، چه، چَند، چِطور، کُجا، کُجایی، چِرا، کِی

۱. آن ـــــ است؟ آن اُستادِ مَن است. ۲ . این کِتاب ـــــ است؟ این کِتابِ سارا است.

۳. ـــــ تا بَرادَر داری؟ دو تا بَرادَر دارَم. ۴ . حالِ تو ـــــ است؟ خوبَم، مِرسی.

۵. پِدَر و مادَرِ تو ـــــ هَستَند؟ آنها دَر نیویورک هَستَند؟ ۶. دوست پِسَرِ تو بَرای اینکه خِیلی ـــــ. ۷. ـــــ سَرِ حال نیستی؟ بَرای اینکه خِیلی خَسته ام.

۸. ـــــ بِه نیویورک میایی؟ فَردا میایم.

26. Translate the sentences below into Persian. Note that in Persian, when we count things and persons the counted items are used in singular, that is, *two brother*, *three cousin*.

روز تولد /roozeh ta-va-lod/ birthday

(1) Where does your family live? My family lives in New York. (2) How many brothers and sisters does your mother have? My mother has one brother and one sister. (3) What does your brother study? My brother studies engineering. (4) What is the name of your professor in the Persian class? The name of my professor in the Persian class is _____. (5) Why are you not in class today? (6) Who lives in that house? (7) Is your maternal cousin also a student? Yes, she is also a student. (8) Is your friend single? She has a boyfriend. (9) Where is your girlfriend from? My girlfriend is Iranian. (10) When is your birthday?

27. Look at the photo of the family below. Write sentences comparing this family to yours. Prepare to read your sentences aloud in Persian. You can use words وَلی (but), اما (however), هم (also), و (and) to construct comparative sentences, for example, there are three people in this family, and there are three people in my family. Remember to structure the two parts of your sentence according to the standard word order in Persian.

28. Draw your own family tree. Include uncles, aunts, cousins and grandparents. For every family member, write in Persian the name and the word that describes that person's relationship to you.

29. A review presentation. Prepare a brief presentation on the topic of this chapter in the way that is applicable to you. Review the vocabulary and topic of this chapter and address the questions below in your presentation. Your presentation must be entirely in Persian. Your objective is to create a coherent and flowing narrative and speak continuously for a couple minutes in the target language. Be prepared to answer your classmates' questions about your presentation.

(1) How many people are there in your family? How many sisters and brothers do you have?

(2) What are your parents' names and ages?

(3) What are your siblings' names and ages?

(4) Where are your parents from? Where do they live now?

(5) How many brothers and sisters does your mother have? Where do they live?

(6) How many sisters and brothers does your father have? Where do they live now?

(7) How many paternal and maternal cousins do you have?

(8) What are your grandparents' names and ages?

(9) Where are your grandparents from? Where do they live now?

(10) Which family member are you very close to?

IN CLASS   دَر کِلاس

30.   You will work with a classmate to arrange the given words into proper sentences. Translate your sentences into English.

Statements:

۱. زِندِگی میکُنَم – دَر – نیویورک – مَن

۲. مَن – خانِواده – پَنج – نَفَر است

۳. من – خواهَر – سال – دارد – بیست

۴. مَن – بَرادَر – است – دانِشجو

Questions:

۱. کجا – است – تو – دوست – ؟

۲. با کی – زِندِگی میکُنی – تو – ؟

۳. عَمه – تو – چه – اسم – است – ؟

۴. کی – آن – است – ؟

۵. است – دوستِ تو – دانِشجو – ؟

31.   Working with a classmate, write a short story with the given words. Use all the words. You may repeat words from the list. Prepare to read your story aloud.

یِک، دوست، است، میخواند، رامین، مَن، اِسم، بَلَد، مُهَندِسی، تِهران،او، دارَم، و

، انگلیسی،خانِوادِه، ایرانی، از، فارسی.

86

32. Work with a classmate. Create as many questions as you can for the sentence below. Say your questions aloud and ask a classmate from a different group to translate it into English. Use question words such as کُجایی، چَند تا، کُجا، آیا، مَگَر، چِه نُوع

دَر شَهرِ ما یِک رِستورانِ خوبِ ایرانی هَست و دوستِ ایتالیایِی مَن دَر آن رِستوران کار میکُند.

33. **Definitions**. You will be working with a classmate. You will receive a card with series of words written in Persian. The words are from this chapter. Your task is to speak only in Persian and provide definitions of the words on your card to your classmate, so that s/he can guess the words and write them down in Persian. Do not say the words that are written on your card. Your classmate will do the same for you. At the end, the instructor will come to check whether the words you wrote down are the exact same words that appear on your classmate's card.

Instructor, please see the appendix Instructor's Resources.

34. Your instructor will assign one topic and three question words to you from the list below. Using those words and topic, come up with three meaningful questions in Persian which you could ask your classmates. Now, approach three random classmates and ask them your questions. Be ready to answer their questions.

Question words	Topics
What, Who, When, How many/much, Why, Where, Where from, How	**Me and my family** **University and classes**

35. You will be working all together as one group. Ask your instructor questions about his/her family and draw on the board your instructor's family tree. Include uncles, aunts and cousins. For every family member, write in Persian the word that describes that person's relationship to you instructor.

LISTENING  شِنیداری

Listen to Ashkan as he describes his family.

Pre-listening 1. Make a list of the words in Persian that you think you will encounter in a narrative about a family. Don't forget to write verbs. Pronounce aloud the words you have written so that you identify them when you listen to the audio.

Pre-listening 2. Think of your family and answer the following questions aloud.

۱. تو کُجا زِندِگی میکُنی؟ ۲. چَند تا بَرادَر و خواهَر داری؟ ۳. چَند تا عَمه و عَمو داری؟ ۴. چَند تا پِسَرعَمو و دُختَرعَمو داری؟ ۵. چَند تا دایی و خاله داری؟ ۶. اِسمِ پِسَرخاله‌ی تو چه است؟ ۷. اِسمِ دُختَردایی تو چه است؟ ۸. پِدَربُزُرگ و مادَربُزُرگِ مادَری تو کُجا زِندِگی میکُنَند؟ ۹. پِدَربُزُرگ و مادَربُزُرگِ پِدَری تو کُجا زِندِگی میکُنَند؟

Listening assignment. Listen and answer the questions in Persian. Say your answers several times aloud until you can easily pronounce them. You will have to say your answers in class.

سوالات:

۱. خانواده اشکان چَند نَفَر است؟ (خونِواده اشکان چَند نَفَر ٥؟)

۲. اشکان چَند تا خواهَر دارد؟ (اشکان چَن تا خاهَر داره؟)

۳. اِسمِ بَرادَر اشکان چه است؟ (اِسمِ بَرادَر اشکان چیه؟)

۴. اشکان چَند تا دُختَرعَمو و پِسَرعَمو دارد؟ (اشکان چَن تا دُختَرعَمو و پِسَرعَمو داره؟)

۵. خانواده‌ی خاله‌ی اشکان چَند نَفَر است؟ (خونِواده‌ی خاله‌ی اشکان چَن نَفَره؟)

۶. پِدَربُزُرگ و مادَربُزُرگِ اشکان کُجا زِندِگی میکُنَند؟ (پِدَربُزُرگ و مادَربُزُرگِ اشکان کُجا زِندِگی میکُنَن؟)

۷. خانواده‌ی کی در تَبریز زِندِگی میکُنَند؟ (خونواده‌ی کی در تَبریز زِندِگی میکُنَن؟)

Follow-up 1. Make one statement in Persian about Ashkan and his family and relatives.
Follow-up 2. State one similarity and one difference between Ashkan's family and your family.

E.g. اشکان یِک خواهَر دارد. مَن هَم یِک خواهَر دارَم (اشکان یِه خاهَر داره. مَنَم یِه خاهَر دارَم). اشکان عَمو دارد. مَن عَمو ندارَم (اشکان عَمو داره. مَن عَمو ندارَم).

Follow-up 3.  You will be working with a classmate. Create a brief dialogue where you will talk about your families. You will be yourself and your classmate will be Ashkan from the audio presentation. Imagine that Ashkan is your classmate in Persian class and you got to talking about families. Ask Ashkan about his family. He will do the same for you.

TRANSLATION   تَرجُمه

Translate the following passage into Persian and write it down.

بَچه های آنها their children

كامران Kamran	تارا Tara	مینا Meena	ساسان Sasan	پارسا Parsa
	زیبا Zeeba	پَریسا Parisa	كِیوان Keyvan	بابَک Babak

Hi, my name is Parsa. I live with my family in New York. There are five people in my family: my mother, my father, my older sister, my younger brother and myself. My dad's name is Sasan, and my mom's name is Meena. My sister's name is Tara, and my brother's name is Kamran. I have one paternal uncle. His name is Babak. My uncle Babak has one son and one daughter. My paternal cousins live in New York with their father and mother. I don't have a paternal aunt. I have one maternal uncle. His name is Keyvan. My uncle Keyvan has three children— two boys and one girl. My uncle Keyvan, his wife Parisa and their children live in Tehran. I have one maternal aunt. Her name is Zeeba. My aunt Zeeba has one daughter. My aunt Zeeba lives in Kashan with her husband and daughter. My paternal grandfather and grandmother live in California, and my maternal grandfather and grandmother live in Kashan.

فَصلِ سِوُم
Chapter 3

کار و پیشه
Occupation and Profession

Musicians playing a violin and melodica in Golestan Mall in Tehran. Increasingly large numbers of young Iranian artists pursue Western genres of music and art.

Function Talking about what you do and what you study, asking and telling time, talking about your schedule, how to describe objects. Key verbs: *to start, to end, to last, to like, to dislike.*

Listening I have to run to class!

Reading A letter from Roya, your new pen pal in Iran.

Structures The connector glide *eh/yeh* (the *ezafeh*), Connecting the word to its modifiers.

91

🔊 Listen and repeat. Say each word and phrase several times aloud until you can easily pronounce them.

Profession and Occupation		
Occupation, job	shoq-l	شُغل
Professor	os-tãd	اُستاد
Student	dã-nesh-joo	دانِشجو
Assistant	dast-yãr	دَستیار
Teaching assistant (TA)	dast-yãreh ãmoozeshee / dast-yãreh tadrees	دَستیارِ آموزِشی / دَستیارِ تَدریس
Middle or high school student	dãnesh-ã-mooz	دانِش آموز
Employer	kãr-far-mã	کارفَرما
Employee of ...	kãr-man-deh ...	کارمَندِ...
Employee of the bank	kãr-man-deh bãnk	کارمَندِ بانک
Office	ed-ã-reh	اِداره
Office clerk	kãr-man-deh ed-ã-reh	کارمَندِ اِداره
Lawyer	va-keel	وَکیل
Doctor, physician	dok-tor, pe-zesh-k	پِزِشک، دُکتُر
Dentist	dan-doon pe-zesh-k	دَندان پِزِشک
Engineer	mo-han-des	مُهَندِس
Civil engineer	mohandeseh omrãn	مُهَندِسِ عُمران
Electrical engineer	mohandeseh barq	مُهَندِسِ بَرق
Athlete	var-zesh-kãr	وَرزِشکار
Artist	ho-nar-mand	هُنَرمَند
Movie actor	ho-nar-pee-sheh, bã-zee-gar	هُنَرپیشه، بازیگَر
Celebrity	sho-h-reh, se-tã-reh	شُهره، سِتاره
Scientist	dã-nesh-mand	دانِشمَند
Nurse	pa-ras-tãr	پَرَستار

Profession and Occupation		
Journalist	kha-bar-ne-gãr	خَبَرنگار
TV host	moj-ree	مُجری
Musician	moo-zee-see-an	موزیسیَن
Singer	khã-nan-deh	خواَننده
Writer	ne-vee-san-deh	نویسَنده
Movie director	kãr-gar-doon	کارگردان
Waiter	peesh-khed-mat	پیشخِدمَت
Architect	me-mãr	مِعمار
Designer	tar-rãh	طَراح
Businessperson	bã-zar-gãn	بازرگان

Miscellaneous		
Experienced	mo-jar-rab	مُجَرَب
Nice, kind	meh-ra-boon	مِهرَبان
Nice people	ã-da-mã-yeh meh-ra-boon	آدَم های مِهرَبان
A lot, many	zee-ãd	زیاد
A little, few	kam	کَم
Private company	sher-ka-teh khoo-soo-see	شِرکَتِ خُصوصی
State-run company	sher-ka-teh dow-la-tee	شِرکَتِ دُولَتی
My favorite actress/actor	ho-nar-pee-she-yeh mow-re-deh alã-qeyeh man	هُنَرپیشهِ مُوردِ عَلاقهِ مَن
Linguistics	zabãn she-nã-see	زَبان شِناسی
Computer Science	oo-loomeh rã-yã-neh	عُلومِ رایانه
Film, a movie	feelm	فیلم
Cinema, movies	see-na-mã	سینَما
My favorite film	feel-meh mow-re-deh alã-qe-yeh man	فیلمِ مُوردِ عَلاقهِ مَن

Verbs and Phrases		
What is your occupation?	shoq-le shomã chee-eh?	شُغلِ شما چه است؟
What is her/his occupation?	shoq-leh oon chee-eh?	شُغلِ او چه است؟
I work in an office	dar ed-ã-reh kãr mee-ko-nam	دَر اِداره کار میکُنَم
Common profession	shoq-leh rã-yej	شُغلِ رایج
I like my job	shoq-la-moh doost dã-ram	شُغلَم را دوست دارَم
S/he likes her/his job	shoq-leh khod-ro doost dã-reh	شُغلِ خود را دوست دارد
S/he does not like her/his job	shoq-leh khod-ro doost nadã-reh	شُغلِ خود را دوست نَدارد
What's your favorite team?	tee-meh mow-re-deh alã-qat chee-eh?	تیمِ مُوردِ عَلاقه ات چه است؟
Tell (me) about yourself	az kho-det ta-reef kon	اَز خودِت تَعریف کُن

HOMEWORK   تَکلیف

1. **Read the sentences and look at the images. Based on the information from the sentences write in Persian digits the age of each person next to their names under the images.**

تینا   آقای کاشانی   تارا   سینا

۱. تینا هُنَرمَند است. او بیست و هفت ساله است.

۲. تارا دانِشجوی دُکتُرا است. او بیست و چهار ساله است.

۳. سینا موزیسیَن است. او بیست و شش سال دارد.

۴. آقای کاشانی کارمَندِ اِداره است. او پنجاه سال دارد.

2. 🔊 Listen and read along as Tara is talking about her family members and their occupations. Complete the transcript with words you hear. Now, based on what you have heard and read, complete the English translation.

سلام، اِسمِ من تارا است. اَهلِ لُس آنجِلِس هستم، ولی آلان در نیویورک زندگی میکنم. دانِشجوی دانِشگاه نیویورک هستم. ـــــــ من در لُس آنجِلِس زندگی میکنند. ـــــــی من مُهَندِسِ عُمران است. ـــــــ من اُستادِ دانِشگاه است. من یک ـــــــ دارم. ـــــــ من بیست و هفت ساله است و در یک بانک کار میکند. ـــــــی من یک ـــــــ دارد. اسم ـــــــ ـــــــی من امیر است. امیر ـــــــی من است. ـــــــی من مِثلِ ـــــــی من مُهَندِس است. ولی ـــــــی من مُهَندِسِ بَرق است. ـــــــی من یک ـــــــ دارد. اسم آن ـــــــ لیلی است. لیلی ـــــــ من است. ـــــــ من پَرَستار است. ـــــــ من یک ـــــــ و یک ـــــــ دارد. ـــــــ من بازَرگان است و ـــــــ ـــــــ من وَکیل است.

Hello, my name is Tara. I am from LA, but I live in NY now. I am a student at New York University. My _____ live in LA. My _____ is a civil engineer. My _____ is a university professor. I have one _____. My _____ is twenty-seven years old and works in a bank. My _____ has one _____. My _____ name is Amir. Amir is my _____. Like my _____, my __ ___ is an engineer. But, my _____ is an electrical engineer. My _____ has one _____. That _____ name is Leylee. Leylee is my _____. My _____ is a nurse. My _____ has one _____ and one _____. My _____ is a businessperson, and my _____ is a lawyer.

3. Write the name of a job that you associate with each one of the following individuals. Use the internet if needed. Prepare to say aloud what you have written.

Shakespeare, Michael Jackson, Van Gogh, Isaac Newton, Kafka, Avicenna, Serena Williams, Audrey Hepburn, Giorgio Armani, Warren Buffett and Larry King.

4. Listen to Reza, who is talking about his family and their occupations. Complete the transcript based on what you hear. Complete the English translation. Now, prepare to compare his family and their occupations to your family members and their professions. Prepare to say your sentences fluently in class. Examples:

مامانِ رِضا دُکتُر است، مامانِ مَن أستاد است. (مامانِ رِضا دُکتُره، مامانِ مَن أستاده.)

رِضا عَمه دارد، مَن عَمه نَدارم (رِضا عَمه داره، مَن عَمه نَدارم).

سَلام دوستان، اسم من رِضا است. دانشجوی ـــــ در دانشگاه شریف هستم. من یک خواهر و یک برادر دارم. خواهر من ـــــ است. برادر من ـــــ ـ ی حقوق در دانشگاه تهران است. بابای من ـــــ ـــــ است و مامان من ـ ـــــ بانک است. عموی من ـــــ است. عموی من هَم در ایران هَم در آمریکا زندگی میکند. زن عموی من ـــــ انگلیسی در دانشگاهِ تهران است. دایی من دندان ـــــ است. خاله من ـــــ است و در یک ـــــ خُصوصی در لس آنجلس کار میکند.

Hello, friends! My name is Reza. I am an _____ student at the Sharif University. I have one sister and one brother. My sister is a _____. My brother is a law _____ at the University of Tehran. My dad is an _____, and my mom works in a _____. My paternal uncle is a _____. My paternal uncle lives in both Iran and the USA. My paternal uncle's wife is a ___ of English at the ___ of Tehran. My maternal uncle is _____. My maternal aunt is a __ and works in a private firm in LA.

5. Do research online and find answers for the following questions. Prepare to say your answers fluently in class.

ایالَت /e-yā-lat/ state, province

رایِج /rā-yej/ common

۱. سه تا شُغل رایِج دَر آمریکا کُدام هَستَند؟

۲. سه تا شُغل رایِج دَر ایران کُدام هَستَند؟

۳. سه تا شُغل رایِج دَر ایالَتِ شُما کُدام هَستَند؟

6. 🔊 Prepare to ask and answer the following questions in Persian.

his/her (own) job کارِ خود (کارِ خودِش)

Does s/he like her/his job? (اون کارِ خودِشو دوسِت داره؟) او کارِ خود را دوسِت دارد؟

- Do your parents work?
- What does your father do? On what days of the week does he work? Does he like his job?
- Is your mother a professor, doctor, TV host, actress, designer, artist or engineer?
- Is your brother a student, PhD student, lawyer or dentist? Where does he work?
- What is your sister's job? Where does she work? Does she like her job?
- Is there a celebrity, lawyer, businessperson, professor or doctor in your family?
- What do you do? Where? What is your field?

7. Do research and find out the following information about the Iranian individuals listed below.

- شُغلِ او چه است؟

- چَند ساله است؟

- کُجا زِندِگی میکُند؟

Anoushe Ansari, Benyamin Bahadori, Shirin Ebadi, Majid Majidi, Christiane Amanpour, Marjane Satrapi, Niki Karimi, Mohsen Namjoo, Yara Shahidi, Firouz Naderi and Pierre Omidyar.

8. 🔊 Listen to Kamran who is talking about what he does. Answer the questions in Persian.

his (own) job کارِ خود (کارِ خودِش)

١. شُغلِ کامران چه است؟ (شُغلِ کامران چیه؟)

٢. کامران کُجا کار میکُند؟ (کامران کُجا کار میکُنه؟)

٣. کامران کارِ خودِش را دوسِت دارد؟ (کامران کارِ خودِشو دوسِت داره؟) چِرا؟

۴. کامران زیاد کار میکُند؟ (کامران زیاد کار میکُنه؟)

۵. شِرکَتِ کامران دُولَتی یا خُصوصی است؟ (شِرکَتِ کامران دُولَتی یا خوصوصیه؟)

IN CLASS

دَر کِلاس

9. Talk to your classmates and ask the following questions in Persian. Find out how many people share your preference for your favorite designer, actress and so on.

چه کَسی هُنَرپیشه، کارگَردان،خوانَنده، نِویسَنده، وَرزِشکار، طَراحِ مُوردِ عَلاقه ِ تو اَست؟

(چه کَسی هُنَرپیشه ِ مُوردِ عَلاقه ِ تو ه؟)

10. Talk to your classmates and find out if anyone's family members have the same jobs as your family members. Report the results to the class. For this activity, you will use the verb in first, second, third person singular. For example,

پِدَرِ او مِثلِ پِدَرِ مَن ... اَست (پِدَرِ اون مِثلِ پِدَرِ مَن .... ه).

11. Your instructor will place on the table several cards face down. You will pick a random card. It will tell you whether you are an "employer" or "employee."

If you are an "employee," the card will describe your professional skills. Prepare to say your skills fluently in Persian, as you will not be reading off the card during the activity.

If you are an "employer," the card will tell you what professionals you are looking to hire. As an "employer," you will interview all "employees" in class to find and hire the professionals you need. Prepare to say what you are looking for in Persian, as you will not be reading off the card during the activity. Think of the questions that you will have to ask in Persian during the interview. Your objective is to hire as many people as you can find with the necessary qualifications, so interview everyone in class. At the end, present to the class whom you have hired and explain why.

Instructor please see the appendix Instructor's Resources.

12. Read the following passage about Tina who is the narrator's best friend. Now, describe your best friend. You can use the passage below as an example.

بِهتَرین دوستِ من.

اِسمِ بِهتَرین دوستِ مَن تینا است. تینا نوزدَه ساله است. او از کالیفُرنیا است و آهلِ شَهرِ لُس آنجِلِس است. تینا یِک بَرادَر و یِک خواهَر دارد. آنها با پِدَر و مادَر دَر لُس آنجِلِس زِندِگی میکُنَند.

تینا آلان دَر شَهرِ نیویورک زِندِگی میکُند و دانِشجوی دانِشگاهِ کُلُمبیا است. او مِعماری میخواند. او دَر خوابگاه زِندِگی میکُند.تینا دانِشجوی خوبی است. تینا سینَما و غَذای ژاپُنی دوست دارد.

اِسم ...

سِن ...

خانِواده ...

کُجایی است ...

آلان کُجا زِندِگی میکُند ...

شُغل ...

رِشته ...

GRAMMAR   دَستورِ زَبان

How to connect a word to its modifiers, the connector glide *eh/yeh* (the *ezafeh*)

Contrary to English, Persian speakers first name the object and then describe it, that is, in Persian they say: *house big*, *book interesting*, *brother mine*. In order to connect the object (i.e., *house*, *book*, *brother*) to its modifiers (i.e., *big*, *interesting*, *mine*), an unstressed glide *eh/yeh* is pronounced between the object and each modifier. The glide *eh/yeh* can connect a noun to a noun, a noun to an adjective, a noun to a pronoun and so on.

This connector glide *eh/yeh* is called *ezafeh*, which means *addition* as it is used to add modifiers to the word. The *ezafeh* is a basic grammatical element of the Persian language that connects words to form meaningful phrases. Missing or misusing the connector glide will either change the meaning of your phrase or render it meaningless. Compare:

دَرِ أُتاق /dar-eh otãq/ the door of the room

دَر أُتاق /dar otãq/ in the room

این دانِشجوی ایرانی اسـت. /een dãneshjoo-yeh eerãnee ast/ This is an
Iranian student.

این دانِشجو ایرانی است. /een dãneshjoo eerãnee ast/ This student is Iranian.

این دانِشجوی سارا است. /een dãneshjoo-yeh Sara ast/ This is Sarah's student.

این دانِشـجو سـارا است. /een dãneshjoo Sara ast/ This student is Sarah.

Pronunciation
The connector glide is always pronounced *eh* after consonants, and *yeh* after vowels.

Spelling
The connector glide is only spelled as an **unconnected** letter ی after the word's final letter آ /ã/
and the word's final letter و (when it represents the vowels *oo* or *o*), for example, پای مَن /pã-
yeh man/, عموی تو /amoo-yeh to/, رادیوی تِهران /rãdeeo-yeh Tehran/.

After other letters the connector glide is pronounced but not spelled, for example, دوسـت من
بستنی /doost-eh man/, دانشگاه شـما /dãneshgãh-eh shomã/, صندلی تو /sandalee-yeh to/,
من /bastanee-yeh man/, خانه او /khooneh-yeh oon/, نی مولانا /ney-yeh mowlãnã/.

In the cases when the connector glide is not spelled with the letter ی but clarification and
disambiguation are still needed, the diacritic representing the vowel sound /e/ can be used to
mark the presence of the connector glide, for example, در اتاق /dar-eh otãq/.

Function
Use the glide to connect any word to its modifiers. These can be a noun and an adjective, a
noun and a noun, an *-ing* verb and an adjective, or a preposition and a noun.

هوای گَرم، أُتاقِ پِدَر، روی میز

When the connector glide is used to express possession, it is somewhat similar to the English
word *of*. In this case, the glide may connect a noun to a noun, pronoun, geographical or proper
names. The glide also connects Persian first and last names, as well as names to titles.

پایتَختِ کِشوَر، دوستِ مَن، شَـهرِ تِهران، اِیالَتِ نیویورک، ماشـینِ کامران،
نَزدیکِ ما، دانِشجوی ما، أَحمَدِ شاملو، آقای کاشانی، خانُمِ کاشـانی

Stacking (the modifiers)

If the word has several modifiers, the modifiers follow that word in a continuous sequence with the glide *eh/yeh* pronounced between all modifiers. If a **possessive pronoun** is present, that possessive pronoun is placed at the end of the entire phrase, for example,

friend good [of] mine	دوستِ خوبِ مَن
friend good [of] family [of] mine	دوستِ خوبِ خانواده ِ من
car new [of] friend [of] mine	ماشینِ جَدیدِ دوستِ مَن

The indicative pronoun is placed right before the word to which it refers:

the book [of] **that** Iranian student   کِتابِ آن دانِشجوی ایرانی

Adverbs are placed before the adjective to which they refer within the chain of modifiers, for example,

house **very** big   خانه خِیلی بُزُرگ

friend **very** good [of] mine   دوستِ خِیلی خوبِ من

Numbers are placed before the word which they enumerate. Remember that nouns modified by numbers are used in the singular form.

three house big   سه خانه ِ بُزُرگ

two student Iranian   دو دانِشجوی ایرانی

HOMEWORK   تَکلیف

13. In the paragraph below insert the glide in the underlined spaces as needed.

عَلی دوست _ ایرانی _ مَن _ است.
خانِواده _ او _ دَر شَهر _ تِهران زِندِگی میکُنَند. بابا _ عَلی _ دَر دانِشگاه _ تِهران کار
میکُند. مامان _ عَلی _ دَر دَبیرِستان کار میکُند.
عَلی دانِشجو _ دانِشگاه _ نیویورک _ است.
او رِشتِه _ ریاضی _ میخواند.

14. 🔊 Distinguish between the /e/ sound of the word's root and the connector glide *eh/yeh* between two different words. Listen carefully to the phrases. When you hear the connector glide *eh/yeh* between different words, mark it in writing either with the letter ی or the diacritic for the vowel sound /e/. When you hear the root sound /e/ of the word, spell it with the letter ه at the end of the word. Remember, the connector glide between separate words in unstressed, whereas the final root sound /e/ that is part of the word is stressed.

۱. خال... مَن. ۲. خال... او

۳. رِشت... تاریخ. ۴. رَشت... زیبا

۵. اید... خوب. ۶. عید... نُوروز

۷. کَلَم... بَرگ. ۸. کَلَم... فارسی

۹. خان... ایرانی. ۱۰. خان... مَن

۱۱. تَخت... جَمشید. ۱۲. تَخت... شَطرَنج.

۱۳. تُخم... مُرغ. ۱۴. تُخم... کَدو

۱۵. حال... شُما.

۱۶. بیم..... سَرما. ۱۷. بیم..... بِهداشتی

15. Translate into Persian the following phrases. Use the connector glide as needed.

1.   My friend has a new car. (2) My new friend has a car. (3) Tom is my brother's friend. (4) Tom is my friend's brother. (5) That's her family's house. (6) Her new friend's name is Tom. (7) Their house is on (pers.: *in*) our street. (8) My new friend's apartment is in this building.

16. 🔊 Listen to Sam as he talks about himself. Listen carefully, identify places where Sam uses the connector glide between words and insert it in the transcript as needed, using either the letter ی or the diacritic.

مَن خودَم /man khodam/ as for me, I myself

سَلام، حال شُما! اِسم مَن سام است. فامیل مَن بَختیار است. مَن آهل لُس آنجِلِس هَستَم. خانِواده مَن دَر یک خانه بزرگ دَر لِس آنجلِس زِندِگی میکُنَند. بابا مَن مُهَندِس است. مامان مَن اُستاد است. مَن یِک بَرادَر و یِک خواهَر دارم. بَرادَر مَن دانِشجو ریاضی دَر دانِشگاه نیویورک است. بَرادَر مَن دانِشجو خیلی خوبی است. خواهَر مَن هفده سال دارد و دَر یِک دَبیرِستان دَر

لس آنجلس درس میخواند. مَن خودَم دانِشجو هَستم و دَر دانِشگاه کالیفرنیا رِشته زیسـت شیناسـی میخوانَم. به نَظَر مَن، رِشته مَن خِیلی جالِب است.

17. In the following exercise make sure to use the connector glide correctly. Ask your classmate if his/her:

- last name is Persian, dad is a professor, maternal uncle is an engineer, maternal aunt is a teacher, friend is Iranian, cousin's name is Persian, paternal uncle has children.
- house is big, house is new, dorm is good, Persian class is big, family is from Iran, father and mother are from New York, brother and sister are students, boyfriend/girlfriend speaks Persian.

For example, باबای تو اُستاد است؟ / bābāyeh toh ostādeh?/

18. In the dotted spaces insert the connector glide as needed. In the underlined space, provide the information relevant to you. Use Persian digits for numbers. Prepare to read the completed sentences fluently in class.

اِسـم... مَن ــــــــــــــ ــــــــــــــ است.

خانِواده... مَن ــــــــــــــ ــــــــــــــ نَفَر است.

اِسم بابا... مَن ــــــــــــــ ــــــــــــــ است.

اِسـم... مامان... مَن ــــــــــــــ ــــــــــــــ است.

عَمو... مَن ــــــــــــــ ــــــــــــــ ساله است.

عَمه... مَن ــــــــــــــ ــــــــــــــ ساله است.

اِسـم... دایی... مَن ــــــــــــــ ــــــــــــــ است.

خاله... مَن ــــــــــــــ ــــــــــــــ ساله است.

اِسـم... بَرادَر... مَن ــــــــــــــ ــــــــــــــ است.

خواهَر... من ــــــــــــــ ــــــــــــــ ساله است.

بِهتَرین دوست ... مَن ــــــــــــــ ــــــ ساله است.

Asking and Telling Time

Listen and repeat. Say each word and phrase several times aloud until you can easily pronounce them.

Translation	Pronunciation	Spelling
Hour, o'clock	sã-at	ساعَت
Minute	de-ee-qeh	دَقیقه
Second	sã-nee-yeh	ثانیه
Time	vaq-t	وَقت
How much time do you have?	che-qad vaqt dã-ree?	چِقَدر وَقت داری؟
How many hours?	chan sã-at	چَند ساعَت؟
What time is it?	sã-at chan-deh	ساعَت چَند است؟
It's five thirty	sã-at pan-jo nee-meh	ساعَت پَنج و نیم است
At 3 o'clock	sã-ateh seh	ساعتِ سه
Starts	shoo-roo mee-sheh	شُروع میشود
Ends	ta-moom mee-sheh	تَمام میشود
Lasts (about duration)	tool mee-ke-sheh	طول میکِشد
5:20	pan-jo beest de-ee-qeh	پَنج و بیست دقیقه
6:30 (i.e., six and a half)	shee-sho neem	شِش و نیم
6:15 (i.e., six and a quarter)	shee-sho rob	شِش و رُبع
5 a.m. (i.e., five in the morning)	pan-jeh sob	پَنجِ صُبح
5 p.m. (i.e., five in the afternoon)	pan-jeh bad az zoh-r	پَنجِ بَعد از ظُهر
10 at night	dah-eh shab	دَه شَب
Evening	asr	عَصر
From 10 o'clock to 1 o'clock	az sãateh dah tã sãateh yek	آز ساعَتِ دَه تا ساعَتِ یِک

1. **Hours**. In order to count hours, first say the number and then say the word *hour* (ساعَت). Similarly, in order to ask: "How many hours?" first say the word *how many* (چَند) and then say the word *hour* (ساعَت).

How many hours?	چَند ساعَت؟
Five hours.	پَنج ساعَت.
How many hours a day do you work?	روزی چَند ساعَت کار میکُنی؟
I work eight hours a day.	روزی هَشت ساعَت کار میکُنَم.
My class lasts 50 minutes.	کِلاسَم پَنجاه دَقیقه طول میکِشد.

2. **O'clock.** In order to ask: *At what time*, first say the word ساعَت followed by the connector glide *eh/yeh*, and then say the modifier (a number or چَند). Literally, you will be asking: *At what hour?*

کِلاس ساعَتِ چَند شُروع میشَود؟   At what time does the class start?

/kelãs sãateh chan shooroo meesheh?/

کِلاس ساعَتِ دَه شُروع میشَود.   The class starts **at** 10 o'clock.

/kelãs sãateh dah shooroo meesheh/

In colloquial language, the word ساعَت is omitted if that does not impede understanding.

کِلاس ساعَتِ دَه ـِ صُبح شُروع میشَود. /kelãs sãateh dah-eh sob shooroo meesheh/

کِلاس دَه ـِ صُبح شُروع میشَود. /kelãs dah-eh sob shooroo meesheh/

How to ask and tell the time: to ask the time, first say the word ساعَت and then say چَند است (چَنده). To answer, first say the word ساعَت and then say the number.

ساعَت پَنج است.   ساعَت چَند است؟
It is five o'clock.   What time is it?

Compare:

ساعَتِ دَه at ten o'clock /sãateh dah/   دَه ساعَت ten hours /dah sãat/

If the minute arrow is before the 30-minute mark, we say how many minutes it is **past** the hour.

105

After the arrow has passed the 30-minute mark, we say how many minutes it is **to** the top of the hour.

5:45 یِک رُبع به شش		5:10 پَنج و دَه	
5:50 دَه به شش		5:15 پَنج و رُبع	
		5:30 پَنج و نیم	

HOMEWORK   تَکلیف

19. Listen and write down the references to time that you hear. Use Persian digits to write down the hours. Use the colon to separate hours from minutes, for example, 12:45 – ۱۲:۴۵

۶.	۱.
۷.	۲.
۸.	۳.
۹.	۴.
۱۰.	۵.

20. Prepare to say the hours aloud in Persian. Don't forget to pronounce the connector glide *eh/yeh* between the hour and the time of the day.

ساعَت چَند است؟ (ساعَت چَنده؟)

نُه و رُبعِ صُبح (نُه و رُبِ صُب)

دَوازدَه و نیمِ بَعد از ظُهر

هَفت و بیست و پَنج دقیقهِ عَصر (هَفت و بیست و پَنج دِیقهِ عَصر)

یازدَه و رُبعِ شَب (یازدَه و رُبِ شَب)

دَه دقیقه به هَشتِ صُبح (دَه دِیقه به هَشتِ صُب)

یِک رُبع به شش (یه رُب به شیش)

نُه و پانزدَه دَقیقه و دَه ثانیه (نُه و پونزدَه دِیقه و دَه ثانیه)

از ساعَتِ نُه تا ساعَتِ یازدَه

21. Prepare to answer and ask the following questions in Persian.

مَعمولا /ma-moo-lan/ usually

۱. آلان ساعَت چَند است؟ (آلان ساعَت چَنده؟)

۲. کِلاسِ فارسی ساعَتِ چَند شُروع میشود؟ (کِلاسِ فارسی ساعَتِ چَن شورو میشه؟)

۳. کِلاسِ فارسی چِقَدر طول میکِشد؟ (کِلاسِ فارسی چِقَد طول میکِشه؟)

۴. کِلاسِ فارسی ساعَتِ چَند تَمام میشود؟ (کِلاسِ فارسی ساعَتِ چَن تَموم میشه؟)

۵. دَر دانِشگاهِ شُما یِک کِلاس مَعمولا چَند دَقیقه طول میکِشد؟ (تو دانِشگاهِ شُما یه کِلاس مَعمولَن چَن دیقه طول میکِشه؟)

22. Listen to the audio presentation and complete the sentences. Write the hours using Persian digits.

۱. بِبَخشید، _____ چَند _____ ؟ _____ .

۲. فیلم ساعَتِ _____ شُروع میشود؟ _____ شَب.

۳. کِلاس چِقَدر طول _____ ؟ _____ ساعَت و _____ دَقیقه.

۴. کِلاسِ تو ساعَتِ چَند _____ میشود؟ _____ صُبح.

۵. ساعَتِ چَند _____ میشود؟ _____ بَعد از ظُهر.

23. Translate the following sentences to Persian. Prepare to say your sentences in Persian.

Useful words:

to, till تا	from اَز	for بَرای
Excuse me بِبَخشید	equals بَرابَر با ... اَست	

(1) Excuse me, do you have five minutes? I have a few questions about the exam.
(2) How much time do we have for the exam? We have two hours.
(3) From what time till what time does our exam last? Our exam lasts from 10:30 a.m. till 12:30 p.m.

(4)   At what time does the Persian class end? Persian class ends at 3:20 p.m.
(5)   What time is it now? It's 2:25 p.m.
(6)   At what time do you usually have (pers.: eat) lunch? Usually, I don't have time for lunch.
(7)   At your university, one credit equals how many hours of work? At our university, one credit equals three hours of work.

24.   🔊⁗ Think of your favorite show and prepare to answer the following questions. Think of the days of the week and the hours during which it airs. Prepare to ask these questions in Persian. Your ultimate objective is to find out if and when anyone in class watches the same shows that you do.

Words:

سریال مُورِدِ عَلاقهِ من /seree-āleh mow-redeh alā-qeyeh man/ my favorite TV series

بَرنامهِ مُورِدِ عَلاقهِ من /barnā-meyeh mow-re-deh alā-qeyeh man/ my favorite TV program

پَخش میشود /pakhsh mee-sheh/ airs, is broadcast

آخبارِ جَهان /akh-bāreh ja-hān/ world news. خَبَر news (singular), آخبار news (plural)

اِسمِ بَرنامهِ مُورِدِ عَلاقهِ تو چه است؟ (اِسمِ بَرنامهِ مُورِدِ عَلاقهِ تو چیه؟)

آن بَرنامه چَندشَنبه ها پَخش میشود؟ (اون بَرنامه چَنشَمبه ها پَخش میشه؟)

از ساعَتِ چَند تا ساعَتِ چَند پَخش میشود؟ (از ساعَتِ چَن تا ساعَتِ چَن پَخش میشه؟)

آخبار تَماشا میکُنی؟

خَبَرِ ایران و جَهان را تَماشا میکنی (خَبَرِ ایران و جَهانو تَماشا میکنی)؟

ساعَتِ چَند آخبار تَماشا میکُنی؟

25.   A review presentation. Prepare a brief presentation on the topic of this chapter in the way that is applicable to you. Review the vocabulary and topic of this chapter and address the questions below in your presentation. Your presentation must be entirely in Persian. Your objective is to create a coherent and flowing narrative and speak continuously for a couple minutes in the target language. Be prepared to answer your classmates' questions about the topic of your presentation.

(1)   List all your family members and say their names (parents, siblings, grandparents).
(2)   Say how old your family members are.
(3)   Are you an undergraduate or graduate student?
(4)   What is your major or field of study?

(5) Do you also work this semester? Where and how many hours a week do you work?
(6) Are your siblings also students? What do they study? Where?
(7) What are the professions or fields of specialization of your parents?
(8) Where do they work now?
(9) What are the professions or fields of specialization of your grandparents?
(10) Do you grandparents work? What do they do?

IN CLASS  دَر کِلاس

26. Pronounce the following phrases. Pay special attention to the pronunciation of the connector glide *eh/yeh* after the vowels and consonants. Make sure to pronounce the sounds *eh/yeh* and *ee* differently.

دوستِ من، حالِ شُما، شَهرِ نیویورک، خیابانِ بوفالو، دانشگاهِ نیویورک،
بابای تو، آقای آمیری، دانشجوی لیسانس، عَموی مَن، خانهِ آنها، دانِشکدهِ هُنر
و عُلوم، خالهِ او، کِلاسِ فارسیِ ما، داییِ تو، فامیلیِ او، دوستِ ایرانیِ مَن.

27. Look at the following phrases. They all have the connector glide in between the two words. Read the phrases aloud and pronounce the connector glide correctly. Remember, the connector *eh* is unstressed, while the final root vowel *eh* is stressed.

گُلدانِ مَن	حالِ شُما
دانهِ گُل	خالهِ مَن
	خالِ تو
بیمِ سَرما	
بیمهِ خوب	رِشتهِ مَن
	رَشتِ خوشگِل
تَختِ جَمشید	دَشتِ کَویر
تَختهِ مَشق	دامَنِ نُو
تَختِ شاهی	دامَنهِ کوه

28. Translate the following phrases into Persian using the connector glide where needed. Be ready to pronounce your Persian sentences and pronounce the connector glide correctly and clearly.

109

(1) That is a new house. That house is new.
(2) She is an Iranian student. That student is Iranian.
(3) That's Keyvan's student. That student is Keyvan.
(4) That's Mr. Tehrani. That gentlemen is Tehrani (i.e., a resident of Tehran).

29. Write meaningful phrases using the following words. Choose which word should go first and which words should follow. Connect the words using the connector glide appropriately. Be ready to pronounce and translate your Persian phrases to English.

۱. مَن کِلاس فارسی.

۲. تِلِفُن تو دوست

۳. خانه مَن پِدَر و مادَر

۴. خوابگاه اُتاق تو در

۵. کِلاس دانِشجو مَن

۶. بابا او ماشین

30. You will work with a classmate. Pick one of the topics below. Now, write as long a sentence as you can on that topic. Pass your sentence to the group next to you. They will have to write: one narrative statement, one statement with a negated verb, one question (with question words or the word آیا) and one question with a negated verb (with the word مگر). You will have to do the same for the sentence that you will receive from another group. Your instructor and classmates will help you check the sentence you write.

Topics: مَن دوستِ بِهتَرین، خانِواده، دانِشگاه.

31. Prepare to answer your classmate's questions about your best friend. Prepare to ask questions about your classmate's best friend. Now introduce to the class your conversation partner's best friend. Use the following clues:

اِسم
کُجایی است
آلان کُجا زِندِگی میکُند (آلان کُجا زِندِگی میکُنه)
شُغل
چه رِشته ای میخواند (چه رِشته ای میخونه)
چَند ساله است
بَرادَر و خواهَر

خانِواده او کُجا زِندِگی میکُنَند (خونِواده ِ اون کُجا زِندِگی میکُنَن)

32. Your instructor will place on the table several cards facing down. You will pick a random card and see your topic for this activity. Ask your classmates in Persian any three questions related to your topic. Answer their questions.

Instructor, please see the appendix Instructor's Resources.

33. Talk to your classmate in Persian and complete his/her schedule of classes. Speak only Persian. Under ساعت write in Persian digits the hours of your classmate's classes. Under the names of the days of the week, write the word کلاس in the time slot when the class occurs.

The questions you will need for this drill are:

دوشَنبه چَند تا کِلاس داری؟ (دوشَمبه چَن تا کِلاس داری؟)

کِلاس ساعَتِ چَند شُروع میشود؟ (کِلاس ساعَتِ چَن شورو میشه؟)

کِلاس ساعَتِ چَند تَمام میشود؟ (کِلاس ساعَتِ چَن تَموم میشه؟)

جمعه	پنج شنبه	چهار شنبه	سه شنبه	دو شنبه	یک شنبه	شنبه	ساعت

34. You will pick a card with a schedule of classes. Talk to your classmates and find out who has classes on the same days and during the same hours (from–to) that you do. You will then present to the class your findings by saying:

او مِثلِ مَن روزِ .... ساعَتِ .... کِلاس دارد (اون مِثلِ مَن روزِ .... ساعَتِ ..... کِلاس داره).

او مِثلِ مَن روزِ .... کِلاس نَدارد (اون مِثلِ مَن روزِ .... کِلاس نَداره).

Instructor, please see the appendix Instructor's Resources.

35. Look at the map. (1) Pick a city and ask your classmate what time it is in that city. Make sure your classmate says whether it is a.m. or p.m. (2) Now, ask the same classmate about the time difference between that city and another city on the map. Speak only in Persian.

Useful words:

اِختِلافِ زَمان بِینِ ..... و ....چِقَدر است؟ (اِختِلافِ زَمون بِینِ ..... و ....چِقَده؟)

/ekh-te-lãf-eh zamoon beyneh ... va ... cheqadeh?/

am صُبح (صُب)

pm بَعد آز ظُهر

36. Interview. The instructor will call on you to be interviewed by your class-mates. Each person in your class will ask you one question in Persian on one of the topics listed below. Once you have answered all the questions, the instructor will appoint a different student to be interviewed, and this time you will get to ask one question on one of the given topics.

If your class is too big for this format of activity, your instructor might divide the class into groups of three, where you will find yourself with two other students who will interview you. Each of the two students will ask you in Persian at least three questions on the given topics.

Topics: اِسم و فامیل، کجایی، خانواده، بِهتَرین دوست، دانِشگاه و کِلاس، شُغل

LISTENING   شِنیداری

Listen to the dialogue between two students as they talk about their schedules this semester. The speakers mention the days of the week and hours when their classes start and end. They also name the various classes that they take this semester.

Pre-listening. Considering the topic of the conversation, make a list of the most common words you expect to encounter in this conversation. If the word you wrote down is a noun, think of the verb that would go with it in the given context. If the word that you wrote is a verb, think of a noun that might go with it in this conversation. Now, read aloud the words you have written.

Follow-up. Answer the questions in Persian.

۱. کِلاسِ دُختَر ساعَتِ چَند شُروع میشود؟ (کِلاسِ دُختَر ساعَتِ چَن شورو میشه؟)

۲. این پِسَر هَم مِثلِ دُختَر آلان کِلاس دارد؟ (این پِسَرَم مِثلِ دُختَر آلان کِلاس داره؟)

۳. آیا پِسَر یا دُختَر هَم صُبح هَم بَعد از ظُهر کِلاس دارد؟ (آیا پِسَر یا دُختَر هَم صُب هَم بَد از ظُهر کِلاس داره؟)

۴. کِلاسِ پِسَر ساعَتِ چَند تَمام میشود؟ (کِلاسِ پِسَر ساعَتِ چَن تَموم میشه؟)

۵. این پِسَر هَر روز کِلاس دارد؟ (این پِسَر هَر روز کِلاس داره؟)

۶. این دُختَر جُمعه ها چَند تا کِلاس دارد؟ (این دُختَر جُمعه ها چَن تا کِلاس داره؟)

113

٧. این پِسَر جُمعه ها تا ساعَت چَند کِلاس دارد؟ (این پِسَر جُمه ها تا ساعَت چَن کِلاس داره؟)

READING

خواندَنی

Pre-reading. You will read a letter from Roya, your new pen pal from Iran. In the letter, she describes her life in college and also talks about her family. Before reading the text, think of the most common words that you might encounter in this reading. Write those words down. If they are nouns, think of the verbs that might go with them in an excerpt on the above-mentioned topic. If the words you wrote down are verbs, think of nouns that might go with them in the given context. Read carefully the list you have written down, so that you can visually identify those words if you see them in the excerpt.

(1)   The following are composite verbs with the second component missing. Complete the verbs.

آنها زِندِگی ـــــــ   من کار ـــــــ   من دَرس ـــــــ

(2)   Think about yourself, and complete the following Persian sentences with the information applicable to you.

۱.من رشته ـــــــ میخوانم. ۲.این ترم زبانِ ـــــــ میخوانم. ۳. من ـــــــ روز در هفته کلاس دارم. ۴. دانشگاه من در شَهرِ ـــــــ است. ۵. من اهلِ ـــــــ هستم. ۶. خانواده من در شَهرِ ـــــــ زندگی میکنند.

Before you read Roya's letter, look through these useful words:

A little bit /yeh kam/	یِک کَم	Big	بُزُرگ
About yourself	از خودِت	Linguistics	زَبان شِناسی
Tell (me)!	تَعریف کُن	Language	زَبان
Every day /har rooz/	هَر روز	Coffee shop	کافی شاپ
A movie	فیلم	Cinema, movies	سینَما
American movies	فیلم های آمریکایی	Busy with classes	دَرگیرِ کِلاس ها
I love my family very much /khoone-vădamoh khe-eelee doost dãram/			خانِواده آم را خِیلی دوست دارَم!

Prepare to read the following letter from Roya. Prepare to read it aloud in class. Before coming to class, read the letter aloud several times until you can easily read the entire text.

سَلام دوستِ من! حالِ تو چِطور است؟ اِسمِ من رویا کاشانی است. من آهلِ شَهرِ تِهران در ایران هستَم. بیست و یک ساله هستَم. دانشجوی زبان شناسی در دانشگاهِ تِهران هستَم. دانشگاهِ تِهران در شَهرِ تِهران است. دانشگاهِ من خِیلی بُزُرگ است. من این تِرم هَم دَرس میخوانم هَم کار میکُنَم. من یک روز دَر هَفته در یک کافی شاپ در تِهران کار میکنم. این تِرم خیلی درس میخوانم. در پَنج تا کِلاس هستم و هَر روز ۳-۲ کِلاس دارَم. سَرَم خِیلی شُلوغ است. این تِرم زَبانِ انگلیسی هم میخوانم.

خانواده‌ِ من در تِهران زِندگی میکُنَند. من یک برادر دارَم. اِسمِ برادر من آمیر است. امیر بیست ساله است. او دانشجو است و رِشته‌ِ عُلومِ رایانه میخواند. امیر دانشجوی خیلی خوبی است و هَمیشه دَرگیرِ کِلاس ها است. او هَم فارسی هم انگلیسی بَلَد است. امیر فوتبال خیلی دوست دارد. من یک خواهر دارَم. اِسمِ خواهرِ من پَریسا است. پَریسا هِفدَه ساله است و در یک دَبیرِستان در تِهران دَرس میخواند. پَریسا فیلم و سینَما دوست دارد. او فیلم های آمریکایی خیلی دوست دارد.

من هم فیلم های آمریکایی خیلی دوست دارَم. مامانِ من دُکتُر است و بابای من اُستادِ عُلومِ رایانه در دانِشگاه است. مامانِ من چِهل و هَفت سال دارد و بابای من چِهل و نُه سال دارد. من خانِواده آم را خِیلی دوست دارَم! خانِواده‌ِ تو بُزُرگ است؟ چَند تا برادر و خواهر داری؟ این تِرم چَند تا کِلاس داری؟ یِک کَم از خودِت تَعریف کُن.

مُخلِصِ تو،

رویا

Questions. Answer the following questions in Persian. Prepare to say your answers aloud and fluently in class.

۱. اِسمِ و فامیلِ او چه است؟ (اِسمِ و فامیلِ اون چیه؟)

۲. او کُجایی است؟ (اون کُجاییه؟)

۳. او دَرس میخواند یا کار میکُند؟ (اون دَرس میخونه یا کار میکُنه؟)

۳. او چه رِشته ای میخواند؟ (اون چه رِشته ای میخونه؟)

۴. او هَر روز کار میکند؟ (اون هَر روز کار میکنه؟)

۵. خانوادهِ او چَند نَفَر است؟ (خونوادهِ اون چَند نَفَره؟)

۶. رِشتهِ چه کَسی (کی) در خانوادهِ رویا عُلومِ رایانه است؟ (رِشتهِ چه کَسی در خونوادهِ رویا عُلومِ رایانه هَست؟)

۷. شُغلِ مامانِ او چه است؟ (شُغلِ مامانِ اون چیه؟)

۸. شما هَم مِثلِ رویا هَر روز ۲-۳ کلاس دارید؟

۹. شُما آهلِ کجا هستید؟

۱۰. شما هَم مِثلِ رویا هَم دَرس میخوانید هَم کار میکُنید؟

Follow-up 1. Complete the sentences in comparing Roya's description to the realities of your life. You can use the words وَلی *but*, هَم *also* and و *and* to write the second part of the sentences.

مامانِ رویا اُستاد است. مامانِ مَن هَم اُستاد است (مامانِ رویا اُستاده. مامانِ مَنَم اُستاده).

۱. رویا دانِشجو است ــــــــــــ

۲. رویا اهل تِهران است ــــــــــــ

۳. رویا بیست و یک ساله است ــــــــــــ

۴. رویا یِک بَرادَر و یِک خواهَر دارد ــــــــــــ

۵. خانِوادهِ رویا دَر تِهران زِندِگی میکُنند ــــــــــــ

۶. بابای رویا مُهَندِس است ــــــــــــ

۷. مامانِ رویا اُستاد است ــــــــــــ

۸. رویا این تِرم در پنج تا کلاس است ــــــــــــ

Follow-up 2. Tell Roya's story from the perspective of an individual other than Roya, that is, Roya's father, Roya's mother or Roya's sibling. Pick one of those characters and prepare to say your narrative fluently.

Follow-up 3.  You will work in pairs. Imagine you are talking to a friend at school. You have told your friend about receiving a letter from your new pen pal Roya in Iran. Create a brief dialogue where your friend will ask you different questions about Roya and you answer those questions based on the information from the Reading.

TRANSLATION   تَرجُمه

Write a Persian translation of the following passage about Keyvan (کیوان). Pay special attention to the spelling of the connector glide after the consonants and vowels. Before turning in your translation, check your sentences for spelling, grammar and word order.

Keyvan is a very good friend of mine. He is from Iran. Keyvan's last name is Kashani. He is 21 and is an engineering student at NYU. Keyvan is a very good student. He studies a lot. This semester Keyvan is taking four classes and is very busy. Keyvan's family is from Tehran. Keyvan has one brother and one sister. His sister is also a student. She studies linguistics at the University of Tehran. Keyvan's brother is 17 and is a high school student in Tehran. Keyvan's dad is a professor of engineering at the University of Tehran. Keyvan's mom is a teacher of English in a high school in Tehran. Keyvan's siblings and parents speak English very well.

WRITING   اِنشا

You will now write your first essay in Persian. By now, you have learned enough words and structures to complete this task successfully.

Roya is your pen pal in Iran. Write your response to Roya's letter. Write in Persian a paragraph of a minimum of 60 words about yourself, your classes and university, and your family. Your objective is to write as much as you can. You can use Roya's letter as an example for the format and content of your letter.

Start with a greeting and state your name. Write where you are from and where you live now. Write about your studies (which university, where it is, your field, the number of classes you take this semester, etc.). Write about your family (parents, siblings, their occupations, where they live). Add any other information you see fitting.

Close your paragraph with the phrase مُخلِصِ تو *Sincerely Yours* and sign it in Persian.

فَصلِ چَهارُم
Chapter 4

کارهای روزانه
My Daily Activities

Going out for kabobs. An outdoor cafe in Tehran. Steam of humidifiers makes Tehran's dry air more pleasant.

Function Talking about recurrent events, describing events in near future, communicating the information acquired from a third person, expressing your opinion, explaining a cause of events, Key verbs: *to come, to go, to think, to say*.

Listening I am so busy this semester!

Reading Kamran's daily routine.

Structures Present tense conjugation. Future tense. How to build sentence with multiple clauses using the words *that* and *because*, using adverbs of time and common prepositions and conjunctions.

🔊 Listen and repeat each word and phrase several times until you can easily pronounce it. The verbs are given in first person singular (e.g., I do). To conjugate the verbs in the Present tense, simply change the verb's ending to reflect the Subject.

Parts of the Body				
Nose / da-mãq, beenee/	دماغ، بینی		Face /soo-r-at/	صورَت
Mouth / da-han/	دهان (دَهَن)		Hands /das-tã/	دَست ها
Ear /goosh/	گوش		Head /sar/	سَر
Leg /leng/	لِنگ		Hair / moo-ã/	مو ها
Foot / pã/	پا		Tooth, teeth / dan-doon, dan-doonã/	دَندان، دندان ها

Miscellaneous				
Restroom / das-shoo-ee/	دَستشویی		Clothes /le-bãs-ã/	لِباس ها
Game / bã-zee/	بازی		Protein bar /shokolãteh poro-te-eenee/	شُکلاتِ پروتئینی

Time		
Day	rooz	روز
Afternoon	bad az zohr	بَعد اَز ظُهر
Night	sha-b	شَب
Yesterday, last night	dee-rooz, dee-shab	دیروز، دیشَب
Today, tonight	em-rooz, em-shab	اِمروز، اِمشَب
Tomorrow	far-dã	فَردا
This morning	sobeh em-rooz	صُبحِ اِمروز
Tomorrow morning	far-dã sob	فَردا صُبح
Breakfast	so-boo-neh	صُبحانه
Lunch	nã-hãr	ناهار
Dinner	shãm	شام
Always	ha-mee-sheh	هَمیشه

Time		
Never	heech vaq-t	هیچ وَقت
Sometimes	ba-zee vaq-tã	بَعضی وَقت ها
Early, soon, quickly	zood	زود
Late	dee-r	دیر
Till late	tã dee-r vaq-t	تا دیر وَقت
After the …	ba-daz …	بَعدَاز ...
Before the …	qab-laz …	قَبل از ...
After that,	ba-daz oon,	بَعدَاز آن،
During, at the time of …	hengãmeh …	هِنگامِ ...

Prepositions		
About	rã-je-beh	راجِع به
Because	choon, ba-rã-yeh een-keh	چون، بَرايِ اینکه
Because of …	be-da-leeleh	به دَلیلِ ...
From … to (referring to time)	az…tã	از...تا...
From … to (referring to space)	az … beh	از...به...
With	bã	با
Together	bã ham	با هَم
Without	be-doo-neh …	بِدونِ...
Again	bã-zam	باز هَم
That/which/who (a conjunction)	keh	که

Verbs		
I wake up	bee-dãr mee-sha-m	بیدار میشَوم
I take a shower	doosh mee-gee-ra-m	دوش میگیرَم
I brush my teeth	(dan-doo-nã-moh) mes-vãk mee-za-nam	(دَندان هایم را) مِسواک میزَنم

Verbs		
I brush my hair	moo-ã-moh shoo-neh mee-kon-am	موهایم را شانه میکُنَم
I wash my hands and face	das-toh soo-rata-moh mee-shoo-ram	دَست و صورَتَم را میشورَم
I get dressed	le-bã-sã-moh mee-poo-sham	لِباس هایم را میپوشَم
I have breakfast	so-boo-neh mee-khor-am	صُبحانه میخورَم
I go to work (class, office)	sa-reh kãr (beh ke-lãs, beh daf-tar) mee-ra-m	سَرِ کار (به کِلاس ، به دَفتَر) میرَوم
I walk to …	beh … pee-ã-deh mee-ra-m	به ... پیاده میرَوم
I go by bus (car, bicycle)	bã oo-too-boos (mã-sheen, do-char-kheh) mee-ra-m	با اُتوبوس (ماشین، دوچَرخه) میرَوم
I study	dars mee-khoo-nam	دَرس میخوانَم
I do homework	takleef an-jãm mee-dam	تَکلیف آنجام میدهَم
I read	ke-tãb mee-khoo-nam	کِتاب میخوانَم
I review lessons	dar-sã roh moo-roo-r mee-kon-am	دَرسها را مُرور میکُنَم
I talk with … on the phone	bã … telefonee so-bat mee-kon-am	با... تِلِفُنی صُحبَت میکُنَم
I call … on the phone	beh … zang mee-zan-am	بِه ... زَنگ میزَنَم
I exercise, work out	var-zesh mee-kon-am	وَرزِش میکُنَم
I play football	foot-bãl bã-zee mee-kon-am	قوتبال بازی میکُنَم
I rest	es-te-rã-hat mee-kon-am	اِستِراحَت میکُنَم
I get tired	khas-teh mee-sha-m	خَسته میشَوم
I have fun	hãl mee-kon-am	حال میکُنَم
I chat with …	bã … gap mee-zan-am	با ... گَپ میزَنَم
I sleep	mee-khã-bam	میخوابَم
I sleep very little	khe-ee-lee kam mee-khã-bam	خِیلی کَم میخوابَم
I return to …	beh … bar mee-gar-dam	به ... بَرمیگَردَم

122

Verbs		
I watch TV	te-le-vee-zee-oon ta-mã-shã mee-ko-nam	تِلویزیون تَماشا میکُنَم
I listen to music	ã-hang goosh mee-kon-am	آهَنگ گوش میکنَم
(It) starts	shoo-roo mee-sheh	شُروع میشود
(It) ends	ta-moom mee-sheh	تَمام میشود
Till one o'clock	tã sã-a-teh ye-k	تا ساعَتِ یِک
From two to five (o'clock)	az doh tã pan-j	اَز دو تا پَنج
What are you doing tonight?	em-shab chee-kãr mee-ko-nee?	اِمشَب چه کار میکُنی؟
I meet up with …	bã … molã-qãt meekonam	با … مُلاقات میکُنَم
I stay up	bee-dãr mee-moo-nam	بیدار میمانَم
I go to bed early	zood mee-khã-bam	زود میخوابَم
I am busy	sar-am shoo-loo-qeh	سَرَم شُلوغ است
Busy schedule	bar-nã-meh-yeh shoo-looq	بَرنامه ِ شُلوغ
I arrive home	beh khooneh mee-re-sam	به خانه میرسَم

HOMEWORK

تَکلیف

1. Read the description of the daily routine of a young office worker. Complete the English translation based on the Persian original.

معمولا ساعت هفت و نیم صبح بیدار میشوم، دوش میگیرم، مِسواک میزَنم و بعد صُبحانه میخورم. ساعت هشت و نیم سر کار میروم. معمولا با اتوبوس سر کار میروم. در اتوبوس مَعمولا آهَنگ گوش میکنم یا اِس اِم اِس های جدید را در گوشی اَم میخوانم. من در یک اِداره کار میکنم و روزِ کاریِ من ساعَتِ نُه ِ صُبح شُروع میشود. سَرِکار، معمولا روی پروژه کار میکنم یا در جَلَسه هستم. ساعت دوازده ناهار میخورم و بعد باز هم کار میکنم. روزِ کاریِ من ساعت پَنج تَمام میشود. بعد از کار، معمولا به باشگاه میروم یا با دوست ها در یک کافی شاپ

مُلاقات میکنم و ما قَهوه یا چای میخوریم و گَپ میزَنیم. دو روز در هفته بعد از کار کلاس فارسی دارم.

معمولا حُدود ساعت هشت به خانه میرسم. برای کلاس فارسی درس میخوانم و بعد یِک کَم اِستِراحَت میکنم. مَعمولا کتاب میخوانم یا بَرنامهِ مُورِدِ عَلاقه ام را تماشا میکُنَم. معمولا ساعت ده میخوابم.

I usually _____ at 7:30 a.m., take a _____, _____, and then have breakfast. At 8:30 a.m. I _____ to _____. I usually _____ to work. On the bus, I usually _____ _____ or read new messages on my phone. I work in an _____, and my working day _____ at 9 a.m. At work, I usually _____ on projects or have _____. At 12 noon, I _____ and then work again. My working day _____ at 5 p.m. After work, I usually go to the _____ or meet up with friends in a _____ and we drink coffee or tea and _____. Two days a week, after work I have _____. I usually _____ at around 8 p.m. I _____ for my Persian class, and then _____ a little. Usually, I either read or _____ my favorite show. I usually go to _____ at 10 p.m.

2. Complete the sentences using the given verbs. Make sure to choose the correct verb for compound verbs that are missing the second component. You can use some of the verbs repeatedly.

میکنم، میشـوَم، میگیرَم، میزَنَم، میخورَم، میروَم، میگَردَم، میشـورَم، میخوابَم، میزَنیم، میخوریم.

مَعمولا ساعت ۷ بیدار _____ و دوش _____ ، مسواک _____ و موهایم را شانه _____ . بعد، صبحانه _____ و به اداره _____ . مَعمولا با ماشین به اداره _____ و در ماشین آهنگ گوش _____ . تا ساعت یک در اداره روی پروژه ها کار _____ . ساعت یک و ربع ناهار _____ . بعد، باز هم در اداره کار _____ . بعد از کار با دوست ها در کافه یا رستوران ملاقات _____ و ما شام _____ و گپ _____ . مَعمولا ساعت نه به خانه بر _____ . در خانه کَمی اِستِراحَت _____ و بعد، دست و صورتم را _____ ، مسواک _____ و _____ . مَعمولا ساعت یازده و نیم میخوابم.

3. 🔊 Listen and read along as a student describes his daily routine. Complete the English translation based on what you hear and read. This audio presentation was not scripted so that you could be exposed to the completely natural speech of the native speaker. You will encounter a couple of unfamiliar structures, but you do not need to know them at this point in order to understand the narrative and complete the task.

جیم=باشگاه   only, just فَقَط

من یک دانشجوی سال دو معماری هَستَم. چهار روز در هَفته کلاس دارم و بایَد به دانشگاه بِرَوم. مَعمولا هر روز ساعتِ هفتِ صُبح بیدار میشوم و دوش میگیرم. سه روز در هفته کلاسَم ساعتِ هشتِ و نیمِ صُبح شُروع میشود، و من بَعد از بیدار شُدَن دَست و صورتم را میشورم و صُبحانه میخورم و به کلاس میرَوم. فَقَط یک روز در هفته کلاسِ بَعد از ظُهر دارم و صُبحِ آن روز بعد از بیدار شُدَن از خواب، اول دَندان هایم را مِسواک میزَنم و به جیم میرَوم. مَعمولا ساعتِ پنجِ بَعد از ظُهر از دانِشگاه به خانه بَر میگَردَم و برای کلاس های بَعدی آم دَرس میخوانم. شَب ها حُدودِ ساعتِ یازدَه میخوابم و هَر هَفته یِک روز را اِستِراحَت میکنم.

I am a second-year architecture student. Four days a week, I _____ and have to go to the university. Usually, every day at seven o'clock in the morning I _____ and _____. Three days a week, my classes _____ at 8:30 in the morning, and after waking up, I _____ and eat _____ and _____ to class. Only one day a week, I have an afternoon class, and, in the morning of that day, after waking up from sleep, I first _____ and _____ to the gym. __ ___, at five o'clock in the afternoon, I _____ home from the university and _____ for my next [day's] classes. At night, I go to _____ at around 11 p.m., and one day a week I _____.

4. 🔊 Listen to a daily routine of another student. Complete the translation based on what you hear. Note how the speaker, who is speaking in colloquial Persian, uses the word تو /too/ *in, inside* instead of the word دَر *in*. Don't confuse the word تو /too/ *in, inside* with the word تو /toh/ *you*. The two words are spelled the same way, but are pronounced differently.

Hello. I am a second-year linguistics _____. This _____, I am taking five classes. I _____ to the university five days a week. I usually _____ at 8.30 a.m., _____ my hands and face, ___ __ and _____ to the university. I usually _____ breakfast and only _____ a protein bar and drink water. My class _____ at 10:10 a.m., and I _____ to class. On the way to class, I ___ __ to _____. I usually _____ to Persian music.

I am in classes till 1:30 p.m. After classes, I have _____. Then, I go to the library and _____ there till 5–5:30 p.m. Around 6:30 p.m., I have _____. I usually _____ dinner at the university together with my friend, Parsa. We eat food and _____. After dinner, I study again for one–two hours, and then I _____ to my room in the dorm. I _____, _____, and _____.

5. Think of your daily activities. For each of the following statements mark either *always*, *sometimes* or *never* according to your routine. Prepare to say the statements aloud in Persian.

Always /ha-mee-sheh/	هَمیشه		Early, soon /zood/	زود
Never /heech-vaqt/	هیچ وَقت		Till late /tā dee-r vaqt/	تا دیر وَقت
Sometimes /bazee vaqtā/			بَعضی وقت ها (بَعضی أوقات / گاهی أوقات)	

E.g., مَن هَمیشه صُبحانه میخورَم.

هیچ وقت	بعضی وقت ها	همیشه	
			صُبحانه میخورَم
			صُبح دوش میگیرَم
			به کِلاس پیاده میرَوم
			ناهار میخورَم
			زود میخوابَم
			دَر کِلاس ایمیل میخوانَم
			هَر روز به باشگاه میرَوم
			صُبح کِلاس دارَم
			بَعداز ظُهر کِلاس دارَم
			دَر کِلاس میخوابَم

6. Prepare to describe for your class in Persian your daily routine on Mondays. You can model your description after the Homework exercises above. Prepare to say your sentences fluently.

IN CLASS   دَر کِلاس

7. Think of three different time periods during the day and ask your classmates what they do at those times. Use the words *today, tonight* and *usually* to give your questions temporal context. Find out who is doing the same thing as you at those times. For example,

اِمروز ساعَتِ یِک چه کار میکُنی؟

What are you doing today at one?

مَعمولا دوشَنبه ها ساعَتِ ۱۰ چه کار میکُنی؟ (مَمولَن دوشَمبه ها ساعَتِ ۱۰ چه کار میکُنی؟)

What do you usually do on Mondays at 10?

8. Think of three activities that you are doing today but are not doing tomorrow (or another day of the week). Name those activities in Persian. For this drill, you will have to negate the verbs. For example,

اِمروز به باشگاه میرَوم وَلی فَردا به باشگاه نِمیرَوم (اِمروز باشگاه میرَم وَلی فَردا باشگاه نِمیرَم).

I am going to the gym today, but I am not going to the gym tomorrow.

9. Think of several activities that you do on specific days of week. Name those activities and the day accordingly.

Useful words:

دوشَنبه ها (دوشَمبه ها)

سه شَنبه ها (سه شَمبه ها)

چَهار شَنبه ها (چار شَمبه ها)

Example:

مَعمولا دوشَنبه به باشگاه میرَوم (مَمولَن دوشَمبه باشگاه میرَم).

جُمعه ها به کِلاس نِمیرَوم (جُمه ها کِلاس نِمیرَم).

127

GRAMMAR

دَستورِ زَبان

VERB CONJUGATION IN PRESENT TENSE

When to use the present tense

Persian present tense is, in many aspects, similar to English present simple tense. We use Persian present tense to describe facts and standing truths, repetitive and habitual actions and state of being.

What is conjugation   To conjugate a verb in Persian means to say *who* or *what* is doing the action described by the verb. Conjugation is done by adding special endings to the ends of the verbs. There are six conjugational endings, and each conjugational ending corresponds to one grammatical person (i.e., I, you [casual], you [formal and also plural], s/he, we, they). There is no irregular conjugation in Persian, that is, all Persian verbs (besides two exceptions *to be* and *to have*) form their present tense in the exact same manner. The set of the six conjugational endings is the same for all verbs and tenses in Persian language. They are only used to describe *who* or *what* is doing the action (i.e., the subject), and do not serve to show the tense of the verb. You will not need to learn any other endings for conjugation in any tense. The endings are:

Subject	Conjugation Endings	
	Pronounced	Written
I	...am (*m* after the vowel ã)	م...
You (تو)	...ee	ی...
S/he, it	eh (*d* after some vowels)	د...
We	...eem	یم...
You (شما)	...een	ید...
They	...an	ند...

How to conjugate verbs in the present tense   To use a verb in present tense, first say "*mee*" (the universal stressed prefix for verbs in present tense), then say the present tense root of the verb, and then say the conjugational ending that corresponds to the person or thing who is doing the action.

Let's conjugate in Present tense the verb *to do* whose Present tense Root is /*kon*/ کُن.

mee-kon-**am**	میکُنَم	I do
mee-kon-**ee**	میکُنی	You (تو) do
mee-kon-**eh**	میکُنَد	S/he, does
mee-kon-**eem**	میکُنیم	We do
mee-kon-**een**	میکُنید	You (شُما) do
mee-kon-**an**	میکُنَند	They do

Let's conjugate in present tense the verb **_to come_** whose present tense root is pronounced *ã*, but is spelled آی.

mee-ã-**m**	میایم	I come
mee-ã-**ee**	میایی	You (تو) come
mee-ã-**d**	میاید	S/he, it comes
mee-ã-**eem**	میاییم	We come
mee-ã-**een**	میایید	You (شُما) come
mee-ã-**n**	می آیند	They come

In **compound verbs**, the prefix *mee* and conjugational endings are attached to the second word in the compound, that is, to the actual verb, for example,

بیدار میشوم	کار میکنم
بیدار میشوی	کار میکنی
بیدار میشود	کار میکند

The prefix *mee* can be written separately (for clarity) or together with the word. The current trend is to write it separately.

In the base (i.e., one-word) verbs the primary stress falls on the prefix می (می کنم), while in compound verbs the primary stress falls on the first component of the verb (درس می خواند).

Negation. To negate the verb in the Present tense simply say /*ne-mee*/ instead of /*mee*/, for example,

نِمیکُنَم	I do **not** do
نِمیرَوم	I do **not** go

The negation prefix *ne/na* is stressed and is written together with the verb as shown above. In compound verbs, only negate the second word in the compound, for example,

کار نِمیکنم   I do **not** work

بیدار نِمیشوم   I do **not** wake up

The only element that changes in the process of conjugation of a given verb is the conjugational ending that identifies the person or thing that is doing the action (the subject). Thus, once you know the first person singular conjugation of a verb (for example, میکَنم), you can easily conjugate that verb for any other subject (you, s/he, we, etc.) by replacing the conjugation ending with the one that corresponds to the needed subject (e.g., میکنی، میکند، میکنیم، میکنید، میکنند).

Omitting the subject   As the Conjugational Endings reflect the subject that does the action, you do not need to mention the subject if that subject is a pronoun, for example:

I work کار میکنم

The Two Exceptions that slightly deviate from the common rule for present tense conjugation are the verbs *to do* and *to have*. These two verbs do not need the *mee* in the beginning; otherwise, they follow the same rule as other verbs, for example,

To do	To be	Subject
دارَم	هَستَم	I
داری	هَستی	you (تو)
دارد	اَست/هَست	S/he, it
داریم	هستیم	We
دارید	هَستید	You (شما)
دارَند	هستَند	They

In the case with the two verbs that are the exception, which do not need *mee*, the negation marker is attached directly to the beginning of the verb, for example,

نَدارَم   I do not have

نیستَم   I am **not**

130

How to find the present tense root of the verb   As you can see, all Persian verbs are conjugated with the same prefix *mee* and have the same conjugational endings. Thus, the only thing that differentiates one verb from another in conjugation is verb's **Tense Root**. Present tense root is usually found in the dictionaries in parentheses right after the *ing* form (the gerund) of the verb. In dictionaries, all Persian verbs appear in the *ing* form. For example, here is the verb *to do* with its present tense root (in parentheses) that you can use for conjugation in present tense for any subject:

کردن (کن) To do

You can find present and past tense roots of most common Persian verbs in the appendix to this textbook.

VERB CONJUGATION IN FUTURE TENSE

Present tense = Future tense in Persian. Aside from its regular meaning of an action occurring in present, the present tense form is also used in Persian to describe an action in near future. Additional words and context are used to show that the verb is in future tense.

فَردا به باشگاه میرَوَم.

I'll go (I am going) to the gym tomorrow.

USING THE WORDS *THAT* AND *BECAUSE* TO BUILD SENTENCES WITH MULTIPLE CLAUSES

As you remember, Persian sentence normally follows the word order shown below:

SIMPLE SENTENCE:

3. Verb	2. Object	1. Subject
میخوانیم	از کتاب فارسی	ما
read	from a Persian book	We

A typical Persian sentence starts with the subject. The subject is followed by the object with its modifiers. The sentence concludes with the Verb. If the sentence contains more information, then the extra words are placed between the subject and object(s), for example,

5. Verb	4. Object	3. Place	2. Time	1. Subject
میخوانیم	از کتاب فارسی	در کلاس	امروز	ما
read	from Persian book	in class	today	We

131

In compound sentences, where the words *that* and *because* (called conjunctions) appear in the middle in order to connect the different parts (clauses) of the sentence into a meaningful and cohesive narrative, each part of the sentence in itself has the same basic word order as described above, for example,

5. Verb	4. Object	3. Place	2. Time	1. Subject	Conjunction	2. Verb	1. Subject
میخوانیم	از کتاب فارسی	در کلاس	امروز	ما	که	میگوید	استاد
(will) read	from a Persian book	in class	today	we	that	says	Professor

The different parts (clauses) of such compound sentence may all have the same subject or each part of the sentence may have a different subject of its own.

Compound sentence with one subject

Clause 2 with the same Subject (we)	Conjunctions	Clause 1 with *We* as the Subject
امروز در کلاس از کتاب فارسی میخوانیم	که	ما خیلی خوشحال هستیم
today in class we (will) read from a Persian book.	that	We are very happy

Clause 2 with the same Subject (We)	Conjunctions	Clause 1 with *We* as the Subject
امروز در کلاس از کتاب فارسی میخوانیم	برای اینکه	ما خیلی خوشحال هستیم
today in class we (will) read from a Persian book.	because	We are really happy

Compound sentences with multiple subjects

Clause 2 with the a different Subject (gym).	Conjunction	Clause 1 with *I* as the Subject
باشگاه اِمروز بَسته اسـت.	برای اینکه	من امروز به باشگاه نمیروم
the gym is closed today.	because	I am not going to the gym today

Clause 2 with a different Subject (We).	Conjunction	Clause 1 with *Professor* as the Subject
ما امروز در کلاس از کتاب فارسی میخوانیم.	که	استاد میگوید
today in class we (will) read from a Persian textbook.	that	Professor says

HOMEWORK   تَکلیف

10. 🔊 You will hear a series of verbs conjugated in the present tense. The verbs are missing the conjugational ending. Listen and read along. Complete the verbs with the conjugational endings you hear. Then, based on the ending you have written, write a pronoun that corresponds to the subject of the verb.

١. بیدار میشـو...

٢. دوش میگیر...

٣. دست ها میشور...

٤. لباس ها میپوش...

٥. صبحانه میخور...

٦. به کلاس میرو...

٧. زود میخواب...

11. 🔊 For each phrase you hear, write a corresponding pronoun based on the conjugational ending of the verb. Pay special attention to the conjugational endings *ee* and *eh*.

٦.		١.	
٧.		٢.	
٨.		٣.	
٩.		٤.	
١٠.		٥.	

12. 🔊 You will hear series of verbs. Listen and identify the verbs in present tense. Write the verbs you hear in present tense in the column below. For each verb you write, add the subject (a pronoun) that agrees with the verb's conjugational ending.

133

Present tense	
Subject	**Verb**

13. Complete the sentences using the given verbs in present tense. The verb root needed for present tense conjugation is given in the parentheses.

من معمولا ساعت ۷ بیدار (شو) ـــــــ و دوش (گیر) ـــــــ . دندان هایم را

مسواک (زن) ـــــــ ، موهایم را شانه (کن) ـــــــ و لباس هایم را (پوش) ـــــــ .

بعد، صبحانه (خور) ـــــــ و به اداره (رو) ـــــــ . تا ساعت یک در اداره کار (کن)

ـــــــ ، و ساعت یک و ربع ناهار (خور) ـــــــ . بعد، باز هم در اداره کار (کن) ـــ

ـــ . ساعت پنج یا پنج و نیم از اداره به خانه (رو) ـــــــ . معمولا ساعت شش

به خانه (رس) ـــــــ .

14. Conjugation of the verbs **to come** and **to go.** Complete the following sentences with the given verbs. For the negative, replace the prefix می with its negative form نِمی.

بِدونِ ...   without ... /be-doo-neh .../   with ... /bā .../   با

رَفتَن (رَو) To go

۱. مَن آز خوابگاه به کِلاس ـــــــ .   ۴. مَن و دوستَم اِمروز به سینَما ـــــــ .

۲. تو اِمروز به کِلاس ـــــــ ؟   ۵. شُما ساعَتِ چَند به اِداره ـــــــ ؟

۳. او ساعَتِ ۸ سَرِ کار ـــــــ .   ۶. آنها به رِستوران ـــــــ .

آمدن (آی) To come

۷. مَن ساعَتِ ۸ به خانه ـــــــ .   ۱۰. شُما کِی به کِلاس ما ـــــــ ؟

۸. تو اِمروز به کِلاس نِمی ـــــــ ؟   ۱۱. ما ساعَتِ ۱۰ به خوابگاهِ تو ـــــــ .

۹. او بِدونِ دوستِ دُختَرِش نِمی ـــــــ .   ۱۲. آنها هَم با ما ـــــــ ؟

15. Answer the following questions in Persian. Also, prepare to ask those questions in Persian. Before class, say your sentences aloud few times until you can easily pronounce them.

134

۱.آوَل صُبحانه میخوری و بَعد مِسواک میزَنی یا آوَل مِسواک میزَنی و بَعد صُبحانه میخوری؟ (آوَل صُبونه میخوری و بَد مِسواک میزَنی یا آوَل مِسواک میزَنی و بَد صُبونه میخوری؟)

۲.آوَل دوش میگیری و بَعد صُبحانه میخوری یا آوَل صُبحانه میخوری و بَعد دوش میگیری؟ (آوَل دوش میگیری و بَد صُبونه میخوری یا آوَل صُبونه میخوری و بَد دوش میگیری؟)

۳.مَعمولا هَر روز چَند ساعَت اِستِراحَت میکُنی؟ (مَمولَن هَر روز چَن ساعَت اِستِراحَت میکُنی؟)

۴.مَعمولا هَر روز چَند ساعَت میخوابی؟ (مَمولَن هَر روز چَن ساعَت میخابی؟)

۵. وَرزِش میکُنی؟ باشگاهِ تو کُجا است؟ (وَرزِش میکُنی؟ باشگاهِ تو کُجاس؟)

۶. آیا هَر روز آخبار میخوانی؟ (هَر روز آخبار میخونی؟)

16. Read Ali's statements about his daily activities. Go over every sentence and compare his activities to your daily activities, for example, Ali wakes up at 8 a.m., but (وَلی) I wake up at 7 a.m.; Ali usually has breakfast, and I also (هَم) have breakfast. Make sure to use the verbs correctly in first person singular as well as third person singular. Before class, prepare to say your Persian sentences fluently.

e.g. عَلی صُبحانه میخورد وَلی مَن صُبحانه نِمیخورَم (عَلی صُبونه میخوره وَلی مَن صُبونه نِمیخورَم).

again /bāzam/ باز هَم

۱) سَلام،اِسمِ مَن عَلی است، مَن دانِشجوی مُهَندِسی هَستَم (سَلام،اِسم مَن عَلیه، مَن دانِشجوی مُهَندِسی هَستَم).

۲) مَعمولا ساعَتِ ۷:۳۰ بیدار میشَوم (مَمولَن ساعَتِ ۷:۳۰ بیدار میشَم).

۳) هَر صُبح دوش میگیرَم. (هَر صُب دوش میگیرَم)

۴) مِسواک میزَنَم

۵) ساعَتِ ۸ صُبحانه میخورَم (ساعَتِ ۸ صُبونه میخورَم).

۶) بَعد، به کِلاس میرَوم (بَد، میرَم کِلاس).

135

۷) به کِلاس پیاده میرَوم (به کِلاس پیاده میرَم).

۸) کِلاسَم ساعَتِ ۹ شُروع میشود (کِلاسَم ساعَتِ ۹ شورو میشه).

۹) ساعَتِ ۱ ناهار میخورَم.

۱۰) بَعد آز ناهار، به کِتابخانه میرَوم و دَرس میخوانَم (بَد آز ناهار، میرَم کِتابخونه و دَرس میخونم).

۱۱) ساعَتِ ۵ شام میخورَم.

۱۲) بَعد آز شام، باز هَم به کِتابخانه میرَوم (بَد آز شام، بازَم میرَم کِتابخونه).

۱۳) بَعد از آن، به خوابگاه بَر میگردَم (بَد از اون، به خوابگاه بَر میگردَم).

17. Translate the following sentences into English. Prepare to identify the two clauses of each sentence and explain whether the two clauses have the same or different subjects.

Useful phrases:

با	with /bā /	from /az/	از
با هَم	together /bā ham/	to (directional preposition) /beh /	به
أصلا	at all /as-lan/	never (when used with a negative verb) /har gez/	هَر گِز

۱. او میگوید که فَردا به کلاس نمیاید. ۲. أستاد میگوید که امتحانِ ما سَخت نیست. ۳. میگویم که بِدونِ او أصلا نِمیایم. ۴. میگوید که بَعد از کِلاس به باشگاه میرود. ۵. میگوید که آز باشگاه به کافه تریای دانِشگاه میرود. ۶. میگوید که با أتوبوس سَرِ کار میرود. ۷. میگوید که آز خانه به کِلاس پیاده میرود. ۸. میگویم که قَبل آز ساعَتِ ۱۱ کِلاس نَدارَم. ۹. میگویم که بَعد آز کِلاس به تو زَنگ میزَنَم. ۱۰. میگویم که جُمعه ها کِلاس نَدارَم. ۱۱. میگویَند که هَر روز دَر کافه تریای دانِشگاه غَذا میخورَند. ۱۲. میگویَند که هَر گِز نوشابه نِمیخورَند. ۱۳. میگویَند که امتِحانِ بَعدی سَخت است. ۱۴. میگویند که این کِلاس اِمتِحان نَدارد. ۱۵.میگویَند که بَرای فَردا تَکلیف نَداریم.

18. Translate the following sentences to Persian. These are compound sentences with two clauses connected by the conjunction *that* که. Be mindful of the subject of the two

clauses and make sure that your verbs agree in conjugation with the corresponding subject. Prepare to say your Persian sentences aloud.

Useful words:
To tell = to say (the present tense root is spelled گوی, but is pronounced /g/)

فَقَط	Just, only /fa-qat/	From far away /az rāh-eh doo-r/	از راهِ دور
راست	Truth /rāst/	On time /sareh vaqt/	سَرِ وَقت
	we don't have any more exams / deegeh emtehān nadāreem/		دیگر اِمتِحان نَداریم
	I like more /beesh-tar doost dāram/		بیشتَر دوست دارم

(1) What does she say? She says that she is busy in the afternoon.
(2) What does he say? He says that he is coming from far away and will not arrive on time.
(3) Are you saying that you don't like NY? I am not saying that I do not like NY, I am just saying that I like LA more.
(4) What do they say about the class? They say that the class is not too hard.
(5) Are you telling (saying) the truth? Yes, I am telling the truth.
(6) What does he say? He says that we don't have class tomorrow.
(7) What does the professor say? She says that we don't have any more exams.

19. Prepare to answer the following questions aloud. Also be ready to ask those questions in class.
   * Insert the name of the town where your University is located.

راجِع به /rājeh beh/ *about*

۱. دوست های تو راجِع به دانِشگاهِ ما چه میگوییَند؟ (دوستای تو راجه به دانِشگاهِ ما چی میگَن؟)

۲. دانِشجو ها راجِع به شَهرِ ____* چه میگوییَند؟ (دانِشجو ها راجه به شَهرِ ____ چی میگَن؟)

۴. پِدَر و مادَرِ تو راجِع به دانِشگاهِ ما چه میگوییَند؟ (پِدَر و مادَرِ تو راجه به دانِشگاهِ ما چی میگَن؟)

۵. به مادَر و پِدَرِ تو هَمیشه راست میگویی؟ (به مادَر و پِدَرِ تو هَمیشه راست میگی؟)

20. 🔊 Complete the statements after the word *that* که. Prepare to say your complete statements aloud.

مادَرِ مَن هَمیشه میگوید که ـــــــ (مادَرِ مَن هَمیشه میگه که)

پِدَرِ مَن هَمیشه میگوید که ـــــــ (پِدَرِ مَن هَمیشه میگه که)

أستادِ مَن هَمیشه میگوید که ـــــــ (أستادِ مَن هَمیشه میگه که)

21. Translate the following sentences to English. Note that the phrase بَرای اینکه *because* is usually used in the middle of the sentence. The word چون *because* is slightly more formal and can be used to start a sentence with *because*.

اینقَدر this much, so /een-qad/

۱. اِمروز به کِلاس نِمیایم بَرای اینکه حالَم خوب نیسـت.

۲. به مِهمانیِ اِمشَب میایی؟ نَه، نِمیایم بَرای اینکه اِمشَب خِیلی کار دارَم.

۳. چِرا اینقَدر زود میروی ؟ بَرای اینکه فَردا صُبح زود اِمتِحان دارَم.

۴. چِرا چیزی نِمیگویی؟ بَرای اینکه خِیلی خَسته هَستَم.

۵. اِمروز ناهار نِمیخورَم بَرای ایکنه وَقت نَدارَم.

۶. چون اِمتِحانِ شیمی خِیلی سَخت است، شَنبه و یِک شَنبه تَمامِ روز بَرای اِمتِحانِ شیمی دَرس میخوانَم.

22. Translate the following sentences to Persian. Remember the word order in Persian. Prepare to say your Persian sentences aloud.

۶	۵	۴	۳	۲	۱
Verb	Indirect object (object with a preposition)	Direct object (object without a preposition)	Place	Time	Subject

بَرای اینکه because

(1) I am not going to gym today because I am very tired. (2) I usually study in the library because my room in the dorm is not comfortable. (3) I am not having breakfast today because I do not have the time. (4) I almost never eat in that dining hall because that dining hall is always very crowded. (5) That dining hall is always crowded because the food there is really good.

23.   Arrange the words into proper question sentences. Translate them into English.

۱. این – اَست – کِلاس – کی – که – سَخت – میگوید - ؟

۲. آیا – چه – اَست – تَکلیفِ فَردا – میگوید – که - ؟

۳. آیا – کی – است – اِمتِحان – میگوید – که – اُستاد - ؟

۴. روزِ جُمعه – اَست – اِمتِحانِ بَعد – میگوید – که -.

۵. آیا – میگوید – کُجا – اَست – که – اِمتِحان - ؟

۶. چه – ؟ – او – میگوید

۷. چیزی – نِمیگویی – چِرا - ؟

۸. کِلاس – چه – راجِع به – میگویَند – دانِشجو ها-؟

۹. به – آنها – میگویی – ؟ – چه

۱۰. میگویَند – ؟ – چه – آنها

24.   🔊 You will hear several statements in Persian. Listen to the statements and say what Sam, the person making the statements, thinks. Note how Sam who is speaking in colloquial Persian, uses the word تو /too/ *in, inside* instead of the word دَر *in*. Don't confuse the word تو /too/ *in, inside* with the word تو /to/ *you*. The two words are spelled the same way, but are pronounced differently.

E.g.,

سام فِکر میکُند که فارسی شیرین اَست.

sweet	شیرین	خوشمَزه	delicious, good-tasting

25.   🔊 Compete the following phrases with what you think. Prepare to say your sentences fluently.

۱. فِکر میکُنم که آمریکا ____ (فِک میکُنم که آمریکا)

۲. فِکر میکُنم که دانِشگاهِ مَن ____ (فِک میکُنم که دانِشگاهِ مَن)

۳. فِکر میکُنم که غَذای دانِشگاه ____ (فِک میکُنم که غَذای دانِشگاه)

۴. فِکر میکُنم که زَبانِ فارسی ــــــــ (فِک میکُنم که زَبانِ فارسی)

۵. فِکر میکُنم که اُتاقِ مَن در دانِشگاه ــــــــ (فِک میکُنم که اُتاقِ مَن تو دانِشگاه)

26. A review presentation. Prepare a brief presentation on the topic of this chapter in the way that is applicable to you. Review the vocabulary and topic of this chapter and address the questions below in your presentation. Your presentation must be entirely in Persian. Your objective is to create a coherent and flowing narrative and speak continuously for a couple minutes in the target language. Be prepared to answer your classmates' questions about the topic of your presentation.

Describe your normal daily routine on a weekday (e.g., on Wednesday) and during the weekend (e.g., on Saturday).

(1) When do you normally wake up?
(2) Do you normally take a shower in morning?
(3) Do you normally wash up, brush your teeth, comb your hair in the morning?
(4) Do you normally have a breakfast? Where? Is it a quick meal or a hearty breakfast?
(5) What do you normally do after your breakfast on that day?
(6) At what time do you go to your class on that day?
(7) How do you normally get to your class (by bus, car, riding a bicycle or walking)?
(8) Till what time are you normally in classes on that day?
(9) What do you normally do after your classes on that day are over?
(10) Do you normally have a lunch on that day? Where?
(11) Do you normally go to the gym on that day?
(12) Do you go to the library on that day?
(13) At what time do you normally have dinner? Where? Do you normally dine alone?
(14) What do you normally do after dinner on that day?
(15) At what time do you normally go to bed on that day?

IN CLASS   دَر کِلاس

27. Complete the sentences with pronouns and verbs as needed.

۱. ــــــ ــــــ دَر نیویورک زِندِگی میکُنَند. ۲. ــــــ دَر کِتابخانه دَرس میخواند. ۳. ــــــ ــــــ دانِشجو است. ۴. پِدَر و مادَرَم دَر نیویورک زِندِگی ــــــ ۵. ــــــ دَر دانِشگاه کار میکُنید؟ ۶. آنها سه تا بَچه ــــــ ۷. تو کُجا کار ــــــ؟ ۸. شُغلِ شُما چه ــ ــ؟ ۹. ما کوکاکولا ــــــ ۱۰. تو هَم عَمو هَم دایی ــــــ؟ ۱۱. ــــــ کُجا میروید؟

28. Translate the following sentences to Persian. Prepare to say your Persian sentences aloud. Arrange the words in your sentences according to the standard sentence structure in Persian. Place the question word where the word that answers the question would usually go in the statement.

←————————————————————————

Verb	Indirect object	Direct object	Place	Time	Subject
	(with a preposition)	(without a preposition)			

(1) At what time do you usually wake up? (2) Do you usually take shower in the morning (صُبح ها)? (3) Do you usually eat breakfast? (4) At what time do you go to class? (5) Do you walk or take a bus to class? (6) Do your classes start in the morning or in the afternoon? (7) At what time do your classes usually end? (8) What (چه کار) do you do after that? (9) At what time do you return to your room on Mondays? (10) At what time do you usually go to bed? (11) Do you study on Sundays (یکشنبه ها)? (12) Do you sleep enough (به اندازهِ کافی) during the semester? (13) Where do you usually eat? (14) Do you eat three times a day? (15) Do you usually eat in the dining hall or in your room?

- "to eat" is a compound verb in Persian. It has to be combined with the word "food" if a specific dish or meal are not mentioned. For example, we usually eat in the dining hall:

مَعمولا دَر سِلفِ دانِشگاه غَذا میخوریم.

29. Ask your classmate questions (in Persian) about their routine activities shown in the table and complete the table with the times at which they complete those activities. Your instructor will ask you questions about the daily routine of your conversation partner.

For this drill, you will use the verbs in I s., II s. and III s. person.

E.g., مَعمولا ساعَتِ چَند بیدار میشوی؟ (مَمولَن ساعَتِ چَن بیدار میشی؟)

ساعت

بیدار میشود (بیدار میشه)

دوش میگیرد (دوش میگیره)

صُبحانه میخورد (صُبونه میخوره)

سَرِ کِلاس میرود (سَرِ کِلاس میره)

ناهار میخورد (ناهار میخوره)

کِلاس ها تَمام میشوند (کلاسا تموم میشَن)

شام میخورد (شام میخوره)

به خوابگاه بَر میگَردد (به خابگاه بَرمیگَرده)

میخوابد (میخابه)

30. Work with a classmate and create the daily routine of a typical student at your university. You instructor will place you together with a student from your field or major. Once you have written the sentences, divide them between the two of you and prepare to say your sentences in Persian to class.

31. Talk to your classmates and find out who has a lifestyle and habits similar to yours. State what those similarities are in complete sentences,

E.g., سارا مَعمولا دَر خوابگاه دَرس میخواند. مَن هَم مَعمولا دَر خوابگاه دَرس میخوانم.

۱. دَر کِتابخانه / خوابگاه دَرس میخواند (تو کِتابخونه / خابگاه دَرس میخونه)

۲. هَر روز تَکلیف دارد (هَر روز تَکلیف داره)

۳. کَم / زیاد میخوابد (کَم / زیاد میخابه)

۴. مَعمولا زود / دیر میخوابد (مَمولَن زود / دیر میخابه)

۵. دَر خوابگاه / شَهر زِندِگی میکُند (تو خابگاه / شَهر زِندِگی میکنه)

۶. اَغلَب به مِهمانی میرود (اَغلَب به مِهمونی میره)

۷. هَم دَرس میخواند هَم کار میکُند (هَم دَرس میخونه هَم کار میکُنه)

۸. هَر روز کِلاس دارد (هَر روز کِلاس داره)

۹. یِک شَنبه ها دَرس میخواند (یه شَمبه ها دَرس میخونه)

۰۱. هَر روز دو - سه بار غَذا میخورد (هَر روز دو - سه بار غَذا میخوره)

32.   Talk to a classmate and find out what s/he will be doing tomorrow morning, noon or afternoon. Compare his/her plans for tomorrow to your plans. For this drill, you will use verbs in II s. and I s. forms.

Example: تینا فَردا صُبح به کِلاس میرود، وَلی مَن فَردا صُبح به کِلاس نِمیروم.

(تینا فَردا صُب به کِلاس میره، وَلی مَن فَردا صُب به کِلاس نِمیرَم)

33.   Make three statements about your university. You can express a popular opinion, rumor or state a fact. Your sentences may be a true or false statement. Start you sentences with:

راسِت میگویند (راسِت میگَن)! ... they say that ...

and then ask:

تو فِکر میکنی ... (تو فِک میکنی ...) do you think ...

First, make one statement and call on a random classmate to respond to your statement. Your classmates will respond to your statement by agreeing or disagreeing with it:

راسِت میگویند (راسِت میگَن)! they are right!

بَله، فِکر میکنم که ...... (بَله، فِک میکنم که ...).

نَه، فِکر نِمیکنم که ... (نَه، فِک نِمیکنم ...).

34.   Peer review. Your instructor will put you in a group with one or two other students. Work together to write three sentences: (1) a question with a question word; (2) a question without a question word (you may use آیا، مگر); (3) a statement. Once you are done, pass your sentences to next group. You will receive sentences from another group. Check their sentences for spelling, grammar and word order and return the corrected sentences to the respective group.

35.   Complete the following sentences:

بَرای اینکه because /barãyeh eenkeh/

بَعضی وَقتها sometimes /bazee vaq-tã/

یاد میگیرم I learn [yãd mee-gee-ram/

143

۱. زادگاهِ مَن را خِیلی دوست دارَم بَرای اینکه ـــــــ (زادگاهِ مَنو خِیلی دوست دارَم بَرای اینکه)

۲. مَن زَبانِ فارسی یاد میگیرم بَرای اینکه ـــــــ (مَن زَبانِ فارسی یاد میگیرم بَرای اینکه)

۳. بَعضی وَقتها صُبحانه نِمیخورَم بَرای اینکه ـــــــ (بَضی وَقتا صُبونه نِمیخورَم بَرای اینکه)

36. Interview. The instructor will call on you to be interviewed by your class-mates. Each person in your class will ask you one question in Persian on any of the topics listed below. Once you have answered all questions, the instructor will appoint a different student to be interviewed, and this time you will get to ask one question on any of the given topics.

If your class is too big for this format of activity, your instructor might divide the class into groups of threes, where you will find yourself with two other students who will inter-view you. Each of the two students will ask you in Persian at least three questions on the given topics.

Topics: اسمِ و فامیل، کجایی، خانِواده، بِهتَرین دوست، دانِشگاه و کلاس، شُغل، کارهای روزانه

LISTENING   شِنیداری

Listen to the conversation between Sara and Kamran. The speakers are talking about whether or not they are busy this semester, how many classes and credits they are taking, what time of the day their classes usually start and what they do after classes.

Pre-listening. (1) Considering the topic of the conversation, make a list of most common words you expect to encounter in this conversation. If the word you wrote down is a noun, think of the verb that would go with it in the given context. If the word that you wrote is a verb, think of a noun that might go with it in a conversation on the given topic. Pronounce the words you wrote aloud so that you identify them when you listen to the conversation. (2) The verbs in the conversation appear in present tense. Think of the present tense marker and of how the verbs usually look with that marker in the beginning and the conjugational endings at the end. Are there exceptions to the rule? The speakers will use the verbs in first person

144

singular (I …) and second person singular (you …) forms. Write and pronounce your verbs in those forms, so you can identify them when you listen to the conversation.

Assignment. Listen to the conversation and for each person, mark the activities they do. Prepare to say aloud in Persian what activities each person does, for example,

سارا هَر روز به کِلاس میرود (سارا هَر روز به کِلاس میره).

سارا	کامران	🔊
		هَر روز به کِلاس میرود (هَر روز به کِلاس میره)
		قَبل آز صُبحانه دوش میگیرد (قَبل از صُبونه دوش میگیره)
		بَعد از صُبحانه دوش میگیرد (بَد از صُبونه دوش میگیره)
		هَر روز تَکلیف دارد (هَر روز تَکلیف داره)
		هَر روز به باشگاه میرود (هَر روز به باشگاه میره)
		هَم صُبح ها هَم بَعد از ظُهرها کِلاس دارد (هَم صُبا هَم بَد از ظُهرا کِلاس داره)
		هَر هَفته به مِهمانی میرود (هَر هَفته میره مِهمونی)
		مَعمولا قَبل و بَعد از کِلاس آهَنگ گوش میکُند (مَمولَن قَبل و بَد از کِلاس موزیک گوش میکُنه)
		کَم میخوابد (کَم میخابه)
		آخَر هَفته ها ساعَتِ ۱۱ یا ۱۲ بیدار میشود (آخَر هَفته ها ساعَتِ ۱۱ یا ۱۲ بیدار میشه)

READING   خواندَنی

Read the text aloud several times until you can read it fluently.

Pre-reading. Read Kamran's description of his average day. Before reading the text, think of the most common words that you might encounter in such a reading. Write those words down so that you can visually identify them when you encounter them in the reading. If they are nouns, think of the verbs that might go with them in the given context. If the words you wrote are verbs, think of nouns that might go with them.

My schedule is very busy بَرنامِه ام خِیلی شُلوغ اسـت.

/bar-nã-mam khe-ee-lee shoo-loo-qeh/

یِک روز دَر زِندِگیِ مَن.

سَلام، اِسمِ مَن کامران است. مَن دَر نیویورک زِندِگی میکُنَم و دانِشجو هَستَم. دَر یِک آپارتمان زِندِگی میکُنَم. هَم اُتاقی نَدارَم. دانِشجویِ سالِ دُوُم هَستَم و بَرنامه آم خِیلی شُلوغ است.

مَعمولا ساعَتِ ۷:۳۰ بیدار میشَوم. دوش میگیرَم، مِسواک میزَنَم، لِباسهایم را میپوشَم، و صُبحانه میخورَم. مَعمولا صُبحانهِ سادِه میخورَم. فَقَط یِک شَنبه ها صُبحانهِ کامِل میخورَم.

بَعد از صُبحانه، با دوچَرخه به کِلاس میرَوَم. کِلاسَم ساعَتِ ۸:۳۰ شُروع میشود. صُبح ها مَعمولا یِک یا دو کِلاس دارَم. حُدودِ ساعَتِ ۱۲، به سِلفِ دانِشگاه میرَوَم و ناهار میخورَم.

بَعد از ظُهر هَم یِک یا دو کِلاس دارَم. بَعد از کِلاس ها، به کِتابخانه میرَوَم و تا ساعَتِ ۵ دَرس میخوانَم. ساعَتِ ۵ مَعمولا با دوستَم پارسا به باشگاه میرَوَم. بَعد از باشگاه، من و پارسا به کافه تِریایِ دانِشگاه میرَویم، شام میخوریم و با هَم صُحبَت میکنیم. بَعضی وَقت ها، من هِنگامِ شام به خانواده آم زَنگ میزَنَم.

بَعد از شام، به اُتاقَم بَر میگَردَم و دَرس میخوانَم. مَعمولا ساعَتِ ۱۲ یا ۱۲:۳۰ میخوابَم. وَلی این هَفته یِک اِمتِحانِ مُهِمی دارَم. دانِشجو هایِ سالِ پیش میگویَند که آن اِمتِحان خِیلی مُشکِل است. پَس، مَن و دو تا از هَمکِلاسی هایم هَر روز بَعد از شام به کِتابخانه میرَویم و با هَم دَرس میخوانیم. تا دیر وَقت دَر کِتابخانه میمانیم و دَرس میخوانیم بَرای اینکه این اِمتِحان بَرایِ مُعَدِلِ ما در این تِرم خِیلی مُهِم است.

سوالات:

از چه لَحاظی in what terms /az cheh la-hãzee/

از لَحاظِ ... in terms of ... /az la-hãzeh .../

۱. آیا زِندِگیِ سام در دانِشگاه مِثلِ زِندِگیِ دانِشگاهیِ شُما است؟

۲. از چه لَحاظی زِندِگیِ سام مِثلِ زِندِگیِ شُما است؟

۳. از چه لَحاظی زِندِگیِ سام با زِندِگیِ شُما فَرق دارد؟

Follow-up 1. Read the following statements.

If you think that the statement is correct say:

/baleh, een jomleh sa-hee-heh/

and then reiterate the statement using the verb in third person singular (S/he form) referring to Kamran. For example,

/baleh, een jomleh sa-hee-heh, Kamran sãateh 7:30 beedãr meesheh/.

If you think that the statement is not accurate, say:

/nah, een jom**leh** sa**heeh neest**/

and then make a correct statement using the verb in in third person singular (S/he form) referring to Kamran.

أَصلاً   at all (in negated phrases) /aslan/

اِمتِحانِ این هَفته آسان است و مَن أَصلاً نِگران نیستَم.

هَر روز با ماشین به دانِشگاه میرَوَم.

این تِرم خِیلی دَرس میخوانَم.

هَر روز صُبحانهِ کامِل میخورَم.

مَعمولا دَر آپارتِمان شام میخورَم.

مَعمولا هَم صُبح ها هَم بَعد اَز ظُهر ها کِلاس دارَم.

مَعمولا بَعد اَز ظُهرها به باشگاه میرَوَم.

هَمیشه تَنهایی به باشگاه میرَوَم.

مَعمولا شَب ها تا دیروَقت بیدار میمانَم.

Follow-up 2. Complete the phrases according to the reading. Prepare to say your complete sentences in Persian. Use the verb in first person singular (I …).

۱.تا ساعَتِ دَوازدَه یا دوازدَه و نیم نِمیخوابَم بَرای اینکه ــــــ .

۲.اِمشَب مَن و دوستَم تا دیر وَقت دَر کِتابخانه میمانیم و دَرس میخوانیم بَرای اینکه ــــــ

۳.بَرای اِمتِحانِ این هَفته خِیلی دَرس میخوانَم بَرای اینکه ــــــ

۴.دَر سِلفِ دانِشگاه هِنگامِ شام هَم غَذا میخورَم هَم و هَم ــــــ

۵.ماشین ندارَم و مَعمولا با دوچَرخه ــــــ

Follow-up 3. Now, prepare two questions about the reading for class. Your questions must follow standard word order of Persian sentence. You must use at least two different verbs (one per sentence).

TRANSLATION   تَرجُمه

Translate the following passage to Persian. Write your sentences according to the standard sentence structure in Persian. Before turning in your translation, check your sentences for spelling, grammar and word order.

at about 10 o'clock /hoo-doo-deh sã-a-teh 10/. حدودِ ساعت ۱۰

by then /oon-vaqt/ آنوقت

Hello, my name is Sam. I am an engineering student. I live in an apartment. I do not have a roommate. My schedule is very busy. I usually wake up at 7:30 a.m. I take shower and brush my teeth. Then, I change and have breakfast at 8:15 a.m. After that, I go to class. I usually go to class by bus. My class starts at 9:05 a.m. I have classes until 12 noon. I have lunch at 12:20 p.m. At 12:45 p.m., I go to the library and study until 4 p.m. Then, I go to the gym and work out for about 30–40 minutes. From the gym, I go to the dining hall and have dinner. I eat and talk on the phone with my friend. Sometimes I call my parents. From the dining hall, I go to the library again and usually stay there until late. The library is very comfortable and I usually study there. After the library, I go back to my room in the dorm. I am usually very tired by then and fall asleep very quickly. On Sundays, I usually wake up at about 11 a.m. and have breakfast at 11:30 a.m. or 12. My friends say that I study too much. They are right! ☺
(راسـت میگویند / حق دارند)

WRITING   اِنشا

Write a 50-word paragraph and describe your typical day at the university.

فَصلِ پَنجُم
Chapter 5

دانِشگاه
My University

Computer Science students at Amir Kabir University in Tehran celebrate graduation by throwing their caps in the air.

Function Talking about your academic schedule and life at university, describing the order of events, counting (hundreds, thousands), describing your origin, saying on what date and where you were born, Persian names of the months. Key verbs: *to learn, to study, to teach, to be born, to need.*

Listening My schedule for next semester.

Reading Your pen pal Roya writes to you about her university in Iran.

Structures Stressed ending *ee*. Ordinal numbers.

Listen to the pronunciation of the words and repeat each word aloud several times until you can easily pronounce them. Try to imitate the native speaker's pronunciation and intonation.

	University and Classes			
PhD student	دانِشجوی دُکتُرا		University	دانِشگاه
Favorite	مُوردِ عَلاقه		College (within an university)	دانِشکَده
My favorite class	کِلاسِ مُوردِ عَلاقه ِ من		Campus	مُحَوطه ِ دانِشگاه، پَردیزه، پَردیس،
Athletic team	تیمِ وَرزِشی		Lab	آزمایِشگاه
Grade (for an assignment)	نُمره		Library	کِتابخانه (کِتابخونه)
(academic) credit	واحِد		Cafeteria, dining hall	کافه تِریا، سِلفِ دانِشگاه
Meaning, i.e., in other words	یَعنی		Office (of a professor)	دَفتَر
Really	واقِعا (واقِعَن/واقَعَن)		Department	بَخش
Native language	زَبانِ مادَری ام (زَبونِ مادَریم)		Dorm	خوابگاه
Foreign language	زَبانِ خارِجی (زَبونِ خارِجی)		Professor	اُستاد
Reference to HW at university	کار		Advisor	اُستادِ راهنَما
generic word for HW	مَشق، تَکلیف		Classmate	هَم کِلاسی
Oral exam	اِمتِحانِ گُفتاری/ اِمتَحانِ گُفتاری		Roommate	هَم اُتاقی
Written exam	اِمتِحانِ نوِشتاری		Housemate	هَم خانه (هَم خونه)
Final exam	اِمتِحانِ آخَرِ تِرم		Freshman / sophomore / junior / senior	دانِشجوی سالِ اَوَل/ دُوُم/سِوُم/چَهارُم

University and Classes			
Middle Eastern Studies	مُطالِعاتِ خاوَرِ میانه / خاوَرشیناسی	Undergraduate student	دانِشجوی لیسانس
New words	کَلِمه های جَدید	graduate student, MA student	دانِشجوی فُوقِ لیسانس
Text, reading	مَطلَب		

Stationery			
Notebook	دَفتَرچه	Pencil	مِداد
Dictionary	لُغَت نامه	Pen	خودکار
Phone, Cellphone	تِلِفُن، موبایل، گوشی	Eraser	پاک کُن
Class notes	جُزوه	(Black)board	تَخته
Class handout	بَرگهِ کِلاس	Bag (my bag, your bag)	کیف (کیفَم، کیفِت)
Email	ای مِیل/ایمِیل	Computer	کامپیوتِر
Internet	اینتِرنِت	Textbook	کِتابِ درسی
Headphones	هِدفون، دوگوشی	Lesson	دَرس

College Life			
Important	مُهِم	Money	پول
Interesting	جالِب	Tuition	شَهریهِ دانِشگاه
Fun	با حال	Scholarship	بورسیه
All of the classes	هَمهِ کِلاسها (هَمهِ کِلاسا)	Semester	تِرم، نیمسال
One day a week	هَفته ای یک روز، یک روز دَر هَفته	Academic year	سالِ تَحصیلی

151

College Life			
In my opinion	به نَظَرِ مَن	Break, vacation	تَعطیلات
Various	مُختَلِف	Winter break	تَعطیلاتِ زِمِستانی (تَعطیلاتِ زِمِستونی)
Approximately	تَقریبا (تَقریبَن)	Spring break	تَعطیلاتِ بَهاری
Only	فَقَط	Experience	تَجرُبه

Verbs	
I have a question	سوال دارَم (سُاَل دارم)
S/he teaches Persian	فارسی دَرس میدهد (فارسی دَرس میدِه)
I am learning Persian	فارسی یاد میگیرَم
I study architecture	مِعماری میخوانَم (مِعماری میخونَم)
I take exam	اِمتِحان میدَهم (اِمتِحان میدَم)
What things do you need?	چه چیزهایی (را) لازم داری؟ (چه چیزایی (رو) لازم داری؟)
I do an exercise	تمرین اَنجام میدَهم (تَمرین اَنجام میدَم)
I make an appointment with …	با … وَقت میگیرَم
I have an appointment with …	با … وَقت دارم
I put, place	میگُذارَم (میذارَم)
I am taking three classes	سه تا کِلاس بَر میدارَم
I took three credits	سه واحِد بَرداشتَم
What is HW?	تَکلیف چه داریم (تَکلیف چی داریم)؟

Numbers: Hundreds

۹۰۰	۸۰۰	۷۰۰	۶۰۰	۵۰۰	۴۰۰	۳۰۰	۲۰۰	۱۰۰
نُهصَد	هَشتصَد	هَفتصَد	شیشصَد (شیشصَد)	پانصَد (پونصَد)	چَهارصَد (چارصَد)	سیصَد	دویست (دیویست)	(یک)صَد (دیویست)

152

Numbers: Thousands

۹۰۰۰	۸۰۰۰	۷۰۰۰	۶۰۰۰	۵۰۰۰	۴۰۰۰	۳۰۰۰	۲۰۰۰	۱۰۰۰
نُه هِزار	هَشت هِزار	هَفت هِزار	شیش هِزار (شیش هِزار)	پَنج هِزار	چَهار هِزار (چارهِزار)	سه هِزار	دوهِزار	(یک)هِزار

(یک) میلیارد	(یک) میلیون
one billion	one million

To construct numbers such as *one hundred twenty-one, two thousand thirty-five* in Persian, say: *(one) hundred **and** twenty **and** five, two thousand **and** thirty **and** five,*

E.g., (یک) صَد و بیست و یِک ، دو هِزار و سی و پَنج

For the ease of pronunciation and fluency, the word و (and) is pronounced as *oh* in such numbers, for example:

۱۲۵ /sadoh beestoh panj/

۱۹۹۴ /hezãroh noh-sadoh na-va-doh chãr/

۲۴۳۵ /do he-zãroh chãr-sadoh seeoh panj/

۲۰۱۴ /do he-zãroh chãr-dah/

The Months of the Western Calendar			
sep-tãmbr	سِپتامبر	zhãn-veeyeh	ژانویه
ok-tobr	اُکتُبر	fev-reeyeh	فِوریه
novãmbr	نُوامبر	mãrs (mãrch)	مارس (مارچ)
desãmbr	دِسامبر	ãvreel	آوریل
the month of March	ماهِ مارس	meh (mey)	مِه (مِی)
Spring	بَهار	zhoo-an	ژوئَن
Summer	تابِستان (تابِستون)	zhoo-yeh	ژوییه
Fall	پاییز	oot (ãgost)	اوت (آگوست)
Winter	زِمستان (زِمِستون)		

153

HOMEWORK  تَکلیف

1. Tina is getting ready for her Persian exam. Read and then mark the images of the items that Tina says she is taking to the exam. Be prepared to say in Persian what these items are.

امروز ساعت سه در کلاس فارسی اِمتِحان میدَهم. بَرای این اِمتِحان یک کامپیوتر و هدفون، دو تا مِداد و پاک کُن، و یک خودکار توی کیفَم میگُذارَم. کتابِ فارسی و لُغَت نامهِ فارسی به انگلیسی و انگلیسی به فارسی را هم تو کیفَم میگُذارَم. این اِمتِحان بَرای نُمرهِ من در این کلاس خیلی مُهِم است.

2. Listen to the series of words and read along. Each series is missing one word in the written text. Listen for that missing word and write it down. Once you have completed all the series, circle the word that does not belong with the other words in the given series.

۱. خودکار، مداد، پاک کن، دفترچه ، ـــــــ

۲. استاد، هم کلاسی، استاد راهنما، دانشجوی سال اول ، ـــــــ

۳. دفتر، دانشکده، کتاب درسی، بخش ، ـــــــ

۴. لازم دارم، اِمتِحان میدهم، درس میدهد ، یاد میگیرم ، ـــــــ

۵. برگه کلاس، جزوه، کتاب درسی ، ـــــــ

3. Listen to the list that Kamran has prepared. From the list that Kamran will read for you, write in the YES column the items he will need for his exam in Persian, and place the items he will not need in the NO column. Write your words in Persian.

Prepare to say in Persian which items Kamran will need for the exam. Use the verb *he needs/will need* ... لازم دارد and the word بَرای for ... /barãyeh .../

Start your sentence by saying:

کامران بَرای اِمتِحانِ فارسی... و ... لازم دارد (کامران واسه اِمتِحانِ فارسی ... و ... لازم داره).

کامران بَرای اِمتِحانِ فارسی... و ... لازم ندارد (کامران واسه اِمتِحانِ فارسی ... و ... لازم نداره).

Note that Kamran uses the quantifier word دانه (دونه) when he enumerates single items. This word serves the same function as quantifier تا, except that the latter is not used to refer to a single item.

نه	بله

155

4. 🔊 A student is preparing to go to class and is putting various items in the bag. Listen and complete the transcript by filling in the missing words. Prepare to read the completed sentences aloud.

امروز سه تا کِلاس دارم. واسهِ کِلاسهایم یک دانه ____ ، چَند تا ____ ، چَند تا ____ و چَند تا ____ توی کیفَم میگذارَم. واسهِ کِلاسِ فارسی یک دانه کتاب ____ ، یک دانه ____ و ____ کلاسی را هم توی ____ میگذارَم.
تو معمولا واسهِ کِلاسهایت چه چیزهایی را توی کیفِت میگذاری؟

5. 🔊 Listen to Mitra and Kamran and mark which classes each one of them takes. Then, tell the class what classes both of them are taking this semester. Say your sentences in Persian:

این تِرم هَم میترا هَم کامران در کِلاسِ ... هَستند.

کامران	میترا	کلاس
		History of Theater
		History of Middle East
		Chemistry
		Persian
		Biology
		Math

6. 🔊 Use the words from this chapter's glossary to complete the statements as applicable to you. Say your completed sentences aloud in Persian.

۱. من در دانِشکَدهِ ____ دانِشجوی ____ هَستم و ____ میخوانم (من در دانِشکَدهِ ____ دانِشجوی ____ هَستم و ____ میخونم).
۲. این تِرم در ____ تا کِلاس هَستم (این ترم در ____ تا کلاس هستم.)
۳. این تِرم به آزمایشگاه ____ .
۴. این تِرم در خوابگاه زِندِگی ____ و هَم اُتاقی / هَم خانه ____ (این تِرم تو خابگاه زِندِگی ____ و هَم اُتاقی / هَم خونه ____).

۵. کِلاسِ فارسیِ ما ـــــــ واحِد است (کِلاسِ فارسیِ ما ـــــــ واحِده).

۶. این تِرم کِلاسِ مُورِدِ عَلاقهِ من ـــــــ است (این تِرم کِلاسِ مُورِدِ عَلاقهِ من ـــــــ ه/هَست).

۷. اسمِ اُستادِ راهنَمای من ـــــــ است (اسمِ اُستادِ راهنَمای من ـــــــ ه/هَست).

۸. اُستادِ راهنَمای من در بَخشِ ـــــــ کار میکند و در کِلاسِ ـــــــ دَرس میدهد (اُستادِ راهنَمای من تو بَخشِ ـــــــ کار میکنه و تو کِلاسِ ـــــــ دَرس میده).

۹. مَعمولا در کِلاسِ فارسی نُمرهِ ـــــــ میگیرَم (مَمولَن تو کِلاسِ فارسی نُمرهِ ـــــــ میگیرَم)

7. 🔊 Listen to Keyvan, who is talking about his classes this semester. Complete the transcript with the words that you hear. Make five statements in Persian about Keyvan.

واقِعا عاشِقِ فارسی هستم I really love Persian!

یَعنی meaning, in other words

دانِشجوی سالِ ـــــــ شَهرسازی در ـــــــ مِعماریِ ـــــــ کُلُمبیا هستم. این ـــــــ در چهار تا کِلاس هستم. یکی از آن کلاس ها با خانُمِ امیری اُستادِ ـــــــ ی من است. خانمِ امیری اُستادِ ایرانشیناسی است و در ـــــــ مُطالِعاتِ خاوَرِ میانه در ـــــــ کُلُمبیا کار میکند. خانمِ امیری در کلاس های تاریخِ خاوَرِ میانه و تاریخِ ایران ـــــــ میدهد .کِلاس های خانُمِ آمیری خیلی جالِب هستند.من این ـــــــ در کلاسِ فارسی هَم هستم. کِلاسِ زَبانِ فارسی کلاسِ مُورِدِ ـــــــ من است. در کلاسِ فارسی، ما هر روز به فارسی ـ ـــــــ میکنیم، از کتابِ فارسی مَطلَب میخوانیم و کَلَمه های جَدیدِ فارسی ـــــــ میگیریم.. کِلاسِ فارسی چهار ـــــــ است، یَعنی من هفته ای چهار روز به کلاسِ فارسی میروم. واسهِ کِلاسِ فارسی هَر روز کار دارم، وَلی به نَظَرِ من، کلاسِ ـِ فارسی کلاسِ خیلی سَختی نیست. ما یک ـــــــ نوِشتاری، یک اِمتِحان ـــ ـ و یک ـــــــ آخَرِ تِرم داریم. زَبانِ فارسی خیلی زیبا و شیرین است. من واقِعا عاشِقِ فارسی هستم.

8. Prepare to answer and ask these questions in Persian.

– چه رِشته ای میخوانی؟ (چه رِشته ای میخونی؟)

– این تِرم دَر چَند تا کِلاس هَستی؟

– چه کِلاسی کِلاسِ مُوردِ عَلاقه تو است؟ (چه کِلاسی کِلاسِ مُوردِ عَلاقه تو ه؟)

– این تِرم به آزمایشگاه هَم میروی؟ (این تِرم به آزمایشگاهَم میری؟)

– اِسمِ اُستادِ راهنَمای تو چه است؟ (اِسمِ اُستادِ راهنَمای تو چیه؟)

– رِشتهِ اُستادِ راهنَمای تو چه است؟ (رِشتهِ اُستادِ راهنَمای تو چیه؟)

– دَفتَرِ او دَر چه ساختِمانی است؟ (دَفتَرِ اون دَر چه ساختِمونیه؟)

– چه کِلاسی در این تِرم برای تو سَخت تَرین کِلاسی است؟ (چه کِلاسی تو این تِرم واسهِ تو سَخت تَرین کِلاسیه ؟)

– چه کِلاسی در این تِرم برای تو آسان تَرین کِلاسی است؟ (چه کِلاسی تو این تِرم واسهِ تو آسون تَرین کِلاسیه ؟)

– دَر چه کِلاسی خِیلی کار داری؟

Now, based on your answers, write brief sentences about your academic interests. Prepare to say your sentences in Persian.

در دانِشکَدهِ ـــــ دَرس میخوانَم.

رِشتهِ ـــــ میخوانم.

کِلاسِ مُوردِ عَلاقه ِ من ـــــ است.

زَبان ـــــ یاد میگیرم.

9. Listen to Neeloo and read along. Complete the transcript by filling in the missing words. Neeloo is talking about her classes. Answer the questions in Persian. Prepare to say your answers fluently in class.

اِسمِ مَن نیلو است. من دانِشجوی ـــــ سیُوم در ـــــ هُنَر و عُلوم در ـــــ نیویورک هستم. ـــــ من مُطالِعاتِ خاوَرِ میانه است. این ـــــ در چهار تا کِلاس هستم. هَمهِ کِلاس های من در این تِرم جالِب هستند. کِلاسِ مُوردِ ـــــ من کلاس فارسی است. در کلاس فارسی ما هَر روز به فارسی ـــــ میکنیم، از کِتابِ فارسی ـــــ، و ـــــ های با حالی را ـــــ میدهیم. من این ترم هَفته ای چهار

158

روز کِلاس دارم و یک روز هَم به آزمایشگاه میروم. جُمعه ها به ـــــــ میروم. فَردا، بَعد از ـــــــ، با ـــــــ کِلاس فارسی ـــــــ دارم. ما روزِ دوشَنبه در کِلاسِ فارسی اِمتِحانِ مُهمی داریم و من راجِع به آن ـــــــ با استادِ فارسی ـــــــ میکنم. من راجِع به ـــــــ فارسی خِیلی سُوال دارم. این آخَر هَفته، من با یکی از هم کِلاسی هایم به ـــــــ میرویم وآنجا بَرای اِمتِحانِ فارسی با هَم ـــــــ میخوانیم.

سُوال ها:

۱. نیلو این تِرم دَر چَند تا کِلاس است؟ (نیلو این تِرم تو چَن تا کِلاسه؟)

۲. به نَظَرِ نیلو ، کِلاسِ فارسی کِلاسِ خوبی است؟ (به نَظَرِ نیلو ، کِلاسِ فارسی کِلاسِ خوبیه؟)

۳. اِمروز بَرای نیلو چَندشَنبه است؟ (اِمروز بَرای نیلو چَن شَمبَس؟)

۴.این شنبه و یکشنبه نیلو چه کار میکند؟ (این شَمبه و یه شَمبه نیلو چی کار میکُنه؟)

۵. چرا نیلو با أُستادِ کِلاسِ فارسی وَقت دارد؟ (چرا نیلو با أُستادِ کِلاسِ فارسی وَقت داره؟)

۶. نیلو چَندشَنبه با استاد کلاس فارسی وَقت دارد؟ (نیلو چَن شَمبه با أُستادِ کِلاسِ فارسی وَقت داره؟)

۷. نیلو دانِشجوی سالِ چَندُم است؟ (نیلو دانِشجوی سالِ چَندُمه؟)

۸. نیلو چه رِشته ای میخواند؟ (نیلو چه رِشته ای میخونه؟)

۹. آیا شما هَم مِثلِ نیلو دانِشجوی دانِشکِدهِ هُنَر و عُلوم هستید؟

10. Using the verb *to need*, prepare to ask and answer these questions in class.

۱. تو هَر روز بَرای کِلاسِ فارسی چه چیزهایی لازِم داری؟ (. تو هَر روز بَرای کِلاسِ فارسی چه چیزایی لازِم داری؟)

۲. تو بَرای زِندِگیِ خوب و شاد چه چیزهایی لازِم داری؟ (تو بَرای زِندِگیِ خوب و شاد چه چیزایی لازِم داری؟)

۳. یک دانِشجو بَرای تَجرُبهِ خوبی در دانِشگاه چه چیزهایی لازِم دارد؟ (یه دانِشجو بَرای تَجرُبهِ خوبی تو دانِشگاه چه چیزایی لازِم داره؟)

IN CLASS

دَر کِلاس

11. Look at the following items and say in Persian which ones you need and which ones you don't need for today's classes.

12.  Pick a few things you have brought today to class. Show them to your conversation partners and tell them in Persian what those items are and how many of them you have with you today. Tell them what classes those items are for. Now, your classmates will do the same for you.

Now, tell the class if either of your conversation partners is going to the same class as you are, and what items both of you brought today for those classes.

13. Ask your classmate the following questions in Persian and complete the table as applicable to your classmate.

	اِسمِ دانشجو
	سِنِ دانشجو
	او اَهلِ کُجا است (او اَهلِ کُجاس)
	او دانِشجوی سالِ چَندُم است (اون دانِشجوی سالِ چَندُمه)
	رِشتهِ او چه است (رِشتهِ اون چیه)

160

	این تِرم در چَند تا کِلاس اَست (این تِرم تو چَن تا کِلاسه)
	این تِرم چَند واحِد بَرمیدارد (این تِرم چَن واحِد بَرمیداره)
	کِلاسِ مُوردِ عَلاقهِ او چه اَست (کِلاسِ مُوردِ عَلاقهِ اون چیه)
	اِسمِ اُستادِ راهنَمایِ او چه اَست (اِسمِ اُستادِ راهنَمای اون چیه)

14. Talk to your classmates and find those who have something in common with you as far as the following activities are concerned. Speak in Persian.

- usually studies in the library or in the dorm
- has a lab this semester
- sleeps only a little, not enough (به اندازه کافی)
- has an exam this week
- works as well as takes classes (هم کار میکند هم درس میخواند)
- goes to parties once a month
- lives in a dorm or in the town
- favorite class this semester
- has classes every day
- has a roommate/housemate
- is in the same college

Now, tell your class in Persian what you have in common with your conversation partners. For example,

او مِثلِ مَن این تِرم زَبانِ فارسی یاد میگیرد (اون مِثلِ مَن این تِرم زَبانِ فارسی یاد میگیره).

Don't forget to conjugate the verbs correctly in third person singular. (s/he form).

15. Go over the Homework about Neeloo. Make two statements about Neeloo. One of your statements has to have a negated verb.

16. Choose one or two items in the classroom and ask a classmate how many of those items are in the classroom right now. The respondent will answer using the quantifiers تا for multiple items and یک دانه (یه دونه) for a single item without naming the items. Follow the example below to formulate the answers:

E.g., دَر این کِلاس چَند تا تَخته اَست؟ - دو تا.

GRAMMAR  دستورِ زَبان

1. How to say where you are from (the stressed ending ی)

The stressed ending of origin ی /ee/ is attached to the end of the names of countries, toponyms and ethnonyms in order to describe one's origin or nationality, for example,

English – انگلیسی	England – انگلیس
American – آمریکایی	America – آمریکا

Spelling

After the consonants, write the ending together with the word whenever possible, for example,

مکزیک – مکزیکی   چین – چینی

After the vowels ا /ã/ and و /o, oo/, write two joined letters ی. Only pronounce one /ee/.

آمریکایی   /ãmreekã-ee/ American

پرتوریکو یی   /porto-riko-ee/ Puerto-Rican

After the vowel ه /e/, write ای and pronounce /ee/.

کره ای   /koreh-ee/ Korean

جاوه ای   /jãveh-ee/ Javanese

Some adjectives of origin do not follow the pattern described above:

تُرکیه – تُرک	گرجِستان – گرجی
روسیه – روس	تاجیکِستان – تاجیک

Note that in some cases the adjective that describes an inanimate object, differs slightly from the adjective that describes a person from the same country:

روسیه	روسی	روس
Russia (the country)	Russian (about an inanimate object, i.e., food, language, etc.)	A Russian person
تُرکیه	تُرکی	تُرک
Turkey (the country)	Turkish (about an inanimate object)	A Turkish person

162

2. Ordinal numbers

Ordinal numbers describe the order of things in a set or a row, for example, first, tenth, twenty-sixth, and so on. Most ordinal numbers in English are formed using an ending (*th*) attached to the end of the adjective. Persian speakers do the same, but use the ending /om-een/. The /een/ syllable in this ending is stressed.

پَنجُمین روز /panj-**omeen** rooz/ fifth day

چهارُمین شَهرِ بُزُرگ /char-**omeen** shahreh bozorg/ fourth largest city

Similarly to English, Persian words *first*, *second*, *third* and *last* are formed differently:

First day /av-val-een rooz/ اَوَّلین روز	First /av-val-een/ اَوَّلین
Last day /ā-khar-een rooz/ آخَرین روز	Second /dov-vomeen/ دُوُّمین
	Third /sev-vomeen/ سِوُّمین
	Last /ā-khar-een/ آخَرین

Persian has another ending to describe the order of things, which is /om/ (the short version of /omeen/). This second ending /om/ is more commonly used and it turns the number into an adjective that will follow the word it describes with the connector glide /eh/ appearing between the word and the ordinal number.

روزِ پَنجُم /rooz-eh panj-om/ the fifth day

شَبِ هَفتُم /shab-eh haft-om/ the seventh night

However, the commonly used variants of the words *first* and *last* are formed without this ending, even though they follow the same word order.

دَفعهِ اَوَّل /dafe-yeh av-val/ First time

دَفعهِ آخَر /dafe-yeh ā-khar/ Last time

سالِ دُوُّم /sāl-eh dov-vom/ Second year

دَرسِ سِوُّم /dars-eh sev-vom/ Third lesson

Note that if the word *first* is part of a compound number, its ordinal form is based on یک / yek/:

سی و یِکُم /see-oh yekom/ Thirty-first   بیست و یِکُم /beestoh yekom/ Twenty-first

In order to say *the first one*, *the second one*, simply pronounce the stressed ending /ee/ at the end of the number, for example,

/dov-vo-mee/ – the second one

/sev-vo-mee/ – the third one

/av-va-lee/ – the first one

آن آوَلی خِیلی خوب است /oon avvalee khe-eelee khoobeh/ – That first one is very good.

How to say a date using ordinal numbers

Persian speakers say the day first and then the month, that is,   5th of March.

To say a date in Persian, first say the number with the ending *om* (...*th*) followed by the connector glide *eh*, and then say the name of the month, for example,

| 5th of March | /pan**jom-eh** march/ | ۵ مارچ |

In colloquial speech, it is acceptable to say /panjeh march/

To ask what the date is today, say:

/em-rooz chan-do-meh?/   اِمروز چَندُم است؟

To answer the question, say:

/em-rooz pan-jom-eh mãrseh/   اِمروز پَنجُمِ مارس است

HOMEWORK   تَکلیف

17.   You will hear and see the names of places (e.g., Iran) along with adjectives of origin (e.g., Iranian). Distribute them accordingly into the two columns in the table below.

ایرانی، چین، تاجیکی، آمریکایی، هِند، ایتالیایی، اُروپا، آفریقایی، کُره ای، جاوه،
تُرکیه، تُرکی، ایتالیا، هِندی، ایران، تاجیکِستان، آفریقا، آمریکا، کُره، چینی،
اُروپایی ، جاوه ای، افغانِستان، افغان

Adjective of Origin	Name of Country

18. For each country, write a word that describes a person from that country, for example, أُسترالیا – أُسترالیایی Prepare to read both words aloud in Persian.

	ایران		آمریکا
	تُرکیه		کانادا
	أُروپا		مِکزیک
	اِسپانیا		آلمان
	پرتوریکو		فَرانسه
			روسیه

19. Translate the following sentences into Persian. Pay special attention to the orthography of the suffix ee ی / یی of origin.

Roya	رویا
Rome	روم

(1) I am an American and I live in New York now. (2) I am a student at NYU. (3) I have one Iranian friend and one Italian friend. (4) My Iranian friend's name is Roya and she is from Tehran. (5) My Italian friend's name is Gina and she is from Rome.

20. Name two or three of your favorite dishes from different countries and tell your class-mates where those dishes are from. Use adjectives of origin in your sentences. Name foods from at least three different countries. Do research online if needed. For example, say:

پیتزا غَذای ایتالیایی است (پیتزا غَذای ایتالیاییه).

21. Listen and write down the numbers you hear. Prepare to read aloud the numbers you have written down.

۱۱.	۶.	۱.
۱۲.	۷.	۲.
۱۳.	۸.	۳.
۱۴.	۹.	۴.
۱۵.	۱۰.	۵.

22. Prepare to ask and answer the following questions in Persian. Look up the information online if needed.

Persian speaker /fārsee zabān/ فارسی زَبان, world /jahān/ جَهان

* insert the name of the town where your university is located.

۱. کِشوَرِ تو چَند سال دارد؟ (کِشوَرِ تو چَن سال داره؟)

۲. شَهرِ تو چَند سال دارد؟ (شَهرِ تو چَن سال داره؟)

۳. دانِشگاهِ تو چَند سال دارد؟ (دانِشگاهِ تو چَن سال داره؟)

۴. دَر دانِشگاهِ تو چَند تا دانِشجو است؟ (در دانِشگاهِ تو چَن تا دانِشجو هَست؟)

۵. در دانِشگاهِ تو چَند تا أُستاد است؟ (تو دانِشگاهِ تو چَن تا أُستاد هست؟)

۶. در شَهرِ تو چَند نَفَر زِندِگی میکُنَند؟ (تو شَهرِ تو چَن نَفَر زِندِگی میکُنَن؟)

۷. دَر آمریکا چَند نَفَر زِندِگی میکُنَند؟ (تو آمریکا چَن نَفَر زِندِگی میکُنَن؟)

۸. دَر شَهرِ _____* چَند نَفَر زِندِگی میکُنَند؟ (تو شَهرِ _____* چَن نَفَر زِندِگی میکُنَن؟)

۹. چَند میلیون نَفَر دَر جَهان فارسی زَبان هَستَند؟ (چَند میلیون نَفَر تو جَهان فارسی زَبان هَستَن؟)

23. Listen and read the following dates in Persian. Prepare to read these dates fluently in class. Don't forget to pronounce the connector glide between the ordinal numbers and the names of the months.

۱. چَهارُمِ ژوییه. ۲. بیست و پَنجُمِ دِسامبر. ۳. اَوَّلِ ژانویه. ۴. چَهاردَهُمِ فوریه.
۵. یازدَهُمِ نُوامبر. ۶. بیست و یِکُمِ مارس. ۷. سی و یِکُمِ دِسامبر. ۸. سیوُّمِ آگوست. ۹. دُوُّمِ آوریل. ۱۰. نُهُمِ اُکتُبر.

24. Pick a month or a day of the week. Ask in Persian which month or day it is in the correct order. Prepare to ask your question fluently in class. Be ready to answer similar questions from your classmates.

دِسامبر چَندُمین ماهِ سال است؟ (دِسامبر چَندُمین ماهِ ساله؟)
دوشَمبه چَندُمین روزِ هَفته است؟ (دوشَمبه چَندُمین روزِ هَفتَس؟)

25. Read this description of the days in a week in Iran and answer the questions in Persian.

هَم دَر آمریکا هَم دَر ایران یِک هَفته هَفت روز است. دَر ایران اَوّلین روزِ هَفته شَنبه است و آخَرین روزِ هَفته جُمعه است. دَر ایران یِک هَفته شِش روزِ کاری و یِک روز تَعطیل دارد. روزِ جُمعه تَعطیل است. در ایران اَوّلین روزِ کاری شَنبه است.

۱. دَر ایران یِک هَفته چَند روز است؟ (دَر ایران یه هَفته چَند روزه؟)
۲. دَر ایران، چه روزی، روزِ اَوَّلِ هَفته است؟ (دَر ایران، چه روزی، روزِ اَوَّلِ هَفتَس؟)
۳. دَر ایران، چه روزی، روزِ آخَرِ هَفته است؟ (دَر ایران، چه روزی، روزِ آخَرِ هَفتَس؟)
۴. دَر ایران، یِک هَفته چَند روزِ کاری دارد؟ (دَر ایران یه هَفته چَن روزِ کاری داره؟)
۵. دَر ایران، یِک هَفته چَند روز تَعطیل دارد؟ (دَر ایران یه هَفته چَن روز تَطیل داره؟)

Now, based on the information you heard from the audio presentation, complete the following sentences about the week in Iran and also in the United States.

در ایران

اَوّلین روزِ هَفته شَنبه است.
ـــــــــ روزِ هَفته سه شَنبه است.
ـــــــــ روزِ هَفته چَهارشَنبه است.

_____ هَفته پَنج شَنبه است.

آخرین روزِ هَفته _____ است.

در آمریکا

اَوَّلین روزِ هَفته _____ است.

_____ روزِ هَفته سه شَنبه است.

_____ روزِ هَفته چَهارشَنبه است.

_____ هَفته پَنج شَنبه است.

آخَرین روزِ هَفته _____ است.

26. Prepare to ask and to answer the following questions in Persian in class. For this drill you will use the verb *to come* in first person singular, second person singular, and third person singular in past tense.

آمَد /oo-mad/ is the Past tense root of the verb *to come*.

آمدم	/oomadam/ I came
آمدی	/oomadee/ you came
آمد	/oomad/ S/he came
به دُنیا آمَدَم (به دُنیا اومَدَم)	I was born

دَر آوریل به دُنیا آمَدَم (دَر آوریل به دُنیا اومَدَم). I was born in April

دَر چه سالی به دُنیا آمَدی؟ (دَر چه سالی به دُنیا اومَدی؟)

دَر چه ماهی به دُنیا آمَدی؟ (دَر چه ماهی به دُنیا اومَدی؟)

دَر چه تاریخی به دُنیا آمَدی؟ (دَر چه تاریخی به دُنیا اومَدی؟)

کُجا به دُنیا آمَدی؟ (کُجا به دُنیا اومَدی؟)

27. Do research and find out the following information about these individuals. Prepare to say in Persian the information you have found out about each personality.

Anoushe Ansari, Benyamin Bahadori, Shirin Ebadi, Christiane Amanpour, Marjane Satrapi, Niki Karimi, Mohsen Namjoo, Ali Javan, Firouz Naderi, Pierre Omidyar and Yara Shahidi.

- شُغلِ او چه است؟ (شُغلِ اون چیه؟)
- دَر چه سالی به دُنیا آمَد؟ (دَر چه سالی به دُنیا اومَد؟)
- کُجا به دُنیا آمَد؟ (کُجا به دُنیا اومَد؟)
- چَند ساله است؟ (چَن ساله هَست؟)
- کُجا زِندِگی میکُند؟ (کُجا زِندِگی میکُنه؟)
- کُجا کار میکُند؟ (کُجا کار میکُنه؟)

28. Write in Persian the sentences that state the **month** and **year** when you, your brother, sister, mother and father were born. Use the sentence below as an example. Prepare to ask and to answer in Persian when your classmate, her or his brother, sister, mother and father were born.

مَن دَر آوریلِ ۱۹۹۵ به دُنیا آمَدَم (مَن دَر آوریلِ ۱۹۹۵ به دُنیا اومَدَم).

29. A review presentation. Prepare a brief presentation on the topic of this chapter in the way that is applicable to you. Review the vocabulary and topic of this chapter and address the questions below in your presentation. Your presentation must be entirely in Persian. Your objective is to create a coherent and flowing narrative and speak continuously for a couple minutes in the target language. Be prepared to answer your classmates' questions about the topic of your presentation.

(1) What is the name of your university or college?
(2) Where is your university located?
(3) Is it a state or private university or college?
(4) Is it a big or a small college? How many students and professors are there in your university?
(5) What do you study? What is your major?
(6) What college are you in within your university?
(7) Are you an undergraduate student or graduate student?
(8) What year are you studying in?
(9) How many classes are you taking this semester?
(10) How many credits are you taking this semester?
(11) Do you have classes every day of the week? On what days do you not have classes?
(12) What is your favorite class this semester?
(13) Do you also work this semester?
(14) How many credits is your Persian class?
(15) How many days a week do you go to Persian class?
(16) What types of exercises and activities do you usually do in Persian class?
(17) How many students are there in your Persian class this semester?
(18) What is the name of your professor in Persian class?

(19) In what department does your Persian language professor work?
(20) What is your mother tongue? Do you speak any other languages?

IN CLASS

دَر کِلاس

30. You will work with a classmate and each of you will receive from the instructor a card with the names of countries. Your cards have the names of different countries on them. Read to your classmate the names of the countries from your card. Your classmate's objective is to say the adjective of origin that corresponds to that name and to also write that adjective down on his card. Now switch the roles. Your instructor will come to check the spelling of the adjectives you have written down.

Instructor, please see the appendix Instructor's Resources.

31. You and one other student will come to the board. Your instructor will say the names of two random countries that end in different letters. Write the adjective of origin or nationality for each of the two countries. The person who writes the two adjectives correctly first will sit down. The other person will face the next student at the board.

32. Work with a classmate and translate the following sentences into Persian. Pay special attention to the stressed ending /eel/ ای / ی / یی of the adjectives of origin.

(1) I live in a dorm and have a roommate. (2) My roommate is from Korea. (3) I don't speak Korean, but my roommate speaks English very well. (4) My parents live in San Francisco. (5) There is a good Spanish restaurant on (pers.: in) their street. (6) Every Friday my parents have a lunch or dinner at that restaurant because they like Spanish food very much.

33. Look at the images and answer your instructor's questions. You will need the following words for this exercise:

ریال Rial /reeãl/ Iranian currency

۱۰۰۰ ریال   1000 Rials /hezãr reeãl/

Your instructor will ask you the following questions about one of the images below.

این پولِ کُجا است؟

اِسمِ این پول چه است؟ (اِسمِ این پول چیه؟)

این چند ریا ل است؟ (این چند ریا له؟)

34. Talk to your classmates and find out their phone numbers. Remember, Persian speakers divide phone numbers into tens and hundreds and say whole numbers.

For example, the phone number 607-255-2060 would be pronounced as six hundred seven – two hundred fifty-five – twenty sixty, that is, /*sheesh sadoh haft, deeveestoh panjahoh panj, beest, shast*/

Example:

شُماره‌ِ تِلِفُنِت چَند است؟ (شُماره‌ِ تِلِفُنِت چَنده؟)

شُماره‌ِ تِلِفُنَم هَست ...

اسم هَمکِلاسی	شُماره تِلِفُن

35. Make a list of foreign cuisines from a country that you like (e.g., ایرانی، غَذای چینی غَذای etc.). Ask if your classmates like those cuisines as well. Write down their answers. Your objective is to talk in Persian to everyone in class and to: (1) Find classmates who like the same cuisine(s) as you do; (2) Find out what the favorite cuisine is in your class. Share your findings with the class. For this drill, you will use the verb *to like* in I person (I form), II person (You form) and III person (S/he or They form).

The words you might need would be:

غَذای آمریکایی، ایتالیایی، هِندی، چینی، فَرانسَوی، ژاپُنی، ایرانی، یونانی،

مِکزیکی، ویتنامی.

دوسـت دارَم، دوسـت داری، دوسـت دارد (دوسـت داره).

36. Working with a classmate, come up with as many questions as you can about the following sentence. Your questions must be in Persian. Then, pick a person in class (not from your group) and ask him/her one of your questions.

هَم أتاقیِ گُره ایِ مَن فارسی بَلَد نیست و ما هَمیشـه به اِنگلیسـی صُحبَت میکُنیم.

37. You will be working with a classmate to translate these questions into Persian. Once you have done this, prepare to pronounce them aloud. Your instructor will assign to you another classmate, while your former group mate will be assigned to yet another student in class. Your objective is to interview the new group mate in Persian using the questions that you have translated.

(1) How many languages do you speak? (2) What languages do you speak? (3) What is your native language? (4) What is your favorite language? (5) What language do you speak at home? (6) Does your father or mother speak Persian?

38. Look at the image of the calendar. Pick a classmate and ask him/her two questions about the date and day of the week. You can structure your questions after the following sentences:

دوشَنبهِ اَوَلِ این ماه چَندُم است؟ (دوشَمبهِ اَوَلِ این ماه چَندُمه؟)

دَهُمِ نُوامبر چَندشَنبه است؟ (دَهُمِ نُوامبر چَن شَمبَس؟)

39. Pick a holiday from the list below. Say the date on which that holiday takes place, but don't name the holiday. Pick a classmate and say the date to him/her. Your classmate will listen to the date you say and will name the holiday.

اَوَلِ ژانویه چه عِیدی است؟ (اَوَلِ ژانویه چه عِیدیه؟)

January 1	New Year	سالِ نُو
December 25	Christmas	کریسمَس
February 14	Valentine's Day	روزِ والِنتاین / روزِ عُشاق
March 21	Norooz (Iranian New Year)	نُوروز

July 4	Independence Day	روزِ اِستِقلال
November 11	Veteran's Day	روزِ جانباز

Now, pick a holiday and ask a random student in class on what date that holiday takes place.

Now, tell class what your favorite holiday is, the date on which it falls this year and why it is your favorite holiday.

40. Pick a question and a classmate. Ask that classmate one of the following questions in Persian.

پاییز fall /pãeez/

بَهار spring /bahãr/

۱. اِمروز چَندُم اَست؟ (اِمروز چَندُمه؟)

۲. دَر دانِشگاهِ شُما تِرمِ پاییز دَر چه ماهی شُروع میشود؟ (تو دانِشگاهِ شُما تِرمِ پاییز دَر چه ماهی شورو میشه؟)

۳. تِرمِ پاییز دَر چه ماهی تَمام میشود؟ (تِرمِ پاییز دَر چه ماهی تَموم میشه؟)

۴. تِرمِ بَهار دَر چه ماهی شُروع میشود؟ (تِرمِ بَهار دَر چه ماهی شورو میشه؟)

۵. تِرمِ بَهار دَر چه ماهی تَمام میشود؟ (تِرمِ بَهار دَر چه ماهی تَموم میشه؟)

41. Talk to your classmates and find out how many of them were born in the same year, month, day of the week, date or place as you were. Useful words:

روز	ماه	سال	تاریخ
day	month	year	date

42. You will be working in groups of three. Ask the following questions in Persian. Ask your group mates at least three questions each, that is, six questions in total.

in the same city   دَر هَمان شَهر (تو هَمون شَهر)

- When was your mom born? Where was she born?
- When was your dad born? Where was he born?

- When was your sister born? Where was she born?
- When was your brother born? Was he born in the same city?
- When was your best friend born? Where was s/he born?

43. When Persian speakers name several related items in a row (nouns, adjectives) they tend to pronounce the word و (and) as /oh/ for the sake of fluency and ease of pronunciation. The same phenomenon occurs in established phrases. Pronounce the following words and phrases following the rule described above.

پِدَر و مادَر، بَرادَر و خواهَر، مِداد و خودکار، میز و صَندَلی، آی پد و کامپیوتر و تِلِفن و موبایل، خَرج و مَرج، سَر و صِدا، خِرت و پِرت.

44.  An interview. You will be working in groups of three. One of you will be a star celebrity (سِتاره), while the other two classmates will be reporters. The reporters will interview the celebrity. You will receive from your instructor cards indicating your role and topics for the questions. The two reporters have different topics and questions to ask. Once you have completed the interview, pass your card to the right and switch roles. Conduct the interview again.

Instructor please see the appendix Instructor's Resources.

LISTENING   شِنیداری

Listen to the conversation between two students, Parsa and Sara. Sara is helping Parsa to put together his academic schedule. The speakers are talking about the number of credits and classes, hours at which classes start and end, and they name various courses.

Pre-listening. (1) Considering the topic of the conversation, make a list of most common words you expect to encounter in the conversation. If the word you wrote down is a noun, think of the verb that would commonly go with it in the given context. If the word that you wrote is a verb, think of a noun that may go with it in this conversation. Pronounce the words you have written so that you identify them when you listen to the conversation. (2) The verbs in the conversation appear in present tense. Think of the present tense marker and how the verbs usually look with that marker in the beginning and with the conjugational endings at the end. Are their exceptions to the rule? The speakers will use the verbs in First Person Singular (I ...) and Second Person Singular (you ...) forms. Write and pronounce your verbs in those forms, so you can identify them when you listen to the conversation.

175

Listen to the conversation and answer the questions in Persian. Prepare to say your answers fluently.

سُوالات:

۱. پارسا چَند تا کِلاسِ دیگَر لازِم دارد؟ (پارسا چَن تا کِلاسِ دیگه لازِم داره؟)

۲. کِلاسِ تاریخِ خاوَرِ میانه چِرا بَرای او خوب نیست؟

۳. کِلاسِ فَلسَفه چِطوره؟

۴. بِالاخَره پارسا بَرای چه کِلاسی ثَبتِ نام میکُند؟ (بِالاخَره پارسا بَرای چه کِلاسی ثَبتِ نام میکُنه؟)

Follow-up 1. Make one statement in Persian about Parsa and his schedule of classes this semester.

Follow-up 2. You will be working in pairs. Prepare in Persian a brief dialogue about your classes and schedules. You can use the following questions and the Listening section to put together your dialogue. Questions:
- How many classes are you taking this semester?
- How many credits are those classes?
- Are you liking those courses?
- What is your favorite class this semester and why (e.g., interesting topic *mo-oo-zoo-esh jãlebeh*, good professor, convenient hours, etc.)?
- Is that class big?
- In which department /dar cheh bakhshee/ is it?
- Is it a difficult or an easy class?
- What is the mean grade /moãdel/ in that class?
- Who is the professor in that class?

Follow-up 3. You will be working in groups of three. Ask your group mates questions in Persian about their classes and schedules this semester. Find out and tell the class one similarity and one difference between your and the schedules of your group mates. You can use the questions of the preceding Follow-up activities and the Listening section in order to design your questions.

READING

خواندَنی

Read the following letter from your pen pal Roya. Prepare to read the entire text fluently in class.

Pre-reading. You will read a new letter from Roya, your pen pal in Iran. In the letter, she describes her university. Before reading the text, think about your university, its location, about your major, about the number of classes that you are taking this semester, your favorite classes and about the breaks you have during the year.

(1)   Now, complete in Persian the following sentences with the information applicable to you.

۱.من رِشتهِ ـــــ ـــــ میخوانم.۲. این تِرم زَبانِ ـــــ ـــــ یاد میگیرَم. ۳. این تِرم در ـــــ ـــــ تا کلاس هَستم. ۴. این تِرم سَرم شلوغ ـــــ . ۵. در این تِرم درس میخوانم و کار ـــــ . ۶. کلاس مورد علاقه من ـــــ است. ۷. دانشگاه من در شَهرِ ـــــ است. ۸. در دانشگاه من ـــــ دانشجوی لیسانس و ـــــ دانشجوی فُوقِ لیسانس درس میخوانند. ۹. در دانشگاه من تَعطیلاتِ تابستانی از ماه ـــــ تا ماه ـــــ است. ۱۰. در دانشگاه من ـــــ تا دانشکده هَست.

Useful words:

I am writing a letter	نامه مینویسَم	dear friend	دوستِ عَزیز
more than	بیش از	was founded	تاسیس شُد (تَسیس شُد)
that, which	که	holiday	عید
Norooz, which falls on March 21 or 22, is the official New Year holiday in Iran.	نُوروز	program	بَرنامه

سَلام، دوستِ عَزیز! حالِ تو چِطور است؟ باز هَم یِک نامه بَرای تو مینویسَم. در این نامه یِک کَم از دانشگاهِ مَن بَرای تو تَعریف میکُنَم. مَن دانِشجوی زَبان شِناسی در دانشگاهِ تهران هَستَم. این تِرم در پَنج تا کِلاس هَستَم و هَمیشه دَرگیرِ کِلاس ها هَستَم. هَر روز دو سه تا کِلاس دارَم.

مَن این تِرم هَر روز دو سه تا کِلاس دارَم. یِک روز دَر هَفته در یِک کافی شاپ در تِهران کار میکُنَم. این تِرم سَرَم خِیلی شُلوغ است وَلی خِیلی خوشحال هَستَم. دانِشگاه و کِلاس هایم را دوست دارَم. کِلاسِ مُوردِ عَلاقهِ مَن در این تِرم کِلاسِ اِنگلیسی است.

دانِشگاهِ مَن خِیلی بُزُرگ است و چَندین پَردیس در چَندیدن شَهرِ ایران دارد. مَن در پَردیسِ مَرکَزی در شَهرِ تِهران دانِشجو هَستَم. دانِشگاهِ تهران در سالِ ۱۹۳۴ در شَهرِ تهران تاسیس شُد. دانِشگاهِ مَن از بیش از سی و سه هِزار دانِشجو دارد: بیش از پانزدَه هِزار دانِشجوی لیسانس و بیش از هِجدَه هِزار دانِشجوی فُوقِ لیسانس. دانِشگاهِ تِهران بیست و پنج دانِشکَده و یِک صَد و پَنجاه و شیش بَرنامهِ دُکتُرا دارد. مِثلِ آمریکا، ما هَم دو تا تِرم داریم: تِرمِ اَوَل که از ماهِ آگوست تا ماهِ ژانویه طول میکِشد و تِرمِ دُوُم که از ژانویه تا ژوئَن طول میکِشد. تَعطیلاتِ زِمِستانیِ ما در ماهِ ژانویه است، و تَعطیلاتِ تابِستانیِ ما در ماهِ ژوئَن شروع میشود و در ماهِ آگوست تَمام میشود. تَعطیلاتِ مُوردِ عَلاقهِ مَن تَعطیلاتِ نُوروزی است بَرای اینکه نُوروز یِک عِیدِ بُزُرگ و مُهِمی بَرای ما ایرانی ها است. تَعطیلاتِ نُوروزی در بَهار، در ماهِ مارچ شروع میشود و دو هفته طول میکِشد.

اِسمِ دانِشگاهِ تو چه است؟ دانِشگاهِ تو کُجا است؟ تو چه رِشته ای میخوانی؟ کِلاسِ مُوردِ عَلاقهِ تو چه است؟ یِک کَم از دانِشگاه و کِلاس های خود تَعریف کُن. مُخلِصِ تو.

رویا

Follow-up 1. Complete the sentences comparing the statements about Roya to the realities of your life. You can use the words وَلی *but* or هَم *also* to write the second part of the sentences, for example,

مامانِ رویا اُستاد اَست – مامانِ مَن هَم اُستاد اَست (مامانِ رویا اُستاده – مامانِ مَنَم اُستاده).

١. رویا زبان شیناسی میخواند (رویا زبان شیناسی میخونه) ـــــــــــــ

٢. اِیر تِرم رویا در پَنج تا کِلاس اَست (این تِرمِ رویا تو پَنج تا کِلاسه) ـــــــــــــ

٣. رویا هَم دَرس میخواند هَم کار میکُند (رویا هَم دَرس میخونه هَم کار میکُنه) ـــــــ

٤. کِلاسِ مُوردِ عَلاقه رویا انگلیسی اَست (کِلاسِ مُوردِ عَلاقه رویا انگلیسیه) ـــــــ

٥. تَعطیلاتِ مُوردِ عَلاقه رویا تَعطیلاتِ نُوروزی اَست (تَطیلاتِ مُوردِ عَلاقه رویا تَطیلاتِ نُوروزیه) ـــــــ

Follow-up 2. Prepare to ask your classmates two questions about the excerpt. Your questions must have two different verbs (one per sentence). Structure your question sentences correctly.

۶	۵	۴	۳	۲	۱
Verb	Indirect object (object with a preposition)	Direct object (object without a preposition)	Place	Time	Subject

Follow-up 3. Use the data about the university given in the excerpt and compare it to the data about your university. Describe the similarities and differences between the universities.

Follow-up 4. You will work in pairs. Imagine you are talking to a friend at school. You have told your friend about receiving a letter from Roya, your new pen pal in Iran. Create a brief dialogue where you share with your friend what you have learned from Roya's letter about her university in Iran. Your friend will ask you questions about similarities and difference between Roya's university and your university. Useful phrases:

179

بَر خَلاف دانِشگاهِ ما

Unlike our university

مِثلِ دانِشگاهِ ما

Like our university

TRANSLATION   تَرجُمه

Write down a Persian translation of the following passage. Use a dictionary if needed.

Curriculum	بَرنامه آموزِشی	Eram Garden	باغِ اِرَم
was designed by ...	تَوَسُطِ...طَراحی شُد	Part	قِسمَت
with the help from ...	با کُمَکِ..	Important fields	رِشته های مُهِم

University of Shiraz

The University of Shiraz was founded in 1946. The curriculum of this university was designed with the help from the University of Pennsylvania and was similar to curriculum in American universities. The building of the University of Shiraz was designed by an American architect M. Yamasaki. Today the University of Shiraz has over 20,000 students: 11,839 undergraduate students, 7,189 postgraduate students and 1,683 doctoral students. There are 700 professors working at the University of Shiraz. The University of Shiraz has 200 BA programs, 300 MA programs and 150 PhD programs. The University of Shiraz has 12 athletic teams. The University of Shiraz has 21 dorms. The beautiful Eram Garden is part of the University of Shiraz. Important fields at this university are engineering, agriculture and computer science. The language of all classes is Persian, but in some classes, the textbooks are in English.

WRITING   اِنشا

Read again the letter from Roya, your pen pal in Iran. Now, write your response to her letter. Write in Persian a paragraph of a minimum of 150 words to describe your university, your classes and what you do this semester. Your objective is to write as much as you can. You can use Roya's letter and the Translation section as examples for the format and content of your letter.

Start your letter with a greeting and close it with the phrase مُخلِصِ تو *Sincerely Yours*. Sign your letter in Persian.

خانه و مَنزِل
My House
and Home

Traditional Iranian house concept with a pool or fountain and a garden in the front yard. Moqaddam house, Tehran

Function Describing the layout of your house, the rooms and furniture, describing the location of objects in relation to other objects, describing possession.

Listening Marjee describes her room.

Reading Our house in Lahijan.

Structures Possessive endings.

Listen and repeat. Try to imitate the native speaker's pronunciation. Repeat each word and phrase a few times aloud until you can easily pronounce them.

Rooms			
Stairs, stairway	راه پله	Room	أتاق
I take the stairs	از پِله میرَوم (از پِله میرَم)	Bedroom	أتاقِ خواب
Hallway	راهرُو	Living room	(أتاقِ) نِشیمَن، هال، پَذیرایی
Roof	بام	Dining room	أتاقِ ناهارخوری
Floor, story (of a building)	طَبَقه	Study, home office	أتاقِ کار
Wall	دیوار	Nursery, child's room	أتاقِ کودَک
Floor	کَف	Kitchen	آشپَزخانه (آشپَزخونه)
Ceiling	سَقف	Restroom	دَستشویی (دَسشویی)
Door	دَر	Bathroom	حَمام (حَموم)
Window	پَنجِره	Attic	زیرشیروانی (زیرشیروونی)
Laundry room	أتاقِ لِباس شویی	Basement	طَبَقهِ زیرزَمین
House	خانه (خونه)	Space to park (at home), garage	پارکینگ، گاراژ
Home, place	مَنزِل	Yard	حَیاط
Apartment	آپارتمان	Elevator	آسانسور
Three-bedroom apartment	آپارتمانِ سه خوابه	I take the elevator	با آسانسور میرَوم (با آسانسور میرَم)
Building	ساختمان (ساختِمون)	Rental apartment / house	آپارتمانِ / خانهِ اِجاره ای
		I am renting (I've rented) a house	من یِک خانه اِجاره کِرده آم (من یه خونه اِجاره کردم)

In the House			
Photo, picture	عَکس	Curtain	پَرده
Poster	پوسیِر	Lamp	چِراغ، آباژور
Mirror	آیینه	Chandelier	لوسیِر
Heating	گَرمایِش	Painting, wall art	تابلو
AC system Air conditioner	تَهویهِ مَطبوع (تَهویه) کولِر		

Furniture			
Carpet	قالی	Furniture	مُبلِمان
Fridge	یَخچال	TV	تِلِویزیون
Stove	فِر	Table	میز
Microwave	ماکروفِر	Desk	میزِ تَحریر
Faucet	شیراب	Chair	صَندَلی
Tidy	مُرَتَب	Armchair	صَندَلیِ راحَتی
Untidy	نامُرَتَب	Sofa	مُبل
Clean	تَمیز	Bed	تَختِ خواب
Dirty	کَثیف	Dresser	کِشُو (کِشو)
Cozy	دِنج		

Position	
In the middle of the room	دَر وَسَطِ اُتاق
In the corner of the room	دَر گوشهِ اُتاق
On the right of ...	دَر سَمتِ راستِ ...
On the left of ...	دَر سَمتِ چَپِ ...
In front of ...	جِلُوی ...
Behind ...	پُشتِ ...
Above ...	بالای ...

Position	
On the ... (on the surface of ...)	روی... (رو ...)
Under ...	زیرِ...
Between ...	بینِ...
Next to ...	کِنارِ...
On the wall	روی دیوار (رو دیوار)
On the floor	روی کَف (رو کَف)
Upstairs	بالا
Downstairs	پایین
On which floor?	در طَبَقهِ چَندُم؟
On the first/second/third floor	دَر طَبَقهِ اَوَل/دُوُم/سِوُم
Ground floor	طَبَقهِ هَمکَف
What rooms?	چه اُتاق هایی (چه اُتاقایی)؟
In which neighborhood?	دَر چه مَحَله ای؟
Fits	جا میشود (جا میشه)

HOMEWORK

تکلیف

1. Listen and read along. Complete the translation based on what you hear and see in the Persian original.

خانهِ من سه طَبَقه است. در طَبَقهِ اَوَل یک اُتاق ناهارخوریِ بزرگ، یک آشپَزخانه،
یک اُتاقِ پَذیراییِ بزرگ، یک حَمام و یک دَستشوییِ هست. در طَبَقهِ دُوُم یک اُتاق
خوابِ بزرگ، دو تا اُتاق خوابِ کوچِک و دو تا حَمام هست. طَبَقهِ سِوُم یک اُتاق
خواب، یک حَمام و یک اُتاق کار دارد. خانهِ من حَیاطِ بزرگ و پارکینگ دارد.

My house has three _____. On the _____ floor, there is one _____ dining room, a kitchen, one large _____ room, a _____ and restroom. On the second _____, there is one large ___ __, two _____ bedrooms, and two baths. On the _____ floor, there is one _____ and bathroom and a study. My _____ has a large _____ and a parking space.

2. Look at the image of the house and complete the description.

خانه من سه طبقه است. در طبقه اول دو تا اتاق هست ‑ یک ـــــــ و یک ـــــــ در طبقه دوم هم دو تا اتاق هست ‑ یک ـــــــ و یک ـــــــ طَبَقه سیُوُم زیرشیروانی است و یک اُتاق ـــــــ دارد.

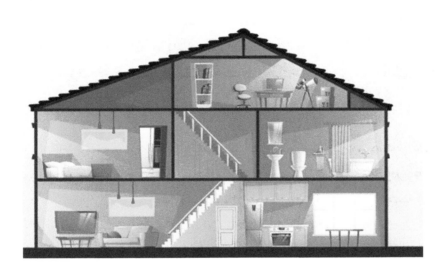

3. Listen and read along. Complete the translation based on the Persian text. Answer the questions in Persian. Prepare to say your answers aloud and fluently.

بابایم (بابام) = بابای من

سلام، دوستان! من در خانهِ مامان و بابایم در تهران زندگی میکنم. خانه ما دو طبقه است. در طَبَقه اَوَل یک آشپَزخانه، یک اُتاقِ ناهارخوری ، یک اُتاقِ پَذیرایی و یک دَستشویی هست. در طَبَقه دُوُم سه تا اُتاق خواب و دو تا حَمام هست. خانه ما زیرشیروانی هم دارد. زیرشیروانی خانه ما بزرگ نیست و یک اتاق کار کوچک دارد. خانه مامان و بابای من حیاط بزرگ و پارکینگ هم دارد.

Hello, friends! I live in my parents' ____ in Tehran. Our house has two _____ On _____ floor, there is a kitchen, a _____, a _____ and a restroom. On the second _____, there are three _____ and two _____. There is also an _____ in our house. The _____ in our house is not big and has one _____ study. My parents' house also has a large _____ and _____.

سُوال ها:

۱. خانه مادر و پدر او چَند طَبقه است؟ (خونه‌ِ مامان باباى اون چَن طَبَقَس؟)

۲. خانه مادر و پدر او چَند تا اتاق خواب دارد؟ (. خونه‌ِ مامان باباى اون چَن تا اتاق خاب داره؟)

۳. در طَبَقه‌ِ اول چه اُتاق هایى هستند؟ (تو طَبَقه‌ِ آوّل چه اُتاقایى هستن؟)

۴. در طَبَقه‌ِ دوم چه اُتاق هایى هستند؟ (تو طَبَقه‌ِ دُوُم چه اُتاقایى هستن؟)

۵. اُتاق کار در طَبَقه‌ِ چَندُم است؟ (اُتاق کار تو طَبَقه‌ِ چَندُمه؟)

۶. حَیاطِ خانه‌ِ او بزرگ یا کوچک است؟ (حَیاطِ خونه‌ِ اون بزرگ یا کوچیکه؟)

4. Look at the image of the house and complete the description.

خانه من سه طبقه است. در طبقه اول دو تا اتاق هست. در سمت راست طبقه اول ____ است و در سمت چپ آشپزخانه ____ است. در طبقه دوم دو تا اتاق هست. وسط طبقه دوم ____ است. سمت راست راه پله ____ است و سمت چپ راه پله اتاق ____ است. طبقه سوم کوچک است و یک اتاق ____ دارد.

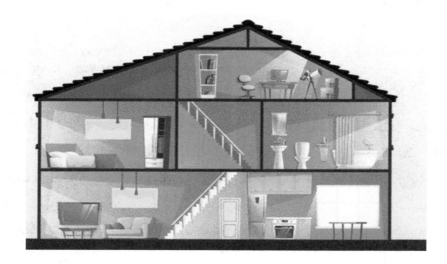

5. Listen to the description of the apartment and draw its outline . Write in Persian the names of the rooms in your drawing.

6. Prepare to describe in Persian your parents' house. Say how many floors it has and what rooms are on each floor. Say if it has an attic and basement and whether or not it has a yard. You can use the text from Exercise 3 above as an example.

7. Prepare to say these questions fluently in class. Be ready to answer the questions.

مَعمولا دَر چه اُتاقی غَذا میخوری؟ (مَعمولَن تو چه اُتاقی غَذا میخوری؟)

دَر چه اُتاقی میخوابی؟ (تو چه اُتاقی میخابی؟)

دَر چه اُتاقی کار میکُنی؟ (تو چه اُتاقی کار میکُنی؟)

ماشین را کجای خانه میگُذاری؟ (ماشینو کجای خونه میذاری؟)

در چه اُتاقی غَذا دُرُست میکُنی؟ (تو چه اُتاقی غَذا دُرُست میکُنی؟)

در چه اُتاقی از مِهمان ها پَذیرایی میکُنی؟ (تو چه اُتاقی از مِهمونا پَذیرایی میکُنی؟)

8. Complete the sentences with appropriate words from the glossary of this chapter.

۱. در ـــــــ ما یک تَختِ خواب، دو تا صَندَلی، و یک کِشُو هست.

۲. ما مَعمولا دَر آشپَزخانه صُبحانه میخوریم، وَلی دَر ـــــــ شام میخوریم.

۳. در ـــــــ ما یک یَخچال بزرگ، یک ماکروفِر، یک شیراب، و یک میز بزرگ با چهار تا صَندَلی هست.

۴. در اُتاقِ ـــــــ ما یک مُبل، سه تا صَندَلیِ راحَتی، یک میزِ کوچک، یک لوستر، یک قالیِ بزرگ و یک تِلِویزیون هست.

۵. در ـــــــ خانه ما دو ماشین جا میشود.

۶. خانهِ ما دو ـــــــ است. در ـــــــ اَوَل دو تا اُتاق خواب و در ـــــــ دُوُم سه تا اُتاق خواب هست.

۷. هوای شهر ما خیلی گرم است و همه خانه ها و ساختمان ها ـــــــ دارند.

9. Listen and complete the sentences with the words you hear. Translate the sentences into English.

۱. ـــــــ ما خِیلی برزگ است و یک ـــــــ مَخصوص هَم دارد.

۲. در طَبَقهِ اَوَل یک آشپَزخانه، یک هال، یک اُتاق خواب و یک ـــــــ هست. در ـــــــ دُوُم دو تا اُتاق خواب و یک حَمام هست.

۳. اُتاق من در خوابگاه دو تا ـــــــ بزرگ دارد.

۴. در شهر ما همهِ خانه ها و ساختِمان ها ـــــــ دارند.

۵. در ــــــ من یک ــــــ ، یک صَندَلی ، دو تا صَندَلی ــــــ ، یک ــــــ ، و یک میز هست. روی ــــــ یک تابلوی بزرگ و روی ــــــ یک آباژور هست. اُتاقِ من دو تا ــــــ بزرگ دارد. اُتاقِ من خیلی بزرگ نیست ولی خیلی ــــــ است.

10. Listen to Parisa and Neema who are talking about the furniture they need for their rooms. Complete the transcript according to what they say. Now, based on the items they mention, identify the three rooms that they have to furnish.

بَرای این اُتاق یک ــــــ ، دو تا صَندَلیِ راحَتی، و یک تِلِویزیونِ بُزُرگ لازِم داریم. و بَرای آن یکی اُتاق یک تَختِ خواب بُزُرگ و دو تا ــــــ ، و یک ــــــ لازِم داریم. دَر طَبَقهِ دُوُم هَم یک ــــــ ناهار خوریِ بُزُرگ و چَند تا صَندَلی ــــــ .

11. Take a photo of your room, classroom or office. Prepare to describe the room and its furniture in Persian. In class, you will be working with a classmate who will listen to your description and draw on paper your room with furniture in it. See how accurately you can help your classmate to draw the image that you describe. Make sure your description is not too complicated.

12. Look at the image below and ask your classmates about the position of various items in the room in relation to each other and to the walls and window.

13. Look at the two images and find differences. Say in Persian what are the differences and similarities between the two rooms.

14. Prepare to describe the location of each number in the table in relation to other numbers, for example, 3 is under 7, 12 is above 5 and so on. In class, you will be working with a classmate who will have the numbers as separate pieces of a puzzle, and you will have to help him/her to arrange the numbers in the correct order by describing the location of each number. For example, پونزدَه بالای شیشه، ده در سَمتِ راستِ شـونزدَهه

۱	۳	۷	۱۵
۱۶	•	۹	۶
۹	۴	۵	۸

15. Think of your dream house خانه رویایی ام (خونه‌ِ رویاییم). Think of how many floors it has, what rooms are on each floor, whether it has an attic, a basement, garage and so on. Think of the basic furniture items in the rooms. Prepare to describe this house to your classmate, so that s/he can draw the general outline of the house with the basic furniture pieces in it.

IN CLASS  دَر کِلاس

16. Once everyone has answered the questions about the parents' house from Homework 3 above, make one statement to compare your parents' house to the house of the narrator (راوی) in Homework 3. You can say what rooms both houses have, or what rooms one house has that the other does not have.

17. Ask a classmate a question about his or her current room, apartment or house at the university. Ask a question about the number of floors, rooms, parking, for example,

اُتاقِ تو در طَبَقهِ چَندُم است؟ (اُتاقِ تو در طَبَقهِ چَندُمه؟)

18. Look at the image of the house from Homework 2. Ask a classmate a question about the house, its floors and rooms, for example,

این خانه چَند تا اُتاق خواب دارد؟ (این خونه چَن تا اُتاق خاب داره؟)

19. Look around you and say in Persian who is on your right and who is on your left in the classroom, for example,

سَمتِ راستِ من تارا است و سَمتِ چَپِ من کامران است (سَمتِ راستِ من تاراه و سَمتِ چَپِ من کامرانه).

20. Think of your parents' house. Say in Persian what room is your favorite room in their house. Say on which floor that room is located and describe its location in relation to other rooms, for example,

اُتاقِ مُوردِ عَلاقهِ من در خانهِ مامان و بابایم اُتاق پَذیرایی است. اُتاقِ پَذیرایی آنها در طَبَقهِ اَوَل، سَمتِ راستِ اُتاق ناهارخوری و سَمتِ چَپِ اُتاق خوابِ کوچک است

(اُتاقِ مُوردِ عَلاقهِ من در خونهِ مامان و بابام اُتاق پَذیراییه. اُتاق پَذیراییِ اونها تو طَبَقهِ اَوَل، سَمتِ راستِ اُتاق ناهارخوری و سَمتِ چَپِ اُتاق خابِ کوچیکه)

21. You will work in groups of three. Two people will be speaking and the third person will be following directions. The two people will receive from the instructor a sheet with a complete floor plan of a house. The third person will receive several cards with one room of that same house on each card. The cards are to be arranged in correct order and position so as to reconstruct the floor plan of the house. The objective of the two speakers is to help the third classmate arrange the rooms in correct order and reconstruct the floor plan of the house featured on their sheet. Useful words:

در طَبقهِ اَوَل، سَمتِ راست ....، سَمتِ چپ ... ، وَسَطِ ....

Instructor, please refer to the appendix Instructor's Resources.

22. Now, look at the plan of the house that you have reconstructed, and make one statement in Persian about the number or location of rooms in that house. For example,

این خانه دو اُتاق خواب دارد (این خونه دو تا اُتاق خاب داره)، آشپَزخانه در طَبَقهِ اول است (آشپَزخونه تو طَبَقهِ اوله).

23. Now, pick a classmate and ask them one question in Persian about the floor plan of the house that you have reconstructed. Ask your question about the number or location of the rooms in the house. For example,

در طَبَقهِ دُوُم چَند تا اُتاق هست؟ (تو طَبَقه دُوُم چَن تا اُتاقه؟) چه اُتاقی سَمتِ راستِ پَذیرایی است؟ (چه اتاقی سَمتِ راستِ پَذیراییه؟) آشپَزخانه در طَبَقهِ چَندُم است؟ (آشپَزخونه تو طَبَقه چَندُمه؟)

24. Read these phrases aloud. Your instructor will give you feedback on pronunciation.

۶. روی دیوار (رو دیوار)	۱.دَر طَبَقهِ بالا
۷.حَمام (حَموم)	۲. زیرِ میز
۸. دَستشویی	۳. دَر وَسَطِ اُتاق
۹.مَحَلهِ آرام (مَحَلهِ آروم)	۴.هال
۱۰. جِلوی پَنجِره	۵.اُتاق خواب

25. Think of a person in class and describe his/her location in relation to other people in class. Do not name the person. Your classmates will listen to your description and guess who that person is. Use the words of location that you have learned, for example,

This person is sitting between Sara and Tom.

این شَخص بِینِ سارا و تام است (این شَخص بِینِ سارا و تامه).

26.   **Arrange the numbers.** You will be working in pairs. Your instructor will give you a table with Persian digits arranged in random order. Your conversation partner will receive those same numbers, but in the form of individual cards. Help your conversation partner to arrange his/her numbers in the exact same way that they are on your table. Your instructor will come to check the arrangement. Your partner will ask you about the position of a number in relation to the other numbers. You can also pick a number and describe its position in relation to the numbers that your partner has already arranged. Speak only in Persian. Use words of location in your sentences such as:

row	رَدیف	between	بِینِ
on the right of	سَمتِ راستِ	below	پایینِ
on the left of	سَمتِ چَپِ	above	بالایِ

Instructor please see the appendix Instructor's Resources.

27.   Ask your classmates the following questions in Persian. Think of your room at the university when you answer the questions. Construct your sentences according to standard sentence structure in Persian. The question word goes where the word to which it refers would usually go in a statement.

1	2	3
Subject	Object	Verb

(1)   Is your desk in front of a window or in front of a wall?
(2)   What is behind the desk?
(3)   Is the door on the right or to the left of the bed?
(4)   Is there a lamp on the desk?
(5)   Is there anything under the bed?

28. **Interior Designer.** You will be working with two other classmates. Two of you will be speaking, and the third person will be following directions. The two people will be interior designers and will tell the third person where to place the furniture. The two designers will get an image of a room with the furniture in it, while the third person will get the image of the same room but without furniture. You will have to communicate with each other in Persian, so that the person with the image of an empty room can draw the furniture pieces in the room according to the image with the furnished room.

Instructor, please see the appendix Instructor's Resources.

29. **Locate your state on the map.** You will be working with a classmate. Both of you will receive a map of the United States with some states missing from the map. The states missing from your map are different from those missing from the other classmate's map. Talk to your conversation partner, describe the location of your missing states in relations to other states that you see, and ask what states those are. Complete your map with the name of the states.

Instructor, please see the appendix Instructor's Resources.

30. 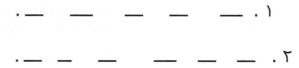 **Sentence charade**. You will receive a sentence written in Persian. Provide a definition for each word in your sentence to your classmate without saying the word. Your classmate will listen to you, try to guess the words and write down your exact sentence without seeing it. She/he will write the sentence by filling in the blanks, that is, your classmate knows how many words are in your sentence. Once you are done, switch roles. Your classmate has a sentence for you to guess.

Instructor, please see the appendix Instructor's Resources.

‫۱. ‫——   ——   ——   ——   ——.‬

‫۲. ‫—— — ——   ——   —   ——.‬

31. Read Sara's statements about her parents' house. Go over each statement and compare their house to your parents' house. You can use the words *am-mã* (but), and *ham* (also) to build your comparative sentences.

پدر و مادر سارا در لُس آنجِلِس زندگی میکنند، و پدر و مادر من در نیویورک زندگی میکنند.

خانه اشان بُزُرگ است (خونَشون بُزُرگه).

پدر و مادَرَم دَر سانفرانسیسکو زِندِگی میکُنَند (پدر و مادَرَم تو سانفرانسیسکو زِندِگی میکُنَن).

خانه اشان بُزُرگ است (خونه اشون بُزُرگه).

خانه اشان سه طَبَقه است (خونَشون سه طَبَقَس).

خانه اشان زیرزَمین نَدارد (خونَشون زیرزَمین نَداره).

خانه اشان زیرشیروانی دارد (خونَشون زیرشیروونی داره).

خانه اشان هَم راه پله هَم آسانسور دارد (خونَشون هَم راه پله هَم آسانسور داره).

خانه اشان پَنج تا اُتاق خواب دارد (خونَشون پَنج تا اُتاق خاب داره).

خانه اشان چَهار تا حَمام و یِک دَستشویی دارد (خونَشون چار تا حَموم و یه دَسشویی داره).

خانه اشان یک آشپَزخانه و یک اُتاقِ ناهارخوریِ بُزُرگ دارد (خونَشون یه آشپَزخونه و یه اُتاقِ ناهارخوریِ بُزُرگ داره).

خانه اشان پارکینگ دو ماشینی دارد (خونَشون پارکینگِ دو ماشینی داره).

خانه اشان حَیاطِ بُزُرگ دارد (خونَشون حَیاطِ بُزُرگ داره).

32. You will be working in groups. Write a short advertisement for a house on sale. Your instructor will assign to you a four- or three-bedroom house, or a two-bedroom apartment. Your objective is to come up with the rest of the description. Start by stating where your house is located. Then state how many floors, bedrooms and baths the house has; whether it has a dining room or only a kitchen; whether the rooms are large or small, whether the house has a yard, garage, and so on. Prepare to say your advertisement aloud in Persian.
  – Where
  – Floors
  – Rooms
  – What special features it has

33. **Guess that word.** The instructor will give you a list of five words related to a house and household items. Describe the words in Persian without naming the word. Your classmates will try to guess your words and write them down.

Instructor, please see the appendix Instructor's Resources.

GRAMMAR   دستورِ زَبان

How to express possession using possessive endings (suffixes)

Possessive endings are attached to the end of the word in order to indicate to whom the item described by that word belongs. Possessive endings can be attached to a noun or to a modifier.

In everyday colloquial speech, the use of possessive endings is widely preferred over the use of pronouns (من، تو، او). Thus, instead of saying بابای من /bãbã-yeh man/ *my dad*, a native speaker would say بابایم /bãbã-m/ *my dad*. The difference between the two ways of describing the possession is that the use of pronouns is an emphatic form and it is used when it is necessary to emphasize that *the dad* is *mine* as opposed to, or compared to *someone else's* dad.

Stacking

If you must add a possessive ending to a word, and that word is followed by modifiers, say the possessive ending at the end of the last modifier, for example,

my good friend /doos-teh khoob-**am**/ دوستِ جوبَم
my older brother /barã-dareh bo-zorg-am/ بَرادرِ بزرگَم

Pronunciation   Possessive endings are pronounced slightly differently, depending on whether they follow the final vowel or the final consonant of the word they describe.

Pronunciation of Possessive Endings		
after consonant	after a vowel	
doost-am	**bãbã-m**	my
doost-et	**bãbã-t**	your
doost-esh	**bãbã-sh**	her/his/its
doost-emoon	**bãbã-moon**	our
doost-etoon	**bãbã-toon**	Your (شما)
doost-eshoon	**bãbã-shoon**	Their

As you can see, when possessive endings follow the final consonant of the word, a vowel glide is pronounced between that final consonant of the word and the possessive ending so as to avoid pronouncing two consonants in a row.

You might have also noticed in the table above that the possessive endings are the first consonant letters of the pronouns to which they correspond. For example, the possessive ending م /m/ *my*, is the first consonant of the pronoun مَن /man/ that we use to say *my*. The possessive ending ت /t/ *your* is the first consonant of the pronoun تو /to/ that we use to say *your*. For the possessive ending ش /sh/ *his/her/its*, think of the formal pronoun ایشان /ee-shoon/ *he/she* and you will see the same pattern.

Spelling   Possessive endings are attached directly to the final consonant of the word.

When the possessive ending follows a word with a final vowel *ã* or *oo*, that possessive ending starts with the joined letter ی.

When the possessive ending follows a word with a final vowel *eh* or *ee*, that possessive ending starts with symbol ا. This separator ا is, sometimes, not used with plural endings, for example, خانه مان، دایی تان،

These separator letters ی and ا are written, but are not pronounced. Think of them as of the apostrophe written in the English phrases, *I'll*, *We'll* and so on. In those words, the apostrophe is not pronounced but is written for the purposes of clarification.

Spelling of Possessive Endings			
after the vowels ه and ی	after the vowels و and آ	After any consonant	
خانه ام	بابایم	دوستَم	My
خانه ات	دانشجویت	دوستِت	Your
دایی اش	بابایش	دوستِش	her/his/its
خانه امان	دانشجویمان	دوستِمان	Our
دایی اتان	بابایتان	دوستِتان	Your (pl./formal)
دایی اشان	دانشجویشان	دوستِشان	Their

HOMEWORK

تَکلیف

34.  Listen and read along. Next to each phrase, write in English the possessive (e.g., my, your, etc.) that you hear and see in Persian.

۱. آشپَزخانه ام

۲. دانِشجو یتان

۳. پَذیرایی امان

۴. میزِت

۵. اُتاق ها یش

35. Listen and for each word write in Persian the possessive ending that you hear. Write the English translation (with possessive) of each word.

۱. ماکروفِر

۲. دانِشگاه

۳. طَبَقه

۴. اُتاق

۵. هال

۶. آباژور

36. Prepare to read the following words with possessive endings in class. Read each word aloud several times until you can easily pronounce it.

۱. جایم (جام)، پِسَر عَمویم (پِسَر عَموم)، اُتاق خوابم، مَحَله ام (مَحَلَم)، صَندَلی ام (صَندَلیم)

۲. آشپَزخانه ات (آشپَزخونَت)، عَمویت (عَموت)، قالی ات (قالیت)، هَم خانه ات (هَم خونَت)، خوابگاهِت

۳. ماکروفِرِش، آیینه اش (آیینَش)، دَستشویی اش (دَستشوییش)، پِسرعمویش (پِسرعموش)، پوسترِ هایش (پوستِراش)

۴. زیرشیروانی امان (زیرشیروونیمون)، اُتاقِمان (اُتاقِمون)، مَحَله امان (مَحَلَمون)، عَکس هایمان (عَکسامون)

۵. اُتاقِ ناهارخوری اشان (اُتاقِ ناهارخوریشون)، میزِتان (میزِتون)، خانه اتان (خونَتون)، صَندَلی اتان (صَندَلیتون)

37. Insert either the separator ی or ا between the words and possessive endings as necessary. If no separator is necessary, connect the possessive ending to the word where possible.

۱. یَخچال   م

۲. دانشگاه مان

۳. پنجره ها ش

۴. صندلی ت

۵. آشپِزخانه تان

۶. دانشجو شان

38. Based on the English translation, complete the Persian phrases with possessive endings.

1. My room	اُتاق_____
2. Her chair	صَندَلی_____
3. Your (sing.) place	جا_____
4. Your (pl.) uncle	عَمو_____
5. Our neighborhood	مَحَله_____
6. Their kitchen	آشپِزخانه_____

39. Translate the following sentences into Persian. Use possessive endings to describe possession.
(1) How many bedrooms are there in your house? There are four bedrooms in my house.
(2) Is your dining room big? Yes, our dining room is very big.
(3) Is your AC working? No, our AC is not working.
(4) Is your neighborhood close to the university? Yes, my neighborhood is very close to the university.
(5) Is your university in New York City? No, my university is in Los Angeles.

(6) On which floor is your room? My room is on the third floor.

(7) Does your room in the dorm have heating? Yes, my dorm has heating.

40. 🔊 Listen and read along. Pay special attention to the pronunciation of the possessive endings. Prepare to read the text aloud in class. Practice before class to achieve fluency in reading.

سلام، اسمِ من میترا است. اهل نیویورک هستم و در دانشگاه نیویورک ریاضی میخوانم. خانواده ام در نیویورک زندگی میکنند. بابایم در نیویورک یک خانه و یک آپارتمان دارد. بابایم معمار است.

بابایم و عمویم در نیویورک یک شِرکتِ معماری دارند. شِرکَتِ معماری اشان بزرگ است. مامانم وکیل است. من یک برادر و یک خواهر دارم. خواهرم دانشجو است و رشته اش حقوق است. برادرم هم دانشجو است و معماری میخواند. من خانواده ام را خیلی دوست دارم.

41. 🔊 Listen to the audio presentation and answer the questions in Persian. Pay special attention to possessive endings. Give complete answers and use possessive endings in your answers.

سُوال ها:

۱. چه کسی زیست شِناسی میخواند؟

۲. دانشکده چه کسی عُلوم و هُنر است؟

۳. آیا کلاس فارسی ام صبح ها یا بَعد از ظُهر ها است؟

۴. آیا دوستم هَم اُتاقی ام است؟

۵. فوتبال ورزش مورد علاقه چه کسی است؟

42. A review presentation. Prepare a brief presentation on the topic of this chapter in the way that is applicable to you. Review the vocabulary and topic of this chapter and address the questions below in your presentation. Your presentation must be entirely in Persian. Your objective is to create a coherent and flowing narrative and speak continuously for a couple minutes in the target language. Be prepared to answer your classmates' questions about the topic of your presentation.

Describe the place and building where you currently live as a student at your university.

(1)   Do you live in a dorm or a rental apartment or a house
(آپارتمان، خانه اجاره ای)?

(2)   Where is your dorm or apartment located?

(3)   On what floor is your room?

(4)   How many floors are there in your building?

(5)   Is your room close to or far from your classes?

(6)   How do you usually get from your place to your classes (by bus, car, bicycle or on foot)?

(7)   What rooms does your apartment have?

(8)   Do you have a parking space?

(9)   Does your place have a yard?

(10) What furniture is there in your place?

(11) Do you have a roommate, or do you live alone?

(12) Do you like your place? Why?

IN CLASS   دَر کِلاس

45.   From each pair of the words with possessive endings pick the one that is spelled correctly. Explain why it should be spelled that way. Translate the word.

مُبل ام	مُبلم
طَبَقهِم	طَبَقه ام
دانشگاه ام	دانشگاهِم
حَمام ت	حَمامت
أتاق هام	أتاق هایم
پسرعمو ام	پسرعمویم
پنجرهِش	پنجره اش
خوابگاه ت	خوابگاهت
آیینهت	آیینه ات
صَندَلیم	صَندَلی ام

46. Say in Persian the following words with the possessive ending *my*.

After the consonants:

أتاق، آباژور، تَختِ خواب، مُبل، یَخچال

After the vowel ٥ (e):

مَحَله، پَنجِره، آیینه، پَرده، آشپَزخانه (آشپَزخونه)

After the vowel آ (ã):

بابا، ماشـین بابا، کلاس ها، جا، موها

After the vowel ی (ee):

صَندَلی، دوستِ ایرانی، دَستشویی (دَسشویی)، قالی، چای

After the vowel و (oo):

عَمو، دانِشجو، رو، پِسَر عَمو، جارو

47. Read Neema's statements. Go over every sentence and make a comparative statement referring to Neema and yourself. Use possessive endings to express possession. You will use two possessive endings (*my* and *his*) in this exercise.

نیما خانواده اش از تهران هسـتند ، و من خانواده ام از نیویورک هسـتند (نیما خونوادَش از تِهران هَسـتَن ، و من خونوادَم از نیویورک هَسـتَن).

His family is from Tehran, and **my** family is from New York.

نیما خواهَرِش دانِشـجو اسـت، و من خواهرم دانِشجو اسـت (خاهَرِش دانِشـجو ﻩ، خواهرم هم دانِشجو ﻩ).

His sister is a student; and my sister is a student.

اسـم من نیما اسـت.
فامیلی ام کاشانی اسـت (فامیلیم کاشـانیه).
خانواده ام از تهران هسـتند (خونوادَم از تِهران هَسـتَن).

بابایِم استاد است (بابام استاده).

مادَرَم استاد اسـت (مادَرَم استاده).

بَرادَرَم دانشجو است (بَرادَرَم دانشجو ه/هَست).

خواهَرَم دانش آموز دبیرستان است (خواهَرَم دانش آموز دبیرسـتونه).

رِشته ام تاریخ است (رِشتَم تاریخه).

بِهتَرین دوستَم دانشجو است (بِهتَرین دوستَم دانشِجو ه/هَست).

بِهتَرین دوستَم my best friend

48. You will be working in pairs. Ask your classmate the following questions. Pay special attention to the pronunciation of the possessive endings. Take note of your classmate's answers. Your instructor will ask you to share with the class some of the information you have received from your classmate. Use possessive endings in your statements. Be ready to answer the questions below. For this exercise you will use possessive suffixes *my* (first person singular), *your* (second person singular) and *her/his* (third person singular).

۱. اسـم بابایت چه است؟ (اسم بابات چیه؟)

۲. اسم مامانت چه ست؟ (اسمِ مامانِت چیه؟)

۳. خانه اشان کجا است؟ (خونَشون کجاس؟)

۴.اسـم برادِرت چه است؟ (اسم برادِرت چیه؟)

۵. شُغلِ عمویت چه است؟ (شُغلِ عَموت چیه؟)

۶. شُغلِ عَمه ات چه است؟ (شُغلِ عَمَت چیه؟)

۷. دایی ات کجا زندگی میکند؟ (داییت کُجا زِندِگی میکُنه؟)

۸. خاله ات کجا زندگی میکند؟ (خالَت کجا زندگی میکُنه؟)

49. You will be working in groups. Talk to two students in class. Ask them what items they have in their room. Tell them what you have in your room. Now, tell the class what similar items you have in your rooms and what the main differences between your rooms are. For this exercise, you will use verbs in first person singular, second person singular and third person singular. Use possessive endings to ask and answer the questions.

Now, ask your instructor what are the main items s/he has in the office. Use possessive endings in your questions.

50. You will be working in pairs. Talk to your classmate and describe your best friend to him/her. Provide basic information such as where the person is from, name, last name, age, occupation, major, college, likes and dislikes, and place of residence. Use possessive endings to describe possession. Your classmate might ask you additional questions for which s/he will use possessive endings (e.g., beh-tar-een doos-tet). Now switch roles. Take note of your classmate's answers. Your instructor will ask you to share something from your classmate's statements. Use possessive endings in your sentences. For this exercise, you will use possessive endings *my* (first person singular) and *her/his* (second person singular).

بِهتَرین دوسـتَم	بِهتَرین دوسـتِش
My best friend	His/her best friend

51. Bring a photo of your room and describe it to your classmates. To say the phrases such as, *my room*, *in my room*, use the possessive endings. You can also bring a photo of a different room (of a celebrity, famous designer, a famous family, an image of a random room online, etc.) and describe it to your class.

52. Your instructor will say the definitions of words pertaining to the vocabulary of this lesson. Circle the words that your instructor describes.

آشپَزخانه   اُتاقِ ناهارخوری   آباژور

پارکینگ   حَمام   یَخچال

آیینه   شـیراب   ماکروفِر

53. You will be working in pairs. Ask your classmate questions about his/her parents' house. Complete the table with the information you find out. Use possessive endings for the questions and answers, for example, پَذیرایی اشان بزرگ است (پَذیراییشـون بزرگه)؟.

بُزُرگ یا کوچک	
	Floors
	Bedrooms
	Baths
	Guest room
	Dining room
	Kitchen

54. Complete the sentences with the words from the list below.

شیراب، کامپیوترش، میز، آباژور، گوشه، کِشُو، پَنجِره، دیوار، وَسَطِ

۱.عَکس ها روی ـــــ هستند. ۲.تارا ـــــ را رُوشـن میکند. ۳. تارا ـــــ را توی کیف میگُذارد. ۴. آیینه بالای ـــــ است. ۵. آباژور روی ـــــ است. ۶. زیرِ تلویزیون ـــــ است. ۷. کِشُو در ـــــ اُتاق است. ۸. تَختِ خواب کِنارِ ـــــ است. ۹. تابلو روی ـــــ است. ۱۰. میزِ بزرگِ ناهارخوری ـــــ اُتاق است.

55. Think about yourself and complete the sentences in Persian. Use possessive endings in your sentences. Say your completed sentences in Persian.

When I come to my room, I put my bag _____
When I come to class, I put my _____, _____, and _____ on the table.
When I study in a library, I usually need _____, _____, _____, and _____ .
When I go to class, I put _____, _____, _____, and _____, in my bag.
I always bring _____ to class.
When I go to the library, I bring _____.

56. Look at the image. Say what items Parisa is still missing for this living room, for example,

پَریسا یک مُبل برای هال لازم دارد (پَریسا یه مُبل برای هال لازم داره).

57. Think of a few things that are characteristic to a specific room in a house. Name those things in Persian without saying which room you intend them for. Your classmates will try to guess what room you have in mind.

58. Your instructor will ask for two volunteers to stand in front of the board and face the classmates. Your instructor will then write on the board a Persian word for a random room. The objective of those sitting in class is to describe in Persian the purpose of the room written on the board without naming the room. The two people standing at the board will listen to the description and try to guess the word written on the board. The student who guesses the word first will sit down. The other student will remain at the board, and will be joined by another volunteer to try to guess the next word written by the instructor.

مَعمولا در این اُتاق میخوابی (مَمولَن تو این اُتاق میخوابی)

Instructor, please refer to the appendix Instructor's Resources.

59. You will be working in groups and will write two questions in Persian on the topic of house and furniture. You will give your questions to the group next to you in class. They will have to read your questions aloud and answer them. Prepare to do the same with questions you receive from another group.

60. Interview. The instructor will call on you to be interviewed by your class-mates. Each person in your class will ask you one question in Persian on one of the topics listed below. Once you have answered all questions, the instructor will appoint a different student to be interviewed, and this time you will get to ask one question on one of the given topics.

If your class is too big for this format of activity, your instructor might divide the class into groups of three, where you will find yourself with two other students who will inter-view you. Each of the two students will ask you in Persian at least three questions on the given topics.

Topics:

اسمِ و فامیل، کجایی، خانِواده، بِهتَرین دوسِت، دانِشگاه و کلاس، شغل،
کارهای روزانه، خانه و مَنزِل

LISTENING  شِنیداری

 Listen to Marjee as she describes her living room. Marjee will name the pieces of furniture that she has in the room and describe their location in relation to each other and in relation to the walls, windows or door.

Pre-listening. Write in Persian a list of the most common furniture pieces you expect to encounter in this audio presentation. Now, think of the verbs and phrases you would use to describe an object's location in a room (e.g., in the middle of ..., on the right of ..., next to the window, on the wall) and write them down in Persian. Read aloud the words you have written down, so that you hear your voice and recognize those words if you hear them in the audio.

Assignment. (1) Listen to Marjee's description of her room and write in Persian the list of furniture pieces and room décor items she names. (2) Now, listen to Marjee again and draw the plan of her room with furniture positioned in it according to her description.

Follow-up 1.   In class, look at the list of furniture pieces you have written down based on Marjee's description of her room. Now, pick an item from your list, pick a classmate and ask them where that item is located in Marjee's room. Compare their answer to where you positioned that item in the room when you drew the plan of Marjee's room.

Follow-up 2. Say one thing that you like about Marjee's room. Now, make one or two comparative statements about Marjee's room and your current room. You can talk about the furniture, windows and doors that the rooms have in common, or talk about furniture that is present in one room but is not present in the other room.

READING  خواندَنی

Prepare to read the following text fluently. Practice before coming to class. Read the text a few times aloud so you hear your voice.

Pre-reading. You will read Daryush's description of his house in the city of Lahijan in Iran. Think of the most common words that you might encounter in such an exercise. Write those words down so you can see them. If they are nouns, think of the verbs that might go with them in such an exercise. If the words you wrote are verbs, think of nouns that might go with them in the given context. Read the words you have written down, so you can visually identify them when you encounter them in the exercise.

That's why, for this very reason	به هَمین دَلیل	North	شُمال
Is famous for tea growing	به چایکاری مَعروف است	Ground floor	طَبَقهِ هَمکَف
Tea factory	کارخانهِ چایسازی	Sink, wash-stand	روشویی
Sugar	شِکَر	Beautiful	زیبا
Saffron rock candy	نَباتِ زَعفِرانی	With lush greenery/ vegetation	سَرسَبز

خانهِ ما در لاهیجان

سلام، اِسمِ من داریوش است. در شَهرِ لاهیجان در شُمالِ ایران زندگی میکُنَم. من هجده ساله هستم و در خانهِ مامان و بابایم در لاهیجان زندگی میکنم. یک بَرادَر و یک خواهَر دارَم.

خانهِ ما سه طَبَقه است. در طَبَقهِ هَمکَف یک اُتاق خواب، یک پَذیرایی، یک آشپَزخانه، یک دَستشویی و یک حَمام داریم. پدر و مادرم در این طَبَقه زندگی میکنند. طَبَقهِ اَوَل دو تا اُتاق خواب، یه آشپَزخانه، یه دَستشویی، یه حَمام و یک روشویی دارد. من و برادَرَم و خواهَرَم در این طَبَقه زندگی میکنیم. من و بَرادَرَم یک اُتاق خواب بَرای خودِمان داریم و خواهَرَم یک اُتاق خوابِ دیگر بَرای خودِش دارد.

طَبَقهِ بالا زیرشیروانی است. زیرشیروانیِ خانهِ ما بُزُرگ است و یک اُتاق خوابِ کوچک، یک هال، یک دَستشویی و حَمام دارد. خانهِ ما حَیاطِ بُزُرگ دارد. خانهِ ما خیلی زیبا و راحَت است. من خانه امان را خِیلی دوست دارم. شَهرِ ما لاهیجان هم خیلی زیبا و سَرسَبز است. به هَمین دَلیل ، من لاهیجان را خیلی دوست دارم. لاهیجان به چایکاری مَعروف است. لاهیجان جای اَوَلین کارخانهِ چایسازی در ایران بود. من چای خیلی دوست دارم و هر روز چای میخورم. معمولا با شِکَر یا نَباتِ زَعفِرانی چای میخورم.

Follow-up 1. Prepare for your classmates two questions in Persian about the excerpt. Use a possessive ending in each sentence.

Follow-up 2. Answer these questions in Persian.

۱. به نَظَرِ شُما، آیا خانه‌ی پِدَرومادَرِ داریوش راحَت است؟

۲. به نَظَرِ شُما، داریوش چِرا خانه‌ی پِدَرومادَرِش را خیلی دوست دارد؟

Follow-up 3. Make two statements. Say one thing that your parents' house has in common with Daryush's parents' house, and then another thing that makes the two houses different.

Follow-up 4. Look through the list of rooms in Daryush's parents' house. Name the rooms that both Daryush's house and an average house in your country would have. Name the rooms or amenities from Daryush's description that an average house in your country would not normally have.

Follow-up 5.  You will be working in groups to create a brief dialogue. Daryush's parents' house is on sale. Create and perform a conversation between a real estate agent and clients. Discuss what the clients are looking for and what the house has to offer in terms of the number and type of rooms, number of floors and the size of a family that the house can accommodate.

real estate agent بُنگاهی، مُشاوِرِ آملاک

TRANSLATION   تَرجُمه

Translate the following passage into Persian. Use possessive endings to describe possession.

My Parents' house in New York

Hello, my name is Sam. I live in New York. I am 18 years old. I have one brother and one sister. I live in my parents' house. Our house has two floors. Our house also has a basement. On the first floor, there is an office, a dining room, kitchen and a bathroom. We usually eat breakfast in the kitchen and eat dinner in the dining room. When we have guests, we always eat in the dining room. On the second floor, there are four bedrooms. One bedroom is for my parents. Their bedroom has a bathroom. My brother has his own bedroom and I have my own bedroom. And, the fourth bedroom is for my sister. In the hallway of the second floor, there is a bathroom. That bathroom is for my brother, my sister and myself. The basement in our house is big. There is a big TV, two couches, and several armchairs in the basement. There is also a ping-pong table in the basement. Our laundry room is also in the basement. Our house also has a garage. Our garage holds two cars. There is a large yard in front and behind the house. I like our house very much!

WRITING  اِنشا

You will be hosting a foreign exchange student at your parents' house. Write (at least 150 words) a description of your house for your guest. Mention which places in the house are your favorite places, describe for the guest the room where s/he will be staying.

فَصلِ هَفتُم
Chapter 7

زادگاهَم
My Hometown and Country

View of North Tehran with the Milad Tower and Alborz mountains in the backdrop.

Function Describing the landscape and basic geographical features of your country, talking about your hometown. Key verbs: *to be located/situated, to border, to be similar, to differ*.

Listening Neeloo talks about her home country.

Reading Letter from your pen pal Roya about her hometown Tehran.

Structures How to make words plural (stressed ending *ã*).

211

Listen, read along, and try to imitate the native speaker's pronunciation. Repeat each word a few times aloud until you can easily pronounce it.

Town and Country			
Square, plaza	مِیدان (میدون)	Country	کِشوَر
Bridge	پُل	State (in the USA)	اِیالَت، آیالَت
Park (green area)	پارک	*ostan*, i.e., a province (an administrative unit in Iran)	اُستان
Tree	دِرَخت	Capital city	پایتَخت
Museum	موزه	Home town	(شَهرِ) زادگاه
Hotel	هُتِل	Village	روستا
Luxury, upscale restaurant	رستورانِ لوکس	Neighborhood	مَحَله
Center of the city, downtown	مَرکَزِ شَهر	Street	خیابان (خیابون)
Places of interest, places to see	جاهای دیدَنی	Alley	کوچه
Tourist attractions	جَذابه های توریستی/ گَردِشگَری	Crowded	شُلوغ (شُلوغ)
Population	جَمعیَت	Not crowded	خَلوَت
Area	مَساحَت	Calm, peaceful, quiet	آرام (آروم)
A view	مَنظَره	Clean	تَمیز
For the sake of …, because of the …	به خاطِرِ …	Highway, expressway	بُزُرگراه
Metropolitan area, metropolis	کَلان شَهر	Sidewalk	پیاده رُو

Landscape			
Mountain range	رِشـتـه کوه	Persian Gulf	خَلیجِ فارس
Sea	دَریا	Atlantic Ocean	أُقیانوسِ أَطلَس
Lake	دَریاچه	Pacific Ocean	أُقیانوسِ آرام
River	رود	Forest	جَنگَل
Desert	کَویر		

Places	
North America, Central America, South America	آمریکای شُمالی، آمریکای مَرکَزی، آمریکای جنوبی (جونوبی)
Asia	آسیا
Europe	أُروپا (اوروپا)
Middle East	خاوَرِ میانه
Africa	آفریقا، اِفریقا
Islamic Republic of Iran	جُمهوری اِسلامی ایران
United States of America	اِیالاتِ مُتَّحِدهِ آمریکا
Midwest (in the United States)	غَربِ میانه
In the north of the country	دَر شُمالِ کِشوَر
On the East/West coast	دَر ساحِلِ شَرقی/ غَربی

Cityscape	
Narrow alleys	کوچه های باریک
Wide streets	خیابان های عَریض (خیابوناى عَریض)
Tall buildings	ساختِمان های بلند (ساختِمونای بُلَند)
Tower	بُرج
Modern buildings	ساختِمان های مُدِرن (ساختِمونای مُدِرن)
Old buildings	ساختِمان های قَدیمی (ساختِمونای قَدیمی)

213

Cityscape	
Sister city	شَهرِ خواهَر خوانده
Tehran has heavy traffic	تِهران تِرافیکِ سَنگین دارد (تِهران تِرافیکِ سَنگین داره)

Directions	
North, northern	شُمال، شُمالی
South, southern	جنوب (جونوب)، جنوبی (جونوبی)
East, eastern	شَرق، شَرقی
West, western	غَرب ، غَربی
Northeast, northwest	شُمالِ شَرقی ، شُمالِ غَربی
Southeast, southwest	جنوبِ شَرقی (جونوبِ شَرقی)، جنوبِ غَربی (جونوبِ غَربی)

Verbs	
America borders the ...	آمریکا با ... مَرز دارد (آمریکا با ... مَرز داره)
It is similar to the ...	آن شَبیهِ ... است (اون شَبیهِ ... هست)
They are like us	آنها مِثلِ ما هَستَند (اونها مِثلِ ما هَستَن)
Is located	قَرار دارد (قَرار داره)
Differs from ...	با ... فَرق دارد (با ... فَرق داره)

HOMEWORK

تَکلیف

1. Complete the sentences with the relevant information.

۱. دانشگاه ما در شَهرِ ـــــ قَرار دارد. ۲. کِشوَرِ آمریکا ـــــ تا اِیالَت دارد.
۳. من در خیابانِ ـــــ زندگی میکنم. ۴. اسم مِیدانِ بزرگ در دانشگاهِ ما ـــــ
است. ۵. پُلِ جورج واشینگتن در شَهرِ ـــــ قَرار دارد. ۶. ـــــ پایتَختِ کِشوَرِ ایران

است. ۷. جَمعیَتِ کِشوَرِ ایران ـــــــ میلیون نَفَر است. ۹. خیابانِ ـــــــ در دانشگاه ما مَعمولا شُلوغ است. ۱۰. مَحَلِهِ ـــــــ در شُمالِ شَهرِ نیویورک قَرار دارد.

2. 🔊 Listen and read along. Fill in the blanks with the words you hear. Translate the sentences to English.

۱. تهران در ـــــــ ایران قَرار دارد. ۲.تهران ـــــــ ایران است. ۳. من در یک ـــــــ آرام در شُمالِ تهران زندگی میکنم. ۴. تهران ـــــــ های مدرن زیادی دارد. ۵. خیابان های مَرکَزیِ تِهران معمولا خیلی ـــــــ هستند.

3. 🔊 Prepare to answer the following questions about your hometown. Practice before class and prepare to say your sentences fluently. In class, everyone will take turns to answer each question so as to give everybody an equal opportunity to speak in the target language.

۱. آهلِ چه شَهری هَستید؟

۲. شَهرِتان چَند نَفَر جَمعیَت دارد؟ (شَهرتون چَن نَفَر جَمعیَت داره؟)

۳. آهلِ چه مَحَله ای دَر شَهرِتان هَستید؟ (آهلِ چه مَحَله ای تو شَهرِتون هَستین؟)

۴. مَحَله اتان آرام یا شُلوغ است؟ (مَحَلَتون آروم یا شولوغه؟)

۵. مَحَله اتان کجای شَهر قَرار دارد؟ (مَحَلَتون کجای شَهر قَرار داره؟)

۶. شَهرِتان در چه ایالَتی قَرار دارد؟ (شَهرتون در چه ایالَتی قَرار داره؟)

۷. شَهرِتان کجای آن ایالَت قَرار دارد؟ (شَهرتون کجای اون ایالَت قَرار داره؟)

۸. آیا شَهرِتان مَرکَزِ آن ایالَت است؟ (شَهرتون مَرکَزِ اون ایالَته؟)

۹. آیا شَهرِ زادگاهِتان را دوست دارید؟ چرا؟ (شَهرِ زادگاهِتونو دوست دارید؟ چرا؟)

IN CLASS   دَر کِلاس

4. Using the given words, say sentences in Persian about your hometown.

۱. زادگاه / اِیالَت / قَرار دارد (قَرار داره)

۲. اِیالَتم / کِشوَرَم / شُمال، جنوب (جونوب)، غَرب، شَرق/ قَرار دارد (قَرار داره)

۳. زادگاه / شَهر / بزرگ

۴. زادگاه / مَرکَز / اِیالَت

۵. جَمعیَت / شَهرَم

5. You will be working in groups of three. Talk to your group mates and ask them the following questions in Persian. Be ready to answer the same questions. Before your start the drill, you will go over the questions together with your instructor to make sure that the translations of the sentences are correct.

(1) What is the name of your home state? (2) What is the capital of your state? (3) Is it a big state? (4) What is the population of your state? (5) Is there a big university or college in your state? (6) Where in the United States is your state located?

GRAMMAR   دَستورِ زَبان

PLURAL MARKER ها HÃ/Ã

To make the plural form of any Persian word, simply say *ã* at the end of it. Say *hã* if the word ends in a vowel. This plural ending *ãlhã* can be added to all and any words in Persian that need to be plural. The plural marker is stressed and is pronounced together with the word as if it were a part of that word. For example,

keshvar – keshvar**ã** (countries)

ãmreekãee – ãmreekãee**hã**/ãmreekãee**ã** (Americans)

kãlã – kãlã-**hã** (products)

am-oo – am-oo**hã** (uncles)

koocheh- koocheh-**hã** (alleys)

rãh – rãh- **h**ã (roads)

You can use the plural ending with nouns, adjectives and adverbs:

polã (bridges)

yekee az oon sefeedã (one of those white ones)

bazee vaqtã (sometimes)

In composite words, the plural ending is pronounced at the end of the last word, for example,

دوسْت دُختَرها

پِدرو مادَرها

Spelling of the plural marker ã/hã   This plural marker is always spelled ها. It can be written together or separately from the word:

خیابانها – خیابان ها، ایرانیها – ایرانی ها

It is written separately if the word ends with the letter ه, for example,

کوچه ها، موزه ها، راه ها

In the handwritten text, it is commonly written together with the word, while in the printed text is it customary to type it separately for the sake of clarity.

Remember that if a word is accompanied by a number, in Persian that word is used in singular, for example,

twenty states – بیست اِیالَت   two cities – دو شَهر

Remember that even though English generic nouns are used in plural, Persian generic nouns are used in singular, for example, I love books. کِتاب خِیلی دوسْت دارَم.

HOMEWORK

تَکلیف

6. (a) Scan through the following words and identify the words in plural.

شَهر، شَهرها، کِشوَر، کِشوَرها، خیابان، خیابان ها، کوچه، کوچه ها، مَحَله، مَحَله ها، راه، راه ها، جا، جاها، روستا، روستاها، ایرانی، ایرانی ها، آمریکایی، آمریکایی ها.

6. (b)  Listen and repeat. Prepare to pronounce the following words in plural in class:

۱. پیاده رُو ها. ۲. مَرزها. ۳. مَحَله ها. ۴. ساختِمان ها. ۵. بُزُرگ راه ها. ۶. اِیالَت ها. ۷. مِیدان های بُزُرگ. ۸. خیابان های بُلَند. ۹. آمریکایی ها. ۱۰. ایرانی ها. ۱۱. کوچه های باریک. ۱۲. خیابان های عَریض. ۱۳. موها. ۱۴. پارک های قَشَنگ. ۱۵. مَحَله های آرام. ۱۶. جاهای دیدَنی. ۱۷. راه ها. ۱۸. شَهرهایی. ۱۹. جاهایی. ۲۰. کِشوَرهایی.

7. For each number, listen and write whether you hear the singular or plural.

۹.   ۸.   ۷.   ۶.   ۵.   ۴.   ۳.   ۲.   ۱.
۱۸.   ۱۷.   ۱۶.   ۱۵.   ۱۴.   ۱۳.   ۱۲.   ۱۱.   ۱۰.

8. Write in Persian the plural of the following words:

(1) City. (2) Country. (3) Square, plaza. (4) Neighborhood. (5) Village. (6) Street. (7) Bridge. (8) Hotel. (9) Restaurant. (10) Museum.

9. Listen to the audio presentation and read along the following questions. Prepare to answer these questions fluently in class.

۱. چه کِشوَرهایی در آمریکای شُمالی قَرار دارَند؟
(چه کِشوَرایی تو آمریکای شُمالی قَرار دارَن؟)

218

۲. چه کِشوَرهایی در آمریکای جنوبی قَرار دارَند؟ (چه کِشوَرایی تو آمریکای جونوبی قَرار دارَن؟)

۳. چه کِشوَرهایی در آمریکای مَرکَزی قَرار دارَند؟ (چه کِشوَرایی تو آمریکای مَرکَزی قَرار دارَن؟)

۴. چه اِیالَت هایی در غَربِ میانهِ آمریکا قَرار دارَند؟ (چه اِیالَتایی تو غَربِ میانهِ آمریکا قَرار دارَن؟)

۵. اِیالاتِ مُتَحِده در شُمال با چه کِشوَری مَرز دارد؟ (اِیالاتِ مُتَحِده تو شُمال با چه کِشوَری مَرز داره؟)

۶. اِیالاتِ مُتَحِده در جنوب با چه کِشوَری مَرز دارد؟ (اِیالاتِ مُتَحِده تو جونوب با چه کِشوَری مَرز داره؟)

۷. چه اِیالَت های بزرگی در ساحِلِ غَربیِ آمریکا قَرار دارَند؟ (چه اِیالَتای بزرگی در ساحِلِ غَربیِ آمریکا قَرار دارَن؟)

۸. چه اِیالَت های بزرگی در ساحِلِ شَرقیِ آمریکا قَرار دارَند؟ (چه اِیالَتای بزرگی در ساحِلِ شَرقیِ آمریکا قَرار دارَن؟)

۹. چه دانِشگاه های بزرگی در ساحِلِ غَربیِ آمریکا قَرار دارَند؟ (چه دانِشگاه های بزرگی در ساحِلِ غَربیِ آمریکا قَرار دارَن؟)

۰۱. چه دانِشگاه های بزرگی در ساحِلِ شَرقیِ آمریکا قَرار دارَند؟ (چه دانِشگاه های بزرگی در ساحِلِ شَرقیِ آمریکا قَرار دارَن؟)

10. 🔊 Listen to Roya as she describes her neighborhood in Tehran. Complete the transcript with missing words in the speech that you hear. Prepare to answer the questions in class.

اسمِ من رویا است. اهل تهران هستم. در تهران به دنیا آمدم و بزرگ شدم. من تهران را خیلی دوست دارم.خانواده ام در یک _____ بزرگ در _____ تهران زندگی میکنند. من تهران و محله امان را خیلی دوست دارم. به نظرم، _____ ام محلهِ خیلی خوبی است چون _____ هایش خیلی _____ و آرام و _____ هایش ئُو و راحَت هستند. یک پارکِ بزرگ و قَشَنگی هم در _____ ام هست.آن _____ نَزدیکِ مَنزِلمان است، و من تَقریبا هر روز بَعد از ظُهر برای قَدَم زَدَن به آن _____ میروم.من قَدَم زَدَن توی آن _____ را خیلی دوست دارم.

۱. آپارِتمانِ خانِواده‌ِ رویا کُجای تهران قَرار دارد؟ (آپارتمانِ خونِواده‌ِ رویا کُجای تهران قَرار داره؟)

۲. مَحَله اشان ساختِمان های نُو یا قَدیمی دارد؟ (مَحَلَشون ساختِمونای نُو یا قَدیمی داره؟)

۳. رویا در یک مَحَله‌ِ شُلوغ یا آرام زندگی میکند؟ (رویا تو یه مَحَله‌ِ شولوغ یا آروم زندگی میکنه؟)

۴. چِرا رویا این مَحَله را خیلی دوست دارد؟ (چِرا رویا این مَحَله رو خیلی دوست داره؟)

11. Prepare for your classmates a brief presentation about your hometown. Make at least four points about your hometown: (1) location, (2) population, (3) appearance (type of streets, building, etc.), (4) points of interest, that is, whether your hometown has universities, museums, tourist attractions, and so on.

12. A review presentation. Prepare a brief presentation on the topic of this chapter in the way that is applicable to you. Review the vocabulary and topic of this chapter and address the questions below in your presentation. Your presentation must be entirely in Persian. Your objective is to create a coherent and flowing narrative and speak continuously for a couple minutes in the target language. Be prepared to answer your classmates' questions about the topic of your presentation.

 (1) Which is your home country?
 (2) Where is it located (North America, Europe, Asia, Africa, etc.)?
 (3) What is the capital city of your country?
 (4) In which city in your country were you born?
 (5) How many provinces or states does your country have?
 (6) What is the population of your country?
 (7) What are the major mountain ranges in your country?
 (8) What are the major rivers in your country?
 (9) Does your country have a sea or ocean coastline?
(10) What other countries neighbor your country in the north, south, east and west?

IN CLASS   دَر کِلاس

13. Close your textbooks. Your instructor will ask you to write on the board the plural form of one of the words from the list below. Some of the words in the list, have the connector glide *eleh* following the plural ending, while others have *leel* یی following the plural ending. Listen carefully and make sure to spell those correctly.

۱. راه. ۲. زادگاه. ۳.موزه. ۴. کوچه. ۵. کِشوَر. ۶. کِشوَرهایی. ۷. اِیالَت هایی.۸ . جاهایی. ۹. جاهای. ۰۱. کِشوَرهای. ۱۱. شَهرهای. ۱۲. پیاده رو. ۱۳. دانِشجو ۱۴. دانِشگاه.

14. You will be working with a classmate. Write in Persian the following words and phrases. After everyone in class is done writing, your instructor will call on random people in class to write the words on the board in order to compare notes.

(1) Iranians. (2) Big cities. (3) Old villages. (4) Modern buildings. (5) My good friends. (6) My favorite places. (7) Large rivers of Iran. (8) Crowded streets of Tehran. (9) My Iranian friends. (10) Northern states of America.

15. Identify the plural form in each pair of the words. Write and say the following words with the possessive ending *its*. Remember that in writing, when the possessive ending follows a word with the final vowels *ã* or *oo*, that possessive ending starts with the silent letter ک, and when the possessive ending follows a word with the final vowels *eh* or *ee*, that possessive ending starts with the silent symbol آ.

شَهر ها	شَهر
خیابان ها	خیابان
پیاده رُو ها	پیاده رُو
دانِشجو ها	دانِشجو
دایی ها	دایی
هَم کِلاسی ها	هَم کِلاسی
مَحَله ها	مَحَله
کوچه ها	کوچه
جاها	جا
راه ها	راه

16. Talk to classmates and ask them the following questions about their hometowns:

۱. اسم شَهرِ زادگاهِتان چه است؟ (اسم شَهرِ زادگاهِتون چیه؟)

۲. شَهرِتان بُزُرگ یا کوچِک است؟ (شَهرِتون بُزرگه یا کوچیکه؟)

۳. آیا شَهرِتان جاهای دیدَنی زیادی دارد؟ (شَهرِتون جاهای دیدَنی زیادی داره؟)

۴.آیا شَهرِتان پارک های زیادی دارد؟ (شَهرِتون پارکای زیادی داره؟)

۵.آیا شَهرِتان رِستوران های لوکس ِ زیادی دارد؟ (شَهرِتون رِستورانای لوکس ِ زیادی داره؟)

۶. آیا شَهرِتان هُتِل های زیادی دارد؟ (شَهرِتون هُتِلای زیادی داره؟)

۷. خیابان های شَهرِتان معمولا شُلوغ یا خَلوَت هستند؟ (خیابوناى شَهرِتون معمولَن شولوغ یا خَلوَت هستن؟)

۸. آیا خیابان های مَرکَزِ شَهرِتان باریک یا عَریض هستند؟ (خیابوناى مَرکَزِ شَهرِتون باریک یا عَریض هستن؟)

۹. آیا بیشتَرِ ساختِمان های شَهرِتان قَدیمی یا مُدِرن هستند؟ (بیشتَرِ ساختِمونای شَهرِتون قَدیمی یا مُدِرن هستن؟)

۱۰. آیا شَهرِتان بُرج ها و ساختِمان های بلند ِ زیادی دارد؟ (. شَهرِتون بُرجا و ساختِمونای بلند ِ زیادی داره؟)

۱۱. آیا معمولا در خیابان های شَهرِتان تِرافیک سَنگین است؟ (معمولَن در خیابوناى شَهرِتون تِرافیک سَنگینه؟)

17. Now, using the information you have collected, report to the class whose hometown appears similar to yours, for example,

شَهرِش شَبیه ِ شَهرَم است بَرای اینکه شَهرِش رِستوران های لوکس ِ زیادی دارد (شَهرِش شَبیه ِ شَهرَمه بَرای اینکه شَهرِش رِستورانای لوکس ِ زیادی داره).

18. Each student in class will say which town they are from, in which state their town is located and in which country and in what part of the world that is.

19. Working in pairs or groups, search for the needed information online and complete the chart below. Prepare to present your findings to the class in Persian. Complete one column of the table with data about Iran. Pick any other country in the world and compare it to Iran by completing the other column of the table.

		ایران
	پایتَخت	

	جَمعیَت	
	مُوقِعیَت	
	با چه کِشوَرهایی مَرز دارد؟	
	چند تا ایالت/ اُستان دارد؟	
	ایالت/ اُستان های بزرگ	
	شَهر های بزرگ	

20. Pick a classmate and ask him/ her one question from the list below. Continue taking turns until the class has exhausted the list of questions.

۱. چه کِشوَرهایی در آمریکای شُمالی قَرار دارند؟ (چه کِشوَرایی در آمریکای شُمالی قَرار دارن؟)

۲. چه کِشوَرهایی در آمریکای جنوبی قَرار دارند؟ (چه کِشوَرایی در آمریکای جونوبی قَرار دارن؟)

۳. چه کِشوَرهایی در آمریکای مَرکَزی قَرار دارند؟ (چه کِشوَرایی در آمریکای مَرکَزی قَرار دارن؟)

۴. چه اِیالَت هایی در غَربِ میانهِ آمریکا قَرار دارند؟ (چه اِیالَتایی در غَربِ میانهِ آمریکا قَرار دارن؟)

۵. ایالاتِ مُتَحِده در شُمال با چه کِشوَری مَرز دارد؟ (ایالاتِ مُتَحِده در شُمال با چه کِشوَری مَرز داره؟)

۶. ایالاتِ مُتَحِده در جنوب با چه کِشوَری مَرز دارد؟ (ایالاتِ مُتَحِده در جونوب با چه کِشوَری مَرز داره؟)

۷. چه اِیالَت های بزرگی در ساحِلِ غَربی قَرار دارند؟ (چه اِیالَتای بزرگی در ساحِلِ غَربی قَرار دارن؟)

۸. چه اِیالَت های بزرگی در ساحِلِ شَرقی قَرار دارند؟ (چه اِیالَتای بزرگی در ساحِلِ شَرقی قَرار دارن؟)

۹. چه دانِشگاه های بزرگی در ساحِلِ غَربی قَرار دارند؟ (چه دانِشگاه های بزرگی در ساحِلِ غَربی قَرار دارن؟)

۱۰. چه دانِشگاه های بزرگی در ساحِلِ شَرقی قَرار دارند؟ (چه دانِشگاه های بزرگی در ساحِلِ شَرقی قَرار دارن؟)

۱۰. دانشگاهِتان کجای آمریکا قَرار دارد؟ (دانشگاهِتون کجای آمریکا قَرار داره؟)

۱۱. دانشگاهِتان در چه شَهری قَرار دارد؟ (دانشگاهِتون در چه شَهری قَرار داره؟)

۱۲. آیا آن شَهر مَرکَزِ ایالَت است؟ (اون شَهر مَرکَزِ ایالَته؟)

۱۳. شما اَهلِ چه شَهری در آمریکا هستید؟ (شما اَهلِ چی شَهری تو آمریکا هستین؟)

۱۴. شَهرِتان در چه اِیالَتی قَرار دارد؟ (شَهرِتون در چه اِیالَتی قَرار داره؟)

۱۵. اِیالَتِتان کجای آمریکا است؟ (اِیالَتِتون کجای آمریکاس؟)

21. You will be working in pairs. Your instructor will give you a map of the United States. Your map will be missing the names of several states on it. Those names are present on the map of your conversation partner. Describe to your partner the location of the states whose names are missing from your map, so s/he can tell you the names. Complete your map and help your classmate to complete his/her map. Speak only in Persian and use the words *north*, *south*, *west*, *east*, *between* and so on. For example,

این اِیالَت شُمالِ تگزاس و غَربِ آرکانزاس قَرار دارد (این اِیالَت شُمالِ تگزاس و غَربِ آرکانزاس قَرار داره).

This state is to the north of Texas and west of Arkansas.

Instructor, please see the appendix Instructor's Resources.

22. Look at this map of Iran. It shows Iran's neighbors and some of Iran's cities. Pick a classmate and ask them a question about the location of Iran, its provinces, neighbors and bodies of water. Use the words north, south, and so on, in your questions and answers. Your instructor might ask couple of sample questions to start off the activity and to demonstrate an example. You can use places on the map as a reference to describe the location of other places, for example,

۱. چه دَریایی در شُمالِ ایران قَرار دارد؟ (چه دَریایی تو شُمالِ ایران قَرار داره؟)

۲. چه اُستانی در شَرقِ ایران و در شُمالِ اُستانِ خُراسانِ جنوبی، قَرار دارد؟
(چه اُستانی تو شَرقِ ایران و تو شُمالِ اُستانِ خُراسانِ جونوبی، قَرار داره؟)

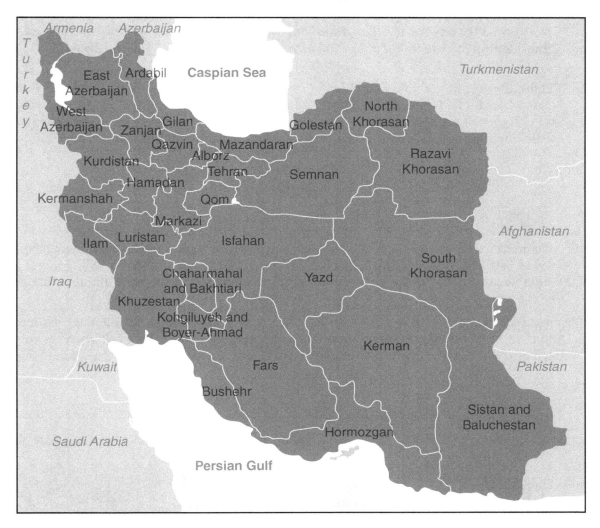

23. Talk to all your classmates and find people who have something in common with you in terms of geography, that is, they are from the same state, town or part of the country (East Coast, West Coast, Midwest, etc.) or the same country. Introduce those individuals to class and say where they are from.

E.g., (اون مِثلِ مَن آهلِ نیویورکه). او مِثلِ مَن آهلِ نیویورک است

24. You will work in pairs. Make at least four descriptive statements about the city in which your university is located. Describe: (1) the city's location, (2) the city's population or size, (3) appearance, in other words, the streets, the type of buildings in the city, and so on, (4) what the city has to offer (restaurants, museums, large malls, luxury hotels, parks, libraries, tourist attractions, etc.). Add anything else you think is noteworthy.

25. Think of your home state and tell your class about its geography. Start by telling your class where in the United States your state is located and what city is the capital of your state. Now, tell your class what rivers, lakes, mountain ranges, deserts or ocean coastline there might be in your home state and describe their location in the state.

26. Interview. The instructor will call on you to be interviewed by your classmates. Each person in your class will ask you one question in Persian on one of the topics listed below. Once you have answered all questions, the instructor will appoint a different student to be interviewed, and this time you will get to ask one question on one of the given topics.

If your class is too big for this format of activity, your instructor might divide the class into groups of three, where you will find yourself with two other students who will interview you. Each of the two students will ask you in Persian at least three questions on the given topics.

Topics:

اسـم و فامیل، کجایی، خانِواده، بِهتَرین دوسـت، دانِشـگاه و کلاس، شُـغل،
کارهای روزانه، خانه و مَنزِل ، شَـهر و کِشـوَر

LISTENING   شِنیداری

Listen and read along as Neeloofar describes her country. She will talk about the geography, landscape and countries that border her homeland.

Pre-listening 1. Write in Persian a list of the most common words related to landscape. Now, think of the words and phrases related to cardinal directions (e.g., north, in the west of …) and write them down as well. Now, think of the most common verbs that you would use to describe where geographical areas are located and what they border. Pronounce aloud the words you wrote so that you hear yourself and can identify those words if you hear them in the narrative.

Pre-listening 2. 🔊 Listen and read along. The following are the names and words you will hear in the narrative.

Alborz Mountain Range	اَلبُرز
Zagros Mountain Range	زاگرُس
Zayandeh-rood River (lit.: life-giving river)	زایَنده رود
Karun River	کارون
Karkheh River	کَرخه
Bible	اِنجیل
Paradise	بِهشت
the Kavir Desert	دَشتِ کَویر
the Lut Desert	دَشتِ لوت
Mars	مِریخ
Caspian Sea	دَریای خَزَر
Persian Gulf	خَلیج فارس
Gulf of Oman	دَریای عُمان
Homeland	وَطَن
Which, that	که
In the capacity of, as ...	به عُنوانِ ...
Is mentioned	ذِکر شُده است (ذِکر شُده)
View	مَنظَره
We spend time	وَقت میگُذَرانیم

Pre-listening 3. Go online and pull up a physical map of Iran. Look for the main bodies of water, mountains and rivers on the map. Now, say aloud in Persian where those mountains, rivers and seas are located. Now, pick Iran's two neighboring countries and say in Persian where they border Iran.

🔊 Now, listen to Neeloo and read along.

سَلام، اسمِ من نیلوفَر است. من در ایران به دُنیا آمدَم و در شَهرِ تهران در ایران زندگی میکنم. وَطَنَم، ایران، در غَربِ آسیا قَرار دارد. پایتختِ ایران شَهرِ تهران است. تهران در شمالِ ایران قَرار دارد.

کِشورم خیلی قَشنگ است. ایران هم جَنگَل دارد هم کَویر ، هم دَریا و هم دَریاچه، هم رود های بزرگ و هم کوه های بُلَند.

ایران دو رشته کوه بزرگ دارد: رشته کوه "الِبُرز" که در شُمالِ ایران قَرار دارد،
و رشته کوه "زاگرُس" که در غَربِ ایران قَرار دارد. رود های معروف ایران "زاینده
رود"، "کارون" و "کرخه" هستند. رودِ کَرخه به عُنوانِ یکی از چهار رودِ بِهِشت
در اِنجیل ذِکر شُده
است. این سه رودِ
ایران در غَرب کشور
قَرار دارند.

دو کویر بزرگ
ایران "دَشتِ کَویر" و
"دَشتِ لوت" هستند.
این دو کویر در شرق
ایران قرار دارند. کَویرِ
ایران خِیلی قَشَنگ
است. به نَظَرَم،
مَنظَره های کَویرِ
ایران شَبیهِ مَنظَره

Town of Sarvelat in the coastal province of Gilan. N. Iran

های مِریخ هستند. در شُمالِ ایران یک دَریای بزرگ به نامِ " دَریای خَزَر" قَرار
دارد. ساحِلِ دریای خزر خیلی قشنگ است. خانواده ام آنجا ویلا دارند و ما هر
تابستان یک دو هفته میرویم ساحِل و آنجا وَقت میگُذَرانیم. فارس و دریای عُمان
در جنوب ایران قرار دارند.
ایران در غرب ، با کشور عراق مرز دارد و در شمال-غربی با کشور ترکیه. در
شمال،ایران با کشورهای آذربایجان، ارمنستان و ترکمنستان مرز دارد. ایران در
شرق با کشورهای افغانستان و پاکستان مرز دارد.
من وَطَنَم را خیلی دوست دارم.

Assignment. Answer the following questions in Persian. Prepare to say your answers fluently in class. Give complete answers and use the key vocabulary of this chapter in your answers.

سوال ها:

۱. چه رِشتهِ کوه و چه رودِ مَعروفی در غَربِ ایران قَرار دارند؟ (چه رِشتهِ کوه
و چه رودِ مَعروفی تو غَربِ ایران قَرار دارن؟)

۲. چه کَویر هایی در شَرقِ ایران قَرار دارند؟ (چه کَویرایی تو شَرقِ ایران قَرار دارن؟)

۳. به نَظَرِ نیلو، کُدام کَویر قَشَنگ اسْت؟ چِرا؟ (به نَظَرِ نیلو، کُدوم کَویر قَشَنگه؟ چِرا؟)

۴. خانواده نیلو کجای ایران ویلا دارد؟ چِرا آنجا ویلا دارند؟ (خونواده نیلو کجای ایران ویلا دارن؟ چِرا اونجا ویلا دارن؟)

۵. خَلیجِ فارس کجای ایران قَرار دارد؟ (خَلیجِ فارس کجای ایران قَرار داره؟)

۶. رود های مَعروفِ ایران کُدام هسْتند؟ (رودای مَعروفِ ایران کُدومَن ؟)

۷. آن رود ها کجای ایران قَرار دارند؟ (اون رودا کجای ایران قَرار دارن؟)

۸. ایران در غَرب با چند تا کِشوَر مَرز دارد؟ (ایران تو غَرب با چن تا کِشوَر مَرز داره؟)

۹. ایران در شَرق با چند تا کِشوَر مَرز دارد؟ (ایران تو شَرق با چن تا کِشوَر مَرز داره؟)

Follow-up. Using the information about Iran given in the text above, point out two or three similarities and differences between the geographies of the United States and Iran. For example,

۱. آمریکا دو رشته کوه بزرگ دارد و ایران هم دو رشته کوه بزرگ دارد (آمریکا دو تا رشته کوه بزرگ داره و ایرانَم دو تا رشته کوه بزرگ داره).

READING خواندَنی

Before coming to class, read the entire text a few times aloud until you can easily and fluently pronounce every sentence.

Pre-reading. You will read a new letter from Roya, your pen pal in Iran. In the letter, she describes her hometown, Tehran. Before reading the text, make a list of the most common words in Persian that you expect to encounter in reading about a big city. If your words are nouns, think of the verbs that might go with them in the given context. If the words you wrote are verbs, think of nouns that might go with them. Write down those words, so that you can visually identify them if you encounter them in the passage.

229

Useful words:

بُزُرگ تَرین	بُلَند تَرین	بُزُرگ تَر larger	مِترو subway
largest	longest		
لوکس upscale, luxury	مایل مُرَبَع square mile	مَجموعه های تاریخی historical complexes	مَکان های میراثِ جَهانیِ یونسکو UNESCO world heritage sites
شَهر خواهَر خوانده sister city	موزهِ هُنر های مُعاصِر تهران Tehran Museum of Contemporary Art, which houses one of the largest and most valuable collections of Western art outside North America and Europe.		

سلام، دوستِ عَزیز! حالِ تو چِطور است؟ باز هَم یک نامه بَرای تو مینِویسَم. در این نامه یک کَم از زادگاهَم تهران بَرای تو تَعریف میکُنَم. من در تهران زندگی میکنم. شَهرِ تهران پایتَختِ ایران است و در شُمالِ کِشوَرِ ایران قَرار دارد. تهران شَهرِ بزرگی با ساختِمان های بُلَند، مِیدان های بزرگ و خیابان های عَریض است. خیابانِ وَلیِ عَصر در تهران بُلَند تَرین خیابانِ خاوَرِ میانه است. مِتروی تهران بُلَند تَرین مِترو در خاوَرِ میانه است. کَلان شَهرِ تهران بزرگ تَرین شَهرِ ایران و پُرجَمعیَت تَرین شَهرِ غَربِ آسیا است. تهران مَرکَزِ اُستانِ تهران است. تهران خیابان ها، کوچه ها و بُزَرگراه های خیلی زیادی دارد. تِرافیک در خیابان های تهران خیلی سَنگین است. مَحَله های شُمالِ تهران ساختِمان های بُلَند و مُدِرن و خانه ها و آپارتِمان های قَشَنگ و لوکسِ زیادی دارند. خانواده من در شُمالِ تهران زندگی میکنند.

230

Resalat Highway, Tehran

من تهران را به خاطِر ِ موزه ها و پارک هایش دوسِت دارم.تهران پارک های خیلی قَشَنگ و بُزُرگی دارد.بُزُرگتَرین پارکِ تِهران پارکِ لَویزان است.مَساحَتِ پارکِ لَویزان ۴ مایلِ ِ مُرَبَع اِست.

تِهران بیش از پَنجاه موزه، و هَمچنین مَکان های میراثِ جَهانی ِ یونِسکو و مَجموعه های تاریخی ِ خیلی زیادی دارد. موزه ِ مُوردِ عَلاقه ِ من موزه ِ هُنر های مُعاصِر ِ تهران است.من دانِشجو هستم و برای من دانِشگاه و کِتابخانه خیلی مُهم هستند.تهران بیش از ۳۰ دانِشگاه و کِتابخانه های زیادی دارد. شَهرِ خواهَر خوانده ِ تِهران در آمریکا شَهرِ لُس آنجِلِس است. تهران هم شَهر ِ مُدِرن و هم شَهرِ تاریخی است. من تهران را خیلی دوسِت دارم.

231

Jamshidieh Park, North Tehran

Prepare to answer these questions in Persian in class. Do online research if needed.

سُوال ها:

۱.آیا رویا در شَهرِ کوچکی یا شَهرِ بزرگی زندگی میکند؟

۲.رویا کجای آن شَهر زندگی میکند؟

۳. خانواده ِ رویا در چه نُوع مَحَله ای مَنزِل دارند؟

۴.رویا به خاطرِ چه چیزی تهران را دوست دارد؟

۵. چرا برای رویا کتابخانه و دانشگاه مُهِم هستند؟

۶. آیا پارکِ لَویزان در تهران یا پارکِ سِنترال پارک در شَهرِ نیویورک بُزُرگ تر است؟

۷. لُس آنجِلِس شَهرِ خواهَر خوانده ِ چه شَهری در ایران است؟

Follow-up 1. Imagine that you are a tour guide in Tehran. Tell the class about Tehran using the facts about Tehran that Roya has included in her letter. Do research online and add one piece of information about Tehran that Roya has not mentioned in her letter.

Follow-up 2. Prepare for your classmates two questions about Roya and her hometown. In your questions, use at least two different new words (one per sentence) from this chapter. Before coming to class, say your questions aloud a few times until you can pronounce them fluently.

TRANSLATION   تَرجُمه

Translate into Persian the following passage about New York.

New York City is located in the northeast of the United States. New York City has many museums, beautiful parks and squares. The streets of New York City are crowded, and there is usually heavy traffic in the center of the city. There are a lot of modern and tall buildings and long avenues in NYC. NYC has many places of interest and tourist attractions. The famous Times Square is located in New York City. With an area of more than 8,000 square kilometers, NYC is the largest city in the world. New York City is located on the Hudson River. New York City is located in the state of New York. New York State borders the states of Pennsylvania and New Jersey in the south, the states of Connecticut, Massachusetts and Vermont in the east and the country of Canada in the north. Lake Ontario is in the north of New York State and Lake Erie is in its west.

WRITING   اِنشا

Read again the letter from Roya. Now, write a response to the letter where you describe your hometown. Start your letter by stating the name of your hometown (provide the English spelling in parentheses after its Persian spelling) and its location in the country and state. State some interesting fact about your hometown (e.g., it is the capital of its state, there is a famous school in it, a famous person was born there, etc.). Add statements that describe the appearance of your hometown (streets, buildings, parks, restaurants, museums, places of interest, hotels, traffic, etc.). Write whether you like your hometown and why.

Your letter must be at least 150 words long in Persian. Your objective is to write as much as you can. You can use Roya's letter and the Translation section as examples in order to structure your letter. Start your letter with a greeting and close it with the phrase مُخلِصِ تو *Sincerely Yours*. Sign your letter in Persian.

فَصلِ هَشتُم
Chapter 8

خَرید
Shopping

Boustan shopping mall in Tehran.

Function Inquiring about price and cost, describing your outfit, talking about colors, how to make requests and suggestions, how to express wishes and intentions, talking about possibilities. Key verbs: *to buy, to pay, to wear, must, have to, want to, to be able to, to need.*

Listening Keyvan is shopping for a new suit.

Reading Persian Gulf Shopping mall in Shiraz.

Structures Subjunctive and imperative (command) verb forms. Prepositional phrases (in order to ..., before/after ...).

🔊 Listen and repeat the words aloud. Repeat each word few times until you can easily pronounce it.

Colors				
Purple	آرغَوانی (آرغَوونی)		Color	رَنگ
Pink	صورَتی		Colorful	رَنگارَنگ
Navy blue	آبیِ دَریایی، سُرمه ای		Red	قِرمِز (سُرخ)
Light (in reference to colors)	رُوشَن		Green	سَبز
Light green	سَبزِ رُوشَن		Yellow	زَرد
Dark (in reference to colors)	تیره		Blue	آبی
Dark green	سَبزِ تیره		White	سِفید
Indigo	نیلی		Black	سیاه، مِشکی
My favorite color	رَنگِ مُورِدِ عَلاقه ام (رَنگِ مُورِدِ عَلاقَم)		Grey	خاکِستَری
What color is that house? (the syllable *gee* is stressed)	آن خانه چه رَنگی است؟ (اون خونه چه رنگیه؟)		Brown	قَهوه ای
What is that color? (the first syllable /ran/ is stressed)	آن چه رَنگی است؟ (اون چه رَنگیه؟)		Orange	نارِنجی
Popular color	رَنگِ مَحبوب		Rainbow	رَنگین کَمان (رَنگین کَمون)
			Navy	سُرمه ای

Clothes				
Clothes	پوشاک، لِباس		Pants, jeans	شَلوار، شَلوار جین
Women's clothes	لِباس زَنانه (لِباسِ زَنونه)		Shorts	شَلوارَک
Men's clothes	لِباسِ مَردانه (لِباسِ مَردونه)		Suit	کُت شَلوار، کُت و شَلوار

Clothes				
Dress	پیراهن زنانه (پیراهَنِ زَنونه)	Jacket	کاپشَن / کاپشین	
Skirt	دامَن	Overcoat	پالتو	
Blouse	بلوز	Hat	کُلاه	
Women's head scarf mandated by Islamic dress code	روسَری	Shoes	کَفش	
Manteau, women's overcoat	مانتو	Sneakers	کَفشِ کَتانی (کَفشِ کَتونی) ، کَفشِ وَرزِشی	
Sweater	ژاکَت	Dress shoes	کَفشِ مَجلِسی	
Shirt	پیراهَن (پیران، پیرَن)	Boots	بوت، چَکمه، پوتین	
T-shirt	تی شِرت	Sandals	صَندَل	
Sleeveless tshirt	تی شِرتِ حَلقه ای	Flip flops	دَمپایِی آبری، دَمپایِی لا اَنگُشتی	
Long sleeve tshirt	تی شِرتِ آستین بُلَند	Watch	ساعَتِ مُچی	
Short sleeve	آستینِ کوتاه	Sunglasses	عِینَکِ آفتابی	
Tank top	پیراهَنِ رِکابی	Prescription glasses	عِینَکِ طِبی	
Belt	کَمَربَند	Backpack	کوله پُشتی	

Places and People				
Mall	مَرکَزِ خَرید، پاساژ	Credit card	کارت، کارتِ اِعتِباری	
Supermarket	سوپِرمارکِت، فُروشگاه (فوروشـگاه)	I'll pay with the credit card, I'll swipe the card	کارت میکِشَم	

Places and People			
Drugstore	دارو خانه	Customer	مُشتَری
Gas station	پمپِ بِنزین	Salesperson	فُروشَنده
Market, traditional Iranian bazaar	بازار	Manager	مُدیر
Cash	نَقد	Store owner	صاحِبِ مَغازه
Sale, promotion	حَراج	Boss, director	رَییس
ATM	عابِر بانک، خودپَرداز	Calling card	کارتِ تِلِفُن
I pay in cash	نَقدی پَرداخت میکنم	I pay, I make payment	میپَردازَم، پَرداخت میکنم
This year	اِمسال	Required course	کِلاسِ اِلزامی
Few issues	یک سِری مُشکِلات (یه سِری مُشکِلات)	I faced, encountered ...	با ... روبِرو شُدَم
I wait	صَبر میکنم	I spend (about money)	خَرج میکنم
Give a discount	تَخفیف بِدهید (تَخفیف بِدین)	15 percent	۱۵ دَر صَد
Second component of words used to describe the type of stores (e.g., shoe store, book store)		فُروشی (کَفش فُروشی، کِتاب فُروشی)	
How much is it?, lit.: how much is its price?		قیمَتِش چَند است (قیمَتِش چَنده)؟	

HOMEWORK

تَکلیف

1. Listen and read along. First, complete the Persian text. Then, based on the Persian original, complete its English translation.

رَنگین کَمان از ــــــ رَنگ تَشکیل شُده است: قِرمِز، نارِنجی، زَرد، سَبز، آبی، نیلی، بَنَفش. رَنگِ قِرمِز در بَخشِ بالایی و ــــــ بَنَفش در بَخشِ پایینیِ رَنگین کَمان قَرار میگیرَند.

نامِ دَیگرِ ـــــــ کَمان در زَبانِ فارسی، تیراژه است که هَمچنین ـــــــ دُختَرانه‌ِ ـــــــ است.

Rainbow comprises seven _____: red, orange, yellow, green, blue, indigo and violet. The color _____ occurs in the upper part of rainbow and the color _____ occurs in bottom part of _____. In Persian, another word for _____ is *teerãzhe*, which is also a Persian name for girls.

2. Complete the sentences with the given words.

بِسیاری از	نا رنگی	لیمو	پَرچَم	مَخلوط کردن	مَرسوم	به دَست می‌آید
many of	tangerine	lemon	flag	mixing	customary	is acquired

زَرد, نارِنجی, سُرخ, سَبز, سِفید, خاکِستَری, آبیِ تیره, آبی, صورَتی

۱. پَرچَمِ ایران رَنگ های ـــــــ و ـــــــ و ـــــــ دارد.

۲. پرچم آمریکا رندگ های ـــــــ و ـــــــ و ـــــــ دارد.

۳. در خاور میانه بسیاری از مردها لباس هایی به رنگ های تیره مثل سیاه و ـ ـــــــ میپوشند.

۴. لیمو ـــــــ است، و نارنگی ـــــــ است.

۵. رنگ قهوه ای با مخلوط کردن رنگ های ـــــــ و ـــــــ و ـــــــ به دست می‌آید.

۶. رنگ ـــــــ با مخلوط کردن رنگ های سیاه و سفید به دست می‌آید.

۷. رنگ مرسوم برای دُختَربَچه ها ـــــــ است.

۸. زنگ مرسوم برای پِسَربَچه ها ـــــــ است.

3. Listen to Sam talk about his family and house. Based on his words, complete the sentences with the words for colors.

(1) Sam's parents' house is _____. (2) They drive _____ Ford. (3) Sam drives a _____ Toyota. (4) The walls in their living room are _____. (5) The walls in Sam's room are _____. (6) His favorite color is _____.

4. For each item below, say what color you imagine when you hear that word. Write and prepare to say the item and your color aloud, for example, گل سُرخ است

Use a dictionary if needed.

؟. توپِ تِنیس	۵. آمریکا	۱. چای
۱۰. شَهرِ ...	۶ . ماه دسامبر	۲ . قَهوه
۱۱ . زادگا هت	۷. ایران	۳. بَستَنی
۱۲. خودِ تو، تو	۸. تاکسی در نیویورک	۴ . پیتزا

5. Prepare to ask and answer the following questions in Persian in class. Before coming to class say your sentences a few times aloud until you can easily pronounce them.

رَسمی   official

(1) What is the color of your house?
(2) What is the official color of your state?
(3) What is the color of your dorm?
(4) What is the color of your car/bicycle?
(5) What is the color of the textbook for Persian class?
(6) What is the color of your favorite shoes?
(7) What is the color of the bus that goes to the university?
(8) Do you like black or green tea?
(9) What is your favorite color?
(10) What color is indigo?

6. Print out an image of the flag of your home state and bring it to class. Tell the class briefly about your state and describe its state colors.

Start by saying the name of your state, its location in the country, its capital city and in which city in the state you live. Then show and describe the colors on the flag of your state. If the flag has symbols and images, tell the class the colors of those symbols.

Useful words:

Flag	پَرچَم
Stripe	نَوار
Star	سِتاره
Circle	دایِره

7. Listen to the announcement of items on sale at a clothing store in Tehran. Next to each item, write the color in which it is available on sale.

رنگ	حراج
	بُلوز
	مانتو
	روسَری
	شَلوار جین زَنانه
	شَلوار جین مَردانه
	تی شِرتِ مَردانه
	پیراهَنِ مَردانه
	ژاکَتِ زَنانه
	کفشِ مَجلِسیِ زَنانه

8. Listen to Neema and then to Tom as they describe what they are wearing. Based on what you hear, decide for what season of the year each person is dressed. Explain in Persian your decision.

9. Write down in Persian a list of clothing items that you most frequently wear. Next to each item write the colors you have them in. Prepare to say in Persian in class what you have written.

10. Do research online and describe the colors of US national soccer team, Iran's national soccer team, Sepahan soccer club (from Esfahan), LA Galaxy soccer club (from Los Angeles), Iran's volleyball team and the US volleyball team.

Useful Words:

تیمِ مِلی	باشگاه	لِباسِ تیم
national team	(athletic) club	team outfit

241

11. 🔊 Listen to the narrator and identify the clothing items you hear. Next to each item, write the price that the narrator said for that item. In class, prepare to ask your classmates how much each item costs.

IN CLASS

دَر کِلاس

12. Pick one of the flags without revealing your choice to class. Name the colors of the flag.
Your classmates will listen to you and try to guess which flag you are describing.

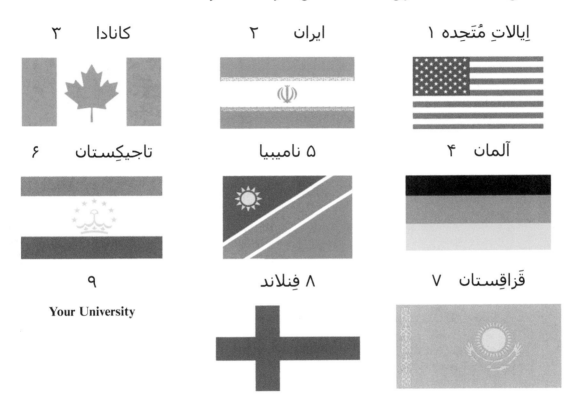

۳ کانادا   ۲ ایران   ۱ اِیالاتِ مُتَّحِده

۶ تاجیکِستان   ۵ نامیبیا   ۴ آلمان

۹   ۸ فِنلاند   ۷ قَزاقِستان

Your University

13. Take turns to say what your favorite colors are.

رَنگِ مُوردِ عَلاقه ام صورَتی است (رَنگِ مُوردِ عَلاقَم صورَتیه).

14.   Talk to everyone in class and find people whose favorite colors are the
same as yours. Useful question:

رَنگِ مُوردِ عَلاقه ات چه است (رَنگِ مُوردِ عَلاقَت چیه)؟

243

Take a note of the colors you hear. Now, say who in class likes the same colors as you do, and also say what the most popular color in your class is.

رَنگِ مَحبوب در کلاس ما ـــــــ است (رَنگِ مَحبوب تو کِلاسیمون ـــــــ ه).

15. You will be working in groups of three. Ask your classmates what the colors of their favorite sports teams are.

16. Take turns to describe what you are wearing today and in what color.

E.g., اِمروز شَلوار جینِ آبی و تی شِرتِ سِفید پوشیدَم

17. Now, take turns and describe what you usually wear to classes during the spring semester when the weather is cold, and during the fall semester when the weather is warm.

در هَوای گَرم مَعمولا ـــــــ و ـــــــ میپوشم.
در هَوای سَرد مَعمولا ـــــــ و ـــــــ میپوشم.

18. Pick a student in class without announcing his or her name. Describe for your class the clothes and colors which that person is wearing today. Your classmates will listen to your description and try to guess the identity of the person you have in mind.

Today Sara is wearing _____ and _____

سارا اِمروز ـــــــ و ـــــــ پوشیده است (سارا امروز ـــــــ پوشیده).

19. Pick a classmate and ask him or her about the color of a clothing item that another student in class is wearing today.

ژاکَتِ کامران چه رَنگی است (ژاکَتِ کامران چه رَنگیه)؟

20. Talk to all your classmates and ask them what they usually wear for classes and what are the colors of those items. Find out who in your class has a taste in clothing that is similar to yours, when it comes to dressing for classes every day.

21. Pick a classmate and ask her/him one of the following questions in Persian.

(1) How many people in this class are wearing jeans? (2) How many people in this class are wearing sneakers? (3) How many people in this class are wearing glasses? (4) How many people in this class are wearing hats today? (5) How many people in this class have watches today?

22. You will be working with a classmate. Put together outfits for the occasions listed below. Name the clothing articles as well as the colors for each one of them.

– a formal dinner in a nice restaurant,
– a job interview,
– to go to the movies with a friend,
– to go to the game of your university team,
– to a party at a friend's house.

23.  You will be working with a classmate. Name an event or place where you have to go within the next few days. Let your classmate suggest an outfit for you to wear to that place.

GRAMMAR   دَستورِ زَبان

Subjunctive

There are three major verb categories in Persian: (1) the Indicative, which is used to communicate facts and describe events in the past, present and future. This category includes present, past and future tenses; (2) the imperative, which is used to communicate orders and commands; (3) the subjunctive, which is used to express an intention, a possibility (that something may or may not have happened), a wish (to do something), speculation or doubt (that something may or may not have happened), obligation (something that needs to be done), condition (for something to happen). In other words, we use the subjunctive when we want to say that we intend (intended) or wish (wished) to do something, we can (could) or cannot (could not) do something, we have (had) to do something, that something may/should/must happen, that something will take place if a condition is met, to suggest to someone to do something.

Formation

Subjunctive in Persian is rather easily recognizable, as it has a special marker /be/ in the beginning of the verb. All Persian verbs (besides the two exceptions *to be* and *to have*) form their subjunctive in the same way. We have already learned the present tense of Persian verbs that starts with the /mee/ prefix. To create the subjunctive of any verb, simply say /be/ instead of /mee/ at the beginning of needed verb.

Subjunctive to express an suggestion, obligation (verb *should buy*)	Present tense to describe a fact (verb *buy*)
بِخَرَم	میخَرم
بِخَری	میخَری
بِخرد	میخَرد
بِخَریم	میخَریم
بِخَرید	میخَرید
بِخَرَند	میخَرَند

In the verbs that start with the vowel آ, the subjunctive marker is spelled and pronounced بی /bee/. Let's conjugate the Subjunctive of the verb *to come* آی /ã/ that starts with the vowel آ and gets بی /bee/ for the Subjunctive marker in the beginning of the verb:

bee-ãm	بیایم	I should come
bee-ãee	بیایی	You (تو) should come
bee-ãd	بیاید	S/he, it should come
bee-ãeem	بیاییم	We should come
bee-ãeen	بیایید	You (شما) should come
bee-ãn	بیایند	They should come

In compound verbs with کُنَم and شَوم, the subjunctive marker /be/ is usually omitted, for example,

You have to wake up. /bã-yad beedãr shee/ بایَد بیدار شوی

I have to work till late. /bã-yad tã deer-vaqt kãr konam/ بایَد تا دیر وَقت کار کُنَم

The Two Exceptions (to be, to have)

The subjunctive of the verb *to be*, is formed using the root /bãsh/ to which then we add the conjugational endings. No subjunctive marker /be/ precedes the root /bãsh/, which makes this verb an exception.

You have to be in class at nine. بایَد ساعَتِ نُه دَر کِلاس باشی.

I want to be home. میخواهم در خانه ام باشَم.

For subjunctive of the verb *to have*, say *dãsh-teh* and then say *bãsh* followed by a conjugational ending.

I hope you have a nice day. ‫أُمیدوارَم روز ِ خوبی داشته باشید.‬

As the conjugational endings reflect the subject, you do not need to mention that subject if that subject is a pronoun, for example,

I must work ‫باید کار کنم‬

Pronunciation and Stress.

In the majority of the verbs, the subjunctive marker is pronounced /be/, but with the verbs where the root vowel is /o/ (e.g., ‫کنم، خورم‬), the subjunctive marker is pronounced /bo/ due to vowel assimilation, for example,

‫بُکُنَم، بُکُنی، بُخورَم، بُخوریم‬
/bo-khoreem, bo-khoram, bo-konee, bo-konam/

In base (single-word) verbs the primary stress falls on the marker *be* (‫بِخَرَم‬), while in compound verbs, the primary stress falls on the first component of the given compound verb (‫رَنگ بِزَنَم‬).

Negation

To form a negative subjunctive, simply say /na/ instead of the marker /be/ in the beginning of the verb, for example, It's better not to go. /beh-tareh keh na-ree/ ‫بِهتَر است که نَروی.‬

For more about negative subjunctive see the appendix Grammarian's Corner.

When to Use the Subjunctive

In many cases, the subjunctive comes after a cue or grammatical trigger:

1. After the words *Must/Have to* /bã-yad/, *May/Perhaps* /shã-yad/:

I must/have to go to the library tonight.

‫اِمشَب باید به کِتابخانه بِرَوم (اِمشَب باید به کِتابخونه بِرَم).‬

I may go to the library.

‫شایَد به کِتابخانه بِرَوم (شایَد به کِتابخونه بِرَم).‬

2. After the verb *Can/Able to* /mee-too-nam/:

I can go to the library tonight.

‫اِمشَب میتوانَم به کِتابخانه بِرَوم (اِمشَب میتونَم به کِتابخونه بِرَم)‬

247

3. After the verbs *Want to/ Would like to* /mee-khām/ doost dā-ram/

I **want to** go to the library.

میخواهَم به کِتابخانه بِرَوم (میخام به کِتابخونه بِرَوم).

I **would like to** go to the library.

دوست دارَم به کِتابخانه بِرَوم (دوست دارَم به کِتابخونه بِرَم).

4. To make polite requests after the word /mee-sheh ...?/ Start your request sentence with the word /mee-sheh/, which stays unchanged regardless of the subject (the person or thing that is asked to do the action) of your sentence, and then say second verb in subjunctive with the necessary conjugation ending in order to show who is asked do the action. The word /mee-sheh/ thus can be rendered in English with the words, *May* I/You/We/ ...? or *Can* I/You/We/ ...? depending on the subject of your sentence. /mee-sheh/ is used to make a request, ask for permission or to ask if someone is willing to do something.

May I (can I) ask a question in English?   میشود (میشه) به انگلیسی سُوال کُنَم؟

May we (can we) talk after the class?   میشود (میشه) بَعد از کِلاس صُحبَت کُنیم؟

Can you (i.e., would you be willing to) write this word in Persian, please?

میشود (میشه) این کلمه را به فارسی بِنویسید؟

Can you repeat your question, please?   میشود (میشه) سُوالِتان را تِکرار کنید؟

5. To convey the meaning of *should*, especially in question sentences, no additional words are used and only the verb itself (in subjunctive) conveys the meaning.

What should we do? چِه کار کُنیم؟

Where should they go? کُجا بِرَوند؟

To whom should I talk about the visa? با چه کسی راجِع بِه ویزا صُحبَت کُنَم؟

In many cases, when in English there are two verbs and the second verb is in infinitive form (to go, to buy, to eat, etc.), in Persian that second verb is used in the subjunctive.

When using the subjunctive, place the object between the subjunctive trigger and the verb in subjunctive, for example, میخواهم به او زَنگ بِزَنَم. I want to call him.

Other Common Cues and Triggers for the Subjunctive

1. Phrases that express hope, suggestion, necessity:

It's possible ممکن است که /mom-ke-neh keh/; It's necessary لازم است که /lā-ze-meh keh/; It is better to/that بهتر است که /beh-ta-reh keh/, ... supposed to ... قرار است که /qa-rā-reh keh .../; I hope that امیدوارم که /o-meed-vā-ram keh/; I have to / I am forced to ... مجبورم /maj-boo-ram/; I tell him/her to ... به او میگویم که /beh oon mee-gam keh/

قرار است که ما در مرکز خرید ناهار بخوریم. we are supposed to have lunch in the mall.

In the trigger phrases with the verb است, that است remains unchanged, and, instead, the verb that stands in subjunctive at the end of the sentence will be conjugated to show the subject of the sentence. By contrast, in the trigger phrases with the ending م/یم, that ending will change along with the ending of the subjunctive verb according to the subject(s) of the sentence.

For further elaborations and illustrative examples of the trigger phrases, refer to the appendix Grammarian's Corner.

2. Prepositional phrases

The subjunctive is also used after prepositional phrases that imply intention, or suggest that the action to which they refer did not happen at all or did not happen until the other event to which they are compared had taken place, for example,

In Order to/So that برای اینکه، تا /barãyeh een-keh, tã/, *Before* قبل از اینکه /qablaz een-keh/, *Without ...* بدون اینکه /bedooneh een-keh/, *Instead of ...* بجای اینکه /beh jãyeh een-keh/

See further elaborations and illustrative examples in the appendix Grammarian's Corner.

Keep in mind that /ba-rã-yeh een-keh/ can also be used as *because*, but in that case, it is followed by a verb in past, present or future tense (i.e., Indicative category that is used to communicate facts). If /ba-rã-yeh een-keh/ is followed by a verb in subjunctive, it means *in order to ...* .

Imperative

We use the imperative to give orders and commands (Come here, please! Read the sentence, please!). The imperative exhibits similarities with the subjunctive.

The imperative marker is /be/ pronounced in the beginning of the verb.

/be-khooneen/ Read!   بِخوانید (بِخونین)!

/be-reen!/ Go!   بِروید (بِرین)!

In compound verbs with کُنَم and شَوم the marker /be/ is normally omitted, especially in colloquial speech.

تِکرار کُنید! بیدار شوید!

With the verbs where the root vowel is /o/ (e.g., کُنم ، خورَم), the marker is pronounced /bo/ due to vowel assimilation.

بُکُنید، بُخورید /bo-khoreen, bo-koneen/

In base (i.e., single-word) verbs the primary stress falls on the prefix /be/ (بِروید!), while in compound verbs the primary stress falls on the first component of the given compound verb (زَنگ بِزَن).

The imperative is only used to address *you* formal/ plural (شما) and *you* singular/ informal (تو).

Formal/plural You: Please, eat!   لُطفا بُخورید (لُطفَن بُخورین)

Informal/singular You: Eat!   بُخور

As you can see from the last two examples, the imperative for informal/singular *you* has no conjugational ending. That ending is implied, and because there is only one other imperative (formal/plural *you* which is identified by its conjugational ending ید) you will not get confused over whether شما or تو is implied.

Negative

To form a negative imperative, simply say /na/ instead of /be/ at the beginning of the verb. This negative marker is used even with compound verbs, where /be/ would usually be omitted.

Don't go! /na-row/   نَرُوا!

Don't work! /kãr na-koneen/   کار نَکُنید!

Don't say! /na-goo/   نَگوا!

The Two Exceptions (the verbs to be *and* to have*)*

Imperative of the verb *to be*.

For *you* informal/singular—simply say /bãsh/. For *you* formal/plural—simply say /bãsh-een/.

	شُما *You* formal/plural	تو *you* informal/singular
Hurry up!	زود باشید	زود باش
Be ready!	آماده باشید	آماده باش

Imperative of the verb *to have*.

For *you* informal/singular—say /dãshteh bãsh/. For *you* formal/plural—say /dãshteh bãsh-een/.

	شُما *You* formal/plural	تو *you* informal/singular
Have!	داشته باشید	داشته باش

HOMEWORK   تَکلیف

24. Look at the following verbs and identify the verbs in the subjunctive. Explain what makes them the subjunctive.

بخرم، میخرم، بپوشم، میپوشم، کارت بکشم، کارت میکشم، بکنم، میکنم، کار کنم، کار میکنم، باشم، هستم، داشته باشم، دارم، بیایم، میام، پرداخت کنم، پرداخت نکنم، پرداخت میکنم، باشم، نباشم، بگویم، نگویم، میگویم، نخرم، نروم، نمیروم، نکنم، نمیکنم، نپوشم، نیستم.

25. Listen and for each number you hear, mark whether you hear the subjunctive (Subj.) or present tense (Pres.) verb.

۶	۵	۴	۳	۲	۱
۱۲	۱۱	۱۰	۹	۸	۷
۱۸	۱۷	۱۶	۱۵	۱۴	۱۳

26. In each numbered phrase, for the red Subjunctive trigger choose a correct verb in black.

۲. میتوانَم کارت بِکِشَم، کارت میکِشَم	۱. میخواهَم بِپوشَم، میپوشَم
۴. لازِم اَست که داشته باشَم، دارَم	۳. بایَد بِخرَم، میخَرَم
۶. قَرار اَست که پِرداخت کنَم، پَرداخت میکنَم	۵. مُمکِن اَست که نَباشَد، نیست
۸. مَجبورَم که بِرَوم، میروم	۷. میشَود تِکرار کنی، تِکرار میکنی؟

27. In each numbered phrase, for the red subjunctive verb choose a correct subjunctive trigger in black.

۲. لازِم هَستم، لازِم اَست بِرَوم.	۱. میتوانم، میتوانی کارت بکشم.
۴. میشَوَد، میشَوی تِکرار کنی؟	۳. مُمکن هستم، مُمکن اَست بپوشم؟
۶. لازِم نیست، لازِم نیستی بیایی.	۵. میشَوم، میشَوَد یِک سُوال کنَم؟

251

28. Read the English phrases and complete the Persian translation with correct conjugational endings.

1. I want to buy بخر____ میخواه____	6. She wants to wear ____بپوش ____میخواه
2. Can I pay with a credit card? ____کارت بکش ____میشو	7. We are supposed to pay. قرار است پرداخت کن____
3. Can you come? بیا____ میتوان____	8. I have to go. باید برو____
4. I would like to go. برو____ دوست دار____	9. I hope you come. ____بیا____ امیدوار
5. We have to wear. بپوش____ باید	10. I hope they come. ____بیا____ امیدوار

29. Listen and write the verbs that are missing in the transcript. Translate the sentences.

فَردا میخوای چه کار ____؟

میخواهم فَردا صُبح به باشگاه ____ .

چِرا نِمیخواهی اِمشَب ____؟

اِمشَب نِمیتوانَم ____ بَرای اینکه اِمشَب بایَد به کِلاس ____ .

30. Translate the following sentences into Persian using the subjunctive as needed. Prepare to read your sentences aloud.

I pronounce	تَلَفُظ میکنم		ATM	عایِر بانک
calling card	کارتِ تِلِفُن		slowly	آهِسته

(1) Can you repeat, please?
(2) Can you speak slowly, please?
(3) Can I bring my homework tomorrow?
(4) Can I email you?
(5) Can you tell me where the bank is?
(6) Can I use this card at the ATM?
(7) Where can I buy a calling card?
(8) I do not want to be late.
(9) I want to talk to you.

31. Think of three things you want to do this coming weekend. Prepare to name those things in class. Do not forget to use the subjunctive as needed. For example,

آخَرِ هَفته‌ِ آینده میخواهم ... (آخَرِ هَفته‌ِ آینده میخام...)

32. Listen to Mitra, Kamran and Mrs. Kermani who are shopping for a birthday gift. For each person, mark only the items they want to buy and note for whom they are shopping. Prepare to say in class in Persian what and for whom each person wants to buy. Do not forget to use the subjunctive after the trigger verb *to want*. For example,

میترا میخواهد بَرای پِدَرِش شَلوار جین و کَفش بِخَرَد

(میترا میخاد بَرای پِدَرِش شَلوار جین و کَفش بِخَره.)

میترا ....

کِراوات	عِینَک آفتابی	پیراهن آستین کوتاه	تی شِرت

کامران...

کمربند	کاپشِن	کفش کَتانی	ساعت مُچی

خانم کرمانی...

پیراهن آستین بلند	شَلوار	جوراب	ژاکت

33. Listen to the narrator and complete the written sentences with the verb you hear. Translate the sentences into English.

۱. میتوانی این را به فارسی _____

۲. میشود این را به فارسی تَلَفُّظ _____

۳. میتوانی این را به فارسی _____

۴. میتوانی این را _____

۵. میتوانی این را به فارسی تَرجُمه _____

۶. بایَد کِی _____

۷. میشود تَکلیفَم را با ایمِیل به شما _____

۸. میخواهی فردا شب با ما به سینِما _____

۹. میشود با شما صُحبَت _____

۱۰. فردا نمیتوانم به کلاس _____

34. Prepare to ask and answer the following questions in class. Before the class, say your sentences a few times until you can pronounce them fluently.

اِستِراحَت کردن to rest

۱. میخواهی چَند سال دَر دانِشگاه دَرس بِخوانی؟ (میخای چَن سال تو دانِشگاه دَرس بِخونی؟)

۲. بَعد از دانِشگاه، میخواهی کجا زِندِگی کنی؟ (بَعد از دانِشگاه، میخای کجا زِندِگی کنی؟)

۳. بَعد از دانِشگاه، میخواهی کار کنی یا اِستِراحَت کنی؟ (بَعد از دانِشگاه، میخای کار کنی یا اِستِراحَت کنی؟)

۴. بَعد از دانِشگاه، میخواهی دَر چه زَمینه ای (رِشته ای) کار کنی؟ (بَعد از دانِشگاه، میخای دَر چه زَمینه ای کار کنی؟)

35. 🔊 Think of three things you must have in life to be happy. Now, prepare to say complete sentences in Persian using the verb *to have* in the subjunctive. In class, you will ask your classmates what they need to have in order to be happy in life, and will find out if anyone in class shares the same values and goals with you.

In order to be happy in life, I must have …

بَرای اینکه در زندگی شاد باشَم بایَد _____ داشته باشَم (بَرای اینکه تو زِندِگی شاد باشَم بایَد _____ داشته باشَم).

36. 🔊 Think of your experiences at your university. Prepare to say in Persian two or three things that, in your opinion, a student at your university should do in order to have a good experience in being a student. Use the subjunctive in your sentences.

به عُنوانِ … as, in the capacity of …

تَجرُبه experience

برای اینکه به عُنوانِ یک دانشجو تَجرُبه خوبی داشته باشی بایَد …

37. 🔊 Listen to Kamran as he talks about what he hopes to accomplish this week, this semester and this year. Complete the sentences referring to Kamran's hopes. Do not forget to use the verbs in the subjunctive, III person singular, in referring to Kamran.

کامران اُمیدوار است که این هَفته …
کامران اُمیدوار است که این تِرم …
کامران اُمیدوار است که اِمسال …

Now, complete the following sentences referring to something that you hope to accomplish or something that you hope happens. Do not forget to use the subjunctive after *I hope*. Prepare to say your sentences fluently in Persian.

اُمیدوارَم که این هَفته …

أُمیدوارَم که این تِرم ...

أُمیدوارَم که اِمسال ...

38. 🔊 Listen and complete the sentences with the verb in subjunctive that you hear. Translate the sentences into English.

نَبایَد	مَجبور نیستی
must not/should not	you don't have to ...

۱. مَجبور نیستی که هَر روز ــــــ.

۲. مَجبور نیستی که این کار را ــــــ.

۳. نَباید این کار را ــــــ.

۴. اینجا مَجبور نیستی که روسَری ــــــ.

۵. نَباید بِدونِ روسَری ــــــ بیرون.

۶. مَجبور نیستی به آن جَلَسه ــــــ.

۷. در این سَرما نَبایَد بِدونِ کُلاه بیرون ــــــ.

۸. در این اِداره مَجبور نیستی هَر روز کُت شَلوار ــــــ.

39. 🔊 Listen to Kamran and complete the transcript by filling in the missing words. Prepare to say in class (in Persian) what Kamran's issues are. Use /maj-boor/ in your sentences. Suggest a solution for each of his problems, if you can. Use /mee-too-neh/ followed by a verb in the subjunctive in your suggestions.

یک سِری مُشکِلات few issues	کِلاسِ اِلزامی required course
اِمسال this year	با ... روبِرو شُدَم ... I faced, encountered
حِسابان calculus	

سَلام دوستان ! من یک دانشجوی سالِ اَوَل هَستم و در خوابگاهِ دانشگاه زندگی میکنم. اِمسال در دانشگاه با یک سِری مُشکِلات روبِرو شُدَم.

۱- دوست ندارم هر روز در کافه تریای دانشگاه غَذا ــــــ، وَلی مَجبورَم این کار را بُکُنم. من آشپَزی بَلَد نیستم.

۲- دوست ندارم صُبح ها زود بیدار ــــــ، وَلی مَجبورَم این کار را بُکُنم. کِلاسِ ریاضی که واسه من اِلزامی است، ساعَتِ ۹ صُبح شُروع میشود.

۳ - کلاسِ حِسابان را اَصلا دوست ندارَم، وَلی مَجبورَم کلاسِ حِسابان را بَر

ـــــــــ، برای اینکه کلاسِ حِسابان یکی از کلاس های اِلزامی است.

۴ - دوست ندارَم در خوابگاه زندگی ـــــــــ، وَلی مَجبورَم این کار را بُکُنم.

در دانشگاهِ ما هَمه‌ِ دانشجوهای سالِ اَوَّل بایَد در خوابگاهِ دانشگاه زندگی

ـــــــــ.

۵ - نِمیخواهَم تَعطیلاتِ آینده به خانه‌ِ پدرومادرَم ـــــــــ، وَلی مَجبورَم

این کار را بُکُنم. در طولِ تَعطیلاتِ دانشگاهی هَمه‌ِ خوابگاه ها بَسته هستَند.

40. Think of three things you do not like, but have to do. Prepare to say these in class in Persian in the form of complete sentences. You can use Kamran's sentences as an example. In class, ask your classmates for solutions.

چی کار کُنَم؟

41. Now, think of three things that you do (or will do), but do not actually have to do. Explain why you do those things. For example,

مَجبور نیستَم در دانشگاه زندگی کنم، وَلی به هَر حال آنجا زندگی میکنم، برای
اینکه مُحَوَطه‌ِ دانشگاه خیلی قَشَنگ است (مَجبور نیستَم تو دانشگاه زندگی کنم،
وَلی به هَر حال اونجا زندگی میکنم، برای اینکه مُحَوَطه‌ِ دانشگاه خیلی قَشَنگه).

42. Translate the following sentences into Persian. You will use the verbs in the Imperative mood. Remember that in Persian the word "please" comes first.

آهِسته slowly	میاوَرَم I bring
صَبر میکُنَم I wait	میبَندَم I close
اِس اِم اِس میدَهم I text, I send a text	پا میشَوم I stand up
کارت میکشم I swipe the (credit) card	مینِشینَم I sit

(1) Please, swipe the card here. (2) Speak slowly, please. (3) Repeat your question, please. (4) Open the book, please. (5) Close the door, please. (6) Please come to class on time. (7) Go to the office number 25, please. (8) Please speak in Persian. (9) Sit down here, please. (10) Please, speak to (با) the manager. (11) Text me your address, please. (12) Please call this number tomorrow after 10 a.m. (13) Please bring one soda for me. (14) Please, wait. (15) Please tell them that I do not speak Persian well. (16) Please, listen. (17) Please, write in English. (18) Please, read. (19) Please, come tomorrow morning.

43. 🔊 Listen and read along. You will hear a conversation between Mitra and Keyvan. Keyvan is phoning Mitra to ask if she would like to come to the movies with a group of classmates.

(a) Listen and fill in the blanks with the verbs that you hear.

(b) In what form are the missing verbs used? Explain what triggered the use of that particular form for those verbs.

(c) Now, go over the rest of the verbs and identify their tenses. Note that in the line 4 (Keyvan), the speaker uses a verb in past tense زَنگ زَدَم *I called* (meaning *I am calling to …*).

میترا – آلو؟

کِیوان – سَلام، میترا جان! کیوانم. چِطوری، خوبی؟

میترا – قربونِت. تو چِطوری؟

کِیوان – خوبَم، مِرسی. زَنگ زَدَم _____ میخای اِمشَب با ما _____ سینَما.

میترا – آره، حَتمَن. کیا میان؟

کیوان – بَچه های کِلاسیمون.

میترا – ساعَتِ چَند؟

کیوان – میخایم ساعَتِ ۹ اونجا _____ .

میترا – عالیه. میتونَم با ماشین _____ دُنبالِت.

کیوان – دَست دَرد_____! مِرسی!

میترا – خواهِش میکنَم! پَس، اِمشَب میبینَمِت.

کیوان – خِیلی خوب. فِعلا خُدا حافِظ.

میترا – فِعلا

(d) Prepare for your classmates two questions in Persian about the dialogue. Your questions must have two different verbs in the subjunctive (one per sentence). Refrain from questions that require Yes/No answers. Prepare to say your questions fluently.

44. 🔊 Listen and read along. Two Tehran residents, Roya and Kamran are referring to the Islamic dress code that is obligatory in all public places in Iran, and describing what type of clothes they usually wear when they go to public places and when they are at home.

سَلام، اسم من رویا است. من در ایران زندگی میکنم. در ایران، طِبقِ قَوانینِ شَرعی، هَمهِ زَن ها چه ایرانی چه خارِجی بایَد در جاهای عُمومی رَعایَتِ حِجاب کنند. به دَلیلِ این قانون، وَقتی من از خانه ام بیرون میرَوم مَجبورم روسَری و مانتو و شَلوار بِپوشم. در تهران هوای تابستانی خیلی گرم است و پوشیدَنِ مانتو و روسری خیلی راحَت نیست، وَلی حِجاب برای هَمهِ زَن ها در هَمهِ جاهای عُمومی در هَر فَصلِ سال اِجباری است. بَنابراین، من نِمیتوانم با تی شیرت یا پیراهَنِ رِکابی یا شَلوارَک یا دامَنِ کوتاهی بِرَوم بیرون. در داخِلِ خانه مُدِ لِباس آزاد است و من مَعمولا در داخِلِ خانه ام پیراهَنِ رِکابی یا یک تی شیرت و شَلوارِ جین میپوشم.

سَلام، اسم من کامران است. من در تهران زندگی میکنم. مَعمولا در ایران تابِستان ها، مَردها بیرون از خانه یا مِهمانی پیراهنِ آستینِ کوتاه یا تی شیرت و شَلوارِ بُلَند میپوشَند مِثلِ جین. من هم وَقتی میرَوم بیرون تی شیرت و شَلوار ِ جین میپوشم. وَلی توی خانه آزاد هَستم، و شَلوارَک و آستینِ حَلقه ای میپوشم. ولی بیرون از خانه سَعی میکنم بیشتر شَلوار های رَنگِ تیره بپوشم و کوتاه نَپوشم.

Now, think of all the clothing items that you know in Persian and make two lists separately for women and men. Make one list of items that can be worn outside, and the other list of items that cannot be worn outside. Tell your class what items you have put on the lists by saying:

در ایران، وَقتی یک زن بیرون میرود، میتواند ـــــ و ـــــ بپوشد (در ایران، وَقتی یه زَن میره بیرون ، میتونه ـــــ و ـــــ بپوشه).

در ایران وقتی یک زن بیرون میرود، نِمیتواند ـــــ و ـــــ بپوشد (در ایران، وَقتی یه زَن میره بیرون ، نِمیتونه ـــــ و ـــــ بپوشه).

IN CLASS

دَر کِلاس

45. (a) Complete the sentences with the correct verb prefix (either *mee* or *be*). Translate the sentences.

۱.میخواهم فردا به پاساژ ـــــــروم.

۲.امروز نمیتوانم به کلاس ـــــــآیم.

۳.باید کاپشن ـــــــخرم.

۴.چطوری میشود به فُروشگاه ـــــــرسم؟

۵. امروز باید لِباس گرم ـــــــپوشم.

۶. امروز تا ساعت ۷ بعد از ظهر کار ـــــــکنم.

۷. امروز لِباسِ گرم ـــــــ پوشم.

۸. با اتوبوس به فُروشگاه ـــــــ رسی.

۹. امروز بعد از کلاس به پاساژ ـــــــرَوم که یک کاپشن زِمستانی ـــــــخَرَم.

45. (b) Your instructor will call on you to come to the board and write in Persian the subjunctive form of one of the following verbs.

میخَرم، میکِشم، میگیرم، نِمیکُنم، نِمیپوشم، میآیَم، میرِسم، میشَوم، پَرداخت میکُنند، دارم، است.

46. Work with a classmate and translate the following sentences into Persian. Pay special attention to the use of the subjunctive.

عابِربانک – ATM

(1) I have to go. (2) What do you have to do now? (3) At what time do you have to be in class? (4) I have to be there at 9:05 a.m. and I don't want to be late for that class. (5) Can I pay with a credit card? (6) Can I use my credit card at this ATM? (7) Where can I buy groceries around here?

47. Talk to several of your classmates and ask what they want to do this coming week. Be ready to answer the same question. Find those in class who have weekend plans similar to yours (study or rest, go out or stay in, etc.).

E.g., آخَرِ هَفته‌ِ آیَنده میخواهی چه کار کُنی؟

259

48. Pick two classmates and address them with polite requests (one per person) using the word (میشه) میشود and one of the verbs listed below or any other verb you know.

میشود (میشه) ...؟

تَلَفُظ کُنی

بِگویی (بِگی)

تَرجُمه کُنی

بِنویسی

بِخوانی (بِخونی)

49. You will work in groups of three. Think of three different times during the day today and ask your classmates where they have to be at those times. Pay special attention to the use of the verb *to be* in the subjunctive.

اِمروز ساعَتِ ۱ بایَد کُجا باشی؟

50. You will work in groups of three. Ask your classmates the questions below. Before you start, you instructor may go over the sentences with you to ensure correct pronunciation.

۱. بایَد هَر روز به کِلاس بِروی (بایَد هَر روز به کِلاس بِری)؟

۲. بایَد هَر روز تَکلیف اَنجام بِدهی (بایَد هَر روز تَکلیف اَنجام بِدی)؟

۳. مَعمولا بایَد ساعَتِ چَندِ صُبح بیدار شوی (مَمولَن بایَد ساعَتِ چَندِ صُب بیدار شی)؟

۴. بَعد اَز این کِلاس، بایَد به کِلاسِ دیگر بِروی (بَد اَز این کِلاس، بایَد به کِلاسِ دیگه بِری)؟

51. You will work in pairs. Think of three most important things you had to do at the beginning of your first year at the university. Now, create a very brief conversation between you and an Iranian student who has just got to your university before the beginning of her or his first freshmen semester. Tell the student what s/he has to do at the beginning of the semester. Use the word must/have to *bã-yad* in your sentences, for example,

اَوَل بایَد .... بَعد بایَد .... بَعد اَز آن، بایَد ....

Let your group mate (the foreign student) ask you questions in order to contribute to the conversation. The question(s) must feature verbs in the subjunctive, for example, *Then, you have to get a university ID. Where can I get a university ID?*

You will present your dialogue to class.

52. You will be working in pairs. Ask the following questions in Persian. Before proceeding, you might go over the questions with your instructor to ensure correct pronunciation.

۱. آیا هَمه‌ی دانشجوهای دانشگاهِتان مَجبور هستند که در خوابگاه زندگی کنند؟ (آیا هَمه‌ی دانشجوهای دانشگاهِتون مَجبورَن که تو خابگاه زندگی کُنَن؟)

۲. آیا هَمه‌ی دانشجوهای رشته تان مَجبور هستند که یک کلاسِ زبانِ خارِجی بَر دارند؟ (آیا هَمه‌ی دانشجوهای رِشتَتون مَجبورَن که یه کلاسِ زبانِ خارِجی بَر دارن؟)

۳. دانشجوهای دانشگاهِتان بایَد در یک تِرم چند تا واحِد بَر دارند؟ (دانشجوهای دانشگاهِتون بایَد تو یه تِرم چَن تا واحِد بَر دارَن؟)

53. Pick a combination of words from the list below. Very politely make a request of a student in your class using that combination in the imperative. Thank that student for honoring your request. The verbs in the table are given without conjugation endings. Decide whether or not you need to add the endings to the verbs in order to say your command sentence correctly.

E.g.,! کامران، لُطفا پایِ تَخته بُرو ... مِرسی!

Verbs that you can use:

پای تَخته بُرو	کِتاب باز کُن
از ... سوال کُن (از ... سُال کُن)	کِتاب بِبَند
به ... جَواب بِده	روی تَخته بِنویس (رو تَخته بِنویس)
نِشان بِده (نِشون بِده)	جُمله بِخوان (جُمله بِخون)
	تَرجُمه کُن

Use more verbs if you need.

54. You will be working in groups. This drill will require you to identify and distinguish various verb forms. Read the following story about Molla Nasreddin, the character featuring in satirical and humorous anecdotes known across the Middle Eastern cultures. Use the verbs given below to complete the anecdote. The verbs are not given in the order in which they should appear in the anecdote. Be prepared to name the form of every verb you use.

هَمه‌ی all of, all the ...	گاز گِرِفت it bit	گاز میگیرد it bites

Verbs to insert:

بِده ، میگیرَند ، بُکُنَم ، بِگیرد

سَگی مُلا را گاز گِرِفت.

بِه مُلا گُفتَند: آگَر نِمیخواهی

سَگ دیگَر تو را گاز ـــــــ ،

غَذا به او ـــــــ .

مُلا گُفت: آگَر این کار را ـــــــ

هَمِهِ سَگ ها مَن را گاز ـــــــ .

55.   Tara is going on an exchange program to Tehran. She is thinking about taking along the following items so that she wears them when she goes out with friends in Tehran. Tell her which items she can wear when she goes out to public places in Iran, and which items she cannot. Use the subjunctive in your sentences.

شَلوار جین، شَلوارَکِ جین، دامَنِ کوتاه، مانتو، کَفشِ وَرزِشـی، کَفشِ مَجلِسـی، پیراهَنِ رِکابی، ژاکَتِ بُلَند. پیراهَنِ آستین بُلَند.

Jake is going on an exchange program to Tehran. He is thinking of taking with him the following items to wear when he goes out with friends in Tehran. Tell him which items he can wear in the street in Tehran, and which items he cannot. Use the subjunctive in your sentences.

شَلوار جین، شَلوارَک، پیراهَنِ آستین کوتاه، پیراهَنِ آستین بُلَند، کَفشِ وَرزِشـی، تی شِرتِ آستین کوتاه.

56.   Think about yourself. If you were to go on an exchange program to Tehran, what you would wear outside, considering the dress code in public spaces in Iran, your gender and your taste. Think of one complete outfit and describe it for class.

57.   Interview. Your instructor will call on you to ask your classmates questions in Persian. Ask each one of your classmates one question in Persian on any of the topics listed below.

If your class is too big for this format of activity, your instructor might divide the class into groups of three, where you will find yourself with two other students. Ask each of the two classmates at least three questions on the given topics.

Topics:

اسم و فامیل، کجایی، خانواده، بِهتَرین دوست، دانِشگاه و کلاس، شغل،

کارهای روزانه، خانه و منزل ، شـهر و کشـور ، لِباس، خَرید

LISTENING  شِنیداری

 Keyvan and his wife Sahar are in a department store shopping for Keyvan's new suit.

Keyvan is trying to choose a suit that he can afford, but also one that he actually likes. Listen to the conversations between Keyvan and Sahar, and between Keyvan and a store associate who helps him choose the right suit. The speakers mention common colors and fabrics used to make men's suits, and discuss the prices of the suits.

Pre-listening. (1) Considering the topic of the conversation, make a list of most common words you might encounter in such a conversation. If the word you wrote down is a noun, think of the verb that would commonly go with it in the context of conversation. If the word that you wrote is a verb, think of a noun that might go with it in a conversation on the given topic. Pronounce the words you wrote aloud so that you can identify them when you hear the conversation.

(2) The verbs in the conversation appear in present tense and in subjunctive. Think of the present tense and subjunctive markers. Think of how the verbs usually look with those markers in the beginning and the conjugational endings at the end of the verb. Are there exceptions to the rule? Now, pronounce the verbs you have written using both present tense and subjunctive forms.

263

3. Using the words you have written down, make a list of the most common Persian phrases that you would use in a department store.

Assignment. Listen to the conversations, and answer the following questions in Persian.

پُلی اِستِر polyester	پَشم wool
تَخفیف discount	قیمتِ مُناسِب reasonable, suitable price
خَرج میکنم I spend	

۱. کِیوان میخواهد برای کُت شَلوار چِقَدر خَرج کند (کیوان میخاد برای کُت شَلوار چِقَد خَرج کنه)؟

۲. کِیوان کُت شَلوار های چه رَنگی را دوست دارد (کِیوان کُت شَلواراى چه رَنگیو دوست داره)؟

۳. کِیوان چرا کُت شَلوارِ ۱۲۰ دُلاری را نِمیخواهد (کِیوان چرا کُت شَلوارِ ۱۲۰ دُلاریو نِمیخاد)؟

۴. در آخر، کیوان چه نُوع کُت شَلواری را میخَرد (در آخر، کیوان چه نُو کُت شَلواریو میخَره)؟

Follow-up 1. Prepare to ask your classmates two questions about the dialogue. Your two questions must have subjunctives of at least two different verbs (one per sentence). Prepare to say your questions fluently.

Follow-up 2. Prepare to summarize the dialogue by saying what type of suit Keyvan wants, what type of suit he can afford, and finally which suit, you think, he will purchase. Use the subjunctive in your sentences as needed, for example,

کِیوان میخواهَد ... بخَرد (کیوان میخاد ... بخَره)

کیوان میتواند ... بخَرد (کیوان میتونه ... بخَره)

کِیوان میتواند ...بخَرد، وَلی نِمیخواهد آن را بخرد (کیوان میتونه ...بخَره، وَلی نِمیخاد اونو بخَره)

Follow-up 3. You will be working with one or two classmates. Create a brief conversation in a clothing store. Divide the roles as a customer and a salesperson or two customers and a salesperson. You can use the conversation from the Listening section for reference, but pick a different clothing item(s) to talk about. You must use at least three subjunctives and the names of any number of clothing items and colors in your dialogue.

READING

خواندَنی

Read the following passage about one of Iran's largest malls called Persian Gulf Mall. Before coming to class, read the text aloud several times until you can easily pronounce all sentences.
Pre-reading. The reading is about one of Iran's largest malls. Think of the most common words that you expect to encounter in this excerpt. Write those words down so you can see them. If they are nouns, think of the verbs that might go with them in the given context. If the words you wrote are verbs, think of the nouns that might go with them in this context. Write down those words as well, so you can visually identify them if you encounter them in the excerpt.

Useful words:

مَرکَزِ هَمایِش ها convention center	شَهرِبازی amusement park
بالگَردِنِشین helipad	چَهار بُعدی 4D

هایپِرمارکِتِ کارفور Hypermarket Carrefour. Carrefour is French-based multinational retailer with branches in over 30 countries.

اِصفَهان سیتی سِنتِر Esfahan City center is one of the largest malls in Iran and Middle East. It is located in the city of Esfahan in Iran.

مَرکَزِ خَریدِ خَلیجِ فارس.

دَر شَهرهای بُزُرگِ ایران مِثلِ تِهران، اِصفَهان، شیراز و مَشهَد پاساژ های بُزُرگ و مُدِرنِ زیادی وُجود دارَند. نامِ یِکی از این پاساژ های بُزُرگِ خَلیجِ فارس است.

مَرکَزِ خَریدِ خَلیجِ فارس دَر شَهرِ شیراز دَر جُنوبِ غَربی ایران قَرار دارد. از لَحاظِ شُمارهِ مَغازه ها، مَرکَزِ خَرید خِلیجِ فارس بُزُرگ تَرین پاساژِ ایران و خاوَرِ میانه است. مَرکَزِ خَریدِ خَلیجِ فارس بیش از ۲۵۰۰ مَغازه دارد. یِک هُتِلِ ۵ سِتاره با ۲۶۲ اُتاق هَم دَر این پاساژ جا دارد. ساختِمانِ این هُتِل ۳۵ طَبَقه است. پاساژِ خَلیجِ فارس هَمچِنین یِک مَرکَزِ هَمایِش ها و یِک بالگَردِنِشین دارد.

پاساژِ خَلیجِ فارس هَم یِک مرکز خرید و هَم یِک مَرکَزِ تَفریحی است. دَر این پاساژ دو شَهرِبازیِ بُزُرگی با اِستاندارد های جَهانی، یِک سالُنِ بولینگ و یِک

سالُنِ سه طَبَقه ای بَرای بیلیارد هَم هست. سینَمای بُزُرگی با ۶ سالُنِ مُدِرن و یِک سالُنِ ۴-بُعدی هم در این پاساژ جا دارد.

پاساژِ خَلیجِ فارس هَمچِنین دو تا اِستَخر، یِک زَمینِ تِنیس، سالُنِ وَرزِشی، سونا، رِستوران ها و کافی شاپ ها دارد. فُروشگاهِ بُزُرگِ هایپِرمارکِتِ کارفور هَم اینجا هَست.

پارکینگِ این پاساژِ بُزُرگ سه طَبَقه است و بَرای ۵۵۰۰ ماشین جا دارد.

پاساژِ بُزُرگِ دیگَرِ ایران اِصفَهان سیتی سِنتِر است. این پاساژ دَر شَهرِ اِصفَهان قَرار دارد و از لَحاظِ مَساحَت، بُزُرگ تَرین پاساژِ ایران و خاوَرِ میانه است.

Follow-up 1. Prepare for your classmates two questions about the excerpt. In your questions, use at least two different verbs in subjunctive (one per sentence). Before coming to class, say your questions few times until you can easily pronounce them.

Follow-up 2. Do research online and add one piece of information about the Isfahan City Center Mall that is not mentioned in the excerpt.

Follow-up 3. On the board, write in Persian one key word from the excerpt. Now that everyone has written their words on the board, pick one or more of those words (except your own word) and ask one of your classmates a question about the mall in her/his hometown.

Follow-up 4. Prepare and say a brief description of the mall in the town where your university is located. Try to include in your description the main key words pertaining to the topic.

TRANSLATION   تَرجُمه

Translate into Persian the following phone conversation. Roya is calling her friend Mitra.

– Hello?
– Hi Mitra! This is Roya. How are you?
– Thank you, dear (قربونت). How are you?
– I am well, thanks.
– What's up?
– All good (سلامتی), I am calling (زنگ زدم) to see if you want to come with me to the mall today. My brother's birthday is next week. I want to go to the mall today in the afternoon

to buy a present for him. I do not want to go by myself (تَنهایی). Do you want to come with me?
– Sure. What kind of present do you want to buy?
– I want to buy a polo shirt or sneakers for him.
– Which mall do you want to go to?
– I don't really know which mall I should go to.
– Well, the mall next to the university has a lot of nice clothing and shoes for young people. For sure we will find a nice T-shirt and shoes for your brother there.
– Ok, great. How about five o'clock? I can pick you up at your place.
– Thank you.
– Sure. See you at five, then.
– Great.
– Bye now.
– Bye.

WRITING  اِنشا

Write a brief passage (at least 100 words) and describe what clothes you usually like to wear to classes every day during the fall as well as the spring semesters. Do not forget to mention the colors. Write where you usually prefer to shop for clothing and shoes. Make sure to use at least three verbs in the subjunctive in your passage.

Stained-glass work in the Masjedeh Naser ol Molk, in Shiraz. Handmade in 1800s.

Function Relating past events, formulating question sentences and responses with the word *because*, using prepositional phrases with past tense. Key verbs: *to be born, to grow up, to go to school, to move, to meet, to get married, to start to*

Listening It was a busy day!

Reading Who is Anoushe Ansari?

Structures Simple Past tense.

GRAMMAR

دسـتورِ زَبان

Verb Conjugation in Simple Past Tense

When to use the past tense. Persian past tense is, for the most part, similar to English simple past tense. It describes:

(a) an event that was completed once in the past, for example,

او دو سـال پیش به آمریکا آمد. She came to America two years ago.

در امتحان قبول شـدم. I passed the exam.

(b) with the verb *to be* it also conveys an event, state of being that continued to be true for some time in past, but has or may have now changed, for example,

آنوقت من در ایران بودم.   I was in Iran then.

او در ایران مهندس عمران بود.   In Iran, he was a civil engineer.

غذا خیلی خوب بود.   The food was very good.

How to Conjugate a Verb in Past Tense

To conjugate a verb in Persian means to show the subject, that is, the person or thing that did the action described by the verb.

All Persian verbs form their past tense in the same manner. To conjugate a verb in the past tense, first say the verb's past tense root, and then say the conjugational ending that corresponds to the subject, that is, the person or thing that did the action. The conjugation endings are the same ones that you have learned for the Present tense, except that we do not need any ending for او, the *she/he/it* form in the Past tense.

Let's conjugate in past tense the verb *to go* whose past tense root is رَفت (raft)

I went	raft-am	رفتم
You (تو) went	raft-ee	رفتی
S/he, it went	raft	رفت
We went	raft-eem	رفتیم
You (شـما) went	raft-een	رفتید
They went	raft-an	رفتند

As the conjugation endings reflect the Subject (i.e., the person or thing that did the action of the verb), you don't need to mention the Subject if that Subject is a pronoun, for example,

کار کردم   I worked

In base (i.e., one-word) verbs the primary stress falls on the root of the verb, while in negated verbs the stress falls on the negation prefix.

Negation. To negate the verb in past tense simply say /na/ at the beginning of the verb, for example,

نَکَردَم /na-kardam/ I did not do

نَخوردَند /na-khordan/ They did not eat

نَبود /na-bood/ It was not

The negation prefix /na/ is stressed and is written together with the verb as shown above. If the verb starts with a vowel آ /ã/, the negation prefix becomes /na-ee/ (نَی):

Negative	Verb
نَیآمَد (نَیومَد) naee-oomad s/he did not come	آمَد (اومَد) oomad s/he came
نَیاوُرد naee-ãvord s/he did not bring	آورد ãvord s/he brought

In order to negate a past tense verb that starts with a vowel carried by a diacritic and introduced by the symbol ا (e.g. أفتادن، آنداختن), drop that symbol in writing and attach the negation prefix نَی /naee/ directly to the first consonant letter of the verb.

Negative	Verb
نَیُفتاد naee-of-tãd s/he did not fall	أفتاد of-tãd s/he fell
نَینداختَم naee-an-dãkh-tam I did not throw	آنداختَم an-dãkh-tam I threw

The verb ایستادَم /ees-tã-dam/ *I stood, stopped* is an exception and the initial ا can be pre-served after /na/, for example,

نایستادَم / نه ایستادَم

For more examples of negated verbs with an initial vowel see the appendix Grammarian's Corner.

How to Find the Verb's Root

When you look up a verb in the dictionary, you will see the verb's past tense root with ن /an/ attached to the end of the verb. That /an/ at the end stands for the gerund (the *...ing* form) of the verb. Usually Persian dictionaries give verbs in the gerund form. So, when you learn a new verb, you are already learning its past tense root.

E.g., To go رَفتَن

Here, رَفت is the past tense root and the ن /an/ at the end is the gerund marker.

The present tense root is, obviously, different from the past tense root. A good dictionary will show the present tense root in parentheses right after the gerund form of the verb, for example,

To go (رو) رفتن

All Persian verbs have only two roots: one root shared by the present tense, subjunctive and imperative and the other for past tense only. As the conjugation endings are almost the same for both past and present tenses, the verb's root is what distinguishes the present tense from the past tense.

For your convenience, a list of the most common verbs with their past tense, present tense and subjunctive forms are listed in the appendices B and C of this textbook.

HOMEWORK   تَکلیف

1. Look at the following verbs. Identify the verbs in the past tense and underline them.

کَردَم، میکُنَم، رَفتَم، میرَوم، شُدَم، میشَوم، گُفتَم، میگویَم، گِرِفتَم، میگیرَم، آمَدَم، میایَم، پوشیدَم، میپوشَم، بودَم، هَستَم، دادَم، میدَهم، دیدَم، میبینَم، گُذَشت، میگُذَرد، داشتی، داری، خواندَم، میخوانَم.

2. 🔊 You will hear a series of verbs. Listen and identify the tense of each verb. Arrange the verbs you hear into two columns: past tense and present tense. You know all the verbs in this exercise from previous lessons.

Past tense	Present tense

3. Look at the following verbs and for each verb write the subject pronoun that corresponds to that verb. The verbs are in the past tense.

رَفتَم. گُفت ، گِرِفتی، خوردَند، پوشیدید ، کَردیم ، آمَدَم ، بودی ، گُذَشت ، دیدَند، دادَم، داشت، خواندی.

4. 🔊 You will hear verbs in Persian. Listen to the verbs and for each verb you hear write the subject pronoun that corresponds to that verb. The verbs are in the past tense.

۷	۴	۱
۸	۵	۲
۹	۶	۳

5. Write the conjugation ending of the verb based on the Subject that you see.

من رفت‌_____ ، تو گفت‌_____ ، شما گرفت‌_____ ، او پوشید_____ ، ما کرد_____ ، آنها آمد_____ ، من بود_____ ، تو دید_____ ، او داد_____ ، آن گذشت_____ ، شما خورد_____ ، من خرید_____ ، ما پدرخت_____ ، او شد_____ .

6. Complete the sentences using the given verbs in the past tense.

دیشب من به مهمانی _____ (رفتن). به هم اتاقی‌ام _____ (گفتن) که با من بیاید، ولی او تصمیم _____(گرفتن) در خوابگاه بماند و برای امتحان درس بخواند. پس، من تنهایی _____ (رفتن). من دوش _____(گرفتن)، لباس های مجلسی_____(پوشیدن)

273

و ____(رفتن). در مهمانی خیلی حال ____(کردن). وقتی بعد از مهمانی به خوابگاه

____(آمدن) به هم اتاقی ام ____(گفتن) که مهمانی خیلی خوب ____(بودن)، به

من خیلی خوش ____(گذشتن) و جایش خالی ____ (بودن).

7. Here is the description of what Ali has done today. Listen and read along. Then, complete the statements with verbs in the past tense in third person singular (he) referring to Ali. Prepare to read the statements aloud in Persian.

باز هَم (بازَم)	تا دیر وَقت
Again	till late

اِمروز ساعَتِ ۸ بیدار شُدَم. دوش گِرِفتَم ، صبحانه خوردَم، و بعد، سَرِ کِلاس

رَفتَم. تا ساعَتِ ۱ دَر کِلاس بودَم. ساعَتِ ۱:۳۰ به کافه تِریای دانِشگاه رَفتَم

و آنجا ناهار خوردَم. بَعد از ناهار، به کِتابخانه رَفتَم و تا ساعَتِ ۵ آنجا بودَم. از

کِتابخانه به کافه تِریا رَفتَم و شام خوردَم. بَعد از شام، باز هَم به کِتابخانه رَفتَم و

تا دیر وَقت آنجا بودَم.

ساعت ۸ بیدار ____

بعد، دوش ____

بعد از دوش، صبحانه ____ (بعد از دوش، صبونه ____)

بعد از صبحانه، سر کلاس ____ (بعد از صبونه، سر کلاس ____)

تا ساعت ۱ در کلاس ____

ساعَتِ ۱:۳۰ به کافه تِریا ____ و ناهار ____

بعد از ناهار، به کتابخانه ____ (بعد از ناهار، به کتابخونه ____)

تا ساعت ۵ در کتابخانه ____ (تا ساعَتِ ۵ تو کتابخونه ____)

از کتابخانه به سیلف ____ و شام ____ (از کتابخونه به سیلف ____ و شام ____)

بعد از شام، باز هَم به کتابخانه ____ (بعد از شام، بازَم به کتابخونه ____)

تا دیر وقت در کتابخانه ____ (تا دیروَقت تو کتابخونه ____)

8. Prepare to say where you were yesterday at 8 a.m., 12 noon and 5 p.m.

For example, دیروز ساعَتِ هَشتِ صُبح دَر خوابگاه بودَم (دیروز ساعَتِ هَشتِ صُب تو

خابگاه بودَم)

9. Prepare to say three main things you did this past weekend. Start your sentences with

هَفتهِ گُذَشته ...

10. 🔊 Listen and read along as Nasreen describes how her day went yesterday. Think of the activities that you also did yesterday and tell class which activities both Nasreen and you did yesterday. For this exercise you will use verbs in past tense in third and in first person singular. For example,

دیروز هم من هم نَسرین به کلاس رَفتیم.

دیروز نسرین دوش گِرِفت، دیروز من دوش نَگِرِفتم.

اِس اِم اِس های جدید   new (text) messages

دیروز ساعت ۸ بیدار شدم. دوش گرفتم، دندان هایم را مسواک زدم و موهایم را شانه کردم. صبحانه کامل خوردم، اِس اِم اِس های جدیدم را خواندم و ساعت ۹:۱۵ به کلاس رفتم. بعد از کلاس ها ناهار خوردم. بعد، به کتابخانه رفتم و ۲ ساعت آنجا درس خواندم. از کتابخانه به باشگاه رفتم و بعد از باشگاه، رفتم سلف دانشگاه شام بخورم. بعد از شام، رفتم پیش دوستم که واسه امتحان با هام درس بخوانیم.

11. 🔊 Listen and read along as Kamran talks about his life. Fill in the blanks with the verbs. Then, answer the questions. Kamran is speaking in first person singular, so you will have to change the conjugation to third person singular in the past and present tenses for your answers.

I met … (i.e., I made …'s acquaintance)	با ... آشنا شُدَم	They call me	من را صِدا میکنند (مَنو صدا میکنَن)
I started to …	شُروع به ... کَردَم	I grew up	بُزرگ شُدَم
Continuation of education	اِدامه تَحصیلات	At the age of 23	در ۲۲ سالِگی
I married …	با ... اِزدِواج کَردَم	I immigrated	مُهاجِرَت کَردَم

سلام دوستان! چطورید! اسم من کامران است، ولی دوست هایم من را کامرون صِدا میکنند. من در آمریکا زندگی میکنم ولی در شهر تهران در ایران به دنیا _____ . من در تهران بزرگ _____ و در تهران به دبستان، دبیرستان و به

دانشگاه ـــــ . در ۲۳ سالگی برای اِدامه‌ی تَحصیلات به آمریکا ـــــ . اَوَل به شَهرِ سانفرانسیسکو ـــــ و در دانشگاهِ سانفرانسیسکو در برنامه‌ی دُکترا شُروع به درس خواندَن ـــــ . بعد از ۵ سال، از سانفراسیسکو به شهر لس آنجلس ـــــ و در یک شرکت مهندسی شروع به کار ـــــ . الان هم در آن شِرکَت کار میکنم و کارم را خیلی دوست دارم. سال اولم در لس آنجلس، من با همسرم آشنا ـــــ و ما چند سال بعد با هم ازدواج ـــــ . آنوقت من ۳۱ ساله ـــــ و همسرم ۳۰ ساله ـــــ . ما الان هم در لس آنجلس زندگی میکنیم. ما لس آنجلس را خیلی دوست داریم. به نظرم، آب و هوای لس آنجلس شَبیهِ آب و هوای تهران است. جَمعیتِ ایرانی ها در لس آنجلس خیلی بزرگ است و به این دلیل، لس آنجلس رستوران های ایرانی خیلی زیادی دارد . هم من هم خائُمَم عاشِقِ غَذای ایرانی هستیم و لس آنجلس برای ما جای خیلی خوبی است.

۱. کامران کُجا به دُنیا آمَد؟ (کامران کُجا به دُنیا اومَد؟)

۲. کامران در ۲۳ سالگی چه کار کَرد؟

۳. او اَوَل به چه شَهری در آمریکا رَفت؟ (اون اَوَل به چه شَهری تو آمریکا رَفت؟)

۴. کامران بَعد اَز ۵ سال زندِگی در سان فرانسیسکو چه کار کَرد؟

۵. کامران چِرا به آن شَهر رَفت؟ (کامران چِرا به اون شَهر رَفت؟)

۶. کامران در لُس آنجِلِس با چه کَسی آشنا شُد؟

۷. کامران در چَند سالِگی اِزدِواج کَرد؟

۸. کامران با هَمسَرِش الان کُجا زندِگی میکُنَند؟ (کامران با هَمسَرِش الان کُجا زِندِگی میکُنَن؟)

۹. آیا کامران در لس آنجلس خوشحال است؟ (کامران تو لس آنجلس خوشحاله؟)

12. 🔊 Listen to Tara as she describes how she was late to class yesterday. Answer the questions starting your answers with the word *because* (برای اینکه). Be ready to say your answers aloud.

۱. چرا این دانشجو با ماشینِش به کلاس نَیامَد؟ (چرا این دانِشجو با ماشینِش به کلاس نَیومَد؟) بَرای اینکه ـــــ

۲. چرا این دانِشجو دیر به کلاس رِسید؟ بَرای اینکه ـــــ

۳. چِرا دیشَب مَشقِ اِمروز را نَنِوِشت؟ (چرا دیشَب مَشقِ اِمروزو نَنِوِشت؟) بَرای
اینکه ـــــــــ

Now, think of the last time you were late for something (e.g., late to class). Explain why that happened. Use the past tense verb in your narrative. You can use the exercise above for reference.

13. **Have you ever …?** Think of something interesting to do (traveling to a place, doing something fun, etc.). Pick a classmate and ask if she/he has ever done the same thing, for example,

هَرگِز به تِهران رَفتی؟   Have you ever been to Tehran?

The word هَرگِز means "ever" in affirmative sentences and questions, and means "never" if used in a negated sentence.

14. Translate the following sentences using the prepositional phrase

بَعد آز اینکه

/bad az een-keh/

Keep in Mind

The word *after* may refer to a noun (e.g., after the exam) or an action (e.g,. after I had lunch). For "after the …," say /bad az …/ in Persian. For "after … *any verb* …," say /bad az een-keh/ in Persian.

For example, **After** I had lunch - بعداز اینکه ناهار خوردم

After the exam – بعداز امتحان

The same rule applies to most prepositions and prepositional phrases that can be used with either a noun or verb (e.g., before, instead of, etc.).

(1) After the class ended, I went to the library.
(2) After the semester started, I did not have time for fun anymore.
(3) After the guests left, I cleaned the room and went to bed.
(4) After I talked to my parents, I went home.
(5) After I saw my grade, I made an appointment with the professor.

با اِستاد وَقت گِرِفتن to make an appointment with a professor

15. Think about yourself and finish these statements using the word "after" correctly. Prepare to say your statements aloud in class.

(1) After I came to the university _____
(2) Today, after I had breakfast _____
(3) Yesterday, after I returned to my room _____

(4)   After I read my acceptance letter from the university _____

(5)   After I turned 18 _____.

16.    Prepare a brief oral presentation about yourself. You will speak in Persian in class. Address the following questions in your presentation.

Learning, study of Persian language   یادگیریِ زَبانِ فارسی

۱. کجا به دُنیا آمَدی (کجا به دُنیا اومَدی)؟ ۲. کجا بُزُرگ شُدی؟ ۳. کجا به دَبیرِستان رَفتی؟ ۴. در چه سالی به دانشگاه آمَدی (در چه سالی به دانشگاه اومَدی)؟ ۵. در چه سالی شُروع به یادگیریِ زَبانِ فارسی کَردی؟ ۶. در دانشگاه چه رِشته ای میخوانی (تو دانشگاه چه رِشته ای میخونی)؟ ۷. سالِ چَندُمِ دانِشگاه هستی (سالِ چَندُمِ دانِشگاهی)؟ ۹. اسمِ بِهتَرین دوستِ تو چه است (اسمِ بِهتَرین دوستِ تو چیه)؟ ۱۰. کِی و کُجا با بِهتَرین دوستِت آشنا شُدی؟

IN CLASS   دَر کِلاس

17.   Fill in the blanks with appropriate verbs in the past tense.

سلام، اسم من علی است. من امروز ساعت ۸ بیدار _____. بعد، دوش _____. بعد از دوش، صبحانه _____ و در موبایلَم اِس اِم اِس های جَدید را _____. بعد، دندان هایم را مسواک _____ و به کلاس _____. امروز فقط دو تا کلاس _____. ساعت ۱۲ به سلف دانشگاه _____ و آنجا ناهار _____. بعد از ناهار، به کتابخانه _____ و تا ساعت ۴ آنجا _____. بعد از کتابخانه، به باشگاه _____ و از آنجا به کافه تریا _____ و شام خوردم. امروز غذای کافه تریا خیلی خوشمزه _____. بعد از شام، به خوابگاه _____، کمی درس _____ و بعد خوابیدم.

18.   Translate the following sentences into Persian.

تَمامِ شَب All night
خَراب شُدن To break, to become broken

(1)   I did not call you because my phone broke.
(2)   I did not go to classes yesterday because I did not feel well.

278

(3) I was late to class, because the bus did not come on time.

(4) I did not do my homework because I was at a party all night.

(5) I was tired because I returned home very late.

19.   Talk to your classmates and ask them where they were at 8 a.m., 12 noon and 5 p.m. Find people in class who were at the same place (lecture, library, etc.) or similar locations at the same time as you were there.

20.   Talk to your classmates and ask them what three things they did last weekend, for example,

آخَر هَفتهِ گُذَشته چه کار کَردی؟

Now, share with the class who in your opinion had a:

fun weekend   آخَر هَفتهِ با حالی

busy weekend   (آخَر هَفتهِ شلوغ) آخَر هَفتهِ شُلوغ

quiet weekend   (آخَر هَفتهِ آروم) آخَر هَفتهِ آرام

21.   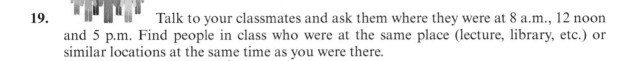 You will be working in pairs. Ask your classmate questions in Persian about the routine activities shown in the table and complete the table with the times at which your conversation partner completed them. Your instructor will ask you questions about the daily routine of your conversation partner, so be ready to say the verbs in III p.s.

ساعتِ چَند بیدار شُدی؟ ,E.g.

	ساعت
Woke up	
Took a shower	
Ate breakfast	

	Went to class
	Had lunch
	Did anything after classes?
	Had dinner
	Returned to the room, home
	Went to sleep

22. Talk to all your classmates and ask them how old they were when they came to your university for their freshmen year. Find out if anyone was of the same age as you were and tell your class about it.

E.g., وَقتی به دانشگاه آمَدی چند ساله بودی؟ (وَقتی اومَدی دانشگاه چن ساله بودی؟)

سارا وَقتی به دانشگاه آمَد، مِثلِ من ۲۰ ساله بود.

(سارا وَقتی به دانشگاه اومَد، مِثلِ من ۲۰ ساله بود)

وَقتی /vaq-tee/ the time when (conditional, not a question word)

23. Think of three places you were at during a specific time yesterday (library, gym, dining hall, class, appointment). Now, ask your classmates where they were at those times, for example,

دیروز ساعت ۳ کجا بودی؟

Now, tell the class:

دیروز وَقتی من در باشگاه بودَم، سارا در کتابخانه بود

(دیروز وَقتی من تو باشگاه بودَم، سارا تو کتابخونه بود)

280

Be prepared to use the verb *to be* in first person singular, second person singular, and third person singular in the past tense.

24. Ask and answer the following questions in Persian. Pay special attention to the use of کِی (question word *When*) and وَقتی که / وَقتی (conditional conjunction *When, the time when …*).

اِنتِخاب کردن to choose

(1) In which year did you come to the university?
(2) How old were you when you came to the university?
(3) When did you choose your major?
(4) When you chose your major, did you talk to your parents?
(5) When are you graduating?
(6) What will you do after you graduate?

25. Pick a classmate and ask him/her a question that starts with, "Do you remember when …?" (yā-det hast ke-ee …?). Use the verb in the second part of your question in the past tense.

E.g., یادِت است کِی با بِهتَرین دوستِت آشنا شُدی؟

(یادِته کِی با بِهتَرین دوستِت آشنا شُدی؟)

Do you remember when you met your best friend?

26. You will be working in pairs. Ask the following questions in Persian. Be ready to also answer these questions. Pay special attention to the verbs in the past tense.

(1) How many credits did you take last semester?
(2) Last semester, did you have classes in the morning or in the afternoon?
(3) Did you go home (during) last fall/spring break?
(4) Last semester, did you have homework every day?
(5) How many finals did you have last semester?
(6) Did you have a roommate last semester?
(7) How many times did you see your advisor this semester?

27. Interview a classmate about his last vacation trip. Ask him/her questions in the past tense using any of the question words below. Use any additional words as needed. You can include your instructor in the activity.

When?	کِی		What?	چه
Whom?	کی را (کیو)		How many?	چند

281

Where?	کجا		Why?	چِرا
With whom?	با کی		On what day?	چه روزی
For whom?	بَرای کی		At what time	ساعَتِ چند
			You had a good time	به تو خوش گُذَشت

28. Interview. Your instructor will call on you to ask your classmates questions in Persian. Ask each one of your classmates one question in Persian on any of the topics listed below. Ask your questions with the verbs in the past tense.

If your class is too big for this format of activity, your instructor might divide the class into groups of three, where you will find yourself with two other students. Ask each of the two classmates at least three questions on the given topics.

Topics:

اسمِ و فامیل، کُجایی، خانِواده، بِهتَرین دوسِت، دانِشگاه و کلاس، شُغل، کارهای روزانه، خانه و مَنزِل ، شَهر و کِشوَر، لِباس، خَرید.

LISTENING   شِنیداری

Listen to the conversation between Sara and Kamran. Sara took an exam and Kamran had a job interview yesterday. Sara and Kamran are sharing their experiences related to the exam and interview.

Pre-listening. (1)   Considering the topic of the conversation, make a list of the words that you would expect to hear in such a conversation. If the word you wrote down is a noun, think of the verb that might go with it. If the word that you wrote is a verb, think of a noun that might go with it in a conversation on the given topic.

(2)   Most of the verbs in the conversation appear in the past tense. Make a list of the most common verbs in the past tense form and pronounce them aloud, so that you can identify them when you listen to the conversation.

(3)   Listen to these words and expressions before you listen to the conversation. You will hear them in the conversation.

We were supposed to study	قَرار بود دَرس بخونیم
I was very worried	خِیلی نِگران بودَم
I prepared whatever way I could	هَر جوری که تونِستَم آماده شُدَم
I hope you passed the exam!	اُمیدوارَم تو اِمتِحان قَبول شُده باشی!
Job interview	مُصاحِبهِ کاری
In-person interview	مُصاحِبهِ حُضوری
I hope you did well with the interview!	اُمیدوارَم که در مُصاحِبه مُوَفَّق شُده باشی!
They will contact me by the end of this week	تا آخرِ این هَفته با من تَماس میگیرَن
Not a problem. Good luck!	خواهِش میکنَم. مُوَفَّق باشی
Thanks, that's very nice of you	مِرسی، لُطف داری

Follow-up 1. Prepare two comparative statements about Sara and Kamran. Make one statement about a similarity and another statement about a difference between Sara and Kamran.

Follow-up 2.  Work with two other classmates and create a conversation about an exam or interview that one of you had recently. Describe what you did that day and how the exam or interview went.

READING

خواندَنی

Pre-reading. The reading is from a brief biography of a renowned Iranian American. Think of the most common words you expect to encounter in a brief biographical blurb. Write those words down so you can see them. If they are nouns, think of the verbs that might go with them in the given context. If the words you wrote are verbs, think of the nouns that might go with them in this excerpt. Write down those words as well, so you can visually identify them when you encounter them in the excerpt.

Useful words:

to move, relocate	نَقلِ مَکان کَردن
shortly after ...	آندَکی بَعد از ...
birth	تَوَلُّد

to immigrate, emigrate	مُهاجِرَت کَردن
to enroll in a university	وارِدِ دانشگاه شُدن
To get a BA diploma	مَدرَکِ لیسانس دَریافت کَردن
to begin working	شُروع به کار کردن
telecommunications company	شِرکَتِ مُخابِرات
together with ...	هَمراه با ...
space explorer	گَردِشگَرِ فَضا
astronaut	فَضانَوَرد
of Iranian origin	ایرانی تَبار
to continue ...	به ... اِدامه دادن
astronomy	سِتاره شِناسی
currently, at present	دَر حالِ حاضِر

انوشه آنصاری

انوشه انصاری در سال ۱۹۶۶ در شِهر مَشهَد
در ایران به دنیا آمد. آندَکی بعد از تَوَلُدِ انوشه،
خانواده اش از مشهد به تِهران نَقلِ مَکان کَردَند.
انوشه در تهران بزرگ شد و همانجا به دبستان
و دبیرستان رفت. در سالِ ۱۹۸۴ خانواده‌ی انوشه
به آمریکا مُهاجِرَت کَردند. در آمریکا، انوشه
وارِدِ دانشگاهِ جُرج مِیسون شُد و در رشته‌ی
مهندسی کامپیوتر مَدرَکِ لیسانس دَریافت کَرد.
بعد از آن، انوشه وارِدِ دانشگاهِ جُرج واشینگتن

Anoushe Ansari in 2006 when she flew to space.

شُد و در رشته‌ی مهندسیِ بَرق مَدرَکِ فُوقِ لیسانس دَر یافت کَرد. بعد از دَریافتِ
مَدرَکِ فُوقِ لیسانس، انوشه در شِرکَتِ ام سی ای شُروع به کار کَرد. در آن زَمان
با حَمیدِ انصاری آشنا شُد. انوشه و حمید در سالِ ۱۹۹۱ با هَم اِزدِواج کَردند . دو
سال بعد، انوشه و شوهرش یک شِرکَتِ مُخابِرات را برای خود تاسیس کَردند.

در سالِ ۲۰۰۶ انوشه هَمراه با یک فَضانَوَردِ آمریکایی و یک فَضانَوَردِ روسی به فَضا سَفَر کَرد. انوشه اَوَلین زَنِ گَردِشگَرِ فَضا، اَوَلین مُسَلمانِ فَضانَوَرد و اَوَلین فَضانَوَردِ ایرانی تَبار است.

پَس از بازگَشت از فَضا، انوشه به تَحصیلاتِ خود اِدامه داد و در رشته‌ِ سِتاره شِناسی از دانشگاهِ سویین بورن در اُسترالیا مَدرَکِ فُوقِ لیسانس دَریافت کَرد. انوشه زَبان های انگلیسی، فارسی، فرانسه و کمی روسی بلد است. در حالِ حاضِر، انوشه و هَمسَرش حَمید در شَهرِ پلانو در تِگزاس زندگی میکنند.

Follow-up 1. Write on the board one key verb from the excerpt, for example, one that reflects a stage in a person's life. Now that everyone in class has written their words on the board, say one sentence about yourself using one of the verbs from the board in the past tense.

Follow-up 2. Do research online and add one fact about Anoushe Ansari that is not mentioned in the passage. Your addition must refer to the events in the past and must be said in past tense.

Follow-up 3. Prepare to ask your classmates two questions about Anoushe Ansari. Use at least two different verbs in the past tense for your questions (one per sentence).

Follow-up 4. Think about your parents. Tell their story briefly in Persian using the verbs in the past tense. Refer to the Reading and Homework sections about Kamran for vocabulary and structures. You can use the cues below to structure your narrative.

- Where is your family from?
- Where was your father born? Where did he grow up?
- Where was your mother born? Where did she grow up?
- Where did they meet?
- When did they get married?
- Did you father go to university? What did he study?
- Did you mother go to university? What did she study?
- Did they move to a different place after they got married?
- Where do they live now?
- When and where were you born? Where did you grow up?

TRANSLATION  تَرجُمه

Write down the Persian translation of the following passage.

Even /hat-ta/	حتی		She came to pick me up	با ماشینِش دُنبالَم آمَد
			We enjoyed ourselves	لِذَت بُردیم

My name is Tara. I am a student. I study a lot this semester. I usually study even on Sundays. However, last week I had a very nice weekend. I woke up at 8 a.m., took shower and brushed my teeth. I had a cup of tea and then texted my best friend, Neeloo. She was asleep and did not answer my text. She texted only after 30 minutes. I asked her where she was. She said she was in her room. I called her and said, "Let's go somewhere and have a nice breakfast. It is very nice outside." She was hungry and said Ok. She came to pick me up in her car. We went to town and had a nice breakfast in a café, and we chatted and enjoyed ourselves.

WRITING

اِنشا

Write a brief autobiography (at least 150 words). Use the following key verbs to describe the various life stages as applicable:

to be born	به دُنیا آمَدَن
to grow up	بُزُرگ شُدَن
to enroll in college	وارِدِ دانِشگاه شُدَن
to move	نَقلِ مَکان کَردَن
to study ...	رِشتهِ ... خواندَن
to start working	شُروع به کار کَردَن
to meet someone	با ... آشنا شُدَن

فَصلِ دَهُم
Chapter 10

آب و هَوا
Weather

Mountain village at dawn. N. Iran

Function How to compare things, understanding the weather forecast. Key verbs: *to shine, to rain, to snow, to blow, to be cold, to be warm.*

Listening What's the best time of the year to visit Tehran?

Reading Tehran during the four seasons.

Structures The Comparative and Superlative.

🔊 Listen and read along. Listen and repeat. Try to imitate the native speaker's pronunciation and intonation. Say each word a few times aloud until you can easily pronounce it.

Weather				
Windy	بادی		Weather	هَوا
Partly cloudy	نیمه آبری		Climate	آب و هَوا، اِقلیم
Heat	گَرما		Temperate	مُعتَدِل
The cold	سَرما		Mild	مُلایِم
Warm	گَرم		Humid	مَرطوب
Cold	سَرد		Dry	خُشک
Spring	بَهار		Wet	خیس
Summer	تابِستان (تابِستون)		Sunny day	روزِ آفتابی
Fall	پاییز		Cloudy	آبری
Winter	زِمِستان (زِمِستون)		Rainy	بارانی (بارونی)
Season (of the year)	فَصل		Snowy	بَرفی
Umbrella	چَتر		Average temperature	میانگینِ دَما
Snow boots	چَکمه‌ِ بَرف، چَکمه‌ِ برفی		Raincoat	بارانی (بارونی)
Thunderstorm	رَعد و بَرق		Cool, fresh	خُنَک

Miscellaneous				
Religious	مَذهَبی		Compared to …	نِسبَت به …
Part	قِسمَت		Place	مَکان
Good-tasting	خوشمَزه		Minority	اَقَلیَت
Bad-tasting	بَدمَزه		Group	گُروه (گوروه)
Most of …	بیشتَرِ …		Issue, problem	مَسئَله (مَسَله)
Majority of …	اَکثَرِ …		Ethnic	قُومی

288

Miscellaneous			
More or less	کَم و بیش	Gender (adj.)	جِنسیَتی
More than	بیش از	Better, best	بِهتَر، بِهتَرین
My younger brother	بَرادرِ کوچَکَم (بَرادرِ کوچیکَم)	My older sister	خواهَرِ بُزُرگَم

Verbs	
It rains	باران میبارد (بارون میباره)، باران میاید (بارون میاد)
It snows	بَرف میبارد (بَرف میباره)، بَرف میاید (بَرف میاد)
Strong wind blows	بادِ شَدیدی میوَزَد (بادِ شَدیدی میوزه)
The sun shines	خورشید میتابَد (خورشید میتابه)
Precipitation occurs	بارِش روی میدهد (بارِش روی میده)
The weather is warm/cold	هَوا گَرم/سَرد است (هَوا گَرم/سَرده)
It gets cold in winter	در زِمِستانِ هَوا سَرد میشود (تو زِمِستون هَوا سَرد میشه)
I'm warm	گَرمَم است (گَرمَمه)
I'm cold	سَردَم است (سَردَمه)
S/he is cold	سَردِش است (سَردِشه)
90 degrees Fahrenheit	۹۰ دَرَجهِ فارنهایت
Weather forecast	پیش بینیِ وَضعِ هَوا
What is the weather like today?	هَوا اِمروز چِطور است؟ (هَوا اِمروز چِطوره؟)
What is the weather forecast?	پیش بینیِ آب و هَوا چه است؟ (پیش بینیِ آب و هَوا چیه؟)

HOMEWORK

تَکلیف

1. Complete the following sentences with the given words. Use all the words.

مُعتَدِل خُشک مَرطوب آفتابی باران باد بَرف

۱.شَهر لُس آنجِلِس در جنوب غربیِ آمریکا است. هَوای لس آنجلس ـــــــ است.

۲.شَهر تامپا در فلوریدا در جنوب شرقیِ آمریکا قرار دارد. هَوای شَهر تامپا ـــــــ است.

۳.شَهر فینیکس در آریزونا در جنوبِ آمریکا قرار دارد. هَوای فینیکس ـــــــ است.

۴.ایالت مونتانا در شمال آمریکا قرار دارد. در مونتانا در زِمِستان خیلی ـــــــ میاید.

۵. در لس آنجلس در تابِستان هَوا مَعمولا خیلی ـــــــ است.

۶.در شَهر تامپا در تابِستان مَعمولا خیلی ـــــــ میاید.

۷.در شَهر بوستون در بَهار مَعمولا ـــــــ میوَزد.

2. Listen to the descriptions of weather conditions and read along. For every sentence, mark a matching image with the number of the sentence.

۱. امروز بَرف میاید (امروز بَرف میاد). ۲. امروز هَوا بارانی است (امروز هَوا بارونیه). ۳. امروز هَوا آفتابی است (امروز هوا آفتابیه). ۴. امروز رَعد و بَرق است (امروز رَعد و بَرقه). ۵. امروز نیمه آبری است (امروز نیمه آبریه). ۶. امروز باد میوَزد (امروز باد میوَزه). ۷. امروز بَرف و باران میبارد (امروز بَرف و بارون میباره).

3. ▶️ Listen to the individuals who describe the climate in their hometowns and complete the sentences.

۱.سلام، من رِضا هستم. تهران زندگی میکنم. هَوای تهران در شُمال ـــــ
است و در جنوب تهران ـــــ است.

۲.سلام، من رویا هستم. در شهر چالوس زندگی میکنم. هَوای چالوس ـــــ
ـ است.

۳.سلام، اسم من از عَلی است. اهل شهر یَزد هستم. هَوای یزد ـــــ است.

۴. سلام، اِلی هستم. اهل شهر هَمِدان هستم. در همدان ـــــ خیلی ـــــ میاید.

۵. سلام، من مَرجان هستم و در شهر رَشت زندگی میکنم. در رشت در ـــــ
خیلی ـــــ میاید. رَشت مَعروف به ''شهرِ باران ها'' است.

۶. سلام، مُحسِن هستم و در شهر آهواز زندگی میکنم. اینجا هَوا هَمیشه
خیلی ـــــ و ـــــ است.

291

٧. سلام، اسم من امیر است. من اهل شهر مَنجیل هستم. شهر منجیل
در شُمالِ ایران است. در مَنجیل خیلی ـــــــ شَدید ـــــــ . مَنجیل مَعروف به
"شهرِ توربین های بادی" است.

4. Using the previous assignment as example, briefly describe the climate in your hometown. Describe the weather in your hometown during at least two seasons.

5. You are hosting a student from Iran who will be attending classes at your university. Describe to him/her the climate in your university town and tell him/her what type of clothes to bring. Describe the weather in the spring and fall semesters. Use the subjunctive when you give advice, for example,

It's better if you bring ... بِهتَر است که ... بیاوری (بِهتَره که ... بیاری)

6. Pick a city (e.g., Tehran, Tabriz, Esfahan, Shiraz, Mashhad, Rasht or Bushehr) or a region in Iran and research online what the weather is like there. In class, briefly describe in Persian the climate in that place.

7. Look for weather forecast in your hometown for tomorrow. Prepare to describe the weather conditions for that day in your hometown.

IN CLASS  دَر کِلاس

8. Describe for you classmates your favorite type of weather. Now describe the outfits you like to wear in that weather.

9. Think of where you would like to spend your next spring break, summer vacation or winter break. Tell your class what the weather is like in that place, and why you would like to spend time there.

10. Look at these images of the weather forecast. Pick a day from the forecast, analyze the weather conditions and tell the class what type of clothes and accessories you would wear, if you were to travel to that city on that day. For example,

اگر دوشَنبه به آن شَهر بِرَوم، بایَد ... و ... بِپوشَم.
(آگه دوشَمبه به اون شَهر بِرَم، بایَد ... و ... بِپوشَم)

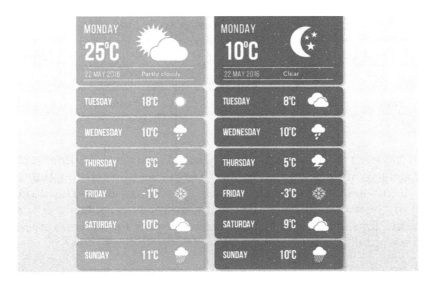

11. You will be working in pairs. Describe for your class a weather-specific outfit, but do not say for what type of weather the outfit is intended. You can include accessories to make it more specific. Your classmates will listen and guess the weather conditions for which you are suggesting the particular outfit.

12. Talk to your classmates and ask them what the weather is like in their hometown today. See if you can find somebody whose hometown has the weather similar to your hometown.

اِمروز در شَهرت هَوا چِطور اَست؟ (اِمروز تو شَهرت هَوا چِطوره؟)

GRAMMAR

دَستورِ زَبان

COMPARATIVE AND SUPERLATIVE FORMS OF ADJECTIVES

We use comparative adjectives to compare objects to each other, for example, the elephant is *bigger* than the mouse. There may be equal and unequal comparisons.

In English, unequal comparisons are formed with the word *more*, or by adding the suffix *er* to the adjective, for example, taller, more expensive. In Persian, all comparative adjectives are formed by saying تَر /tar/ at the end of the adjective.

293

higher	بالاتَر		Warmer	گَرمتر
further ahead	جلوتَر		more delicious	خوشمَزه تَر
Stronger	قوی تَر		Shorter	کوتاه تَر
Harder	سَخت تَر		more humid	مَرطوبتر

The latest trend has been to always write the ending تَر separately. In older texts, the ending /tar/ is written together with the word, except for a few cases when writing the suffix separately would help the clarity and ease of reading, that is, when: (a) the word ends with the letter ت e.g., سَخت تَر; (b) the word ends with a vowel, for example, آفتابی تَر ، خوشمزه تَر; (c) the word is a composite, for example, کمیاب تَر rarer; (d) writing the suffix together with the word would render the word difficult to read, for example, قهوه ای تَر browner.

The Persian word that represents the English word *than* used in comparison phrases is the word از /az/, for example,

هوای آلاسکا سَردتَر از هوای نیویورک است.

The weather in Alaska is colder than the weather in New York.

او تُندتَر از من حَرف میزَند.

S/he speaks faster than I do.

Say /tā/ تا (than) instead of /az/ از (than) when:

(a) you are comparing two or more actions done by the same person, that is, you are comparing actions (as opposed to adjectives or adverbs) that have the same subject, for example,

من بِهتَر میخوانم تا مینویسم.

I read better than I write.

او بیشتَر با مادرش صحبت میکند تا با پدرش.

S/he talks to her mom more than to her dad.

(b) you are comparing phrases that already have a preposition (either از or a different preposition), for example,

خانه ام دورتَر از یَزد است تا از تهران.

My home is farther from Yazd than from Tehran.

خانه ام نزدیکتَر به دانشگاه است تا به خانه تو.

My home is closer to the university **than** to your house.

Compare: آیا خانه من از اینجا دورتَر است یا خانه شما؟

Is my house farther away from here or (than) your house?

The Persian ending تَر (tar), can also be used to make phrases such as, *as... as ...*, *the ... the ....* For this purpose, it is combined with the phrase هَر چه, that is, تَر ... هَر چه. For example,

هَر چه زودتَر as soon as possible

هَر چه بیشتَر as much as possible; the more ...

هَر چه بیشتَر کار میکنم، بیشتَر خَسته (خَسته تَر) میشوم.

The more I work, the more tired I get.

Equal comparisons   Equal comparisons are used to compare two objects that are equal in a given quality. In English, these are formed with the words *as ... as*, for example, as fast as ..., as tall as .... In Persian, for equal comparisons (*as ... as, as much/many as ...*), use the phrase *beh an-dã-ze-ye* ... به اَندازهِ

For example,

تهران به اَندازهِ نیویورک ترافیک دارد.

Tehran has as much traffic as New York.

هَوای تهران به اَندازهِ هَوای لس آنجلس گَرم است.

The weather in Tehran is as warm as the weather in Los Angeles.

او به اَندازهِ من قَوی است.

She is as strong as I am.

To compare the intensity of an action (as opposed to quality):

او به اَندازهِ من تُند میدود. She runs as fast as I do.

او به اَندازهِ من رَوان حَرف میزند. He speaks as fluently as I do.

Because these comparison phrases end with a verb, you can turn them into unequal comparisons by negating the verb, for example, او به اندازهِ من تُند نمیدود؛

او به اندازهِ من رَوان حَرف نمیزند.

Keep in Mind   Similar to English, there are some Persian words that form their comparative forms from a different root.

good خوب – بِهتَر Better

many زیاد – بیشتَر More

Use the word بیشتَر (more) to compare quantities in Persian, for example,

در این ترم او بیشتَر از من کلاس دارد.   This semester, she has more classes than I do.

او دو تا کلاس بیشتَر از من دارد.   She has two more classes than I do.

در این ترم او بیشتَر از من درس میخواند.   This semester, he studies more (i.e., harder) than I do.

نیویورک را بیشتَر دوست دارم. Also: I like NY more.

بیشتَرِ دانشگاه ها most of the universities   /beesh-ta-reh .../

آکثَرِ دانشجو ها most (majority) of the students /ak-sa-reh.../

Use the phrase بیش از when you refer to a number, that is, *more than* ...number...

کتابخانه ما بیش از صد هزار کتاب دارد. Our library has more than one hundred thousand books.

من کَمتَر از صد کتاب دارم.   I have less than a hundred books.

When not used in comparison phrases, the words بیشتَر and کَمتَر come to mean mostly and rarely, for example,

بیشتَر در خانه غذا میخورم.   I mostly eat at home.

کَمتَر کتاب میخوانم.   I rarely read.

Superlative Form   The superlative form is used to describe an object that is superior in a given quality to all others, for example, the *oldest* building, the *youngest* student.

Example:

In class, I am the oldest one.	دَر کلاس، مَن از هَمه بزرگتَر هَستم.
You are the best.	از هَمه بِهتَر هَستی (از هَمه بِهتَری).
S/he knows the best.	از هَمه بِهتَر میداند.
She works the most, i.e., she works more than all (others).	از هَمه بیشتَر کار میکند.

As you can see, in the above cases the superlative adjectives (oldest, best) are not followed by a noun, that is, they stand independently. If you want to use the superlative adjective together with the person/thing which it describes (e.g., best friend), simply say تَرین /tar-een/ at the end of the adjective (or adverb). For example,

What is the largest state in America? بزرگتَرین ایالت آمریکا کدام است؟

He is my best friend. او بِهتَرین دوست مَن است.

Her best song is…. بِهتَرین آهنگ او … است.

Example: the second largest city دومین شَهرِ بزرگ

As it happens in English, some Persian words form their superlative form from a different root:

| بِهتَرین best | بِهتَر better | خوب good |
| بیشتَرین most | بیشتَر more | زیاد many |

HOMEWORK   تَکلیف

13. Listen and read along. Underline the adjectives in comparative form.

آفتابی، آفتابی تَر، بارانی، بارانی تَر، گَرم، گَرمتَر، سَرد، سَردتَر، شَدید، شَدیدتَر، خُشک، خُشکتَر، مَرطوب، مَرطوبتَر، مُلایِم، مُلایِمتَر، زیاد، بیشتَر، کَم، کَمتَر.

14. Listen and read along. Complete the Englsh translation of the Persian sentences that you hear.

۱. هَوای جنوب ایران گرمتَر از هَوای شمال ایران است. ۲. آب و هَوای جنوب ایران خُشک‌تَر از آب و هَوای شمال ایران است. ۳. شهر رَشت کوچک‌تَر از شهر تَبریز است. ۴. استان البُرز کوچک‌تَر از استان گیلان است. ۵. رودِ سیفیدرود کوتاه تَر از رودِ کارون است. ۶. بُرج میلاد بلندتَر از بُرج آزادی است. ۷. اسم برادر بزرگم کامران است. ۸. کامران کوچک‌تَر از خواهرم است. ۹. به نظرم، هتل اسپیناس پالاس بهتَر از هتل های دیگر تهران است. ۱۰. به نظرم، زندگی کردن در محوطه ِ دانشگاه بَدتَر از زندگی کردن در شهر است. ۱۱. نمره هایم در این ترم بَهتَر از نمره هایم در ترم گذشته هستند. ۱۲. من این ترم بیش از ۱۶ واحِد بَرمیدارم.

(1) The weather in the south of Iran is _____ than the weather in the north of Iran. (2) The cilmate in the south of Iran is _____ climate in the north of Iran. (3) The city of Rasht is _____ than the city of Tabriz. (4) The province of Alborz is the _____ province in Iran. (5) Sefidrud river is _____ Karoor river. (6) Milad Tower is the _____ tower. (7) My _____ brother's name is Kamran. (8) Kamran is _____ than my sister. (9) In my opinion, the hotel Espinas Palace is _____ other hotels in Tehran. (10) In my opinion, living on campus is _____ living in the town. (9) My grades this semester are _____ my grades from last semester. (10) I am taking _____ than 16 credits this semester.

15. 🔊 Complete these sentences using the given words in the comparative form. Prepare to say your completed sentences fluently. You will need these questions to complete a speaking drill in class. In the underlined spaces insert the comparative forms of the given adjectives, and in the dotted spaces insert the name of the town where your university is located.

۱. آیا زادگاهِت ____ (بزرگ، از) از شهرِ ... است؟ ۲. به نَظَرِ تو، آیا زادگاهِت ____ (زیبا، از) شَهرِ ... است؟ ۳. آیا زادگاهِت ____ (شُلوغ، از) شَهرِ ... است؟ ۴. آیا زادگاهِت ____ (زیاد، از) شَهرِ ... دانشگاه و کالِج دارد؟ ۵. آیا زادگاهِت ____ (زیاد، از) شَهرِ ... جاهای دیدَنی دارد؟ ۶. آیا هَوای زادگاهِت ____ (گرم) یا ____ (سَرد، از) هَوای شَهرِ ... است؟ ۷. آیا در زادگاهِت یا در شَهرِ... ____ (زیاد) بَرف میاید؟ ۸. آیا در زادگاهِت یا در شَهرِ... ____ (زیاد) باران میاید؟

16. 🔊 Listen and read along. Distribute the adjectives in the superlative and comparative columns accordingly.

گَرمتَر، گَرمتَرین، از هَمه گَرمتَر، سَردتَر، سَردتَرین، از هَمه سَردتَر، خُشک‌تَر، خُشک‌تَرین، از هَمه خُشک‌تَر، مُلایِمتَر، مُلایِمتَرین، از هَمه مُلایِمتَر، کوچک‌تَر،

کوچکتَرین، از هَمه کوچکتَر، بِهتَر، بِهتَرین، از هَمه بِهتَر، سَخت تَر، سَخت تَرین،
از هَمه سَخت تَر، بُلَندتَر، بُلَندتَرین.

Superlative	Comparative

17. 🔊 Listen and complete the sentences with the superlative and comparative adjectives that you hear. Translate the sentences.

تِهران ـــــــ شهر ایران است.

شهر تِهران ـــــــ از شهر شیراز است.

کوهِ دَماوَند ـــــــ کوهِ ایران است.

خیابان وَلی عَصر که در تِهران قرار دارد ـــــــ خیابانِ خاوَرِ میانه است.

دانشگاهِ تهران ـــــــ دانشگاهِ ایران است.

شهرِ شیراز ـــــــ از شهرِ تِهران است.

18. Translate and complete the following sentences about Iran. Do research online if needed.

(1) The hottest place in Iran is _____

(2) The driest city in Iran _____

(3)   The rainiest part of Iran is _____
(4)   The longest metro (subway) in the Middle East is _____
(5)   The oldest university in Iran is _____
(6)   The coldest month in Tehran is _____

19. Prepare to ask and to answer the following questions in class. Prepare to say your sentences fluently. Your objective will be to see if you can find people in class who feel the same way as you do. Share your findings with the class.

۱. به نَظَرِ تو، چه چیزی در دانشگاه از هَمه سَخت تَر است؟ (به نظر تو، چه چیزی تو دانشگاه از هَمه سَخت تَره؟)

۲. به نَظَرِ تو، چه چیزی در دانشگاه از هَمه آسان تَر است؟ (به نَظَرِ تو، چه چیزی تو دانشگاه از هَمه آسون تَره؟)

۳. چه چیزی را در دانشگاه از هَمه بیشتَر دوست داری؟ (چه چیزیو تو دانشگاه از هَمه بیشتَر دوست داری؟)

۴. چه چیزی را در دانشگاه از هَمه کَمتَر دوست داری؟ (چه چیزیو تو دانشگاه از هَمه کَمتَر دوست داری؟)

۵. در این ترم، سَخت تَرین کلاسهای تو کُدام هستند؟ (تو این ترم، سَخت تَرین کلاسای تو کُدومَن؟)

۶. در این ترم، آسان تَرین کلاسهای تو کُدام هستند؟ (تو این ترم، آسون تَرین کلاسای تو کُدامَن؟)

۷. در چه روز هفته بیشتَر از روز های دیگر درس میخوانی؟ (در چه روزِ هفته بیشتَر از روزای دیگه درس میخونی؟)

۸. چه روزِ هفته را بیشتَر از روزهای دیگر دوست داری؟ چِرا؟ (چه روزِ هَفتَه رو بیشتَر از روزای دیگه دوست داری؟ چِرا؟)

۹. به نَظَرِ تو، غَذای کدام کافه تریای دانشگاه از هَمه خوشمَزه تَر است؟ (به نَظَرِ تو، غَذای کدوم کافه تریای دانشگاه از هَمه خوشمَزه تَره؟)

۱۰. به نَظَرِ تو، چه جایی در دانشگاه قَشَنگ تَرین مَکان دانشگاه است؟ (به نَظَرِ تو، چه جایی تو دانشگاه قَشَنگ تَرین مَکان دانشگاهه؟)

۱۱. چه مَکانی در دانشگاه از همه آرامتَر است؟ (چه مَکانی تو دانشگاه از همه آرومتره؟)

۱۲. به نَظَرِ تو، چه خوابگاهی بِهتَرین خوابگاهِ دانشگاه است؟ (به نَظَرِت، چه خابگاهی بِهتَرین خابگاهِ دانشگاهِه؟)

20. Translate the following sentences into Persian.

   (1)   Is Tehran as large as New York City?
   (2)   Life in Tehran is as expensive as it is in NYC.
   (3)   The climate in Yazd is as dry as it is in Arizona.
   (4)   Tehran's winter is as cold as the New York winter.
   (5)   My room in the dorm is not as comfortable as my room in my parents' house.
   (6)   My chemistry class is as difficult as my physics class.

21. Think of the climate in your hometown. Do research online and find a town, city or area in Iran with similar climate and weather. Prepare to tell the class briefly about your findings in Persian. Practice your speech for fluency before coming to class. Start by saying which place in Iran has a climate similar to your town and where in Iran that place is located. Then proceed with the details.

22. Do research online if needed, and tell class what you found out in response to the following questions. Useful words:

اَقلیَتِ جِنسیَتی	اَقلیَتِ مَذهَبی	اَقلیَتِ قُومی	و غِیره
gender minority	religious minority	ethnic minority	etc.

۱. بزرگ تَرین اَقلیَت های مَذهَبی و قُومیِ آمریکا کدام هستند؟ اَکثَرِشان کجای آمریکا زندگی میکنند؟ (بزرگ تَرین اَقلیَتای مَذهَبی و قُومیِ آمریکا کدومن؟ اَکثَرِشون کجای آمریکا زندگی میکنن؟)

۲. بزرگ تَرین اَقلیَت های مَذهَبی و قُومیِ ایران کدام هستند؟ اَکثَرِشان کجای ایران زندگی میکنند؟ (بزرگ تَرین اَقلیَتای مَذهَبی و قُومیِ ایران کدومن؟ اَکثَرِشون کجای ایران زندگی میکنن؟)

۳. مُهِم تَرین مَسئَله در آمریکای اِمروز چه است؟ (مُهِم تَرین مَسئَله تو آمریکای اِمروز چیه؟)

23. Research online about the cities and provinces of Iran and answer the following questions in Persian. Compare the cities by population and provinces by area. Prepare to say your answers fluently in class. Give complete answers and use the comparative and superlative adjectives in your answers as needed. Useful expressions:

دُوُّمین شَهرِ کوچِک second smallest city	دُوُّمین اُستانِ بُزُرگ second largest province	اُستان province (in Iran)
	یِکی از کوچِکتَرین اُستان ها one of the smallest provinces	یِکی از بُزُرگتَرین شَهر ها one of the largest cities

۱. آیا شَهرِ تِهران بزرگتَر یا کوچکتَر از شَهرِ اِصفَهان است؟ (آیا شَهرِ تِهران بزرگتَر یا کوچکتَر از شَهرِ اِصفَهانه؟) ۲. آیا شَهرِ شیراز بزرگتَر یا کوچکتَر از شَهرِ اِصفَهان است؟ (آیا شَهرِ شیراز بزرگتَر یا کوچکتَر از شَهرِ اِصفَهانه؟) ۳. چه شَهری بزرگتَرین شَهرِ ایران است؟ (چه شَهری بزرگتَرین شَهرِ ایرانه؟) ۴. چه شَهری بزرگتَرین شَهرِ اُستانِ فارس است؟ (چه شَهری بزرگتَرین شَهرِ اُستانِ فارسه؟) ۵. چه شَهری دُوُّمین شَهرِ بزرگِ ایران است؟ (چه شَهری دُوُّمین شَهرِ بزرگِ ایرانه؟) چه شَهری سِوُّمین شَهرِ بزرگِ ایران است؟ (چه شَهری سِوُّمین شَهرِ بزرگِ ایرانه؟) ۶. آیا اُستانِ گیلان که در شُمالِ ایران قرار دارد، بزرگتَر یا کوچکتَر از اُستانِ فارس در جُنوبِ ایران است؟ (آیا اُستانِ گیلان که تو شُمالِ ایران قرار داره، بزرگتَر یا کوچکتَر از اُستانِ فارس تو جونوبِ ایرانه؟) ۷. آیا اُستانِ فارس که در جنوبِ ایران قرار دارد، بزگتَر یا کوچکتَر از اُستانِ گُلِستان در شُمالِ شَرقی ایران است؟ (آیا اُستانِ فارس که تو جونوبِ ایران قرار داره، بزگتَر یا کوچیکتَر از اُستانِ گُلِستان تو شُمالِ شَرقی ایرانه؟) ۸. چه اُستانی بزرگتَرین اُستانِ ایران است؟ (چه اُستانی بزرگتَرین اُستانِ ایرانه؟) ۹. چه اُستانی کوچکتَرین اُستانِ ایران است؟ (چه اُستانی کوچکتَرین اُستانِ ایرانه؟) ۰۱. چه اُستانی دُوُّمین اُستانِ بزرگِ ایران است؟ (چه اُستانی دُوُّمین اُستانِ بزرگِ ایرانه؟) ۱۱. چه اُستانی سِوُّمین اُستانِ بزرگِ ایران است؟ (چه اُستانی سِوُّمین اُستانِ بزرگِ ایرانه؟) ۱۲. آیا شَهرِ هَمِدان یِکی از سَردتَرین یا گَرمتَرین شَهرهای ایران است؟ (آیا شَهرِ هَمِدان یِکی از سَردتَرین یا گَرمتَرین شَهرای ایرانه؟) ۱۳. آیا شَهرِ آهواز یِکی از سَردتَرین یا گَرمتَرین شَهرهای ایران است؟ (آیا شَهرِ آهواز یِکی از سَردتَرین یا گَرمتَرین شَهرای ایرانه؟) ۱۴. آیا اُستانِ تِهران که در شُمالِ ایران قرار دارد، یِکی از بزرگتَرین یا کوچکتَرین اُستان های ایران است؟ (آیا اُستانِ تِهران که تو شُمالِ ایران قرار داره، یِکی از بزرگتَرین یا کوچیکتَرین اُستانای ایرانه؟) ۱۵. آیا اُستانِ فارس یِکی از بزرگتَرین یا کوچکتَرین اُستان های ایران است؟ (آیا اُستانِ فارس یِکی از بزرگتَرین یا کوچیکتَرین اُستانای ایرانه؟)

IN CLASS  دَر کِلاس

24. Complete the following sentences with the given adjectives in the comparative form. Translate the sentences into English.

۱. مَن ـــــــ (کوچِک) از بَرادَرَم هَستم.

۲. هَوای آلاسکا ـــــــ (سَرد) از هَوای فلوریدا است.

۳. ایالَتِ تِگزاس ـــــــ (بُزُرگ) از ایالَتِ نیویورک است.

۴. تابِستانِ تِهران ـــــــ (گَرم) از تابِستانِ نیویورک است.

۵. هَوای آریزونا ـــــــ (خُشک) از هَوای لوییزیانا است.

25. In the following sentences, arrange the words in the correct order. Read your sentences aloud to class and compare with how other groups arranged the words.

۱. نیویورک ـ از ـ من ـ گرم ـ است ـ شهر ـ تَر ـ هَوای

۲. ایالت ـ است ـ آلاسکا ـ ایالت ـ شهر ـ تَرین ـ آمریکا ـ سَرد

۳. از ـ بلد ـ دوست دُختَر ـ من ـ است ـ بِهتَر ـ من ـ فارسی

۴. هَوای ـ مرطوب ـ از ـ غربِ ایران ـ تَر ـ است ـ شُمالِ ایران ـ هَوای

۵. تَرین ـ تِهران ـ است ـ شهر ـ ایران ـ بزرگ

26. Look at the statements from the exercises In Class 24 and 25 (above) and for each statement, ask a question in Persian using a comparative adjective. Address your questions to a random classmate.

27. You will be working in groups. Together with a classmate, translate the following questions into Persian. Your instructor will assign a third person to your group. Interview that third person together and ask the questions in Persian. Fill in the blanks with the name of the town where your university is located.

(1) Is your hometown larger than _____? (2) In your opinion, is your hometown more beautiful than _____? (3) Is your hometown more crowded than _____? (4) Does your hometown have more universities and colleges than _____? (5) Does your hometown have more attractions than _____? (6) Is the weather in your hometown warmer or colder

than in _____? (7) Does it snow more in your hometown or in _____? (8) Does it rain more in your hometown or in _____?

28.   You will be working individually. Take turns to answer each of the following questions, so that every student in class receives equal time to speak in the target language.

is served سِرو میشـود (سِرو میشه)

۱. چه جایی در دانشگاه مَکانِ مُورِدِ عَلاقه ات است؟ (چه جایی تو دانشگاه مَکانِ مُورِدِ عَلاقَته؟)

۲. خوشمَزه تَرین غَذای دانشگاهِت در کُدام کافه تریا سِرو میشـود؟ (خوشمَزه تَرین غَذای دانشگاهِت تو کدوم کافه تریا سِرو میشه؟)

۳. به نَظَرِ تو، چه جایی در دانشگاه قَشَنگ تَرین مَکانِ دانشگاه است؟ (به نَظَرِ تو، چه جایی تو دانشگاه قَشَنگ تَرین مَکانِ دانشگاهه؟).

۴. چه مَکانی در دانشگاه آرام تَرین مَکانِ دانشگاهِت است؟ (چه مَکانی تو دانشگاه آروم تَرین مَکانِ دانشگاهِته؟)

۵. به نَظَرِ تو، چه خوابگاهی راحَت تَرین خوابگاهِ دانشگاهت است؟ (به نَظَرِ تو، چه خابگاهی راحَت تَرین خابگاهِ دانشگاهِته؟)

29.   You will be working individually. Take turns to answer all of the following questions in Persian, so that every student in class receives equal time to practice speaking in the target language.

۱. گِران تَرین پوشاکی که داری چه پوشاکی است؟ (۱. گِرون تَرین پوشاکی که داری چی پوشاکیه؟)

۲. آرزان تَرین پوشاکی که داری چه پوشاکی است؟ (آرزون تَرین پوشاکی که داری چی پوشاکیه؟)

۳.قَدیمی تَرین پوشاکی که داری چه پوشاکی است؟ (قَدیمی تَرین پوشاکی که داری چی پوشاکیه؟)

۴.جَدیدتَرین پوشاکی که داری چه پوشاکی است؟ (جَدیدتَرین پوشاکی که داری چه پوشاکیه؟)

۵.راحَت تَرین کَفشی که داری چه کَفشی است؟ (راحَت تَرین کَفشی که داری چه کفشیه؟)

۶. پوشاکِ مُوردِ عَلاقه ات چه است؟ (پوشاکِ مُورِد عَلاقَت چیه؟)

30. Read Roya's statements about her clothes and respond to each one of them by saying if your clothes are different or similar to hers. Pay special attention to the use of the phrase *most of beesh-ta-reh* …, for example,

بیشتَرِ لِباس های رویا صورَتی هستند. - بیشتَرِ لِباس هایم صورَتی نیستند

(بیشتَرِ لِباسای رویا صورَتی هستن – بیشتَرِ لِباسام صورَتی نیستن)

سَلام، من رویا هَستم. چَند کَلَمه راجِع به لِباس هایم به شما میگویم.بیشتَرِ لِباس هایم یا سِفید یا آبی یا اَرغوانی هَستند.

بیشتَرِ شَلوار هایم جین هستند. بیشتَر تی شِرت هایم به رَنگ های روشَن هَستند. بیشتَر کَفش هایم یا مِشکی یا قِرمِز هستند. بیشتَر لِباس های زِمِستانی ام تیره رَنگ هستند.

31. Complete the following open-ended sentences in Persian. Pay special attention to the use of the phrases *most of* (beesh-ta-reh …) and *majority of* … (ak-sa-reh …)

۱. این ترم بیشتَرِ کلاس هایم_____ (این ترم بیشتَرِ کلاسام_____)

۲. بیشتَرِ کافه تِریا های دانشگاه _____

۳. بیشتَرِ خوابگاه های دانشگاه _____

۴. آکثَرِ دانشجو های دانشگاه _____

۵. آکثَرِ دوست هایم _____ (آکثَرِ دوستام _____)

32. Talk to as many classmates as you can, and find out:

– Who is taking more than twelve credits this semester.
– Who is taking more than two classes every day.
– Who has classes more than four days a week.
– Who has more than two finals this semester.
– Who goes to the gym more than twice a week.
– Who likes the climate in your university town.

33. You will be working individually. Using the words below, say some comparative sentences. Make equal or unequal comparisons as needed. Use از or به آندازهِ accordingly, and use the adjective in the comparative or basic form as needed. Insert verbs as needed.

به آندازهِ ... as much/many as, to the same degree as   از than

۱. غذای رستوران – خوشمَزه – غذای کافه تریای دانشگاه

۲. زِمِستان (زِمِستون) – سَرد – اینجا – زادگاهَم – زِمِستان (زِمِستون)

۳. اِمتِحانِ فارسی – اِمتِحان های دیگرم (اِمتِحاناى دیگه ام) – سَخت

۴. اُتاق خوابگاه – گِران (گِرون) – یک اُتاق در شهر

۵. ترافیک – دانشگاه – در (تو) – شَهرَم – سَنگین – در (تو) – ترافیک

34. Respond to the following statements by agreeing or disagreeing with them. Start your statements with به نَظرِ من، ...

– Persian grammar is as difficult as English grammar.
– USA is as ancient as Iran.
– Family is as important as friends are.
– Your university is as expensive as Harvard University.
– This semester is as difficult as the last semester.

35. You will be working in groups. Think about the question below and discuss it in Persian with your group mates. Tell your class what conclusion you arrived at, as a result of the discussion.

شَخص individual, person

به نَظَرِ تو، آیا یک شَخصِ جَوان بِهتَر است که در شهرِ خود یا دور از شهرِ خود به دانشگاه برود؟ چِرا؟ (به نَظَرِ تو، آیا یه شَخصِ جَوون بِهتَره که تو شهرِ خود یا دور از شهرِ خود به دانشگاه بره؟ چِرا؟)

36. You will be working in groups. Ask your classmates the following questions in Persian.

   – What difficult classes are you taking this semester?
   – What is your most difficult class this semester?
   – In which class do you work the most?
   – Do you speak better in Persian than you write it?

37. Look at the words below. It is a scrambled Persian proverb. Reconstruct the original sequence of the words.

آباد flourishing   خَراب in ruins

دِه – بِهتَر – آباد – خَراب – آست – یِک – شهرِ – آز صَد

38. You will be working individually. Take turns to answer all of the following questions, so that all students in class receive an equal opportunity to speak on the topic of the chapter in the target language.

۱. بزرگ تَرین شهرهای ساحِلِ شَرقی کُدام هستند؟ (بزرگ تَرین شهرای ساحِلِ شَرقی کُدومَن؟)

۲. بزرگ تَرین شهرهای ساحِلِ غَربی کُدام هستند؟ (بزرگ تَرین شهرای ساحِلِ غَربی کُدومَن؟)

۳. مَعروف تَرین دانشگاه های آمریکا کجا قَرار دارند؟ (مَروف تَرین دانشگاه‌های آمریکا کجا قَرار دارن؟)

۴. بزرگ تَرین دانشگاه های ساحِلِ غَربی کُدام هستند؟ (بزرگ تَرین دانشگاه‌های ساحِلِ غَربی کُدومَن؟)

۵. چه شهرهایی گران تَرین شهر های آمریکا هستند؟ (چه شهرایی گرون تَرین شهرای آمریکان؟)

307

۶. چه شهری بزرگ ترین شهرِ ایالتتان است؟ (چه شهری بزرگ ترین شهرِ ایالتتونه؟)

۷. مُهِم ترین زبان های آمریکا کدام هستند؟ (مُهِم ترین زبونای آمریکا کدومَن؟)

39. You will be working in groups. Look at the map of Iran, and ask your classmates comparative questions about the provinces of Iran. Use adjectives in the comparative and superlative forms for your questions. When you ask your question, point out the location of the province in Iran so that it is easier for the respondent to locate it on the map. Useful words and phrases:

یکی از کوچکترین اُستان ها one of the smallest provinces		یکی از بُزُرگترین شهر ها one of the largest cities		اُستان province (in Iran)
	شَرق East	غَرب West	جنوب (جونوب) South	شمال North

Example questions:

۱. اُستانِ فارس که در جنوبِ ایران قرار دارد، بزرگتَر یا کوچکتَر از اُستانِ گیلان در شُمالِ ایران است؟ (اُستانِ فارس که تو جونوبِ ایران قرار داره، بزرگتَر یا کوچیکتَر از اُستانِ گیلان تو شُمالِ ایرانه؟)

۲. اُستانِ کِرمان که در جنوبِ ایران قرار دارد یکی از بزرگتَرین یا کوچکتَرین اُستان های ایران است؟ (اُستانِ کِرمان که تو جونوبِ ایران قرار داره یکی از بزرگتَرین یا کوچیکتَرین اُستانای ایرانه)؟

۳. چه اُستانی یکی از بزرگتَرین استان های غَربِ ایران است؟ (چه اُستانی یکی از بزرگتَرین استانای غَربِ ایرانه)؟

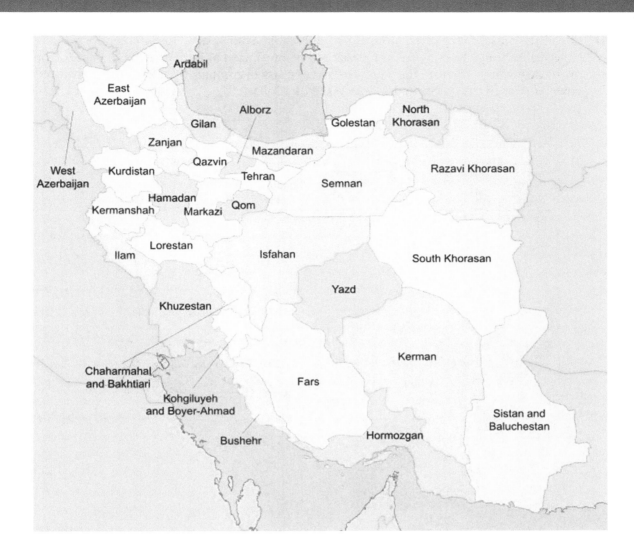

40. Look at the table below. Make comparative statements about the cities in each category (area, population, etc.).

شَهر	جَمعیَت	مَساحَت	تِعدادِ دانشگاه ها
تِهران	12 million	13,692 sq km	50
اِصفَهان	1.7	7,654 sq km	7
شیراز	1.6	240 sq km	5
تَبریز	1.8 million	2,356 sq km	14

41. Read the glossary together. Now, close your book. Your instructor will read for you the anecdote about Molla Nasreddin described below. Listen and then retell the anecdote in your own words. Identify the adjective that appears in comparative form. Now, give your own answer to the question that was asked of Molla.

To illuminate	رُوشَن کَردَن			the Sun	خورشید
Existence	وُجود			the Moon	ماه
Comes out	دَر میاید	To have a benefit, to be beneficial		سود داشتَن /sood/

از مُلا پُرسیدَند: خورشید بِهتَر است یا ماه؟

مُلا گُفت: ماه بِهتَر است!

پُرسیدَند: چِرا ماه بِهتَر است؟

گُفت: بَرای اینکه خورشید دَر روزِ رُوشَن دَرمیایَد، و وُجودِ خورشید سودی نَدارد. اَما ماه شَب ها را رُوشَن میکُند، پَس ماه بِهتَر است!

42. Interview. Your instructor will call on you to ask your classmates questions in Persian. Ask each one of your classmates one question in Persian on any of the topics listed below.

If your class is too big for this format of activity, your instructor might divide the class into groups of three, where you will find yourself with two other students. Ask each of the two classmates at least three questions on the given topics.

Topics:

اِسم و فامیل، کُجایی، خانِواده، بِهتَرین دوست، دانِشگاه و کِلاس، شُغل، کارهای روزانه، خانه و مَنزِل ، شَهر و کِشوَر، لِباس، خَرید، آب و هَوا

LISTENING

شِنیداری

Listen to the conversation between Sara and Kamran. Sara is planning to go to Tehran and is asking Kamran what would be the best time of the year to visit Tehran. The speakers are talking about precipitation, temperature, and humidity and are comparing the weather conditions in Tehran during different seasons of the year.

Pre-listening. 1. (a) Write down in Persian a list of the most common words related to weather and the elements. If the word you wrote down is a noun, think of the verb that would commonly go with it in a text about weather. Think of the seasons of the year and add those words to the list. Pronounce the words from the list aloud so that you hear your voice. Think about how you would ask a question in Persian about the weather, temperature or precipitation. Say your sentences aloud in Persian so that you hear your voice. (b) The verbs in the conversation appear mostly in present tense and subjunctive. Think of the present tense and subjunctive markers and how the verbs usually look with those markers in the beginning and with conjugational endings at the end of the verb. Are there exceptions to the rule? What do you think the conjugational forms of the verbs would be, in a conversation on the above topic? Now, pronounce the verbs you have written down in both the present tense and subjunctive. (c) As the speakers will be comparing the weather during various times of the year, they will be using the comparative (...er) and superlative (...est, most) forms. What are the markers of those two forms in Persian? Look at the adjectives from the list you have made and pronounce those adjectives in comparative and superlative forms.

Pre-listening 2. Listen to these words and expressions before you listen to the conversation. You will hear these words and names in the conversation.

Keshavarz boulevard (one of the main avenues in Tehran, located in the northern part of the city)	بُلوارِ کِشاوَرز
Laleh Park (located on Keshavarz boulevard)	پارکِ لاله
the rainiest	پُرباران تَرین (پُربارون تَرین)
least rainy	کَم باران تَرین (کَم بارون تَرین)
the roads were (had been) closed	جاده ها مَسدود شُده بودَند
about 90 degrees Fahrenheit	حُدودِ ۹۰ درجه فارنهایت
Vali Asr avenue (one of the main north-south avenues in Tehran)	خیابانِ وَلی عَصر (خیابونِ وَلی عَصر)

311

Mellat Park (located in the northern part of Tehran)	پارک ِ مِلَت
Qeytariyeh Park (located in the northern part of the city)	پارک ِ قیطَریه
(they) escape to the North	به شُمال فَرار میکُنَند
one doesn't even feel going out	آدَم حُوصِله ِ بیرون رَفتَنو نَداره

Pre-listening 3. Go online and pull up a climate map of Iran. Look at the map and say in Persian what kind of climate there is in the north, west, south and east of the country. Now say comparative sentences and compare the climate in the four parts of the country.

Listening Assignment. Listen to the conversation and answer in Persian the following questions. Prepare to say your answers fluently in class.

(1)   What is the hottest season of the year in Tehran?
(2)   What is coldest season of the year in Tehran?
(3)   What is the driest time of the year in Tehran?
(4)   What is the most humid time of the year in Tehran?
(5)   What is Kamran's favorite time of the year in Tehran? Why?
(6)   According to Kamran, what is the best time for Sara to go to Tehran, considering her academic schedule and the weather in Tehran?
(7)   How do the weather and climate differ in various parts of Tehran?

Follow-up 1. If you were to go to Tehran, in which season would you have liked to go there considering the weather and climate of Tehran? Explain why.

Follow-up 2. Say what is different or similar between Tehran and your hometown in terms of the weather.

Follow-up 3. Create a dialogue between you and your classmates about the weather in your hometown. Your classmates are planning to visit your hometown and are asking you when would be the best time of the year for them to visit.

READING

خواندَنی

Read the text several times aloud until you can easily pronounce all sentences. Be ready to read it aloud in class.

آب و هَوای شَهرِ تِهران.

تِهران شَهرِ خیلی بزرگی است و آب و هَوای مَحله های مُختَلِفِ تِهران باهَم فَرق دارد. تِهران بینِ رِشته کوهِ اَلبُرز و دَشتِ کَویر قَرار دارد. شُمالِ تِهران به رِشته کوهِ اَلبُرز نَزدیک تَر است و به این دَلیل در مَحَله های شُمالیِ تِهران آب و هَوا مُعتَدِل و کوهِستانی است. جنوبِ تِهران به دَشتِ کَویر نَزدیک تَر است و به این دَلیل جنوبِ تِهران آب و هَوای نیمه خُشک دارد.

هَوای تِهران در بَهار و پاییز مُلایم است، در تابِستان گَرم و خُشک است و در زِمِستان سَرد و مَرطوب است. بیش از ۲۰۰ روز در سال هَوای تِهران صاف و خُشک است. هَوای بَهار و پاییز در تِهران مُلایم است. بارِشِ باران بیشتَر در بَهار و پاییز روی میدهد. فِوریه و مارچ پُرباران تَرین ماه های سال در تِهران هستند. در آوریل، هَوا گَرم تَر میشود و در تابِستان هَوا خیلی گَرم است. میانگینِ دَما در تابِستان ۹۰ دَرَجه فارنهایت است، وَلی به دَلیلِ نَزدیک بودَنِ کوه ها، وُجود ِ پارک ها، بوستان ها، و فَضا های سَبز زیاد در حاشیهِ خیابان ها و بُزُرگراه ها و کَم بودَنِ فَعالیَت های صَنعَتی، هَوای شُمالِ تِهران نِسبَت به هَوای جنوب

ِ تِهران ۴-۳ دَرَجه فارنهایت خُنَک تَر است. ژوییه گَرم تَرین و کَمباران تَرین ماهِ سال در تِهران است. فَصلِ سَرد در آواخِرِ نُوامبر شُروع میشود و در مارچ تَمام

Mellat Park, Tehran

313

میشود. زِمِستانِ تِهران سَرد است. میانگینِ دَما در زِمِستان بِینِ ۳۳ و ۴۱ دَرَجه
فارِنهایت است. به دَلیلِ نَزدیک بودَنِ کوه ها به شُمالِ تِهران، هَوای شُمالِ
تِهران در زِمِستان سَردتَر از هوای جنوبِ تِهران است. سَردتَرین ماهِ سال ژانویه
است. در ژانویه و فِوریه در تِهران بَرف میبارد.

Follow-up 1. Prepare to ask your classmates in Persian three questions about the Reading. Prepare to say your questions fluently. Your questions must be:

(1)   with a comparative adjective,
(2)   with a superlative adjective,
(3)   your free question.

Follow-up 2.    Now, working in pairs, draw a general comparison of two areas in the United States with different climates (e.g., Florida and New York, Northern California and Southern California). You can use the Reading above as an example.

TRANSLATION      تَرجُمه

Translate the following passage into Persian. Use a dictionary if necessary.

Mediterranean-like	شِبهِ مِدیتِرانه	Manjil	مَنجیل
is famous for …	به … مَعروف است	wind turbine	توربینِ بادی
cypress tree woods	جَنگل های دِرَختِ سَرو	olive tree groves	باغ های دِرَختِ زِیتون

Climate of Manjil, the city of cypress groves and olive gardens.

The city of Manjil is located in the north of Iran, in the province of Gilan. Manjil is located between three different climate zones: the mountainous climate of the Alborz Mountains, the humid and warm climate of the Caspian Sea, and the dry climate of the south. Because of this reason, the climate in Manjil is Mediterranean-like and is different from the climate in most places in Gilan. There are numerous groves of olive trees everywhere in Manjil and the villages near it. Because of its Mediterranean climate, the area of Manjil is also famous for vast cypress woods. Manjil has more windy days that any other place in Iran. A strong wind blows from the Caspian Sea during all four seasons. In the past, Manjil was known as the city of seven winds. Today, it is known for its wind energy because of the numerous wind turbines located there.

Manjil wind farm in N. Iran

WRITING

اِنشا

You will be hosting a foreign exchange student at your place. Write, for her/him, briefly (minimum 200 words) about the climate in your hometown. Write about all four seasons of the year. Start by stating the name of your hometown (provide the English spelling in parentheses after its Persian spelling) and its location in the country and state.

Write general information about the weather in each season, including the average temperatures. Give him/her advice as to what type of clothes to bring along. You can describe what type of clothes people in your hometown usually wear every day, so your guest may choose his/her clothes accordingly.

Open you letter with سَلام دوست ِ عَزیز

Close your letter with

به اُمید ِ دیدار،

Sign the letter in Persian

صِفات شَخصیَتی فَصلِ یازدَهُم

Chapter 11   Personality Traits

Happy in blue.

Function Talking about personality traits, describing people's appearances.

Listening I look a lot like my dad.

Reading Do you love me?

Structures Specific Direct Object Marker *o/ro*. High frequency verbs *to do* and *to become* as compound verb builders.

Listen and repeat. Say each word and phrase several times aloud until you can easily pronounce them.

Feelings and State of Being				
Anxious	مُضطَرِب		I am (I'm)	هَستَم - (م)
Thirsty	تِشنه		You are (You're)	هَستی - (ی)
Hungry	گُرسنه (گُشنه)		In good mood	سَرِ حال
I am full	سیر شُدَم		Cute	ناز
Ready	حاضِر		Happy	خوشحال
I'm not feeling well, I'm feeling under the weather	کِسِلَم		Sad, downcast (about person)	دِلگیر
I'm ill, sick	مَریضَم		Excited	هَیجان زَده
Content	راضی (از ...)		Bored; I am bored, s/he is bored	بی حُوصِله؛ حُوصِله آم سَر رَفته (حُوصِلَم سَر رَفته)؛ حُوصِله آش سَر رَفته (حُوصِلَش سَر رَفته)
Dissatisfied	ناراضی		Tired	خَسته
Worried (about ...)	نِگران (از ...)		Angry	عَصَبانی (عَصَبونی)
Occupied, busy doing something	مَشغول		Nervous, panicky	دَستپاچه، عَصَبی
I am busy, I have a lot of things to do	سَرَم شُلوغ است (سَرَم شولوغه)		Upset, sad, uncomfortable	ناراحَت (از ...)
Positive	مُثبَت		Comfortable	راحَت
Negative	مَنفی		I am uncomfortable	راحَت نیستَم
Behavior	رَفتار		I am stressed	اِسترِس دارم

318

				Personality
Studious	دَرسخوان		Personality	شَخصیَت
Punctual	وَقت شِناس		What type of personality do you have?	شُما چه شَخصیَتی دارید؟ (... دارین؟)
Impolite, with no manners	بی اَدَب		What kind of person is s/he?	او چه جور آدَمی است؟ (اون چه جور آدَمیه؟)
Quiet	ساکِت		Cheerful, happy	خوش طَبع (خوش طَب)
Talkative, chatty	پُرحَرف		Cool, fun	باحال
Reserved, of few words, untalkative	کَم حَرف		Emotional person	آدَمِ اِحساساتی
Social	اِجتِماعی، مُعاشِر		Shy	خِجالَتی
Successful	مُوَفَق		Introvert	آدَمِ دَرون گَرا
Kind, nice	مِهرَبان (مِهربون)		Extrovert	آدَمِ بُرون گَرا
Friendly, approachable	خودِمانی (خودِمونی)		Decent	مَحجوب
Stingy	خَسیس		Absentminded	حَواس پَرت
Generous, giving	سَخی		Intelligent	باهوش
Strange	عَجیب		Clever	زِرَنگ
Average, regular	مَعمولی		Likeable	دوست داشتَنی
Snobby	پُرافاده		Hardworking	پُرکار، سَختکوش
Proud	مَغرور		Lazy	تَنبَل
Arrogant	مُتَکَبِر		Caring	دِلسوز
Humble	فُروتَن (فوروتَن)		Candid, straightforward	راستگو
Different	مُتَفاوت		Polite	مُوَدَب
Similar	مُشابه، هَمسان		Fair, just	با اِنصاف، مُنصِف

319

Verbs and Phrases	
I convinced him/her	او را راضی کَردَم
S/he agreed to ...	راضی شُد که ...
Are you sure?	مُطمَئِن هستی (مُطمَئِنی) ؟
Tomorrow's exam makes me anxious	اِمتِحانِ فردا مُضطَرِبَم میکُند
We have a difficult exam tomorrow and I am worried	فردا امتحانِ مُشکِلی داریم و من نِگرانَم
I laugh	میخَندَم
I am scared of ...	از ...تَرسیده اَم
I'm distracted	حَواسَم پَرت شُد
I'm sleepy	خوابَم میاید (خابَم میاد)
S/he is sleepy	خوابِش میاید (خابِش میاد)

HOMEWORK   تکلیف

1. Complete the table by putting what you think are positive and negative qualities in the respective columns. Prepare to read them aloud in class.

مَنفی	مُثبَت

2. Listen and read along. Complete the translation based on what you hear and see.

۱. امروز خیلی خوشحالَم. ۲. چرا دِلگیری؟ ۳. دوست من آدَمِ خیلی مِهرَبانی است. ۴. برادر من آدَمِ بُرونگَرا است، ولی من آدَمِ دَرونگَرا هستم. ۵. نِگرانی؟ ۶. نِگرانِ امتحان هستم. ۷. کِسیلی؟ ۸. نَه، کِسیل نیستم، خیلی خَسته هستم. ۹. او خیلی خِجالَتی است. ۱۰. او آدَمِ کَم حَرفی است.

(1) I'm very _____ today. (2) Why are you _____? (3) My best friend is a very _____ person. (4) My brother is an _____, but I am an _____. (5) Are you _____? (6) I am _____ about the exam. (7) Are you _____? (8) No, I'm not _____, I am very _____. (9) She is very _____. (10) He is_____ person.

3. (a) Listen and fill in the blanks. The missing words are from this chapter's glossary. Complete the English translation.

پدرم و مادرم _____ های مُتَفاوِتی دارند. مادَرَم آدَمی _____ ، پُرحَرف و _____ است. مادَرَم را خیلی دوست دارم بَرای اینکه او آدَم _____ و مِهرَبانی است. پِدَرَم آدَمی _____ ، _____ و _____ است. او آدمی باانصاف و _____ است. پِدَرَم را خیلی دوست دارم بَرای اینکه او آدمی _____ ، _____ و فروتَن است.

My father and mother have different _____ . My mother is an _____ , talkative and _____ person. I love my mother very much, because she is a _____ and kind person. My father is an _____ , _____ and _____ person. He is a fair and _____ person. I love my father very much because is a _____ , _____ and humble person.

(b) Prepare to describe personal qualities of the members of your family using three or four adjectives from this chapter's glossary. Prepare to say in Persian with which family member, you think, you share personality traits. Your classmates will ask you about the personality of some of your family members (parents, siblings, uncles and aunts).

4. Complete the following statements.

بابایِم پدرِ خوبی است بَرای اینکه _____ (بابام پدَر خوبیه بَرای اینکه _____)

مامانِم مادرِ خوبی است بَرای اینکه _____ (مامانم مادَر خوبیه بَرای اینکه _____)

خواهرم آدَمِ خوبی است بَرای اینکه _____ (خواهرم آدَم خوبیه بَرای اینکه _____)

برادرم آدَمِ خوبی است بَرای اینکه _____ (برادرم آدَم خوبیه بَرای اینکه _____)

دوست پسرم/دوست دخترم آدَمِ خوبی است بَرای اینکه _____ (دوست پسرم/دوست دخترم آدَم خوبیه بَرای اینکه _____)

5. Translate the following sentences into Persian.

فَقَط just, only

(1) I'm very happy today. (2). It is very warm today, and I am in a good mood. (3) Why are you (تو) sad? (4) Why are you nervous? (5) I am worried about the exam. (6) Are you feeling under the weather? (7) No, I am not feeling under the weather, but I am very tired. (8) Are you (تو) hungry? (9) No, I'm not hungry, but I am thirsty.

6. Describe your best friend. Start by saying what s/he does, where s/he is and then describe his/her personal qualities that you like. Now compare your best friend's qualities to yours, that is, name the qualities that you both share and then say what qualities you have but s/he does not have.

IN CLASS   دَر کِلاس

7. Talk to your classmates and ask about the personality traits of their family members. Find out if your classmates share any qualities with any of their family members. Tell the class in Persian what you have found out. Also, tell the class if you share personality traits with any of your respondents. Useful question:

پِدَرِت چه جور آدَمی اسـت (پِدَرِت چه جور آدَمیه)؟

8. Describe what is your idea of an ideal boyfriend/girlfriend or best friend, as far as his/her personality is concerned.

9. Pick two individuals from the list below as applicable to you. Compare the personalities of those two individuals.

پدرم – مادرم؛ من – برادرم/خواهرم؛ برادرم/خواهرم – پدرم؛ من – دوستم؛ من – هم اتاقی ام

10. You will be working in pairs. Create and say aloud a brief conversation using at least three words or phrases that describe personality traits. Guidelines: You are talking to a classmate who mentions that yesterday, in the dining hall s/he saw you with somebody. Tell your classmate that it was your best friend. Tell your classmate your best friend's name and describe in brief his or her personality. You do not need to reveal your real best friend's identity, but do think of an actual person you know when you describe his or her personality. During the conversation, your classmate asks you where your

best friend is from, what her or his major is and what year she or he is at the university. Answer those questions.

11. Ask your classmates the following questions. Be ready to answer these questions.

مَعمولا چَند شَنبه ها خِیلی خَسته میشوی؟ (مَمولَن چَن شَمبه ها خِیلی خَسته میشی؟)

از اِمتِحان ِ فارسی نِگَرانی؟

آیا آدَم ِ وَقت شیناسی هَستی؟

12. Are you a morning person? Talk to you classmates and find those who are like you (either or not a morning person). Now, tell your class whether you are a morning person, and then say who in class is like you.

Questions you will need:

آیا صُبح ها مَعمولا سَر ِ حال هَستی؟ (آیا صُبها مَمولَن سَر ِ حالی)؟

آیا صُبح ها حالِت بِهتَر است یا بَعد از ظُهر ها؟ (آیا صُبا حالِت بِهتَره یا بَداز ظُهرا؟)

13. You will be working in groups. Prepare to ask and to answer the following questions in class.

  – How are you feeling today?
  – Were you in a good mood when you woke up today?
  – How were you feeling yesterday?
  – Do you usually feel better in the mornings or afternoons?

14. You will be working in groups. Ask and answer the following questions.

هِنگام ِ ... during, at the moment of ...

مَعمولا وَقتی دِلگیر میشوی چه کار میکنی؟ (مَمولَن، وَقتی دِلگیر میشی چه کار میکنی؟)

وَقتی سَرحال نیستی، مَعمولا چه کار میکنی؟

مَعمولا، وَقتی دَستپاچه هَستی چه کار میکنی؟ (مَمولَن، وَقتی دَستپاچه هَستی چه کار میکنی؟)

323

وَقتی از درس خواندن خَسته میشوی چه کار میکنی؟ (وَقتی از درس خوندن خَسته میشی چه کار میکنی؟)

وَقتی تِشنه میشوی مَعمولا دوست داری آب، نوشابه یا آب میوه بخوری؟ (وَقتی تِشنه میشی مَمولَن دوست داری آب، نوشابه یا آب میوه بُخوری؟)

وَقتی هِنگامِ کلاس گُرسنه میشوی چه کار میکنی؟ (وَقتی هِنگامِ کلاس گُرسنه میشی چه کار میکنی؟)

15.  Think of your favorite movie character or a favorite celebrity. Describe his/her personal qualities that you like the most. Ask your classmates who their favorite movie star or a celebrity is and why.

GRAMMAR   دَستورِ زَبان

How to create compound verbs with شدن **and** کردن

The majority of Persian verbs are compound verbs. Most of those compound verbs have the verbs *to do* کَردن or *to become* شُدَن as their second component. The verbs *to do* and *to become* are useful verbs to know, as you can create new verbs by combining them with nouns, adjectives or adverbs.

شُدَن

(to become, to turn into, to get ...) can be used to:

– describe *becoming, turning into* somebody or something, for example, in reference to professions: میخواهم مُهَندِس شَوم (I want to become an engineer), دُکتُر شُد (s/he became a doctor), or in reference to changing a form of existence, for example, بَرف آب شُد (snow melted, i.e., turned into water).

– describe changing into a state, quality, for example, خَلوَت شد (got crowded), شلوغ شد (got empty, desolate), بزرگ شدم (it got dark), تاریک شد (it increased), زیاد شد (I grew up), دَر باز میشود (the door is opening), کلاس شُروع میشود (class starts).

– describe getting into an emotional state or a health condition, for example, خَسته شُد (she got tired), خوشحال شُدَم (I became happy), مَریض شُدَند (they got sick).

شُدَن *to* بودَن *Compare*

شُدَن With	بودَن With
دَر باز شُد (the door opened)	دَر باز اَست (the door is open)
خَسته شُدَم (I got tired)	خَسته هَستم (I am tired)
سَرِ کار خَسته میشَوم (I get tired at work)	هَمیشه خَسته هَستم (I am always tired)

The verb شُدَن can be thus combined with an **adjective** (e.g., تاریک, خُشک, باز) **verb participles** (sent فِرِستاده, written نِوِشته, ساخته built, دیده seen), **non-verb participles** (e.g., accepted قَبول, forced مَجبور), **nouns** (e.g., invitation, دَعوت, translation, تَرجمه). For example,

از ... پیاده شُدَن (to get off the car, bus, etc.)	پا شُدَن (to stand up)
با ... آشنا شُدَن (to meet the ...)	بُلَند شُدَن (to get up)
حالَم بِهتَر میشود (I will feel better)	وارِد شُدَن (to enter)
چه شُد (چی شُد)؟ (what happened, lit.: what came out of it).	سَوار ... شُدَن (to get on the car, bus, etc.)

کَردَن

(to do, to make into …) can be used with the same adjectives, nouns, participles, and so on as the verb شُدَن, but the verb کَردَن is used when both subject (person or thing who does the action) and object (person or thing to whom the action is done) have to be mentioned in the sentence. For details as to what subject and object mean please refer to the appendix Grammarian's Corner. Thus, کَردَن can be used for describing the action of turning something into a state of being, or making somebody feel and be in certain ways.

کَردَن *to* شُدَن *Compare*

مَن خَسته شُدَم. I got tired.

مَن او را خَسته کَردَم. I made him/her tired.

Here, both sentences use خَسته *tired*. but, the sentence with شدم only has the subject (I), and it only talks about one person (I). By contrast, the sentence with کردم has both subject (I) and object (S/he), and it describes how *I* make *him/her* feel.

The verb کَردَن can be thus combined with an **adjective** (e.g., تاریک,خُشک,باز), **non-verb parti-ciples** (e.g., accepted قَبول, forced مَجبور), **nouns** (e.g., invitation, دَعوَت, translation, تَرجُمه).

Negation. To negate a compound verb with کردَن or شُدَن, simply negate the شدن /کردن part.

باز نَشُد. it did not open

فرستاده نَشُد. it was not sent

شُروع نَکردَم. I did not start

How to say *by, by the means of* in phrases such as *it was built by …, it was translated by … .* You can use either the word تَوَسُّط /ta-va-so-teh …/ *by*, or the word ـِ به وَسیله... /beh va-see-leh-yeh …/ *by the means of … .*

این ساختِمان تَوَسُّطِ یِک معمار ایرانی ساخته شُد.

This building was built **by** an Iranian architect.

It is also possible to use the verb in third person plural (they) in order to describe who did the action.

او قَبول شُد S/he was accepted

or

او را قَبول کَردَند (i.e., they accepted him/her)

Keep in mind. In Persian we don't say تَمام شُدَم to say that you are done with work. Instead say تَمام شُد (تَموم شُد). that is, *it is done*, referring to the work that you have completed.

Specific Direct Object Marker

The Specific Direct Object (SDO) Marker is used in Persian to mark the SDO of the verb in order to make the context and meaning of the sentence unambiguous. For details as to what direct and indirect objects mean, please refer to the appendix Grammarian's Corner.

Pronunciation. The SDO Marker is pronounced *o* if it follows a word that ends in any consonant or the vowel ی *ee* (e.g., pedaram-**o**, sandalee-**o**). It is pronounced *ro* if it follows a word that ends in vowels /bãbã-**ro**/, /amoo-**ro**/. The *o/ro* is pronounced together with the word that it follows, as if it were part of that word.

Spelling. The SDO Marker is always spelled را regardless of pronunciation. It is written separately from the word that it marks. An occasional exception is the combination مَن را (me) that is sometimes written together as مَرا /ma-rã/

Why Is the SDO Marker Needed?

The SDO Marker is very helpful in clarifying the meaning of the sentence. Its use in some cases is crucial to understanding who is the subject (actor of the action) and who is the object (recipient of the action) of the sentence, especially in the sentence where both subject and object appear in the same grammatical person (e.g., third person singular). In order to see clearly the point of using the SDO Marker, let us look at the following examples.

Let us look at the following words that, if arranged correctly, make up a sentence.

نیما / آن دختر / دوست دارد / را

These words can be arranged into a sentence in two different ways, and, depending on the place of the SDO Marker in the sentence, the meaning of the sentence will change.

(1) The sentence can either mean *Neema loves that girl*,

نیما آن دختر را دوست دارد.

or (2) *That girl loves Neema.*

آن دختر نیما را دوست دارد.

Another example that illustrates the need for the SDO Marker is the case of Persian pronouns (I, you, she, etc.). In English, the pronouns that serve as the subject and the pronouns that serve as the object are differentiated from each other by having two separate sets of forms: *I–Me, He–Him, She–Her, We–Us, They–Them, Who–Whom*, where the first word in each pair is the pronoun that serves as the subject (Actor) and the second word in each pair is the pronoun that serves as the object (recipient). By contrast, Persian only has one set of pronouns (I, you, s/he, we, they, etc.) and simply uses the SDO Marker *o/ro* to designate the object (i.e., recipient of the action).

	Subject		Object	
I	من /man/		من را /man-o/	Me
S/he	او /oon/		او را /oon-o/	Her, him
We	ما /mã/		ما را /mã-ro/	Us
They	آنها oonã		آنها را /oonã-ro/	Them
Who	کی /kee/		کی را /kee-o/	Whom

The same marker *o*/*ro* is attached to any other word that, similar to the pronouns above, appears in the sentence in the place and capacity of the object (recipient of the action).

I saw her او را دیدم /oon-**o** deedam/.

I saw my professor استادم را دیدم /ostãdam-**o** deedam/.

In some cases, the use of the SDO Marker in Persian can be compared to the use of English definite article *the* as opposed to indefinite article *a*.

/man nãmeh gereftam/ I received **a** letter.   .نامه گرفتم

/man nãmeh-**ro** gereftam/ I received **the** letter.   .نامه را گرفتم

Thus, the *o*/*ro* marker is used to mark the recipient of the action (the object) in order to distinguish it from the actor of the action (the subject) in the sentence. Using this marker helps to avoid possible ambiguity as to who is the actor and who is the recipient in the sentence. However, in the cases when the roles of actor (subject) and recipient (object) are perfectly clear, the marker is not used.

Simple Rule of Thumb

The SDO Marker is only used for the object that is a Direct Object and is a Specific Object at the same time. A Direct Object means that the Object does not come with the preposition (to, at, from, toward, etc.). A Specific Object means the object that is familiar to the participants of the conversation, either from the context of the conversation, previous knowledge or due to the descriptive words that accompany that object (modifiers, possessive or indicative suffixes and pronouns). If the object only possesses one of the above two characteristics, we do not use the SDO Marker *oh*/*ro* with that object.

Checklist

Always use the SDO Marker with the object when that object is:

(1)   represented by a personal name (Nasreen, Ali, etc.), for example, *I saw Nasreen yesterday*.

دیروز نسرین را دیدم. /deerooz nasreen-o deedam/

(2)   modified by a demonstrative adjective (this, that, those, these), for example, *I love this movie*.

این فیلم را خیلی دوست دارم. /een feelm-o khe-eelee doost dãram/

(3)   modified by a possessive pronoun or suffix (my, his, their, theirs, etc.) or by a superlative adjective, for example, *I love my class very much.*

کلاسم را خیلی دوست دارم. /kelãsam-o khe-eelee doost dãram/

(4)   represented by a pronoun (me, us, him, her, you, them, it, whom). All pronouns are considered specific because they are only used when the participants of the conversation know to whom they are referring without actually naming that person or thing. Other pronouns such as *somebody* کسی /kasee/, *someone* یکی /yeh-kee/, *each other, one another* یک دیگر، همدیگر /hamdeegar, yek digar/, *everyone* همه /hameh/ and the word *...self* خود /khod/ are considered specific and are marked by the SDO Marker.

کی را دیدی؟   Whom did you see?

(5)   modified by the words *what* (چه), *which* (کُدام), *every* (هَر), *all of ...* (هَمه ِ) *other* (دیگر), *one of the ...* (یکی از)

کُدام ژاکت را خَریدی؟ Which sweater did you buy?

Stacking. The SDO Marker immediately follows the object it marks, and follows the last modifier, if that object is described by modifiers.

Examples:

I received the books today.   امروز کتاب ها را گِرِفتَم.
I received the Persian books today.   امروز کتاب های فارسی را گِرِفتَم.
I received my Persian books today.   امروز کتاب های فارسی ام را گِرِفتَم.

HOMEWORK   تَکلیف

16.   Insert کردن or شدن as needed to complete the following sentences. Translate the sentences into English.

مُطمَئِن بودن to be sure, certain   رَفتار behavior   آذیَت کردن to harass, annoy

۱. من از دیدنِ تو خیلی خوشحال ـــــــ .

۲. این هَمه درس خواندن من را خَسته ـــــــ .

۳. او من را خیلی خوشحال ـــــــ .

۴. داستانِ آنها من را خیلی دِلگیر ـــــــ .

۵. من مَعمولا صبح ها خیلی زود بیدار ـــــــ .

۶ ساعَتَم من را خیلی زود بیدار ـــــــ .

۷. صدای بلندِ موسیقی ما را خیلی ناراحَت ـــــــ .

۸. من را آذَیَت ـــــــ !

۹. این فیلم زیاد جالِب نیست. من حُوصِله ام سَر ـــــــ .

۱۰. رَفتارِش با من را عَصَبانی ـــــــ .

۱۱. از آشنایی با شما خیلی خوشحال ـــــــ .

۱۲. آنها را راضی ـــــــ که بیایَند.

۱۳. معمولا سر امتحان خیلی دَستپاچه ـــــــ .

۱۴. چرا عَصَبانی ـــــــ ؟

۱۵. راضی ـــــــ که بیاید.

۱۶. مُطمَئِن ـــــــ که او فارسی بَلَد است.

17. Complete the following sentences using the given verbs with either شدن or کردن verbs as necessary.

E.g., کلاسم ساعت نُه ... (شروع کردن/شدن) – کلاسم ساعت نُه شروع میشود.
کلاسمان را ساعت دَه... (شروع کردن/شدن) – کلاسمان را ساعت دَه شروع میکنیم.

۱. من موبایلت را در کلاس پیدا ـــــــ (شُدَن/کَردَن).

۲. کلاس فارسی دوازده و پنج دقیقه تمام ـــــــ (کَردَن/شُدَن).

۳. کافه تریای دانشگاه ساعت ۶ صبح باز ـــــــ (کَردَن/شُدَن).

۴. من امروز چهار تا کلاس داشتم و خیلی خسته ـــــــ (کَردَن/شُدَن)؟

18. Complete the sentences with the appropriate ending. Prepare to say your sentences aloud.

راضی شُدَم که ـــــــ

ناراحَت شُدَم برای اینکه ـــــــ

خوشحال شُدَم که ــــــــ

خیلی دَستپاچه شُدَم برای اینکه ــــــــ

هَیجان زده شُدَم برای اینکه ــــــــ

19. Read the statements, and for every statement write how, you think, the person who is making the statement feels.

روزِ تَوَلُّدِ من my birthday

۱. فردا بعد از ظهر امتحان مشکلی دارم، ولی وقت ندارم برای امتحان درس بخوانم. نمیدانم در این امتحان قَبول میشَوم یا نه.

۲. فردا روزِ تَوَلُّدِ من است. خیلی مهمان میاید. من مهمانی ها خیلی دوست دارم.

۳. امروز چهار تا کلاس دارم. بعد، باید سر کار بروم و تا ساعت ۸ شب کار کنم. امروز روز خیلی شلوغی است.

۴. امروز هَوا خیلی گَرم است. میخواهم آب خُنَک بخورم.

20. For each English pronoun below, write a corresponding Persian pronoun. Use the SDO Marker where necessary. Prepare to read the Persian pronouns aloud.

Object	Subject
Whom کی را	Who کی
Me من را	I من
Him	He
Her	She
Us	We
Them	They
You	You

21. Translate the following sentences into English. In your translation, use the article *the* as needed to convey the SDO of the Persian sentence.

۱. دیروز کتاب را به کتابخانه دادم.

۲. ماهی یک بار از کتابخانه کتاب میگیرم.

٣. آن کاپشن زرد را در پاساژ خلیج فارسی دیدم.

۴. در نیویورک در زمستان کاپشن لازم است.

۵. شما خیلی کتاب میخوانید.

۶. آن کتاب را نخواندم.

22. Read the passage where Roya describes her neighborhood and says how she feels about it. Look carefully for the SDO Markers and underline the words (and its modifiers) followed by the SDO Marker. Explain why Roya uses the SDO Marker with those words.

سلام، اسم من رویا است. من در تهران زندگی میکنم. تهران خیلی بزرگ و قشنگ است. تهران را خیلی دوست دارم. خانواده من نزدیکِ میدانِ تجریش منزل دارند. ما سال ها است که آنجا زندگی میکنیم. من محله امان را خوب میشناسم. آهالیِ محله امان مَردُمِ خیلی مِهَربان و خودِمانی هستند. من محله ام را دوست دارم.

خانواده ما چهار نفر است. من یک خواهر دارم. اسم خواهرم تارا است. تارا نُه سالش است. او خیلی دوست داشتَنی، مِهَربان و مُوَدَب است. به نَظَرَم، خواهرِ کوچَکَم خیلی ناز است. من خواهرم را خیلی دوست دارم. مامانم آدمی خیلی مِهَربان، باهوش و قُروتَن است. من مامانم را خیلی دوست دارم. بابایم آدمی دِلسوز، مِهَربان و باانِصاف است. من بابایم را خیلی دوست دارم. مامان و بابایم هر روز صبحِ زود سَرِ کار میروند، و من تارا را خودَم به مَدرِسه میرِسانَم. بعد از کلاس ها، مامانم به مدرسه میاید و من و تارا را به خانه میرساند. در خانه، مامانم ناهار درست میکند و من و تارا و مامانم با هم ناهار میخوریم. بعد، من و تارا یکی دو ساعت درس میخوانیم و مشق هایمان را انجام میدهیم. آنوقت بابایم از سر کار میرسد. مامانم شام درست میکند و ما همه با هم شام میخوریم. من خانواده ام را خیلی دوست دارم.

23. Arrange the following series of words into sentences. Pay special attention to the SDO Marker. Translate your sentences into English.

۱. من - خوشحال - را - میکنی - تو

۲. دختر - پسر - دوست دارد - را

۳. مشقم - خوابگاه - را - گذاشتم - در

۴. برادر – خواهر – عصبانی – میکند – را

۵. من – مامانم – ناراحت – کردم – را

24. 🔊 Listen and insert the SDO Marker *o/ro* wherever you hear it. Remember that regardless of the pronunciation, the SDO Marker is always spelled را. Translate the sentences into English.

۱. لطفا در ببندید.

۲. لطفا این کلمه روی تخته بنویسید.

۳. لطفا سوال هایتان تکرار کنید.

۴. کلاس فارسی ساعت ۱۱ شروع میشود.

۵. امروز کتابم به کلاس نیاوردم.

۶. خانواده ام خیلی دوست دارم.

۷. موبایلم در کتابخانه گذاشتم.

۸. نه، من آن فیلم ندیدم.

۹. لطفا این جمله به انگلیسی ترجمه کنید.

۱۰. لطفا جمله ِ اول بخوانید

25. 🔊 In the following sentences, insert the SDO Marker where necessary. Prepare to read the completed Persian sentences aloud.

They did not see me.	۱. مَن ـــــــ نَدیدَند.
I did not see Kamran in class yesterday.	۲. دیروز کامران ـــــــ دَر کِلاس نَدیدَم
Where did you see me?	۳. کجا من ـــــــ دیدی؟
The boy loves the girl.	۴. پسر ـــــــ دختر ـــــــ دوست دارد.
I left my book in the dorm.	۵. کتابم ـــــــ دَر خوابگاه گذاشتَم.
Where did you see us?	۶. کجا ما ـــــــ دیدی؟
I saw you in the library yesterday.	۷. دیروز دَر کِتابخانه شما ـــــــ دیدَم.
I love them very much.	۸. آنها ـــــــ خِیلی دوست دارَم.
He calls (**to**) me every day.	۹. هَر روز به من ـــــــ زَنگ میزَند.
Who is coming **with** you?	۱۰. کی با تو ـــــــ میایَد؟

١١. به او ـــــــ جواب دادم.   I answered (to) her.

١٢. دیگر آن ـــــــ لازِم نَدارَم.   I do not need it any longer.

١٣. کامران ـــــــ سارا ـــــــ خوشحال میکند.   Kamran makes Sara happy.

١٤. با دوست هایم ـــــــ کار میکُنَم.   I work with my friends

١٥. مَن ـــــــ دَر خانه هَستَم.   I am at home.

١٦. آن ـــــــ خِیلی خوب است.   It is very good.

١٧. آنها ـــــــ دَر نیویورک زِندِگی میکُنَند.   They live in NY.

١٨. شما ـــــــ کجا کار میکنید؟   Where do you work?

١٩. ایمیل هایتان ـــــــ نگرفتم.   I did not get your emails.

٢٠. اس ام اسم ـــــــ دیدی؟   Did you see my message?

26.   Prepare to ask and answer the following questions.

(1) What makes you excited? (2) What makes you happy? (3) What makes you sad?
(4) What makes you bored? (5) What makes you nervous?

27.   Translate the following sentences into Persian.

ساعَتِ زَنگدار Alarm	جَلَسه Meeting
پا شُدَن To stand up	بَسته بودن To be closed

(1). The cafeteria opens at 6:30 a.m. (2) They open all cafeterias after the spring break.
(3) My roommate always closes all the windows. (4) It was cold outside, and all windows were closed. (5) The alarm woke me up too early. (6) I usually wake up at 6:30 a.m.
(7) Class ended and we all stood up. (8) Hope you feel better (lit.: your health become
better). (9) We met at a party. (10) Loud noises make me tired. (11) His words made me
upset. (12) At what time did the meeting begin? (13) I finished the book last night. (14)
Open your book, please.

28.   Translate the sentences and phrases into Persian using the verbs in imperative (command)
form. Use the SDO Marker as needed. Note that in Persian the word *please* comes first.

(1) Give me that book, please. (2) Could you write this word in Persian. (3) Translate this
sentence, please. (4) Open your books to (در) page 25. (5) Close your books. (6) Put your
bag under the table. (7) Say this sentence in Persian, please. (8) Open the door, please.
(9) Close the window, please. (10) Give me two tickets, please. (11) Read the next chapter
for tomorrow. (12) Please, say your question in Persian. (13) Take one of these. (14) Bring

two sodas. (15) Give me their phone number, please. (16) Pass me (give me) that chair, please.

29. The following are some of the phrases that *mom always says*. Translate them into Persian. Add one more phrase. Choose a phrase that has an SDO. Prepare to say the sentences fluently in Persian.

(1)   Clean up your room!
(2)   Wash your hands!
(3)   First, brush your teeth and comb your hair.
(4)   First, finish your food!

30.  Translate these questions into Persian. Mark the SDO as needed. Prepare to say and answer these questions fluently in class.

How often? چَند وَقت یِک بار؟

–   How often do you see your parents?
–   How often do you see your brother/sister?
–   How often do you see your advisor?
–   How often do you see your boyfriend/girlfriend?
–   How often do you see your best friend?
–   Do you bring your textbook to class every day?
–   Do you bring your laptop to classes every day?

IN CLASS   دَر کِلاس

31. Look at these Persian sentences and English translations. Explain the reason for the use of the SDO Marker in each case.

۱. این را برای کی آوردی؟ For whom did you bring this?

۲. این را برای تو آوردم. I brought this for you.

۳. امروز کتاب درسی را نیاوردم. I did not bring the textbook today.

۴. مشق فارسی را امشب انجام میدهم. I will do the Persian homework tonight.

۵. صَندَلی را کجا میبَری؟ Where are you taking the chair?

۶. لطفا در را باز کنید. Open the door, please.

۷. میشود سوالت را تکرار کنی؟ Can you repeat your question?

۸. وقتی کسی را دوست داری. When you love somebody.

۹. این فیلم را دیدی؟ Did you see this movie?

32. Choose the correct Persian translation for each English sentence.

(1) The class started. کلاس شروع کرد - کلاس شروع شد.

(2) The book was found. کتاب را پیدا کرد - کتاب پیدا شد.

(3) He got upset. او ناراحت شد - او ناراحت کرد.

(4) They woke up at 6. آنها ساعَتِ شش بیدار کردند- آنها ساعَتِ شش بیدار شُدند.

(5) The car broke down. ماشین خَراب شُد - ماشین خراب کرد.

(6) Car got fixed. ماشین درست کرد - ماشین درست شد.

(7) The meeting ended at 10. جَلَسه ساعت ده تمام کرد- جلسه ساعت ده تمام شد.

(8) The supermarket opens at 7. سوپِرمارکت ساعت هفت باز میشود - سوپرمارکت ساعت هفت باز میکند.

(9) This book was written in Persian. کتاب به فارسی نوشته شد - کتاب به فارسی نوشته کرد.

(10) I broke my computer. کامپیوترم را خراب کردم - کامپیوترم خراب شد.

(11) I got on the bus. سَوارِ اتوبوس شدم- سَوارِ اتوبوس کردم.

(12) I finished my work. کارم را تمام کردم / کارم تمام شدم.

33. Read the following sentences aloud. Pay special attention to the pronunciation of the SDO Marker.

۱. ایمیلت را نگرفتم. (ایمیلتو نگرفتم.)

۲. هنوز مشقم را انجام ندادم. (هنوز مشقمو انجام ندادم.)

۳. موبایلم را کجا دیدی؟ (موبایلمو کجا دیدی؟)

۴. کِی او را دیدی؟

۵. هم اتاقی ات را در مهمانی دیدم. (هم اتاقیتو در مهمانی دیدم.)

۶. کتابم را در کلاس گذاشتم. (کتابمو در کلاس گذاشتم.)

۷. خودکارم را توی کوله پشتی ام گذاشتم. (خودکارمو تو کوله پشتیم گذاشتم.)

۸. کلیدم را به هَم اُتاقی ام دادم. (کلیدمو به هَم اُتاقیم دادم.)

۹. پول بلیت را به کِی دادی؟ (پول بلیتو به کِی دادی؟)

۱۰. ای پدم را از اینترنت خریدم. (ای پدمو از اینترنت خریدم.)

34. Translate the sentences below using the SDO Marker where necessary.

(1) Did you see this movie? (2) Yes, I saw it in Persian. (3) Do you read this book in your class? (4) Yes, we will read it next week. (5) Did you get my message? (6) I have a question. (7) Repeat your question please. (8) Can you say your sentence again, please? (9) Say your sentence in Persian, please. (10) I have many books, but I do not have this book.

35. Your instructor will assign you a word from the list below. Create two phrases or sentences with that noun: (1) a sentence where the noun is an SDO and (2) a sentence where the noun is not an SDO.

کتاب، واژه، مشـقم، جُمله

36. Pick a classmate whom you have seen recently somewhere outside of class and say where you saw him/her. Alternatively, just say that you saw her/him in class. Do not forget to use the SDO Marker.

دو روز پیش سـام را در باشـگاه دیدم (دو روز پیش سـامو تو باشـگاه دیدم)

37. Say who or what makes you happy in life and why. For example,

... من را خوشـحال میکند برای اینکه.... (... منو خوشـحال میکنه برای اینکه...).

38. Share with class what movie, book, story or event makes you:

Happy, Sad, Excited, Worried

39. Go to the board and write a word in Persian. Pick a classmate and ask him/her, "How do you pronounce this word?" Pick another classmate and ask him/her politely to write a Persian word on the board.

Useful phrases:

لُطفا این واژه را به فارسـی تَلَفُظ کنید (لُطفَن این واژه رو به فارسـی تَلَفُظ کنین).

لُطفا واژه ... را به فارسـی بنویسید (لُطفَن واژه ... را به فارسـی بنویسـین).

40. Your instructor will call on you and read a sentence from the list below without saying the final verb of the sentence. Repeat the sentence and complete it with an appropriate form of شـدن or کردن. Another student will translate your completed sentence.

من تکلیف امروز را دیشب _____ (من تکلیف امروزو دیشب _____)

فیلم ساعت چند شروع _____؟ (فیلم ساعت چند شوروع _____؟)

جلسه را شروع _____ (جلسه رو شروع _____)

تَعطیلاتِ زِمِستانی چه روزی تمام _____؟ (تَطیلاتِ زِمِستونی چه روزی تموم _____؟)

کلاست ساعت چند تمام _____؟ (کلاست ساعت چند تموم _____؟)

هَوای آفتابی من را خوشحال _____ (هَوای آفتابی منو خوشحال _____)

از دیدَنِت خیلی خوشحال _____

از درس خواندن خَسته _____ (از درس خوندن خَسته _____)

کار کَردَن در آزمایشگاه من را خَسته _____ (کار کَردَن تو آزمایشگاه منو خَسته _____)

از موسیقی بلند ناراحَت _____

موسیقی بلند من را ناراحَت _____ (موسیقی بلند منو ناراحَت _____)

من دیروز به مهمانی دَعوَت _____

شما را به مهمانیِ تَوَلُّدم دَعوَت _____ (شما رو به مهمانیِ تَوَلُّدم دَعوَت _____)

مَعمولا ساعت ۷ بیدار _____ (مَمولَن ساعت ۷ بیدار _____)

صِدای باران من را _____ (صِدای بارون منو _____)

41. Answer the following questions. Do not forget to mark the SDO as needed in your answers.

۱. آیا دانشگاهِت را دوست داری؟ (آیا دانشگاهِتو دوست داری؟)

۲. آیا خوابگاهَت/اتاقت را دوست داری؟ (آیا خوابگاهتو/اتاقتو دوست داری؟)

۳. کتاب فارسی ات را از کتابخانه یا اینترنت خریدی؟ (کتاب فارسیتو از کتابخونه یا اینترنت خریدی؟)

۴. مَعمولا لباس هایت را از اینترنت یا پاساژ میخری؟ (مَمولَن لباساتو از اینترنت یا پاساژ میخری؟)

۵. کوله پشتی را از کجا خریدی؟ (کوله پشتیو از کجا خریدی؟)

۶. شهرهای بزرگ یا شهر های کوچک بیشتر دوست داری؟ (شهرای بزرگ یا شهرای کوچیک بیشتر دوست داری؟)

۷. آیا شهر _____* را دوست داری؟ (شهر _____* رو دوست داری؟)

*Name of the town where your university is located

42. Ask your classmates the following questions in Persian. Use the SDO Marker as needed. See if anyone in class recently saw the same movie as you did, and if they liked it.

Useful words:

شاد happy   خَنده دار funny   غَم آنگیز sad   فیلم movie

(1) What was the last movie you saw? (2) Was that movie funny, happy or sad? ( ). Did you like that movie? (4) Where did you watch the movie? (5) With whom did you watch the movie? (6) Did s/he also like that movie?

Now, think of a TV show that you like and watch. Ask your classmates if they have seen that TV show and whether they like it or not.

TV show (soap opera, sitcom) – سِریال

بَرنامه ِ تِلِویزیونی TV show

43. Think of all the professors whose classes you are taking this semester. Talk to you classmates and ask if they know those professors. Your objective is to find people in your class who know the same professors as you do. Ask a separate question about each professor of yours. Your question sentence will follow the example sentence given below. Make sure to mark the SDO in your questions and answers. Useful phrases:

آیا استاد ... را می‌شِناسی؟ (آیا استاد ... رو/و می‌شِناسی؟)

بله، استاد ... را می‌شِناسَم. (بله، استاد ... و/رو می‌شِناسَم)

نه، استاد ... را نِمی‌شِناسَم. (نَه، استاد ... و/رو نِمی‌شِناسَم)

Now, share your findings with the class. You will use the verb *to know* in third person singular.

سارا مثل من، استاد ... را می‌شِناسَد. (سارا مثلِ من، استاد ... رو/و می‌شناسه.)

45.   For this exercise, you will need the following phrase:

؟... هَر گِز (*have you ever?*) combined with the verb in the past tense.

For example, هَر گِز ایران رَفتی؟ Have you ever been to Iran?

You will be working in pairs. Come up with questions that combine the above phrase with the verbs below used in the past tense. Your sentence must have an SDO.

- to eat
- to see
- to read
- verb of your choice (with an SDO)

46.   Think of a command sentence with an SDO similar to the sentences below. Ask a classmate very politely to follow the command.

E.g., (لُطفَن دستو بُلَند کُن!) لُطفا دستت را بُلَند کُن!

(لُطفَن کتابِتو باز کُن!) لُطفا کتابت را باز کُن!

(لُطفا خودکارِتو رو دَفتَرچَت بِگُذار!) لُطفا خودکارِت را روی دَفتَرچه ات بِگُذار!

47.   Pick a student in class and ask that student to introduce another student from your class to everyone. Use the following phrase to make your request:

(لُتفَن اونو به کلاس مُعَرِفی کن!) لُطفا او را به کلاس مُعَرِفی کُن!.

The student to whom you directed your request will have to say: the name, last name, place of origin, major and whether she or he is a undergraduate or graduate student, about the person being introduced.

Listen and repeat. Try to imitate the native speaker's pronunciation and intonation. Say each phrase a few times aloud until you can easily pronounce it.

Appearance	
How does s/he look?	او چه شِکلی است؟ (اون چه شِکلیه؟)
I look more like my mother	مَن بیشتَر شِکلِ مادَرَم هَستَم
I have got my father's stature	قَدَم شَبیه ِ پِدَرَم است / قَدَم به پِدَرَم رَفته / قَدَم را از پِدَرَم اِرث بُرده ام (قَدَم شَبیه ِ پِدَرَمه / قَدَم به پِدَرَم رَفته / قَدَمو از پِدَرَم اِرث بُردَم)

	Appearance	
Pretty, beautiful (about a woman)		خوشگِل
Good-looking (about a man)		خوش قیافه
Good-looking. i.e., well-dressed, well-groomed		خوشتیپ
Attractive		جَذاب
Well-built		خوش اَندام
Cute		ناز، لوس
S/he is tall		او بُلَندقَد است (اون بُلَندقَده)
S/he is short		او کوتاه قَد است (اون کوتاه قَده)
S/he is of medium height		قَدِش مُتِوَسِط است (قَدِش مُتِوَسِطه)
Full, plump (about a person)		پُر؛ او پُر است (اون پُره)
Big (in reference to person's physique or stature, also to person's eyes)		دُرُشت
Corpulent		چاق
Chubby		تُپُل
Skinny		لاغَر
Balanced weight		وَزنِ مُتِعادِل
Old		پیر
Middle-aged		میان سال
Young		جَوان (جَوون)
Face		صورَت
Shape of the face		فُرمِ صورَت
Round face		صورَتِ گِرد
Eyes		چِشم ها (چِشما/چِشا)
Nose		دَماغ
Eyebrow		اَبرو
Skin		پوست
Hair		مو ها
Body		بَدَن

	Appearance
Height, stature	قَد
What color is his/her hair?	موهایش چَه رَنگی اسـت؟ (موهاش چه رنگیه؟)
What color is his/her eyes?	چِشم هایش چه رَنگی هَستَند؟ (چِشماش چه رَنگی هَستَن)
S/he has long hair	او موهای بُلَند دارد (اون موهای بُلَند داره)
Short hair	موهای کوتاه
Moustache	سِبیل (سِبیل)
Beard	ریش
He has long beard	او ریشِ بُلَند دارد (اون ریشِ بُلَند داره)
He has short beard/stubble	او تَه ریش دارد (اون تَه ریش داره)
S/he is blond	او موبور است (اون موبوره)
S/he is redhead	او موقِرمِز است (اون موقِرمِزه)
S/he has black hair	او موهای مِشکی (سیاه) دارد (اون موهای مِشکی داره)
Brown hair	موهای قَهوه ای رَنگ، موهای خُرمایی
Grey hair	موهایِ سِفید
Her/his hair is straight	موهایش صاف/لَخت است (موهاش صافه/لَخته)
Her/his hair is curly	موهایش فِر است (موهاش فِره)
His/her hair is wavy	موهایش حالَتدار است (موهاش حالَتداره)
S/he has a fair skin	پوسِتِش رُوشَن است (پوسِتِش رُوشَنه)
S/he is tanned	پوسِتِش بُرُنزه است (پوسِتِش بُرُنزِست)
Relatively	نِسبَتا (نِسبَتَن)
The color of her/his hair is blondish (lit.: of almost golden color)	رنگ موهایش به طَلایی میزَند (رنگ موهاش به طَلایی میزَنه)
olive-greenish (in reference to the color)	به زِیتونی میزَند (به زِیتونی میزَنه)
is ...ish, like, very similar to ...	به ... میزَند (به ... میزَنه)

HOMEWORK تَکلیف

48.  Listen and read along. The narrator is decribing his friend Sarah in the photo below. Complete the translation.

سَلام. این عَکسِ دوستَمِ ساراست. سارا لاغَر است.قَدِش مُتِوَسِط است. موهای بُلَند و لَخت و قَهوه ای رَنگی دارد. سارا دَماغ کوچک و چِشم های قَهوه ای رنگی دارد. سارا مَعمولا رَسمی لِباس میپوشد، و هَمیشه پُرِانِرژی و سَرِحال است.

Hi, this is a photo of my friend Sarah. Sarah is _____. She is of medium _____. She has _____, _____, brown hair. Sarah has a small _____ and brown _____. Sarah usually dresses formally and is always energetic and _____.

49. 🔊 Listen to Koorosh as he describes himself. You will hear his description and see both the Persian transcript and the English translation. Complete the script based on what you hear. Then complete the translation based on your completed transcript.

سَلام، اسم من کورُش اسـت. من فُرم ِ.......َم بیشتَر به خانواده مادَری ام و مادَرم رَفته، وَلی .... و ....َم بیشـتَر شَبیه ِ پدرم اسـت. من وَزن ِ مُتَعادِلی دارم و ....م نِسبَتا .... اسـت. رَنگ پوسـتم روشَن اسـت، ....یم قَهوه ای رَنگ اسـت، و .... هایم به زیتونی میزَند.

Hi, my name is Koorosh. I got my _____ shape more from my maternal family and specifically from my mother, but I got my _____ and _____ more from my father. I have a balanced weight and am relatively _____ My skin is fair. My _____ is brown, and my _____ are kind of olive-colored.

50. Translate the following sentences into Persian. Fill in the blanks with information relevant to you.

(1) I got my _____ from my mom. (2) I got my _____ from my dad. (3) I have _____ eyes.
(4) I have _____, _____ hair. (5) I look more like my _____.

51. 🔊 Listen to the narrator. He describes two of his friends, Tom and Nik. Listen and, based on the descriptions, write a corresponding name to each photo.

52. Look at the images of these individuals and prepare to describe their appearance in class.

53. Think of a person in your family that you look like. Now, prepare to describe to your class that person as well as another random family member. Let your classmates guess which of the two people you describe looks more like you.

IN CLASS      دَر کِلاس

54. Pick a person in class and describe that person's appearance without announcing the name. The class will listen to you and try to guess who that person is.

55. 👥 You will be working in pairs. Think of the country and culture that one of you comes from. Now, describe for your class the standard of beauty for men and women prevalent in that culture or country. One of you will describe the standard of beauty for women and the other will describe the standard of beauty for men.

56. Interview. Your instructor will call on you to ask your classmates questions in Persian. Ask each one of your classmates one question in Persian on any of the topics listed below. Once you are done asking your questions, you will become the interviewee, and each student in class will ask you in Persian one question on any of the topics given below.

If your class is too big for this format of activity, your instructor might divide the class into groups of three, where you will find yourself with two other students. Ask each of the two classmates at least three questions on the given topics.

Topics:

اسم و فامیل، کجایی، خانِواده، بِهتَرین دوست، دانِشگاه و کلاس، شغل،
کارهای روزانه، خانه و منزل ، شَهر و کشور، لباس، خرید، آب و هَوا، شَخصیَت

LISTENING   شِنیداری

Listen to the conversation between two individuals who are describing the appearances of their family members and saying who they look like in the family.

Pre-listening. Considering the topic of the conversation, make a list of the words that you would expect to hear in such a conversation. If the word you wrote down is a noun, think of the verb that might go with it in the given context. If the word that you wrote is a verb, think of a noun that might go with it in a conversation on the given topic. What would the tense of the verbs in such conversation likely be? What is the marker of that tense in Persian? Read aloud the words you have written down so that you hear your voice.

Follow-up 1. Listen and, based on what the speakers mention, describe what similarities the Speaker I and Speaker II have with each other.

Follow-up 2. Make comparative statements. Say a few things that you have in common with either of the speakers and few things that are different.

Follow-up 3. Work with two other classmates and create a brief conversation. Imagine that you are going to a summer school in Tehran. Another person from your group will be your Tehrani classmate. The third member of your group will be your Tehrani classmate's family member in Tehran. Theme: you are arriving at the Tehran airport. Your Tehrani classmate has arranged for you to stay with his or her family in Tehran. One of his or her family members is going to pick you up from the Tehran airport, but you have never seen that person. Ask your Tehrani classmate to describe for you the person who is waiting for you at the airport.

Now, your friend also gave you the phone number of his/her family member who is waiting for you at the airport. Call that person, introduce yourself and describe yourself to him/her so she or he can recognize you at the airport.

READING

خواندَنی

Before coming to class, prepare to read the following dialogue fluently. Read the entire dialogue several times aloud until you can easily pronounce all sentences. In order to reflect the real-world use of the language, the dialogue is transcribed in colloquial style.

Pre-reading 1. The dialogue you will read below is about feelings, emotions and relationships. Think of yourself and think of the adjectives in Persian that describe how you feel 1) after you did great on your final exams; 2) before an exam; 3) before a trip abroad; 4) after a long day; 5) when you go out with good friends.

Pre-reading 2. Read the glossary below, and think how you would say the following phrases in Persian.

1. I want to be happy. 2. Are you content with your life? 3. I forgot that I have an exam tomorrow. 4. At the university, I got used to sleeping only a little. 5. I usually feel anxious before my final exams. 6. I don't want to leave. 7. I love you. 8. It's hard for me to change. 9. I decided to stay. 10. I pretend that I am not worried. 11. Don't be afraid.

any longer دیگر (دیگه)	دِلِت واسهِ مَن میسوزد you feel sorry for me
تو را دوست دارم = دوسِتِت دارم (دوسِت دارم)	دِلشور داشتَم/دارم، I felt/feel anxious / دِلشوره گِرفتَم/میگیرم I got/get anxious
چرا positive response to a negative statement or question	تَظاهُر کردم/میکنم I pretended/pretend
مگر نیستَم (مَگه نیستَم) aren't I	تَرسیدَم/میتَرسَم I was/am afraid
مگر (مَگه) combined with a subjunctive verb means unless	راحَت شُدَم/میشوم I got/get piece of mind, be at ease, not worry
بگذار (بِذار) let, allow (imperative verb)	از یادِت رفت/میرود you forgot/forget

347

بگذرد (بِگذَره) [it] to pass (subjunctive verb)		عادَت کردم/میکنم I got/get used	
جای تو را (جاتو) your place		دُنبالِ بودم/هستم I was/am after ...	
اِنگار as if, it's like ...		تَغییر کردم/میکنم I changed/change [myself]	
من هم (مَنَم) me too, so do I		تَصمیم گرفتم/میگیرم I decided/decide	
به من (بِهِم) to me		از زندِگی راضی بودم/هستم I was/am content with life	

نیما: تو دیگه مَنو دوست نَداری.

پریسا: چرا، خِیلی دوسِت دارم. با تو هستم، مَگه نیستم؟

نیما: تو میخای بِری، وَلی دِلت واسه مَن میسوزه.

پریسا: برای اینکه دوسِت دارم.

نیما: فَقَط تَظاهُر میکنی. میدونَم که میخای بِری، وَلی نِمیری برای اینکه دِلشوره داری. نَتَرس، بُرو، بُرو دور. بِذار چَن ماه بِگذَره، این دِلشوره ها و دِلسوزی ها از یادِت میرَن. راحَت میشی

پریسا: تو راحَت میشی؟ من دِلشوره دارم واسه فَردای تو.

نیما: تو از فَردای بی توی من نِگران نَباش. بِبین، هیچکَس جاتو تو دِلَم نِمیگیره. وَلی آخَرِ کار، عادَت میکنم، راحَت میشَم.

پریسا: نِمیخام که عادَت کنی. من دِلشوره میگیرَم برای اینکه تو حالِت خوب نیست با من. اِنگار دُنبالِ زندگیِ دیگه ای هستی، اِنگار از من خَسته ای. من میخام که خوشحال باشی، شاد باشی، از زندِگیت با من راضی باشی. میخام مَنَم خوشحال باشم، شاد باشم، راحَت باشم. وَلی نِمیتونَم کِنارِ تو خوشحال باشم مَگه تو تَغییر کُنی. میخام هَمینجا هَم برای خود تَصمیم بِگیری و هم بِهِم بِگی دوستَم داری یا نه، میخای بِری یا نه، میخای بِرَم یا نه.

نیما: ...

پریسا: میخای بِری؟ میخای بِرَم؟

نیما: نه.

Prepare to answer the questions in Persian in class. Before coming to class, say your answers aloud several times until your can easily pronounce your sentences.

را تَرک کردن to leave, abandon somebody

سُؤال ها:

۱. به نَظَرِ شما، آیا نیما پریسا را دوست دارد؟

۲. به نَظَرِ شما، آیا پریسا نیما را دوست دارد؟

۳. به نَظَرِ شما، مُشکِلِ نیما چه است؟

۴. به نَظَرِ شما، مُشکِلِ پریسا چه است؟

۵. به نَظَرِ شما، آیا پریسا میخواهد با نیما بِماند؟

۶. به نَظَرِ شما، آیا بهتر است که پریسا بِرود؟

۷. به نَظَرِ شما، آخرِ کار، پریسا نیما را تَرک میکند یا نه؟

۸. به نَظَرِ شما، چرا پریسا نِگرانِ فَردایِ نیما بود؟

۹. به نَظَرِ شما، آیا نیما تَغییر میکند؟ چرا؟

Follow-up 1. Your instructor will assign to you and another student in class the lines of Parisa and Neema. Read out the dialogue for your class. This exercise will test your pronunciation and fluency.

Follow-up 2. Tell your class briefly in Persian what happened between Neema and Parisa. Tell your story as a narrative, not as a sequence of the lines of the two people. In order to provide a context for your narrative, add to your story what you think was the beginning and conclusion of the conversation between Parisa and Neema.

Follow-up 3. Look again through the transcript of the dialogue and the glossary. Pick two different words that describe emotions, feelings or state of being. Now, pick two classmates and ask each classmate one question using those two words. Your questions must be about your classmates.

TRANSLATION

ترجُمه

Translate into Persian the following anecdote about the humorous character Molla Nasreddin. Don't forget to use subjunctive and the SDO Marker where needed.

Molla Nasreddin مُلا

گاز گِرِفتن (گیر) To bite

One day, a dog bit Molla. They told Molla, "If you do not want the dog to bite you again, give it some food." Molla said, "If I do that, all other dogs will bite me."

WRITING

اِنشا

We describe people all the time. It is a part of life. For example, you might describe your new friend at college or your roommate to your family. You might describe someone to your friend, who is going to work with that person. You might need to describe a person to justify your request or claim. Descriptions appear in written material (literature pieces, job descriptions, stories and anecdotes) and in verbal communication. It is very useful to know how to describe people.

Think of a person who has a presence in your life. It may be your best friend, a family member and the like. Write a brief description of that person. Start by describing the person's appearance. Then describe the person's personality, character traits, mannerisms and usual behavior. You can also write couple of your favorite things about that person's personality.

فَصل دَوازدَهُم
Chapter 12

سَفَر به ایران
Traveling in Iran, the *Taãrof*

Tehran International Airport, Iran.

Function Going through customs at the airport, taking a cab, checking in at the hotel, buying a bus ticket, asking for directions. Basics of the Persian social etiquette, the *taãrof*. Key verbs: *to travel, to arrive, to visit, to get on/off the vehicle, to stay, to return, to reserve, to cross, to pass, to turn, to enter, to exit.*

Listening Passport control in the airport, in a cab to the hotel, at the hotel's reception desk, at the bus terminal.

Reading A few tips about flying abroad.

Structures Review: Subjunctive and imperative, simple past tense.

TAÃROF

تَعارُف

Persian social etiquette, the Taãrof

In Iranian culture the interaction and communication between individuals (other than well-acquainted persons) follow a behavioral convention called the *taãrof* (تَعارُف). The *taãrof* is rooted in Iran's social tradition and Iranians' affinity for courtesy and social grace. It is variously translated to English as *Persian social etiquette*, *ritual courtesy*, and *ritual politeness*. The *taãrof* includes both behavioral and verbal aspects. The essential basis of the *taãrof* is a display of politeness and respect for the conversation partner. In practice, the *taãrof* calls for a demonstration of one's humility, humbleness and even deference, while at the same time affirming and preserving the conversation partner's dignity and high status (actual or perceived) throughout the conversation. Usually, both speakers follow this behavioral game, unless superiority (in age, or social, professional or hierarchical status) of one of the speakers is overwhelmingly obvious or is intended to be expressed, in which case the party with superior status is free to resort to a less elaborate form of the *taãrof*. Thus, a younger speaker addressing an older speaker (e.g., a student addressing a professor) would resort to the *taãrof* and use the polite *you* (شـما) and conjugate the verbs in plural, while the older speaker (especially if the age difference is significant) would have a liberty of choosing to use casual *you* (تو) and conjugate the verbs in the singular. If the conversation partners are of equal status, the extent of *taãrof* depends on how well they know each other, that is, two university professors who meet for the first time will resort to the complete *taãrof* register.

It is important to keep in mind that the concept of *taãrof* is different from the difference between the formal and colloquial registers. The *taãrof* can be performed in colloquial as well as formal registers.

The *taãrof* is expressed through behavior, body language, gestures and words. Persian language provides two sets of lexical units for most common verbs and pronouns—one for the *taãrof* and the other for regular speech. Given below are some common examples and cases.

Some of the Basic Behavioral Conventions

1. When several persons arrive simultaneously at the doorway, one is expected to stop and acknowledge the others' presence by insisting that the other person(s) at the door goes first. Usually, the word used in this case is */befarmãeed/*. This action is to be reciprocated by the other(s) with equal persistency and using the words */khãhesh meekonam, befarmãeed/*. After a repeated exchange of */befarmãeed/*, usually the one who is older or has an overwhelmingly higher social/professional status will move first, often apologizing */bebakhsheed/* for taking advantage of the others' courtesy. If the speakers are peers or close friends, usually polite persistence and even gentle physical strength are used, and in this case the one who goes last wins!

2. At social gatherings, when the host invites everyone to the table to get some food, one is expected to show shyness and reservation at first, even if one is hungry. It is considered impolite to "dig right in." The host will encourage the guests again by repeating several times the words /befarmãeed, khãhesh meekonam, befarmãeed/, after which it is acceptable to approach the table and enjoy the food.

3. If given a compliment or praise for one's accomplishments or qualities, it is customary to downplay one's achievements (compare to "You're too kind" in English). Readily accepting the praise and thanking for it will be seen as lack of social grace and a sign of arrogance (compare to "Yes, you are right, I am smart!" in English).

4. If a guest compliments something while visiting someone's house (including a piece of the host's clothing), the guest will be offered that piece as a gift. It is customary to politely reject that offer, even if the host insists.

5. When stopping by at someone's home and being offered food or beverage by the host it is customary to politely refuse it at first, so as to not bother the host. The host will continue to insist, after which it is appropriate to accept the offer. It is considered impolite not to try at least a little bit of food/beverage after it has already been brought to the table.

6. When several persons go out for a meal, usually one of them will insist on paying for everybody. Sometimes, that person will rush to the counter first to pay before others have a chance to do the same.

Most Common Words and Expressions

1. /be-far-mã-eed/ (بفَرمایید) literally means *Command it!* and is one of the most commonly used words in polite Persian speech. It can be roughly translated to English as *Please* combined with appropriate verbs (e.g., Please sit down; Please come in; Please help yourself; Please go ahead, etc.). In Persian, only the word /befarmãeed/ is used in place of all the phrases given above, while the verb of action is implied and becomes clear from the context. /befarmãeed/ is used: (a) when giving someone an object which s/he had requested, in which case the /befarmãeed/ is the equivalent of English "Here you are"; (b) when opening the door to guests and inviting them in, that is, the equivalent of English "Please come in"; (c) when stopping at the door to let the other(s) go first, in which case, it means "After you"; (d) when offering someone a seat and pointing at the chair, in which case /befarmãeed/ means "Please take a seat"; (e) when someone addresses you by name in order to ask a question or make a request and you express your readiness to listen, in which case /befarmãeed/ is the equivalent of English "Please speak", "Please go ahead", and so on.

2. /khã-hesh mee-ko-nam/ (خواهِش میکُنم) literally means *I plead, I request* and is often used to say *You Are Welcome* and as a polite disclaimer. /khãhesh meekonam/ is used: (a) in response to *Thank you!* in which case it means "You are welcome"; (b) in response to a compliment or praise, in which cases it expresses a polite disagreement with the speaker's high opinion and translates to English as "You are too kind". In this context, it is sometimes combined with the phrase /lotf dãreed/ (لُطف دارید); (c) when urging or asking someone to do something, in which case it translates to English as "Please, could you …".

3. /lot-fan/ (اًلطفا) literally means *Kindly* and is the most common word to introduce a request for an action. It is followed by the verb that describes the requested action, for example, /*lotfan tekrãr koneed*/ (Please repeat), /*lotfan tavajoh koneed*/ (Please pay attention).

4. /das-teh-toon dard na-ko-neh/ (دَستِتون دَرد نَکُنه) literally means *May your hand not hurt!* and is used to say *Thank you very much!* when one wants to go beyond simple /mer-see/. It is used to thank a person for a gift or a service s/he has performed. The phrase refers to "the hand" that performed the service or offered the gift. The traditional response is /*sar-eh-toon dard na-koneh!*/ *May your head not hurt*, however, usual /khãhesh meekonam/ can be used as well.

5. /qã-be-leh sho-mã roh nadã-reh/ قابِل شُما رو نَداره is used in response to an expression of gratitude as an equivalent of English *Don't mention it*. Literally it means *It is not worthy of you*. This phrase is also used to ostensibly refuse a compensation for a service or help offered. For example, taxi drivers may say it to refuse your payment after they deliver you to your destination. It is expected that you insist on paying, for which you will use the phrases /*khãhesh meekonam, befarmãeed*/ repeatedly after which the driver will take the money. The other variant of this phrase is /qã-bel na-dãreh/ قابِل نَداره

6. /be-bakh-sheed/ (بِبَخشید) means *Sorry* and *Excuse me*. It is used to: (a) apologize for one's actions. The usual response to it is either /khãhesh meekonam/ and/or /e-eeb nadãreh/ (No problem!); (b) to call for someone's attention in order to ask a question or make a request. The usual response is /befarmãeed/ to encourage the person to speak.

7. /bã e-jã-zeh/ (or bã e-jã-zah-toon) (با اِجازه) means *With [your] permission!* Even if the permission is not obligatory, it is taken to show respect for others by acknowledging their presence. This phrase is used when taking leave from a table, gathering or a conversation that you have to interrupt. The usual responses are /khãhesh meekonam/ or /qorbooneh shomã/.

8. /khas-teh na-bã-sheed/ (خَسته نَباشید) can be rendered with different English words depending on the context. It means something similar to "I hope you are not too tired", "I hope you are not having a hard day". This phrase is used to express the acknowledgement and appreciation for the work, hard labor or valuable service that someone has done or is still doing. You might use this phrase when you see a person who has just organized a successful event, completed a paper, or fixed something around the house or office. Students often say /khas-teh nah-bã-sheed/ to the professor when they exit the classroom after an interesting lecture. The traditional response to this phrase is /salãmat bãsheed/. The phrase /khas-teh nah-bã-sheed/ is also used to greet someone or call for someone's attention in order to introduce a question or request. In such cases, it is used instead of, or in conjunction with the greeting word /salãm/. You might use /salãm, khasteh nabãsheed/ when you enter a store and would like to address the salesperson with a question. It can also be used as an opening line to ask a person in the street for directions.

IN CLASS   دَر کِلاس

1. You will be working in groups. Come up with and perform a brief dialogue where you demonstrate the use of at least one courtesy or *taãrof* phrase or word in Persian.

TRAVELING   سَفَر و مُسافِرَت

Listen and repeat the words. Say each word aloud several times until you can easily pronounce it. Practice before coming to class.

Nouns			
Trip	سَفَر	Taxi	تاکسی
A ticket	بِلیت (بیلیت)	Airport	فُرودگاه (فورودگاه)
Hotel	هُتِل	Flight	پَرواز
A place similar to a hostel; a motel, inn	مُسافِرخانه (مُسافِرخونه)؛ مِهمانخانه (مِهمونخونه)	Bus terminal, bus station	تِرمینالِ اتوبوس
Airplane	هَواپیما	Bus stop	ایستگاهِ اتوبوس
Train	تِرن، قَطار	Train station	ایستگاهِ تِرن/قَطار
Bus	اتوبوس (اوتوبوس)	Foreign country	کِشوَرِ خارِجی
Car	ماشین	Rental car	ماشینِ کِرایه ای

Verbs and Phrases	
To take a trip, to travel	سَفَر کَردَن، مُسافِرَت کردن
To go on a trip	به مُسافِرَت رَفتَن
To buy in advance	پیشدَست خَریدَن
To reserve a room	اُتاق رِزِرو کَردَن
To get on the … (bus, taxi, car, etc.)	سَوارِ … شُدَن

	Verbs and Phrases
To get off the ... (bus, taxi, car, etc.)	از ... پیاده شُدَن
Supposed to ...	قَرار است (قَراره) که ...
To prefer	... را تَرجیح دادَن
To cover expense for gas	هَزینه‌ِ بِنزین را دادن (هَزینه‌ِ بِنزینو دادن)
To pay for gas	پولِ بِنزین را دادَن (پولِ بِنزینو دادن)
To stay in a hotel; I stayed/stay in a hotel	در هُتِل ماندن (در هُتِل موندن)؛ دَر هُتِل ماندَم/میمانَم (دَر هُتِل موندَم/میمونَم)
To return, go back to ... ; I returned/return	به ... بَر گَشتَن؛ بَرگَشتَم/بَر میگَردَم
All of the ...	کُلِ ...
Alone	تَنهایی
With family	با خانواده (با خونواده)
To take along	با خود بُردن (بَر)

HOMEWORK   تَکلیف

2. Complete the following sentences with the words that fit the context. Now compare the writer's travel preferences to yours. Prepare to say your sentences fluently in class.

۱. دوست دارم تَنهایی ـــــــ کنم.

۲. وَقتی قَرار است که با اُتوبوس یا تِرن سَفَر کنم، معمولا بلیت ها را ـــــــ از اینترنت میخَرم.

۳. وَقتی قَرار است که در هُتِل بِمانَم، معمولا اُتاق را پیشدَست ـــــــ

۴. تَرجیح میدَهم سَوار ـــــــ شوم تا سَوارِ هَواپیما.

۵. برای تَعطیلات معمولا به ـــــــ میروم برای اینکه عاشِقِ پلاژ و آفتاب هستم.

۶. ـــــــ فَردا ساعتِ ۶:۳۰ صُبح از فُرودگاهِ لاگواردیا است.

۷. برای رِسیدان به فُرودگاه معمولا سَوارِ ـــــــ میشَوم.

۸. وَقتی من و دوستم با ماشینَم به مُسافِرَت میرویم، دوستم کُلِ ـــــــ بِنزین را میدهد.

356

3. Make a list of your family members and tourist destinations they like to visit (beach, mountains, etc.). Prepare to say your sentences fluently in class.

پدرم دوست دارد برای تَعطیلات به ساحِل برود.

- پدرم

- مادرم

- خواهرم

- برادرم

- من

4. Prepare to ask these questions fluently. Be ready to answer these questions.

۱. تابِستان آیَنده میخواهی کجا بِروی؟

۲. باید با ماشین، اُتوبوس یا هَواپیما آنجا بِروی؟

۳. دوست داری برای تَعطیلات به چه نُوع جایی (کِنارِ دَریا، کَویر، کوهِستان، جَنگَل) بِروی؟

۴. معمولا تَنهایی یا با دوست ها مُسافِرَت میکنی؟

۵. وَقتی با چندین دوست با ماشین به مُسافِرَت میروید، چه کَسی هَزینهِ بِنزین را میدهد؟

۶. وقتی در یک کِشورِ خارِجی مُسافِرَت میکنی، معمولا در یک هُتل یا مُسافِرخانه میمانی؟

۷. به نَظَرِ تو، سَفَر به خارِج با خانواده، دوست ها یا تَنهایی بِهتَر است؟

۸. وَقتی به مُسافِرَتِ دو سه روزه میروی چه چیزهایی را با خود میبَری؟

IN CLASS   دَر کِلاس

5. Share with your classmates what you have to do and what means of transportation you have to use to get from your university to your hometown. Start by saying where your hometown is located, how far it is from your university and what transportation you usually use to get there. Then describe where and how you buy the tickets (in person, online, well in advance or right at the station). Now, walk everyone through what you do to get from your room at the university to your room at your house in your hometown. If you need to get to a bus terminal, train station or airport, do you get a cab or find a ride; do your usually travel during the day or night; and so on. Give as many details as you can.

6. Tell the class about your last trip (where, for how long, with whom, how did you get there, where did you stay, where did you eat, how did you get around while there, did you like it?).

7. You are going on a field trip with your Persian class to a town that is an hour and a half drive away from your university. Answer the following questions about planning that trip.

۱.به نَظَرِ شُما، چه روزی برای این مُسافِرَت بِهتَر است؟

۲.آیا بِهتَر است که با ماشینِ یکی از هَمکِلاسی ها بروید یا بِهتَر است که با یک ماشینِ کِرایه ای بروید ؟

۳. هَزینهِ بِنزین را چِطوری میدهید؟

۴. چه چیز هایی را به مُسافِرَت میاورید؟ غَذای خانه را میاورید یا در آن شَهر در یک رِستوران غَذا میخورید؟

۵.آیا بِهتَر است که در آن شَهر یک شب بِمانید یا هَمان روز به دانشگاه بَرگَردید؟

8. Think of the type of destinations that you like to travel to (coast, mountains, desert, forest, etc.). Now talk to as many in class as you can, and find out if anyone shares your travel preferences.

9. You will be working in groups. The instructor will assign to your group one of the two situations below. Create and perform a brief dialogue based on that situation.

> **Situation one:** Together with friends, plan a trip. Arrange for a ride, discuss what to bring on the trip, where to stay, when to get back, how to share the expenses for gas, hotel, food, and so on. Incorporate verbs in the subjunctive and imperative forms. Use phrases such as "We should …", "It's better to …"
>
> **Situation two**: You are on campus and run into two classmates who are from a foreign country. They are trying to get to the closest mall. Explain to them how to get there (how far it is, whether they can take a bus, taxi, etc. to get there, where they can catch bus, taxi, where they should get off, etc.). Incorporate verbs in the subjunctive and imperative forms. Use phrases such as "You can …", "It's better to …"

10. Two of your classmates just got back from a trip. Ask them questions about their trip and their experiences. Working as a group prepare and demonstrate a short dialogue. Key words for the questions and answers are:

کِی، کجا، با ... (أتوبوس، هَواپیما، ...)، چِقَدر، ماندن، هتل/مُسافِرخانه، بَرگَشتن، خوش گُذَشت.

AT THE AIRPORT

دَر فُرودگاه

Listen and repeat the words. Say each word aloud several times until you can easily pronounce it. Practice before coming to class.

Passport control (In airports)	کُنترُلِ گُذَرنامه	Customs (for arriving passengers)	صَفِ گُمرُک
Passport control officer	مامورِ گُذَرنامه	First time	دَفعهِ اَوَّل، اَوّلین دَفعه
Traveler, passenger	مُسافِر	Tourism	گَردِش
Target, purpose	هَدَف	Business trip	سَفَرِ کاری
How long	چِهِ مُدَّتی، چِقَدر (چِقَد)	You are too kind (a response to a compliment)	خیلی لُطف دارید!
Visa for traveling	ویزا، رَوادید	Welcome!	خوش آمَدید
Baggage claim area	سالُنِ تَحویلِ بار	to intend to … (this verb is a subjunctive trigger)	قصد داشتَن
Suitcase, luggage	چَمِدان (چَمِدون)	To visit somebody, some place	از...بازدید کَردَن

HOMEWORK

تَکلیف

11.   **Pre-listening**. Complete these sentences with the appropriate words.

کُنترُل، گُذَرنامه، مامور، هَدَف، ماندَن، تَحویل، چَمِدان، گُمرُک

بعد از وارد شُدَن به فُرودگاه در یک کشورِ جارِجی ، اَوّل باید به ـــــ گُذَرنامه

بِرَوم و ـــــ را به ـــــ گُذَرنامه بِدَهم. مامورِ گُذَرنامه مُمکِن است از من بِپُرسَد

که ____ سَفَرَم به آن کشور چه است و چه مدتی را در آن کشور ____ . بعد از

کُنترُلِ گُذَرنامه، میتوانم به سالُنِ ____ بار بِرَوم و ____ هایم را بَر دارم. از آنجا

باید به صَفِ ____ بِرَوم. بعد از گُذَشتَن از صَف ____ میتوانم از فُرودگاه خارِج

شَوم و به هُتل بِرَوم.

IN CLASS   دَر کِلاس

12.   **Pre- listening**. Talk to everyone in class and ask them the following questions.

۱. برای سَفَر به چه کشور هایی گُذَرنامه لازِم داری و برای سَفَر به چه کشور هایی گُذَرنامه لازِم نداری؟

۲. وَقتی آوَلین دَفعه به خارِج رفتی به چه کشوری رفتی؟

۳. وَقتی به مُسافِرَت میروی معمولا در هُتل یا مُسافِرخانه میمانی؟

۴. هَدَفِ آخَرین سَفَرت چه بود؟

۵. دَفعهِ آخَری که به مُسافِرَت رفتی چه مُدَتی در آن جا ماندی؟

HOMEWORK   تَکلیف

13. Listen to the dialogue between a passenger and the passport control officer at the airport in Tehran.

کُنترُلِ گُذَرنامه.

مُسافِر - سلام، خَسته نَباشید

مامورِ گُذَرنامه - سلام. گُذَرنامَتون لُطفا

مُسافِر – بِفَرمایید.

مامور – هَدَفِ سَفَرِتون به ایران چیه؟

مُسافِر - گَردِش.

Tehran International Airport, Customs Line for Iranian citizens

مامور – قَصد دارین کُجای ایرانو ببینین.

مُسافِر - بیشتَر در تَهران میمونم، آما میخام از اِصفَهان هَم بازدید کنم و بَعد، بِرَم شُمال کِنارِ دَریا و چَند روزی در سَلمانشَهر بِمونم.

مامور – شُما قَبلا هَم ایران بودین؟

مُسافِر – نَخیر، این دَفعهِ اَوَّلامه در ایران.

مامور – چه مُدَّتی در ایران میمونین؟

مُسافِر – سه هفته.

مامور – این سه هفته کُجا میمونین؟

مُسافِر - تو تَهران در هُتلِ اِسپیناس پالاس اُتاق رِزرو کردم. در اِصفَهان در هُتلِ عَباسی میمونَم، و اگه رَفتَم شُمال ، وَقتی اونجا رِسیدَم یه هُتل یا مِهمانخونه ای پیدا میکنم. خوندَم که هُتلِ اَلماسِ قو خیلی قَشَنگ و راحَته و لَبِ دَریا س.

مامور – شُما چِقَد خوب فارسی حَرف میزَنید.

مُسافِر – خیلی لُطف دارید!

مامور – خیلی خوب.. به ایران خوش اومَدین. اُمیدوارَم که خوش بگَذره

مُسافِر – مِرسی. خُدا حافِظ

مامور – خُدا نِگَهدارِتون

14.   Answer the following questions in Persian.

١. این مُسافِر تا امروز چند دَفعه به ایران رفت؟

٢. مُسافِر قَصد دارد از چه شهرهایی در ایران بازدید کُند؟

٣. آیا مُسافِر با دوست ها یا خانواده در ایران میماند؟

٤. آیا او در هَمه‌ی آن شهر ها در هُتل اُتاق رِزِرو کَرد؟

٥. به نَظَرِ شما، این مُسافِر فارسی خوب بَلَد است؟

٦. آیا شما هَرگِز به ایران رفتید؟ به چه شهرهایی در ایران رفتید؟

Follow-up 1. Your instructor will assign one of the roles to your group: (1) Imagine that you are the passport control officer from the dialogue above. Describe in narrative style to a colleague of yours the conversation you had with the passenger and impressions you have of that passenger. Your colleague will ask you questions about the foreign passenger. (2) Imagine you are the passenger from the conversation above. You are talking to your friends. Tell your friends about the conversation you had with the passport control officer, the type of questions they asked you and the overall impressions you have of your first contact with the border officers in Iran.

Follow-up 2. You will be working in groups. Create and perform a brief dialogue at the passport control area at an airport. One of you will be a passport control officer who checks passports and the other two people will be arriving passengers. Decide whether the two passengers are family or friends and create the dialogue accordingly. You must use at least three key words from the vocabulary and one *taārof* phrase.

Follow-up 3. You will be working in groups in class. Prepare to compare the steps one has to go through after arriving in a US airport to those after arriving in an Iranian airport. What are the similarities and differences?

IN A CAB   در تاکسی

Listen and repeat the words. Say each word aloud several times until you can easily pronounce it. Practice before coming to class.

Cab driver	تاکسی ران (تاکسیرون)
OK, sure (response to a request or command to do something)	چَشم!
Flat rate	نِرخِ ثابِت
As quickly as possible	هَر چه زودتَر
Right at the entrance	دَمِ وُرودی
Shared, common	مُشتَرَک
To arrive (at a destination)	رِسیدَن
To take someone to a destination (e.g., by car)	رِساندَن (رِسوندَن)
How long will it take?	چِقَدر طول میکِشد؟ (چِقَد طول میکِشه؟)
How much do I owe you?	چِقَدر تَقدیم کُنَم؟
Stop! Pull Over! (said to a driver of a vehicle)	نِگَهدارید! (نِگَهدارین)

HOMEWORK   تکلیف

15. Read the description of how Yasamin gets from her dorm to her morning class.

معمولا از خوابگاه به کلاسِ اَوَّلم با اُتوبوس میرَوَم. تَقریبا ۲۰ دقیقه طول میکِشد
که با اُتوبوس به کلاس بِرِسم. بَعضی وَقت ها دوستِ پسرم من را به کلاسِ
اَوَّلم میرِساند، آنوَقت، ۱۰ دقیقه بیشتَر طول نِمیکِشد.

Now, think of how you usually get from your room to your first class of the day. Prepare
to say two sentences using two different verbs from the ones given below, and describe
how long it takes you to get to the classroom.

طول میکِشد، میرِسَم، میرِساند.

16. 🔊 Listen and complete with the given words as you hear them. The verbs are given in
the infinitive, but the speaker uses them in the conjugated form. Write them in the conjugated form as the speaker uses them.

طول کِشیدن، رِسیدن، رِساندَن، دَمِ وُرودی،نِگَهدارین.

363

۱. سَفَرِ اتوبوس از تهران به کَرَج تَقریبا ۱ ساعت و نیم ــــ ــــ ــــ .

۲. اتوبوس دُرُست به در وُرودیِ دبستانم ـ .

۳. ــــ ــــ حَیاطِ دِبستانَم از اُتوبوس پیاده میشوم.

۴. سه روز در هفته مادرم من را به دبستانم ــــ .

۵. به تاکسیران به فارسی گفتم "لطفا همینجا ــــ".

| **IN CLASS** | | دَر کِلاس |

17. Think of the last time you took a cab. Think of the phrases you say to the driver and s/he says to you. Now, retell in Persian how that conversation went. Include in your description the key phrases of that conversation.

18. Read the passage about the types of cabs in Tehran.

در تهران دو نُوع تاکسی وُجود دارند: تاکسیِ خانُم ها و تاکسیِ مُشتَرَک. تاکسیِ خانُم ها که اِسمِش "تاکسیِ بانُوان" است فَقَط برای زَن ها است و هیچ مَردی نِمیتواند سَوارِ آن تاکسی شَود. تاکسیِ خانُم ها به رَنگِ سَبز است و رانَندهِ چنین تاکسی هَمیشه زَن است. تاکسیِ خانم ها تاکسیِ تِلِفُنی است. میتوانید رَنگ بِزَنید و آن هَم به هَر کُجایی که هَستید میرِسد و شما را به هَر جایی که میخواهید میرِساند.

تاکسیِ مُشتَرَک به رَنگِ زَرد است. تَقریبا همه رانَنده های تاکسیِ مُشتَرَک مَرد هستند. هم زن و هم مرد میتوانند دَر عِینِ حال سَوارِ تاکسیِ مُشتَرَک شوند. اگر میخواهید که در تاکسیِ مُشتَرَک تنهایی سَفَر کنید، بایَد به رانَنده بگویید که میخواهید سَواری دَربستی کنید.

سوالها:

۱. به نَظَرِ شما، آیا وُجودِ "تاکسیِ بانُوان" کارِ خوبی است؟

۲. آیا دَر کشورِ شما هم این دو نُوع تاکسی وُجود دارند؟

۳. آیا شما آغلَب از تاکسی اِستِفاده میکنید؟

۴. نَظَرِ شما در مُوردِ سِرویسِ "اوبِر" چه است؟ آیا هَرگِز از آن سِرویس اِستِفاده کردید؟

HOMEWORK  تَکلیف

19. Listen to the dialogue between Sara, who has just arrived in Tehran, and the cab driver.

در تاکسی

سارا – سلام، خَسته نَباشید، حالتون چطوره؟

تاکسیران – مِرسی، شما خوب هَستین؟

سارا – مِرسی. تا هُتلِ اِسپیناس پالاس چِقَد میگیرین؟

تاکسیران – خانوم، ما تاکسیای فُرودگاه هستیم، نِرخِمون ثابِته ، به هَر کُجای تهران ۸۰ هِزار تومَن میشه.

سارا – خیلی خوب. لُطفا مَنو به هُتلِ اِسپیناس پالاس بِرسونید.

تاکسیران – چَشم، خانوم.

سارا – تا هُتل چِقَد راهه؟

تاکسیران – خب، این وَقتِ شَب که ترافیک بَد نیست خیلی طول نِمیکشه. زود میرِسونَمِتون.

...

تاکسیران – رِسیدیم.

سارا – خُب، لُطفا هَمون دَمِ وُرودیِ هُتل نِگَهدارید! صُبحونه تا ساعتِ ۱۱ سِرو میشه.

سارا – بِفرمایید، اینم ۸۰ هِزار تومَن

تاکسیران – قابل نَداره.

سارا – خواهِش میکُنَم، بِفرمایید

تاکسیران – خیلی مَمنون، دَسِتِتون دَرد نَکُنه. به ایران خوش اومَدید!

Follow-up 1. Based on the above dialogue, complete/respond to the following sentences in English.

(1) Sara needs to get to …
(2) Does the cab driver say it takes a long time to get to that hotel?
(3) The cab driver was refusing payment because …
(4) Did Sara pay for the ride at the end?

Follow-up 2. Say in Persian a few summarizing statements about the dialogue between Sara and cab driver by addressing the following key points:

– who
– when
– where
– the outcome of the events

Follow-up 3.  You will be working in groups. Create a dialogue "in a taxi" similar to the one above. Change the location, destination, price, and so on in your dialogue. Add extra lines if needed.

Use the key words – بِرِسانید، میرِسانَمِتان، چِقَدر، طول میکِشد، نِگَهدارید

AT THE HOTEL   در هُتِل

Listen and repeat the words. Say each word aloud several times until you can easily pronounce it. Practice before coming to class.

Reception desk (in hotel)	پَذیرِش
Receptionist	پَذیرِشگَر
Form	فُرم
A view	مَنظَره
To fill out a form	فُرم را پُر کَردَن (فُرمو پُر کَردَن)
The room is facing the …	اُتاق رو به ... اَست (اتاق رو به ... ه)
Breakfast is served	صُبحانه سِرو میشود (صُبونه سِرو میشه)

HOMEWORK

تَکلیف

20.  Listen to the conversation between Sara, who is checking in at the hotel, and the receptionist.

در هتل

پَذیرِشگَر – سلام. به هُتِلِ اِسپیناس پلاس خوش اومَدید!

سارا – سلام، مرسی. حال شما چطوره!

پَذیرِشگَر – خیلی مَمنون. شما خوب هَستین؟ اتاق رِزِرو دارید؟

سارا – بله. از قَبل اتاق رِزِرو کردم. اسمِ من سارا جانسانه.

پَذیرِشگَر – بسیار خوب، خانومِ جانسان.... اُتاقِتون حاضِره. لُطفا این فُرم رو پُر کُنید!

...

سارا – بِفرمایید، اینَم فُرم.

پَذیرِشگَر – مرسی. اُتاقِتون طبقه نُهُمه، شماره‌ِ ۹۰۹.

سارا – اُتاقَم رو به شَهره یا رو به کوه؟

پَذیرِشگَر – اُتاقِتون رو به شَهر ه. مَنظَرهِ خیلی زیبایی داره.

سارا – مرسی، مَمنون.

پَذیرِشگَر – خُب،
اُتاقِتون شامِلِ صُبحانه هست. رِستورانِ ما ساعَتِ ۶ صُب باز میشه. صُبحونه تا ساعتِ ۱۱ سِرو میشه.

سارا – عالیه. مرسی.

پَذیرِشگَر – خواهِش میکُنَم. آسانسور از این طَرَفه.

سارا – مرسی، خُدا حافِظ.

پَذیرِشگَر – خُدا نِگَهدار.

Follow-up 1. Prepare for your classmates two questions about the dialogue. Use two different verbs for your questions.

367

IN CLASS

دَر کِلاس

Follow-up 2. Use one of the words below to make one statement about the individuals and facts from the dialogue above.

پَذیرِشگَر، رِزِرو کردن، اُتاق، مِهمانِ هُتِل، صبُحانه

Follow-up 3. Say in Persian what are the three major things one has to do in order to check into a hotel in your country.

Follow-up 4.  Working in groups, put together and perform a brief dialogue at the reception desk in a hotel. There will be one receptionist and two hotel guests. Your instructor will assign one of the situations to your group:

(1) The guests have already reserved a room.
(2) The guests are looking to rent a room and they have not made any prior reservations.

AT THE BUS TERMINAL

دَر تِرمینالِ اُتوبوس

Listen and repeat the words. Say each word aloud several times until you can easily pronounce it. Practice before coming to class.

Isle seat	صَندَلیِ راهرُو
Windows seat	صَندَلیِ کِنارِ پَنجَره
Round trip ticket	بِلیتِ دوطَرَفه، بِلیتِ رَفت و بَرگَشت (بیلیت...)
Highway	جاده
Unequaled	بی نَظیر
Carry-on	ساکِ دَستی
To depart	حَرَکَت کَردَن
To fold flat	خواباندَن (خابوندَن)

368

HOMEWORK  تَکلیف

21. Listen to the conversation Sara is having at a bus terminal. She is buying a bus ticket to go to Chaloos, a place in North Iran.

در ترمینال اتوبوس

سـارا – سـلام، خَسته نَباشید. اتوبوسِ چالوس سـاعَتِ چند حَرَکَت میکنه؟

کارمَندِ ترمینال – هشتِ شب.

سـارا – سـاعَتِ چند به چالوس میرِسه؟

کارمَندِ ترمینال – حودودِ سـاعتِ یک. سَفَرِ چالوس معمولا ۵ سـاعَت طول میکِشه.

سـارا – هَزینه یه بیلیتِ دوطَرَفه چِقَدره ؟

کارمَندِ ترمینال – ۲۵ هِزار تومَن واسه یک نَفَر.

سـارا – خیلی خوب. یه بیلیت واسه ساعَتِ ۸ میخام. اگه میشه صَندَلیِ کِنارِ پِنجره رو به مَن بِدین و نَزدیکِ دَستشویی هَم نَباشه.

کارمَندِ ترمینال – خُب، پَس، هَمون صَندَلی ۶ خوبه. نَقدی پَرداخت میکنین؟

سـارا – میشه کارت بِکِشَم؟

کارمَندِ ترمینال – بله.

سـارا – راستی، جاده اش قَشَنگه ؟

کارمَندِ ترمینال – بله، جاده اش بینَظیره ، یکی از قَشَنگتَرین جاده های جَهانه.

سـارا – اوتوبوس راحَته ؟

کارمَندِ ترمینال – بله، خیلی. اوتوبوسِ شما اوتوبوسِ وی.آی.پیه، و میتونین پُشتیِ صَندَلیتونو کامِلا بِخابونین. اینَم بیلیتِتون. بِفَرمایید

سـارا – خیلی مَمنون. من یه چَمِدون و یه سـاکِ دَستی دارم.

کارمَندِ ترمینال – چَمِدونو به شاگِرد بِدین. چَمِدونِتونو قِسمَتِ پایین اوتوبوس میذاره.

سـارا – مِرسی. خُدا حافِظ

کارمَندِ ترمینال – خُدا حافِظ

Follow-up 1. Prepare for your classmates two questions about the above dialogue. Be ready to ask your questions fluently.

IN CLASS

دَر کِلاس

Follow-up 2. Pick a word from the above dialogue and describe it in Persian for your classmates. Do not say the word that you are describing. Your classmates will listen and try to guess the word. After the class has guessed the word, write it on the board in Persian. Once everyone's words have been guessed and written on the board, each student will use one or more words from the board and make one statement about the story that unfolded in the dialogue.

Follow-up 3. Make one statement about Sara, true or false. Make another statement about the cashier or the bus, true of false. Make your statements in Persian. The class will listen and say if your statements are true or false.

Follow-up 4. Put together and perform a short dialogue, where you demonstrate the process of buying a ticket to get from the university to the hometown of one of your group members. You can use the dialogue above as a reference, but change the location, destination and means of transportation as needed. Incorporate at least two *taãrof* or politeness phrases, along with the verbs:

حَرَکَت کردن

and

any new verb from this lesson

DIRECTIONS

پُرسیدَن و دادنِ آدرِس

Listen and repeat the words. Say each word aloud several times until you can easily pronounce it. Practice before coming to class.

Translation (verbs are in Command form)	
address	آدرِس

cross the …	از … عُبور کُن
pass the/by …	از … رَد شُو
turn to the right	راسِت بِپیچ
left	چَپ
go straight	مُستَقیم بِرُو
enter the …	وارِدِ …شُو
exit the …	از… خارِج شُو
street	خیابان (خیابون)
alley	کوچه
plaza, square	مِیدان (میدون)
intersection	چَهار راه (چارراه)
building	ساختِمان (ساختِمون)
entrance	وُرودی
exit	خُروجی (خوروجی)
this/that side of the street	این/ آن طَرَفِ خیابان (این/اون طَرَفِ خیابون)
in the direction of …	به سَمتِ …
Excuse me, can you tell me where … is?	بِبَخشید، مُمکِن است بِگویید …کُجا است؟ (بِبَخشید، مُمکِنه بِگین …کُجا است؟)
Excuse me, do you know where … is?	بِبَخشید، میدانید … کُجا است؟ (بِبَخشید، میدونین … کُجاس؟)
Is this the right way to …?	این راه بَرای … دُرُست است؟ (این راه بَرای … دُرُسته؟)
You are going the wrong way	دارید اِشتِباه میروید (دارین اِشتِباه میرین)
Can you show me on the map?	میشود توی نَقشه به من نِشان بِدهید؟ (میشه توی نَقشه بِهِم نِشون بِدین؟)
Take this street	از این خیابان بِروید (از این خیابون بِرین)

HOMEWORK تَکلیف

22. Prepare to give directions to your classmates to get from your Persian classroom to your room on/off campus. You may use the verbs in the imperative (command form) or the subjunctive (combined with بایَد). In either case, stay consistent with the choice of the verb form. Prepare to say your sentences fluently.

IN CLASS دَر کِلاس

23. Your instructor will pick a place on campus (library, cafeteria, university store, health-care center, a landmark on your campus, etc.) and ask you how to get there from your Persian class. Give your instructor precise directions.

24. Tell your classmates the directions to the place on campus where you are going after your Persian class. Do not name the place. Be precise in your description, and mention any transport you have to take to get to the destination. Your classmates will listen and try to guess what building on campus you are going to after your Persian class.

HOMEWORK تَکلیف

25. Translate the following dialogue into Persian. Prepare to read your sentences aloud. Practice for fluency and pronunciation before coming to class.

رَهگُذَر، عابِر passerby

سوپِری supermarket

دَر نَزدیکیِ اینجا nearby

JOHN	Excuse me, sir, is there a supermarket nearby?
PASSERBY	Yes, it is behind the neighborhood park. It is not very far.
J	Can I get there by bus?
P	Yes, and the bus stop is very close from here. Go to the right here until you reach the gas station. The bus stop is across from the gas station. Take the yellow bus. It comes every 20 minutes.
J	Where should I get off?
P	Get off when you see a park. You will be there in 5 minutes. The supermarket is behind the park.

J   Thanks!
P   You are welcome!

IN CLASS  دَر کِلاس

26. Together with your instructor, go over the translation you did for Homework in order to make sure that all lines are translated correctly.

27. Read out the Persian lines in pairs. Aim at fluency.

28. You will be working in pairs. One of you will ask the other person for directions. Create and perform a dialogue similar to the one you translated for Homework.

29. Everyone will say sentences and name all buildings they have to pass in order to get to the Persian class. Use the verb *to pass* in your sentences.

30. Look at the signs below and describe what directions they are meant to communicate. Use the imperative for the verbs in your sentences, for example, do not turn left.

READING

خواندَنی

Pre-reading. Iran. In the text below, the writer describes his trip abroad that started in Tehran, Iran and gives his friend practical advice as to what to expect and do in the airports during the trip. Think of the topic of the excerpt and think of the most common words that you might encounter in such reading. Write those words down so you can see them. If they are nouns, think of the verbs that might go with them in such an excerpt. If the words you wrote are verbs, think of nouns that might go with them in an excerpt on this topic. Write down those words as well, so you can visually identify them when you encounter them in the reading.

This is a longest reading you have done so far. The structures and vocabulary you possess will allow you to comprehend it successfully. Do not be taken aback by a few unfamiliar words that are a natural occurrence in any authentic material. You can easily find those in a dictionary. The reading is about travel abroad, so be prepared to see some non-Persian words spelled in Persian letters as the writer will refer to signs and foreign terms. Read the text several times aloud until you can read it fluently.

Cognates	Persian vocabulary
پاسپورت passport	کارتِ پَرواز boarding pass
"چِک ین" check-in	مِهماندار flight attendant
سالُنِ ترانزیت transit/waiting area	با خونسَردی with calm
موبایل mobile/cell phone	... را اِعلام کَردَن to declare something
دَستگاهِ پُرتابِل portable device	ساعَتِت را با وَقتِ مَحَلی تَنظیم کُن set your watch to local time
لَپ تاپت را شارژ کُن charge the laptop	کارتهایی را میگَردانَند. they distribute (lit: circulate) cards, forms
گِیت gate (in an airport)	دَر نَظَر بگیری you take into consideration
چِک کَردَن to check	پیشنِهاد کَردَن to advise, to suggest

سلام دوستِ عِزیزَم

میدانم که سَفَرِ طولانی در پیش داری و تَصمیم گرفتم از تَجرُبیاتِ خودَم بَرایت بنویسم.گفتم شایَد دوست داشته باشی بخوانی و تَجرُبه های من را در نَظَر بگیری که برای سَفَرت بِهتَر آماده شوی.

از لَحاظِ لِباس پیشنِهادِ من از یک تی شیرتِ آستین کوتاه، رویش یک پیراهَنِ آستین بُلَند، شَلوارِ گُشاد و راحَت و کَفش وَرزشی است. هَمچنین پیشنِهاد میکنم که پاسپورت و قِسمَتی از پولِت را توی کیفِ گَردَنی بگذاری و بَقیهِ پولها را در چند قِسمَت در جیب های مُختَلِف بگذاری

یادِت نَرود که برای پَروازهای خارجی باید لاآقَل دو ساعَت قَبل از وَقتِ پَرواز به فُرودگاه بِرسی که تَمام کارهای قَبل از پَرواز را آنجام بدهی.

مَراحِلِ داخِلِ فُرودگاه: اول به باجهِ چِک یِنِ شیرکَتِ هَوایی ات میروی که بار را تَحویل بِدهی و کارتِ پَرواز بگیری

بعد از چِک یِن به سالنِ ترانزیت میروی. در این مُدَت، یکی دو بار بازرسی میشوی که باید از زیرِ دَستگاه رَد شوی. یادِت باشد که قَبل از اینکه از زیرِ دَستگاه رَد شوی، باید هر چیزِ فِلِزی و حَتی موبایل را توی سَبَد بگذاری که دَستگاه صِدا نَدهد. اِمکان دارد که دَستگاه بازهَم صِدا دهد. این خیلی عادی است و آصلا نِگرانی ندارد. خیلی خونسَرد و آرام هر چه که ماموران میگویند آنجام بِده.

اِمکان دارد که در فُرودگاه به مُدَتِ چند ساعَت مُعَطَل شوی که در این صورَت پیشنِهادَم این است که موبایل و لَپ تاپِت را شارژ کُنی و در فُرودگاه بِگَردی، اما پیش از هَمه گیتِ پَروازِ بَعدی را پِیدا کن که نَزدیکِ پَرواز به مُشکِل نَخوری

یادِت نَرود که در فُرودگاه ساعَتِت را با وَقتِ مَحَلی تَنظیم کنی چون ساعَتِ پَرواز به وَقتِ مَحَلِی فُرودگاه است نه تهران.

در طولِ پَرواز هر چه میخواهی - آب میوه، نوشابه، چای، دَستمال، بالِش - از مِهماندارها بگیر، خِجالَت نَکِش. بالِش اگر نداشتند، پَتو بگیر که در طِی پَرواز بتوانی راحَت بِنشینی و بِخوابی.

نَزدیکِ فُرودگاه مِهماندارها کارتهایی را میگَردانَند. حَتما یکی از آن کارتها را بِگیر و به دِقَت بِخوان و پُر کُن. فِکر میکنم آدرسِ اِقامَت را هم میخواهند. عَلاوه بر این اگر پول بیشتَر از دَه هِزار دُلار داری باید در این کارت اِعلام کنی که اِحتِمالا تو نداری.

قبل از پیاده شدن از هَواپیما دِقَت کُن چیزی را جا نَگذاری.

در فُرودگاه جَمعیَت و تابلوها را دُنبال کُن. اَوَل کُنتِرُلِ گُذَرنامه است که ویزایت را چِک کنند. تَجرُبه‌ی مَن از این است که مامورِ گُذَرنامه فَقَط چند سوال میکند که تو هم آرام و خونسَرد به تَمامِ سوالهایش جَواب بده. بعد از کُنتِرُلِ گُذَرنامه باید بارت را بگیری و به صَفِ گُمرُک بروی.

تَجرُبه‌ی مَن از این است که مامورانِ فُرودگاه خیلی رَفتارِ دوستانه داشتند. هر وَقت مُشکِلی پیش آمد از آنها سوال کن. اگر مُتَوَجه نَشُدی چه میگویند دوباره بِپُرس. یادِت باشد که مامورانِ فُرودگاه هر روز با صَدها مُسافِر که یک کَلَمه هم انگلیسی بَلَد نیستند سَروکار دارند و عادَت دارند به سوال های خارِجی ها چند بار جَواب بِدَهند.

بعد از صَفِ گُمرُک از فُرودگاه خارِج میشَوی.

Follow-up 1. Prepare for your classmates two questions with two different verbs (one per sentence) about the excerpt.

Follow-up 2. Can you give the person to whom the letter is addressed any additional general advice about travelling through foreign airports?

Follow-up 3. Think of your last air travel. Say what you did differently or similarly when compared to the writer's experience.

Follow-up 4. Write on the board one key word from the excerpt. Now, that everyone has written their words on the board, pick one (or more) of them (not your own word) and ask one of your classmates a question using that word. Your question must refer to your respondent's experiences and not to the writer's experiences described in the story.

TRANSLATION

تَرجُمه

Translate the following phrases into Persian.

Gharb	غرب
Azadi	آزادی
Gate	خُروجی، دَرب، گِیت

(1) Excuse me, where is the baggage claim area? (2) It is on the second floor. The elevators are on the left. (3) The baggage claim is after passport control. (4) What is the purpose of your trip to Iran? How long will you stay in Iran? (5) Tourism. I will stay in Iran for two weeks. (6) Take me to the Hotel Azadi, please. (7) Excuse me, where is the Gharb bus terminal(8) Do you have one round-trip ticket to Shiraz? (9) At what time does the Shiraz bus leave? (1) From which gate does the bus leave?

WRITING

اِنشا

Your friend who is a student in a different university is coming to visit you this weekend. Your friend knows how to get to the main plaza on your campus, but does not know how to get from there to your room. Text your friend detailed directions to your place.

377

APPENDIX A: UNDERSTANDING PERSIAN VERBS: WHY DO "THEY ALL APPEAR ALIKE"?

There are two major reasons why Persian verbs might look all so similar: (1) composite verb formation and (2) verb tense and category markers.

1. Composite verb formation. In the Persian language there are composite (compound) verbs and then there are base (single-word) verbs. The vast majority of Persian verbs are the derivative composite verbs, and a small minority of verbs are base verbs. Composite verbs consist of a noun, adjective or adverb that is combined with one of the few base verbs. Base verbs appear at the end of such composite verbs. Because the pool of base verbs is relatively small, large numbers of composite verbs use the same base verb as their second component which makes the end of these composite verbs look the same. In addition, a majority of composite verbs use one of the two کردن or شدن as their base verb which adds to the structural similarity among large numbers of Persian verbs. It might make things easier if we draw parallels between English and Persian. For example, in English, the composite verb *to get ready* is different in meaning from the composite verb To Get Over, and from the composite verb To Get By, although all three have the verb "to get" in them. This is still different from the meaning of the base verb To Get when it is used on its own and not as a part of a composite verb, for example, I got a letter from my friend. Similar phenomenon occurs in Persian. Let's take one of the most common verbs, the base verb شُدَن which, on its own, means To Become. When it is used in a composite verb, the meaning of that verb might not be the same. For example,

To get ready – حاضر شدن

To get tired – خسته شدن

To get better – بهتر شدن

To settle – ساکن شدن

To grow up – بزرگ شدن

To enter – وارد شدن

We see the verb شدن appearing at the end of all these composite verbs, but the meanings of these composite verbs are very different. The verb شدن is a high frequency verb that appears in numerous composite verbs as well as on its own. The same applies to the verb کردن (to do), which is also a high frequency verb that appears in numerous composite verbs as well as on its own, for example,

To do – کردن

To work – کار کردن

To work out (lit.: to do exercise) – ورزش کردن

To start – شـروع کردن

As we can see, in the examples above the two verbs keeps recurring, but the meanings of the verbs are always different. In order to understand the meaning of the verb one has to look at the first, the primary component of the composite verb that carries most of the meaning. The good news is that there are relatively few base verbs in Persian, which means that the number of possibly recurring verbs in composites is limited and can be learned relatively easily. Most of the composite verbs rely on the base verbs شـدن or کردن, both of which we have already used above.

How to Avoid Confusion

The key is to not rush into treating the verb that you hear or see in the sentence at first glance as a base (single-word) verb with its original meaning. That is especially true if you hear or see the verb شدن or کردن. as these two are commonly used to build composite verbs. Instead, see if the verb is a composite one and look for accompanying nouns, adjectives, adverbs or prepositions that may go together with the verb and represent the other component of a composite verb. Usually, that other (first) component of a composite verb would come either immediately before the second component, which is the verb that you already saw, or may be separated from it by modifiers, for example,

I work every day. – هَر روز کار میکُنَم

You did a very good thing. – کارِ خِیلی خوبی کَردی

I entered the room. – وارِدِ أتاق شُدَم

I got on the bus. – سَوارِ اتوبوس شُدَم

It will also help greatly if you master the verbs کردن and شـدن from the beginning. By doing that, you will be able to understand an incredibly large number of verbs, and, importantly, will also be able to build new verbs on your own by combining these two verbs with nouns, adjectives or adverbs that you might have learned before as individual nouns, adjectives, and so on.

For example, combine the adjective خوشحال (happy) that you learned in Lesson 1 with the base verb کردن to build the compound verb "to make somebody happy" – خوشحال کردن

The fact that such a large number of Persian verbs are compound verbs which are made by using the same کردن or شدن can be seen as a glass half-full or glass half-empty scenario. It's up to you, how you approach this matter. For your convenience, this textbook has appendices where high frequency base verbs and high frequency composite verbs are listed in their present, past and subjunctive forms.

Here are few examples of high frequency base verbs and the most common compound verbs in which they appear as the second (conjugated) component:

خواندن	شدن	کردن
کتاب خواندن	بیدار شدن	سوال کردن
درس خواندن	آماده شدن	کار کردن
فارسی خواندن	شروع شدن	شروع کردن
آواز خواندن	تمام شدن	تمام کردن
فرا خواندن	درست شدن	درست کردن

2. Tense and category markers. All Persian verbs (besides the two exceptions *to be* and *to have*) in Habitual tenses start with the same prefix *mee*, which is the Habitual tense marker. These include the high frequency tense – present tense, as well as past habitual tense. Similarly, Persian verbs that are in subjunctive (besides the two exceptions *to be* and *to have*) will start with the prefix *beh*, which is the subjunctive marker. This might make all present tense verbs visually similar and all subjunctive verbs visually similar, but, on the other hand, the use of the markers makes the three most frequently used tenses in Persian, that is, the present tense (with the marker *mee*), subjunctive (with the maker *beh*) and past tense (lacks a marker prefix), easily distinguishable in the sentence.

Past tense	*Subjunctive*	*Present tense*
کردم	بکنم	میکنم
شدم	بِشوم	میشوم
خواندم	بِخوانم	میخوانم
گرفتم	بِگیرم	میگیرم
زدم	بِزنم	میزنم

How to Avoid Confusion

Once you have understood the use of the markers, focus on the root of the verb that immediately follows the marker. The root of the verb carries the verb's meaning, and understanding the verb's root will make all the difference when it comes to understating what is happening in the sentence. Learn the two roots of the verb: present tense root and past tense root.

APPENDIX B:
HIGH FREQUENCY BASE VERBS IN PRESENT, PAST AND SUBJUNCITVE FORMS

These following verbs may be used alone or as a part of a compound verb. The table features conjugated forms of the verbs in the First Person Singular in present tense (e.g., I ask), past simple tense (e.g., I asked) and subjunctive. The verb's final letter shown in red is the conjugational ending attached to the verb's root. English transliteration shows the pronunciation of the root of the verb in corresponding tense and mood. Present tense root is used to conjugate the verb in present tense, subjunctive and imperative forms. Past tense root is used to conjugate the verb in past tense.

	Present tense (e.g., I ask)	Subjunctive (e.g., I should ask)	Past tense (e.g., I asked)
Ask	میپُرسَم	بِپُرسَم	پُرسیدَم
Ask for something	میخواهَم (از ...)	بخواهَم	خواستَم
Be	هَستَم	باشَم	بودَم
Become	میشَوَم	بِشَوَم	شُدَم
Bring	میاوَرَم	بیاوَرَم	آوُردَم
Buy	میخَرَم	بِخَرَم	خَریدَم
Can	میتوانَم	بِتوانَم	تَوانِستَم
Carry, take (from one place to another)	میبَرَم	بِبَرَم	بُردَم
Close	میبَندَم	بِبَندَم	بَستَم
Come	میایَم	بیایَم	آمَدَم
Cook	میپَزَم	بِپَزَم	پُختَم
Count	میشُمارَم	بِشمارَم	شُمُردَم
Cut	میبُرَم	بِبُرَم	بُردَم
Do	میکُنَم	بِکُنَم	کردَم

	Present tense (e.g., I ask)	Subjunctive (e.g., I should ask)	Past tense (e.g., I asked)
Eat, drink	میخورَم	بِخورَم	خوردَم
Fall	می اُفتَم	بیُفتَم	اُفتادَم
Forgive	میبَخشَم	بِبخشَم	بَخشیدَم
Get, receive	میگیرَم	بِگیرَم	گِرِفتَم
Give	میدَهم	بِدهم	دادَم
Go	میرَوم	بِرَوم	رَفتَم
Have	دارَم	داشته باشَم	داشتَم
Hear	میشنَوَم	بِشنَوَم	شِنیدَم
Hit, strike	میزَنَم	بِزَنَم	زَدَم
Know	میدانَم	بِدانَم	دانِستَم
Let, allow	میگُذارَم	بگُذارَم	گُذاشتَم
Lose (e.g., a game)	میبازَم	بِبازم	باختَم
Make	میسازَم	بِسازَم	ساختَم
Pass (by, near)	میگُذَرَم	بِگُذَرَم	گُذَشتَم
Pay	میپَردازَم	بِپَردازَم	پَرداختَم
Pull	میکِشَم	بِکِشَم	کِشیدَم
Put, place, allow	میگُذارَم	بِگُذارَم	گُذاشتَم
Reach	میرِسَم (به ...)	بِرِسَم	رِسیدَم
Read	میخوانَم	بِخوانَم	خواندَم
Recognize	میشیناسَم	بِشیناسَم	شِناختَم
Return, go back	بَر میگَردَم	بَر گَردَم	بَر گَشتَم
Run	میدوَم	بدوَم	دویدَم
Say	میگویَم	بِگویَم	گُفتَم
See	میبینَم	بِبینَم	دیدَم
Send	میفِرِستَم	بِفِرِستَم	فِرِستادَم
Sell	میفُروشَم	بِفُروشَم	فروختَم
Sit	مینِشینَم	بِنِشینَم	نِشَستَم
Sleep	میخوابَم	بِخوابَم	خوابیدَم
Stand	می ایستَم	به ایستَم	ایستادَم
Stay, remain	میمانَم	بِمانَم	ماندَم

	Present tense (e.g., I ask)	Subjunctive (e.g., I should ask)	Past tense (e.g., I asked)
Take, take into hands	میگیرَم	بِگیرَم	گِرِفتَم
Tell	میگویَم	بگویَم	گفتَم
Turn	میپیچَم	بپیچَم	پیچیدَم
Want	میخواهَم	بخواهَم	خواستَم
Wash	میشویَم	بشویَم	شُستَم
Wear	میپوشَم	بپوشَم	پوشیدَم
Win	میبَرَم	بِبَرَم	بُردَم
Write	مینویسَم	بنویسَم	نِوشتَم

High Frequency Verbs with Single-Letter Roots

When pronounced in present tense and subjunctive, these verbs only have one letter, that is, one-sound root. Grey color marks the letters that are spelled but not pronounced. Pronunciation is also shown in parentheses.

	Subjunctive	Persent tense	The root
come	بیایَم (بیام)	میایَم (میام)	
	بیایی (بیای)	میایی (میای)	
	بیاید (بیاد)	میاید (میاد)	آی
	بیاییم (بیاییم)	میاییم (میاییم)	(آ)
	بیایید (بیاین)	میایید (میاین)	
	بیایند (بیان)	میایند (میان)	
give	بِدَهَم (بِدَم)	میدَهَم (میدَم)	
	بِدَهی (بِدی)	میدَهی (میدی)	
	بِدَهد (بِدَه)	میدَهد (میدَه)	دَه
	بِدَهیم (بِدیم)	میدَهیم (میدیم)	(د)
	بِدَهید (بِدین)	میدَهید (میدین)	
	بِدَهند (بِدَن)	میدَهند (میدَن)	

	Subjunctive	*Persent tense*	*The root*
go	بِروَم (بِرَم)	میروَم (میرَم)	رَو
	بِروی (بِری)	میروی (میری)	(ر)
	بِرود (بِره)	میرود (میره)	
	بِرویم (بِریم)	میرویم (میریم)	
	بِروید (بِرین)	میروید (میرین)	
	بِروند (بِرَن)	میروند (میرَن)	
become	بَشوم (بِشَم)	میشوم (میشَم)	شَو
	بَشوی (بِشی)	میشوی (میشی)	(ش)
	بَشود (بِشه)	میشود (میشه)	
	بَشویم (بِشیم)	میشویم (میشیم)	
	بَشوید (بِشین)	میشوید (میشین)	
	بِشوند (بِشَن)	میشوند (میشَن)	
say	بِگویم (بِگَم)	میگویم (میگَم)	گوی
	بِگویی (بِگی)	میگویی (میگی)	(گ)
	بِگوید (بِگه)	میگوید (میگه)	
	بِگوییم (بِگیم)	میگوییم (میگیم)	
	بِگویید (بِگین)	میگویید (میگین)	
	بِگویند (بِگَن)	میگویند (میگَن)	

How to Find the Verb's Roots

In dictionaries, when you look up a verb, what you will see is the verb's Past Tense Root with ن /an/ attached to the end of the verb. That is the gerund (*ing*) form of the verb. Usually Persian dictionaries give verbs in the gerund form. So, when you learn a new verb, you are already learning its past tense root which you will use for conjugation in past tense.

The present tense root is different from the past tense root. A good dictionary will show the present tense root in parentheses right after the gerund form of the verb, for example, To go رَفتَن (رَو)

APPENDIX C: HIGH FREQUENCY COMPOSITE VERBS IN PRESENT, PAST AND SUBJUNCTIVE

The final letter of the verb that appears in red is the conjugational ending. You can use the verb forms below for conjugation in any grammatical person by replacing the conjugation ending with the one that corresponds to the subject of the verb in the given sentence.

	Present (e.g., I add)	*Subjunctive* (e.g., I should add)	*Past tense* (e.g., I added)
Add	اِضافه میکنم	اِضافه بکنم	اِضافه کردم
Agree	مُوافِق هستم (با ...)	مُوافِق باشم	مُوافِق بودم
Answer (to ...)	جَواب میدَهم (به ...)	جَواب بِدَهم	جَواب دادَم
Apologize (to ...)	مَعذِرَت میخواهم (از ...)	مَعذِرَت بِخواهم	مَعذِرَت خواستم
Ask a question	سُوال میکُنَم (از ...)	سُوال کُنَم	سُوال کَردَم
Begin (e.g., it begins)	شُروع میشَوَد	شُروع شَوَد	شُروع شُد
Break (transitive, e.g., to break something)	خَراب میکنم	خَراب کنم	خَراب کردم
Break (intransitive, e.g., something broke down)	خَراب میشود	خَراب شود	خَراب شد
Believe	باوَر میکُنَم	باوَر بِکُنَم	باوَر کَردَم
Call on the phone	زَنگ میزَنَم (به ...)	زَنگ بِزَنَم	زَنگ زَدَم
Call	صِدا میکنم	صِدا بِکنم	صِدا کردم
Change	عَوَض میکنم	عَوَض کنم	عَوَض کردم

387

	Present (e.g., I add)	Subjunctive (e.g., I should add)	Past tense (e.g., I added)
Clean	تَمیز میکُنَم	تَمیز کُنَم	تَمیز کَردَم
Complete, accomplish	آنجام میدَهم	آنجام بِدَهم	آنجام دادم
Continue	اِدامه میدَهم (به ...)	ادامه بِدَهم	اِدامه دادم
Cross (e.g., cross a street)	(از ...) عُبور میکُنَم	عُبور کُنَم	عُبور کَردَم
Decide	تَصمیم میگیرَم	تَصمیم بِگیرَم	تَصمیم گِرفتَم
Describe	تُوصیف میکُنَم	تُوصیف کُنَم	تُوصیف کَردَم
Disagree	مُخالِف هستم (با ...)	مُخالِف باشم	مُخالِف بودم
Drive (to go by car as opposed to walking)	با ماشین میرَوم	با ماشین بِرَوَم	با ماشین رَفتَم
Drive, do driving	رانَندِگی میکنم	رانَندِگی کنم	رانَندِگی کردم
End (e.g., class ends at …)	تَمام میشَوَد	تَمام شَوَد	تَمام شُد
Explain	تُوضیح میدَهم	تُوضیح میدَهم	تُوضیح دادَم
Fall down	زَمین میخورَم	زَمین بخورم	زَمین خوردَم
Feel	حِس میکُنَم	حِس کُنَم	حِس کَردَم
Find	پیدا میکُنَم	پیدا کُنَم	پیدا کَردَم
Finish, end something	تَمام میکُنَم	تَمام کُنَم	تَمام کَردَم
Fix; also fix up, prepare (about food)	درست میکنم	درست کنم	درست کردم
Follow	دُنبال میکنم	دُنبال کنم	دُنبال کردم
Forget	فَراموش میکُنَم	فَراموش کُنَم	فَراموش کَردَم
Get up	بُلَند میشوم	بُلَند شوم	بُلَند شُدَم
Happen	اِتِفاق می اُفتد	اِتِفاق بیُفتد	اِتِفاق اُفتاد
Help	کُمَک میکُنَم (به ...)	کُمَک کُنَم	کُمَک کَردَم
Learn	یاد میگیرَم	یاد بِگیرَم	یاد گِرفتَم
Leave, forget something somewhere	جا میگُذارَم	جا بگُذارَم	جا گُذاشتَم
Lie down	دِراز میکِشَم	دِراز بِکِشَم	دِراز کِشیدَم
Like	دوست دارَم	دوست داشته باشم	دوست داشتَم

High Frequency Composite Verbs in Present, Past and Subjunctive

	Present (e.g., I add)	Subjunctive (e.g., I should add)	Past tense (e.g., I added)
Live	زِندِگی میکُنَم	زِندِگی کُنَم	زِندِگی کَردَم
Listen	گوش میکُنَم (به ...)	گوش کُنَم	گوش کَردَم (به ...)
Look	نِگاه میکُنَم (به ...)	نِگاه کُنَم	نِگاه کَردَم
Look for	دُنبالِ ... میگَردَم	دُنبالِ ... گَردَم	دُنبالِ ... گَشتَم
Lose, to misplace	گُم میکُنَم	گُم کُنَم	گُم کَردَم
Meet	آشنا میشوم (با ...)	آشنا شوم	آشنا شدم
Move (to a different place)	نَقلِ مَکان میکُنَم	نَقلِ مَکان کُنَم	نَقلِ مَکان کَردَم
Move, make a movement	حَرَکَت میکنم	حَرَکَت کنم	حَرَکَت کردم
Need	لازِم دارَم	لازِم داشته باشَم	لازِم داشتَم
Open	باز میکنم	باز کنم	باز کردم
Play	بازی میکُنَم	بازی کُنَم	بازی کَردَم
Prepare, get ready	آماده میشَوَم، حاضِر میشَوَم	آماده شَوَم، حاضِر شَوَم	آماده شُدَم، حاضِر شُدَم
Prepare something	آماده میکُنَم، حاضِر میکُنَم	آماده کُنَم، حاضِر کُنَم	آماده کَردم، حاضِر کَردَم
Push	هُل میدَهم	هُل دَهم	هُل دادم
Recall, remember	به یاد میاورم، یادم میاید	به یاد بیاورم، یادم بیاید	به یاد آوردم، یادم آمد
Remember	یادَم است	یادَم باشد	یادَم بود
Repeat	تِکرار میکُنَم	تِکرار کُنَم	تِکرار کَردَم
Rest	اِستِراحَت میکنَم	اِستِراحَت کُنَم	اِستِراحَت کَردَم
Return, Give back	پَس میدَهَم	پَس بِدَهم	پَس دادَم
Show	نِشان میدَهَم	نِشان بِدَهم	نِشان دادَم
Speak a language, know a skill	بَلَدَم	بَلَد باشم	بَلَد بودَم
Speak	حَرف میزَنم	حَرف بِزَنم	حَرف زَدم
Stand up	پا میشَوَم	پا شَوَم	پا شُدَم

	Present (e.g., I add)	Subjunctive (e.g., I should add)	Past tense (e.g., I added)
Start (to start something)	شُروع میکُنَم	شُروع کُنَم	شُروع کَردَم
Study	درس میخوانم	درس بخوانم	درس خواندم
Succeed	مُوَفَق میشَوم	مُوَفَق شَوم	مُوَفَق شدم
Take off	دَر میاوَرَم	دَر بیاوَرَم	دَر آوُردَم
Take a class	کِلاس بَر میدارَم	کِلاس بَر دارَم	کِلاس بَرداشتَم
Take an exam	اِمتِحان میدَهَم	اِمتِحان بِدَهَم	اِمتِحان دادَم
Talk (to somebody)	صُحبَت میکُنَم	صُحبَت کُنَم	صُحبَت کَردَم
Teach	یاد میدَهَم	یاد بِدَهَم	یاد دادَم
Think	فِکر میکُنَم	فِکر کُنَم	فِکر کَردَم
Translate	تَرجُمه میکُنَم	تَرجُمه کُنَم	تَرجُمه کَردَم
Travel	مُسافِرَت میکُنَم	مُسافِرَت کُنَم	مُسافِرَت کَردَم
Try, attempt	سَعی میکُنم	سَعی کُنم	سَعی کَردَم
Turn	میپیچَم	بپیچَم	پیچیدَم
Turn on	رُوشَن میکنم	رُوشَن کنم	رُوشَن کردم
Turn off	خاموش میکنم	خاموش کنم	خاموش کردم
Understand	مُتَوَجه میشَوَم، میفَهمَم	مُتَوَجه شَوَم، بفَهمَم	مُتَوَجه شُدَم، فَهمیدَم
Use	اِستِفاده میکُنَم (از ...)	اِستِفاده کُنَم	اِستِفاده کَردَم
Wait	صَبر میکُنَم	صَبر کُنَم	صَبر کَردَم
Wake up	بیدار میشَوَم	بیدار شَوَم	بیدار شُدَم
Walk (as opposed to taking a vehicle)	پیاده میرَوَم	پیاده بِرَوَم	پیاده رَفتَم
Watch	تَماشا میکُنَم	تَماشا کُنَم	تَماشا کَردَم
Work	کار میکُنَم	کار کُنَم	کار کَردَم
Write	مینِویسَم	بِنِویسَم	نِوِشتَم

APPENDIX D: A GUIDE TO HIGH FREQUENCY VERB CATEGORIES IN PERSIAN (WITH EXAMPLES)

All verb categories (e.g., tenses and moods) in Persian are divided into those based on the present tense root and those based on the past tense root of the verb. The conjugational endings that reflect the person who is doing the action described by the verb are the same for the present and past. The prefix (mee) می is shared by several present and past forms. So, the part of the verb that distinguishes the verb's present form from its past form is the Root. All Persian verbs have only two Roots – one for present and the other for past.

Present tense formation.

Conjugational endings to show the subject/actor of the verb	Verb's Present tense root	Present tense prefix
م، ی، د	گیر	می
/eh/, /ee/, /am/, etc.	/geer/	/mee/

Subjunctive formation.

Conjugational endings to show the subject/actor of the verb	Verb's Present tense root	Subjunctive prefix
م، ی، د	گیر	به
/eh/, /ee/, /am/, etc.	/geer/	/be/

Past tense formation.

Conjugational endings to show the subject/actor of the verb	Verb's Past tense root
م، ی، د	گرفت
/eh/, /ee/, /am/, etc.	/gereft/

Compare the three forms of the same verb.

Present tense	میگیرم	/mee-geer-am/
Subjunctive	بگیرم	/be-geer-am/
Past	گرفتم	/gereft-am/

How to Find Verb Roots

When you look up a verb in the dictionary what you will see is the verb's past tense root with ن /an/ attached to the end of the verb. That /an/ at the end is the gerund (-*ing* form of the verb) marker. Usually Persian dictionaries give verbs in gerund form. So, when you learn a new verb, you are already learning its past tense root.

For example, To go رفتن

Here, رفت is the past tense root and the ن /an/ at the end is the gerund marker.

The present tense root is, obviously, different from the past tense root. A good dictionary will show the present tense root in parentheses right after the gerund form of the verb, for example,

To go رفتن (رو)

The first two tables below show the verb categories that are based on present tense root and the past tense root respectively. The third table is a comparison of the verb forms that exist in both present and past (e.g., habitual, progressive).

Verb Forms with Present Tense Root Sample verb: (eating) خوردن Present tense root: خور	
present Simple/Habitual I don't eat greasy food.	میخورم غذای چرب نمیخورم.
present Habitual This semester, I eat full breakfast every day.	میخورم این ترم هر روز صبحانه کامل میخورم.
Subjunctive I should eat more vegetables.	بخورم باید بیشتر سبزیجات بخورم.
Imperative (Command form) Please, eat!	بخور لطفا بخور.
Future simple I'll eat later.	میخورم بعدا میخورم.
Present Progressive I am eating right now.	دارم میخورم دارم میخورم.

Verb Forms with Past Tense Root
Sample verb: (eating) خوردن
Past tense root: خورد

Past Simple I did not eat breakfast yesterday.	خوردم دیروز صبحانه نخوردم.
Past Habitual Last semester, I used to eat full breakfast every day.	میخوردم ترم گذشته هر روز صبحانه کامل میخوردم.
Subjunctive in past I had to eat breakfast earlier.	باید میخوردم باید زودتر صبحانه میخوردم.
Past Progressive I was eating breakfast when you called me.	داشتم میخوردم وقتی به من زنگ زدی من داشتم صبحانه میخوردم.
Present Perfect I have not eaten breakfast yet.	خورده ام هنوز صبحانه نخورده ام.
Past Perfect I had never eaten kabob before that.	خورده بودم تا آنوقت هرگز کباب نخورده بودم.

Parallel Verb Forms in Present and Past
Sample verb: خوردن (eating).
Past tense root: خورد Present tense root: خور

	Past		Present
Simple	خوردم I ate		میخورم I eat
Habitual	میخوردم I used to eat		میخورم I regularly eat
Subjunctive	باید میخوردم I had to eat		باید بخورم I should eat
Progressive	داشتم میخوردم I was eating		دارم میخورم I am eating

APPENDIX E: A QUICK GUIDE TO DIFFERENCES BETWEEN SPELLING AND PRONUNCIATION IN PERSIAN

Similar to English, some words in Persian feature spelling that is different from their pronunciation. Not all words in Persian have a discrepancy between spelling and pronunciation. The majority of words in Persian are pronounced according to their spelling. The following represents a summary of the main cases of divergence between spelling and pronunciation in the modern Persian of Iran.

Phonology: Nouns, Pronouns, Adjectives, Adverbs.

1. Written combinations ان (ãn) and ام (ãm) are pronounced *oon* and *oom* respectively:

Written	*Pronounced*
بارانی	بارونی
تمام	تموم
آمد	اومد oomad
مهمانی	مهمونی

2. Letters ح and ه (h) are not pronounced in the middle of the word; at the end of the word, especially after a consonant; in the plural ending ها; in the word هم *also*.

395

Written	Pronounced
چَهار	چار
چِهِل	چِل
صَفحه	صَفه
صاحِبخانه	صابخونه
صبح به خیر	صُب به خِیر
میخواهم	میخام
شما هم	شُمام
ماشین ها	ماشینا
ایرانی ها	ایرانیا
آنها	اونا

3. The diacritic vowel *e* is pronounced as the letter vowel *ee* ی as long as that does not change the meaning.

Written	Pronounced
شِیش	شیش
کوچِک	کوچیک
هِفده	هیفده
آتِش	آتیش
سِبیل	سیبیل

Note that in cases like the word که (ke) *that*, the pronunciation does not change to کی (kee) *who* because the word کی already exists as a different word with its own, specific meaning.

4. When the vowel *o* represented by the diacritic is followed in the next syllable by the vowel *oo* represented by the letter و in the root of the same word, both vowels are pronounced uniformly as *oo* و.

Written	Pronounced
شُلوغ	شولوغ
دُروغ	دوروغ
اُروپا	اوروپا
دُرود	دورود

5. Specific Direct Object Marker را is usually pronounced *ro* after vowels and *o* after consonants and vowel ی:

Written	Pronounced
مامانم را	مامانمو
بابا را	بابا رو
صندلی را	صندلیو
کی را	کیو

6. Combination of consonants *nb* is pronounced *mb*:

Written	Pronounced
شنبه	شمبه
تنبل	تمبل
دنبال	دمبل

7. Miscellaneous:

Written	Pronounced
چه	چی
یک	یه
آگر	آگه
دیگر	دیگه
مَگر	مَگه

Phonology: Verbs

1. The verb است is pronounced *eh* and, sometimes, *s* depending on the last letter in the word that است follows.

Written	Pronounced	After
خوب است	خوبه khoob-eh	any consonant
کی است چه است	کیه kee-eh چیه chee-eh	ی
اینجا است	اینجاس	ا
دانشجو است	دانشجوه dãneshjoo-eh	و
خوشمزه است	خوشمزس khoshmaza-s	ه

2. Conjugational endings in verbs.

Written	Pronounced
میگیرد	میگیره
میگیرید	میگیرین
میگیرند	میگیرَن

3. The و and وی of the verb roots vanish during conjugation in present tense and subjunctive.

Written	Pronounced
میگویم	میگَم
بیاورید	بیارَم
میشوم	میشَم
بروم	بِرَم

4. The letter ه vanishes from the verb's root when conjugated in present tense and subjunctive.

Written	Pronounced
میخواهم	میخام
میدهم	میدَم

5. Altered verb root. The letters either vanish or become replaced with other letters.

Written	Pronounced
میگُذارَم	میذارَم
میگُذَرَم	میذَرَم
مینِشینَم	میشینَم
بَرداشتَم	وَر داشتَم
به ایست	وایستا

7. Subjunctive/imperative marker prefix *beh* (به) is pronounced *bo* in the verbs whose root vowel is *o*. For example,

Spelling and bookish pronunciation	Colloquial pronunciation
بِکُن	بُکُن
بِرُو	بُرُو
بِخور	بُخور
بِبَر	بُبَر
بِدُو	بُدُو

Phonology: Prepositions, Suffixes.

1. Prepositions رو (roo) *on the surface* and تو (too) *inside* are not followed by the glide ی (eh/yeh) in pronunciation.

Written	Pronounced
روی میز	رو میز
رویش	روش
توی کلاس	تو کلاس
تویش	توش

2. The glide (ا or ی) before the possessive suffixes and Object suffixes vanishes in pronunciation if those suffixes follow the word's final vowel.

Written	Pronounced
رویش	روش
تویش	توش
بالایش	بالاش
برایش	بَراش
بابایت	بابات
زندگی ام	زِندِگیم

3. Final *eh* of the word becomes *a* when followed by a possessive ending.

Written	Pronounced
خانه ام	خونَم
دوچرخه ام	دوچرخَم
خاله ام	خالَم

Substitutions.

1. Vocabulary substitutions.

Written and Formal language	Colloquial
بَرای	واسه
گُرسنه	گُشنه
دَر	تو /too/

2. In colloquial speech, the pronouns are replaced with the corresponding suffixes whenever those pronouns follow a preposition.

	Preposition به *to*
Written and formal language	Colloquial
به من	بِهِم / بِم
به تو	بِهِت / بِت
به او	بِهِش / بِش
به ما	بِهِمون / بِمون
به شما	بِهِتون / بِتون
به آنها	بِهِشون / بِشون

	Preposition با *with*
Written and formal language	Colloquial
با من	باهام / بام
با تو	باهات / بات
با او	باهاش / باش
با ما	باهامون / بامون
با شما	باهاتون / باتون
با آنها	باهاشون / باشون

	Other
Written and formal language	Colloquial
بلای آن	بالاش
بَرای آن	بَراش
پُشتِ آن	پُشتش
روی آن	روش
توی آن	توش

Structural Differences: Word Order

The verb of motion in the sentence is placed in front of the word that describes the destination and direction. The directional preposition به *to* is omitted.

Written and formal language	Colloquial
به خانه میروَ م.	میرَ م خونه.
فردا آن را به دفتر میبَرَم.	فَردا میبَرَمِش دَفتَر.
بعد از کلاس به کافه تِریا میرویم.	بَعد از کِلاس میریم کافه تِریا.

APPENDIX F: GRAMMARIAN'S CORNER

What Do Subject and Object Mean?

In a sentence with subject, object and verb, the subject is the person or thing that is doing something or being something. In other words, the subject is the Actor of the action. The object, on the other hand, is the person or thing at which the above action is directed and to which the action is done. In other words, the object is the Recipient or the Target of the action. In the sentence *Kamran cleaned the room*, Kamran is the subject (Actor), as he is doing the action (cleaning), the Room is the object (Target of the action) because the action (cleaning) is done to the Room, and Cleaned is the Verb.

What Is the Indirect Object?

A sentence may have one or more objects. The objects, in turn, may be indirect or direct. Indirect object means the object (Target of the action) that requires a special connector word (preposition) such as *to, at, from, toward* and so on, in order to be used with the verb. This preposition stands in front of the object and thus points to the person or thing at whom the action is directed. In the sentence: *The student looked at the board*, the word *student* is the subject (Actor), while the word *board* is the object. The word *at* is the preposition that points to the object (*the board*). Therefore, the word *board* here is the indirect object as it does not follow the verb directly but rather, it follows a connector word (preposition *at*) which is required in order for the object to be used with the verb correctly. It would be incorrect to say: *The student looked the board.*

What Is the Direct Object?

The direct object, on the other hand, means that the object does not require connector words (Prepositions) in order to be used with the verb correctly. In the sentence *Kamran cleaned the room*, Kamran is the subject (Actor), the word *room* is the object (Recipient of the action). The word *room* here is the direct object, as it does not require any prepositions (such as *to, at, from, toward*, etc.) in order to be used with the verb correctly.

Chapter 7. My Hometown and Country

Alternative Plural Markers

There are other plural endings in Persian that are mostly used in written language and very formal speech.

– *ān* (ان) ending that is used for animates (e.g., humans, some plants) and some body parts, for example, پِسَران، دانِشجویان، آقایان، دَستان، چِشمان

As you can see above, if the word ends in a vowel, a glide ی (ee) appears between the word and this plural ending.

– *gān* and *jāt* endings that are used with the words that end in *eh* ه, for example,

بَچِگان، پَرَندِگان ، کارخانِجات

When these two plural endings are used, the final ه of the word is omitted in spelling.

– *oon* (ون) ending is only used in very formal and written language with several words that end in *ee* sound ی, for example, اِنقِلابیون revolutionaries.
– *een* (ین) ending is only used with a few words in formal and written language for example, مُسافِرین passengers.

Chapter 8. Shopping

Other Common Cues and Triggers for the Subjunctive

Phrases that express hope, suggestion, necessity.

It's possible ممکن است که /mom-ke-neh keh/, It's necessary لازم است که /lā-ze-meh keh/, It is better to/that بهتر است که /beh-ta-reh keh/, ... supposed to ... قرار است که /qa-rā-reh keh .../.

Note that in the trigger phrases above, the verb است will remain unchanged regardless of the grammatical subject of the sentence, and, instead, the verb that stands in the subjunctive at the end of the sentence will be conjugated according to the subject of the sentence.

By contrast, in the following trigger phrases the verb will be conjugated along with the verb that will stand in subjunctive at the end of the sentence according to the same or different subjects depending on the meaning of the given sentence:

I hope that ... امیدوارم که /o-meed-vā-ram keh/, I have to / I am forced to ... مجبورم که /maj-boo-ram/, I tell him/her to ... به او میگویم که /beh oon mee-gam keh/

Examples (unchanging trigger phrases):

مُمکِن است (که) دیر بِرِسیم. It is possible that we will arrive late.

مُمکِن است (که) دیر بِرِسَند. It is possible that they will arrive late.

It is **necessary** that we get to class on time. لازِم اِست (که) سَرِ وَقت به کِلاس بِرِسیم.

It is **necessary** that you get to class on time. لازِم اِست (که) سَرِ وَقت به کِلاس بِرِسید.

It is **better** that we go together. بِهتَر اِست (که) با هَم بِرَویم.

It is **better** that you go together. بِهتَر اِست (که) با هَم بِرَوید.

We are **supposed** to go together. قَرار اِست که با هَم بِرَویم.

I am **supposed** to call them tonight. قَرار اِست (که) اِمشب به آنها زَنگ بِزَنَم.

Examples (conjugated trigger phrases):

I am **forced to** leave. مَجبورَم (که) بِرَوَم

She is **forced to** leave. مَجبور اِست (که) بِرَوَد

I **hope** I get there on time. اُمیدوارَم (که) سَرِ وَقت آنجا بِرِسَم

He **hopes** to get there on time. اُمیدوار اِست (که) سَرِ وَقت آنجا بِرِسَد

I **hope** we get there on time. اُمیدوارَم (که) سَرِ وَقت آنجا بِرِسیم

I tell him to always arrive on time. به او میگویم (که) هَمیشه سَرِ وَقت بِرِسَد

He tells me to always arrive on time. به من میگوید (که) هَمیشه سَرِ وَقت بِرِسَم

Prepositional Phrases

Subjunctive is also used after prepositional phrases that imply intention, or suggest that the action to which they refer did not happen at all or did not happen until the other event to which they are compared had taken place, for example,

In Order to/ So that (tã, ba-rã-yeh een-keh, keh), Before … (qab-laz een-keh), Without … (be-doo-neh een-keh), Instead of … (beh jã-yeh een-keh)

I am going to the library **in order to** study for the exam.

به کِتابخانه میرَوم تا بَرای اِمتِحان دَرس بِخوانم

I am going to the dining hall (in order) to have lunch. به کافِه تِریا میرَوم که ناهار بُخورَم

In order to call my family, I am buying a new phone today.

بَرایِ اینکه به خانواده ام زَنگ بِزَنَم ، امروز تِلِفُن نُو میخَرَم

Keep in mind that the triggers *tã* and *keh* can be omitted all together, especially in colloquial register, for example,

میروم کافه تریا ناهار بخورم

405

Keep in mind that we can start a sentence with *ba-rã-yeh een-keh* (in order to …), but we do not start sentences with *keh* or *tã (in order to …)*

Keep in mind that *ba-rã-yeh een-keh* can also be used as "because," but in that case, it is followed by a verb in past, present or future tense (i.e., Indicative category that is used to communicate facts). If **ba-rã-yeh een-keh** is followed by a verb in subjunctive, it means *in order to … .*

Before going to class, I quickly stopped at the store.

قَبل آز اینکه به کلاس بِرَوم، به فُروشگاه رَفتَم

Without calling my friend, I went to his house.

بِدونِ اینکه به دوستمَ زَنگ بِزَنمَ، به خانه اش رَفتَم

Instead of going to class, I went to the mall.

به جای اینکه به کلاس بِرَوم، من به پاساژ رَفتَم

Subjunctive is also used in cases where it is not clear whether the action will ever happen.

They want us to come at nine. (آنها) میخواهند که (ما) ساعَتِ نُه بیاییم

I am telling them to come at nine. به آنها میگویَم که ساعَتِ نُه بیایند

I will not let them leave early. نِمیگُذارَم که زود بِرَوند

Negation

For negative subjunctive simply say *na* instead of *be* in the beginning of the verb, for example, It's better not to go. (beh-ta-reh keh na-ree)

بِهتَر اسـت (که) نَروی

If the verb starts with a vowel آ /ã/, the negation prefix becomes *naee* (نَی). Let's conjugate in negative subjunctive form the verb *to come* whose subjunctive/present tense root is spelled آی /ãee/ and pronounced /ã/.

نَیایم	naee-ãm	I should not come
نَیایی	naee-ãee	You (تو) should not come
نَیاید	naee-ãd	S/he, should not come
نَیاییم	naee-ãeem	We should not come
نَیایید	naee-ãeen	You (شـما) should not come
نَیایند	naee-ãn	They should not come

In order to negate the subjunctive of the verb that starts with a vowel carried by a diacritic and introduced by the symbol ا (e.g. أفتادن، أنداختن), drop that symbol in writing and attach the negation prefix *naee* directly to the first consonant letter of the verb. This will actually make for a more phonetic spelling of the resulting verb.

Let's conjugate in negative subjunctive form the verb *to fall* whose subjunctive/present tense root is أفت /oft/:

نَیُفتم	naee-oftam	I should not fall
نَیُفتی	naee- oftee	You (تو) should not fall
نَیُفتد	naee- ofteh	S/he, it should not fall
نَیُفتیم	naee- ofteem	We should not fall
نَیُفتید	naee- ofteen	You (شما) should not fall
نَیُفتند	naee- oftan	They should not fall

Chapter 9. Review

Negation. To negate the verb in past simply say *na* in the beginning of the verb. The negation prefix *na* is stressed and is written together with the verb, for example,

نَرفتم /na-raftam/ I did not go

نَرفتی /na-raftee/ you did not go

نَرفت /na-raft/ S/he did not go

If the verb starts with a vowel آ /ã/, the negation prefix become *na-ee* (نَی). Let's conjugate in negative past tense the verb *to come* whose past tense root is آمَد (oomad).

نَیامدم	naee-oomadam	I did not come
نَیامدی	naee-oomadee	You (تو) did not come
نَیامد	naee-oomad	S/he, it did not come
نَیامدیم	naee-oomadeem	We did not come
نَیامدید	naee-oomadeen	You (شما) did not come
نَیامدند	naee-oomadan	They did not come

In order to negate the past tense verb that starts with a vowel carried by a diacritic and introduced by the symbol ا (e.g. أفتادن، أنداختن), drop that symbol in writing and attach the negation prefix *naee* directly to the first consonant letter of the verb. This will actually make for a more phonetic spelling of the resulting verb.

Let's conjugate in the negative past tense form the verb *to fall* whose past tense root is أُفتاد /oftãd/:

نَیُفتادم	naee-oftãdam	I did not fall
نَیُفتادی	naee- oftãdee	You (تو) did not fall
نَیُفتاد	naee- oftãd	S/he, it did not fall
نَیُفتادیم	naee- oftãdeem	We did not fall
نَیُفتادید	naee- oftãdeen	You (شما) did not fall
نَیُفتادند	naee- oftãdan	They did not fall

Let's conjugate in the negative past tense form the verb *to throw* whose past tense root is آنداخت /andãkht/:

نَینداختم	naee- andãkhtam	I did not throw
نَینداختی	naee- andãkhtee	You (تو) did not throw
نَینداخت	naee- andãkht	S/he, it did not throw
نَینداختیم	naee- andãkhteem	We did not throw
نَینداختید	naee- andãkhteen	You (شما) did not throw
نَینداختند	naee- andãkhtan	They did not throw

Chapter 11. Personality Traits

What Do Subject and Object Mean?

The subject is the person or thing that carries out the action described by the verb of the sentence, in other words the subject is the Actor of the action. The Object is the person or the thing at which the action is directed and to which the action is done, in other words the object is the Recipient, or the Target of the action. The action is expressed by the verb of the sentence. In the sentence *Kamran cleaned the room*, Kamran is the subject (Actor), as he is doing the action (cleaning), while the *room* is the object (Recipient) because the action (cleaning) is done to the room.

What Are the Indirect and Direct Objects?

The object (recipient of the action) may be indirect or direct. Indirect object means that the object (Recipient of the action) requires a special connector word (Preposition) such as *to, at, from, toward* and so on, in order to be used with the verb correctly. This preposition stands in front of the recipient of the action (object) and points to the person or thing at whom the action is directed. In the sentence *The student looked at the board*, the word *student* is the subject (Actor), while the word *board* is the object. The word *at* is the preposition that points to the object (*the board*). The word *board* here is the indirect object as it does not follow the verb directly but rather, it requires a connector word (preposition *at*) in order to be used with the verb correctly. It would be incorrect to say *The student looked the board.*

A direct object, on the other hand, means that the object does not require connector words (prepositions) to be used with the verb correctly. In the sentence *Kamran cleaned the room*, Kamran is the subject (Actor), the word *room* is the object (recipient of the action). The word *room* here is the direct object, as it does not require any prepositions (such as *to, at, from, toward, etc.*) in order to be used with the verb correctly.

Now, let's look at the two sentences discussed above in Persian.

1. The student looked at the board. دانشجو به تخته نگاه کرد

Here, دانشجو is the subject, and تخته is the object. It is the indirect object as it follows the preposition به *at*.

2. Kamran cleaned the room. کامران اتاق را تمیز کرد

Here, کامران is the subject, and اتاق is the object. It is the direct object as it does not require any prepositions in order to make a correct sentence. In the absence of prepositions, the SDO Marker را plays the role of pointing to the recipient of the action (object) in the Persian sentence.

CPSIA information can be obtained
at www.ICGtesting.com
Printed in the USA
LVHW062330260421
685675LV00007B/471